PHYSIOLOGY OF THE NERVOUS SYSTEM

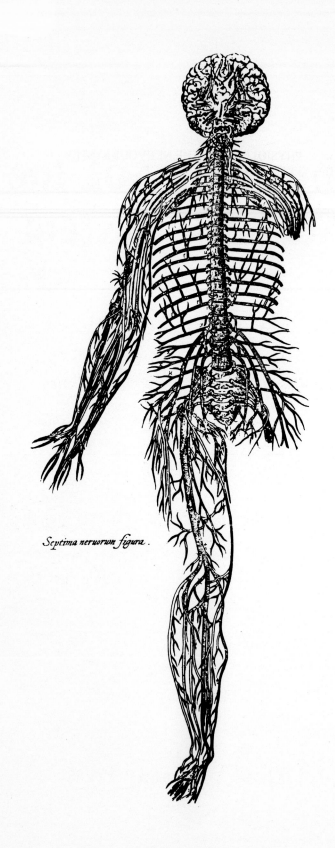

Septima neruorum figura.

Physiology of the Nervous System

DAVID OTTOSON

Department of Physiology II,
Karolinska Institutet, Stockholm, Sweden

New York
Oxford University Press
1983

Published in Great Britain by The Macmillan Press Ltd

Library of Congress Cataloging in Publication Data

Ottoson, David, 1918–
    Physiology of the nervous system.

    Bibliography: p.
    Includes index.
    1. Neurophysiology.   I. Title.   [DNLM:
1. Nervous system – Physiology.   WL 102 091n]
QP361. 0874.   1983   612'.8   82–14171
ISBN 0–19–520409–3
ISBN 0–19–520410–7 (pbk.)

Printed in Hong Kong

Contents

Foreword

Physiology of the Nervous System was originally published in Swedish and immediately became very popular among medical students and university biology students. The reason then, as now, was that there was no other 'middle-sized' book that gave a succinct but still sufficiently scholarly treatment of the nervous system. David Ottoson is able to do just that in his descriptions spanning the biophysics of nerve impulse conduction and synaptic transmission through integration to higher brain functions. The presentation of the physiology is balanced by a description of essential morphological characteristics of the nervous system and a discussion of the neurochemistry of synapses. Thus it is possible to read and enjoy the book even if one has only limited previous knowledge about brain function. The short historical vignettes provide the reader with a useful perspective.

It is increasingly rare for a single author to be able to cover such a wide range of material, and in view of the explosion of new knowledge in neuroscience this is an impressive feat. I find it satisfying to listen to only one voice, just as it is usually preferable to have one teacher in a course, especially if, as in the book, one can sense competence and sound judgement in the selection and interpretation of the material on which the book is based.

As a student I treasured a good textbook — which I defined as a book from which one could get, in a reasonable amount of time, some understanding of, and feeling for, a whole new area of knowledge. Later in life I returned to textbooks for teaching purposes, and also because old textbooks often give one insight into the knowledge and thoughts of an earlier time. Recently I looked at the central nervous system sections of Carpenter's *Elements of Physiology*, published in 1851. The chapters on the cerebellum and cerebrum were thoughtful and carefully reasoned on the basis of the facts available at the time. For example, it was known that the cerebellum was involved with complex movement, but Gall had proposed that it also had to do with sexual sensation. Carpenter did not think there was any evidence for Gall's notion, but gave it serious consideration. To compare this with misconceptions in our own time we need only recall the extensive discussion just a few years ago in regard to the claim that memory could be transferred by intraperitoneal injection of DNA.

Even if our understanding of the cerebral cortex has today reached a more advanced state, it is instructive to read Carpenter's discussion of the cortex, or, as he called it, the 'cerebrum'. At that time the 'sensorium' (the machinery of sensory processing) was thought to be located in subcortical structures, and 'the cerebrum is the instrument of all psychical operations', to 'Ideas', ranked as 'Emotional' and the 'Intelligential . . .', in other words, not too different from the present-day concept about the role of frontal lobes.

I make these comments because it seems appropriate to remind students that 'facts' stated in textbooks may be utterly wrong or may not necessarily give the whole story. At the same time it is true that from the student's point of view 'facts' are facts, particularly for the purpose of taking examinations, and the important thing is that they be stated correctly. It also helps if, as in the present case, the text reads easily and has numerous illustrations.

The decision to update this book and to make an English translation is most welcome, since there is also a real need at colleges and medical schools outside of Scandinavia for this kind of book about the nervous system. As with Carpenter's book, perhaps in 100 years or so someone will pick up Ottoson's text and muse over our misconceptions, but also be impressed by the balance and soundness of the treatise. My prediction is that over many years, students, teachers and historians will find much in this book to learn and enjoy.

Harvard Medical School   Torsten Wiesel
Boston, MA   Professor and Chairman
May 1982

Preface

'It is in the brain that the sensations arise, like seeing, hearing and smelling and out of these sensory perceptions memory and concept evolve; when memory and concepts have become consolidated there is knowledge.' (Plato in the dialogue *Phaidon*)

The cover of this book is from the work of the famous Spanish histologist and Nobel Laureate, Ramón y Cajal. What it shows is a section of the visual cortex with its neurons and intricate network of neuronal connections. When studying such a preparation under the microscope, one looks into a world full of beauty and marvels. It is also a world of secrets and mysteries. When looking at the maze of dendrites and nerve fibres, it is tempting in the fantasy to try to follow the pathways of the signals from one neuron to another. In doing so, in the back of one's thinking the question often arises as to whether neuroscience will ever be able to explain the mind. In the last few decades, a number of new technologies have developed that have provided fascinating possibilities for exploring the functions of the brain, and we are at present beginning to understand some of the basic principles of its machinery.

The present book is an extended version of a textbook in Swedish that was developed from lectures presented to the medical students in their course of physiology. Ever since the first edition of the book appeared, I have also been repeatedly asked to make it available for English-speaking readers. For a long time, I have been reluctant to do this. The main reason for this is that I was deeply aware of the fact that the content of the book reflected my own interests in neuroscience too much. Furthermore, the book in its Swedish version is written in a personal narrative style that might be difficult to maintain in the process of transmutation into a foreign language. When finally I gave way after much persuasion, I tried to eliminate some of the most obvious shortcomings of the Swedish edition. However, when the book is now presented in English, I find that I have only been partly successful in this respect. As in the Swedish version, I have endeavoured to give a 'three-dimensional' account of the present state of our understanding of various aspects of nervous functions, instead of attempting to present a concise summary of available data. My aim has been to tell the story of how various problems in neuroscience have been attacked and solved in the past and how these advances form the basis of today's attempts to unravel the secrets of the nervous system.

It is inevitable that a book like this will reveal the interest of its author. As the reader may soon discover, I have a keen interest in the history of neuroscience; almost every chapter begins with a short historical note. The great emphasis that has been placed on sensory functions reflects a field of even more profound interest to me. However, I have strived not to let these interests encroach upon my aim of presenting an integrated picture of the manifold and marvellous functions of the sensory system.

This book was originally written for medical students. However, it might also be of value to students in psychology and biology as well as to students who, regardless of their scientific background, want to familiarise themselves with specific topics in neuroscience. The neuroanatomy required to understand various functions is presented when relevant in order to make the book suitable for those who are not familiar with these aspects of the nervous system.

As mentioned above, the rapid development of neuroscience in the last few decades has contributed greatly to our understanding of many aspects of nervous functions. However, the day is still certainly remote in the future when we shall be able to explain in physical and chemical terms the higher functions of the brain, such as learning and memory or emotions like love and hate, happiness and sorrow, hope and despair. The inner secrets of the brain will most likely remain hidden from us for an indefinite time in the future. To have the privilege as a neurophysiologist of being able to glance into this world of marvels is a fascinating experience, and I hope that I have been able in this book to convey a little of my own feelings and enthusiasm in this respect.

Stockholm, 1982   David Ottoson

Acknowledgments

The fact that there is only one author of the present book should by no means be understood that this is one man's work. I owe a great debt of gratitude to a number of colleagues who have contributed in one way or another to the completion of the book. First, I should like to acknowledge my deep obligation to Drs Charles Edwards, David Potter and Gordon Shepherd, who read the whole book, and to Drs Åke Flock, Jan Lännergren and Gerald Westheimer and Professor Torsten Wiesel, who read portions of it. Their comments and suggestions have added considerably to the clarity and organisation of presentation. I should like, too, to thank Professor Wiesel for contributing the Foreword. I also have the pleasure of acknowledging the competent editorial work carried out by Mrs Joan Dallos and Mrs Ellen Curtin. Most of the illustrations were drawn by Mrs Sandra Almenberg and Mrs Bibbi Mayrhofer, whose excellent work has added a great deal to the quality of the book.

I should like to extend my thanks to Mrs Grethe Shepherd, who prepared the English translation of the original Swedish edition of the book; her considerable work has formed the basis for this new edition.

Miss Olga Popoff has spent endless hours not only in typing and retyping the manuscript over and over again but also in bringing together all the material involved in the presentation. It is thanks to her unfailing help that it has been possible to complete this book. I would also like to thank Miss Gabrielle Ottoson, who gave me assistance in the final, most difficult, period of the work on the illustrations. Lastly, I wish to give special thanks to Miss Elizabeth Horne, Senior Editor of the Medical Division of Macmillan Press Ltd, for her endless patience and whole-hearted support, and to Mr R. M. Powell, who handled the production matters in a most efficient way.

Section I: Introduction

1

Historical Survey

The history of neurophysiology goes back to a November day in 1786. Luigi Galvani, anatomist and teacher at the University of Bologna, was in his laboratory that day studying the discharge of a Leyden jar, a new and fascinating instrument for the scientists of the time (Fig. 1.1). One of his pupils, dissecting a frog, noticed that the frog twitched each time the Leyden jar discharged sparks. When the frog was connected directly to the Leyden jar with a wire, the same effect was observed, even if the frog was in a separate room, although the muscle response was then weaker. That an electrical discharge could cause muscle to twitch was not a new discovery; a French scientist had demonstrated this phenomenon half a century earlier at the Academy of Sciences in Paris, and

the possibility of using electricity to restore function to paralysed muscles was at this time the subject of much discussion. Indeed, electrical phenomena of all kinds captured the imagination of the scientific world. Franklin had recently published his theory that all matter contains a natural quantity of electricity. It was thought that this amount could be changed in different ways; thus by adding electricity a body would become positively charged, whereas if deprived of its natural charge it would become negative.

Galvani studied the contraction of the frog muscle for several years (Fig. 1.2); in 1791 he published his discovery in a monograph entitled *De Viribus Electricitatis in Motu Musculari Commentarius.* In this he suggested that an inherent electricity

Fig. 1.1 Engraving from the original work of Galvani, 1791, showing the apparatus used in his experiments. At left is an electrostatic machine, and to the right a Leyden jar. (From de Santillana, *Scient. Am.*, 212, 1965. Copyright Burndy Library Collection.)

Fig. 1.2 Luigi Galvani demonstrating to his wife and pupil the effect of electricity on the muscles of a frog. (Radio Times Hulton Picture Library.)

exists in living tissue. Galvani assumed that the brain was the source of electricity and that it was transferred to the muscles through the nerves, where it was stored. This idea was quite in line with speculations current at this time, which depicted electricity as some sort of subtle fluid. What was mystifying to Galvani was the amazing speed of its flow and, still more remarkable, how nerves, lacking electrical insulation, could be effective conductors.

Galvani's discovery aroused enormous interest, and scientists all over Europe began to study the phenomena he had described. It was thought that the *Spiritus animalis* had been found and that this

discovery would unlock the secrets of life. It was suggested that many illnesses could be attributed to disturbances in the electrical charge of particular organs. Galvani himself suggested that electricity might be used for treatment of ischias, epilepsy and nervous diseases.

Galvani's thesis that nerves and muscles have an electrical charge did not remain unchallenged. Volta contended that the twitch did not depend upon an electrical discharge of the muscle, but rather that the muscle was simply stimulated electrically. In some of his experiments Galvani had used a pair of forceps which had one blade of copper and another of zinc. Volta showed that such a pair of forceps acted as an electromotive force when in contact with a fluid, copper being the positive pole and zinc the negative pole; this discovery eventually led to Volta's construction of the first electrical battery (Fig. 1.3). Volta claimed that Galvani had actually stimulated the nerve with the pair of forceps and thus challenged Galvani's explanation that the nerve itself is charged. The battle that ensued between Galvani and Volta (Fig. 1.4) was bitter, protracted and pursued with undiminished force by both sides until Galvani's death. It was an uneven fight, for Galvani was a gentle, withdrawn, almost shy, man, while Volta was outgoing and self-confident. His

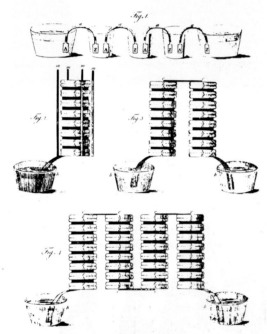

Fig. 1.3 The first electric battery constructed by Volta around 1800. It developed out of the controversy with Galvani. Volta denied the existence of 'animal' electricity and maintained that Galvani's observations could be explained by the fact that metals in contact with fluid form a source of electricity. To prove his theory, Volta started to experiment with different metals. The battery at the top of the picture consists of silver (A) and zinc (Z) plates placed in a salt solution; the other pictures show the plates arranged in stacks with moist paper between each set of plates. (From de Santillana, *Scient. Am.*, 212, 1965. Copyright Burndy Library Collection.)

many discoveries in physics brought Volta much authority as well (Fig. 1.5), and he soon appeared to emerge the victor in the scientific clash with Galvani.

The last years of Galvani's life were very unhappy. He was deprived of his chair at the University for refusing to swear allegiance to the new Republic of Bologna and he became depressed by the spiteful criticism of his ideas, particularly Volta's vituperations. Reinstated at last, Galvani returned to his laboratory but died soon after on 4 December 1798.

A few years before his death, Galvani performed an experiment which finally answered Volta's criticism: he succeeded in eliciting a twitch in the absence of metals by using the electricity of living tissue. The reports of this experiment were published anonymously in 1794, but Galvani's authorship seems indisputable. In this experiment the frog muscle was made to twitch when brought into contact with the spinal cord (Fig. 1.6). In this case the source of the electrical stimulus was the tissue itself. Volta, however, was reluctant to acknowledge even the evidence of this experiment, replying that the muscle twitch occurred because of heterogeneity in the tissues of the preparation, and therefore the effect was comparable to that obtained by stimulation with different metals.

Galvani died convinced that he had emerged the victor in the fight with Volta, but the latter was equally convinced that he had won. Today we know that neither Volta nor Galvani was entirely correct. With the instrumentation available at that time neither of them could ascertain whether animal tissue was electrically charged or not. Not until the construction of the first galvanometer in the 1820s did it become possible to record the weak electrical currents of living tissues. The first measurements with this instrument were done in 1827 by the Italian physicist, Nobili; the electrical current that he recorded from muscles was interpreted as a thermoelectric phenomenon, and he discounted the possible evidence of differences in charge within the muscles themselves. Some years later another Italian scientist, Matteucci, provided conclusive evidence of electrical potentials in living tissue. He showed that at rest there is a potential difference

tacts with secondary neurons. Since dendrites generally convey signals towards the cell body and the axon conducts impulses away from the cell body, the peripheral process may be considered as an elongated dendrite and the central process as an axon. However, the peripheral process possesses all the structural and functional properties of an axon and is therefore generally termed an afferent axon. The bipolar neurons are sensory in function like the unipolar neurons. The cell body is spindle-shaped and has an extension at each pole of the cell. This kind of neuron is found in the organs of special senses such as in the olfactory mucosa, in the retina and in the cochlear and vestibular ganglia. Multipolar neurons are by far the most common in the central nervous system. They have numerous processes and their cell bodies show a wide variation in shape.

According to another more functional scheme of classification, neurons in the central nervous system can be classified into Golgi type I and Golgi type II neurons. The type I neurons have long axons which may leave the central nervous system and become peripheral nerve fibres. Their axons also form the main fibre tracts of the spinal cord and the brain. The type II neurons are small and their axons terminate near the cell body to give them a stellate or star-shaped appearance.

Early light microscope studies suggested that the neuron is a protoplasmic, gelatinous structure enclosed by a thin membrane. With the advent of electron microscopy and other techniques, it became apparent that, besides cytoplasm, the interior of the cell contains a variety of organelles (Fig. 2.1). Later neurophysiological and biochemical studies have provided evidence that these organelles carry out specific functions vital to the neuron. Most of the organelles are wrapped in membranes which separate their contents from the cytoplasm of the cell. The neuron is not, therefore, to be considered as a homogeneous cytoplasmic substance separated from the external environment by a membrane, but rather it is to be considered as composed of a number of structural subunits enclosed by a common membrane. Vast amounts of data accumulated in recent years show, moreover,

that the plasma membrane is itself the primary site of numerous functions, such as the reactions underlying communication between neurons, the release of substances produced inside the neuron and the exchange of metabolic products.

Membrane structure

The membrane delineating the cell is too thin to be seen under the light microscope and so its structure remained unknown until the electron microscope first became available in the late 1940s. In the electron microscope the cell membrane after fixation with osmium appears as two dark lines (Fig. 2.2), each about 25 nm thick, separated by a light space of the same thickness. Early studies revealed that the membrane has the same general appearance not only in all neurons but also in all the cells of the body. These findings led to the proposal of the 'unit membrane model' in 1959, according to which all membranes have the same basic structure. Since cell membranes are composed of proteins and lipids and since osmium, which is used to increase the contrast of electron micrographs, binds strongly to proteins, it was concluded that the two dark lines in electron micrographs represent proteins and the light middle line is a layer of lipids. This hypothesis accords with earlier biochemical findings that lipids constitute about 50% of the membrane and that most of the remainder is protein. The membrane lipids were found to be primarily phospholipids. The head of a phospholipid molecule is electrically charged and hydrophilic, or water attracting, whereas its other end is hydrophobic, or water repelling. Consequently, when phospholipids are mixed with water, they tend to aggregate into micelles or in bimolecular layers: the charged heads face outwards, towards the water molecules, while the other ends of the molecules are oriented towards one another, at the interior of the micelle or bilayer. It was on the basis of his studies of lipid films formed in this way that Danielli suggested in 1935 that cell membranes consist of a bimolecular layer of phospholipids sandwiched between two layers of protein.

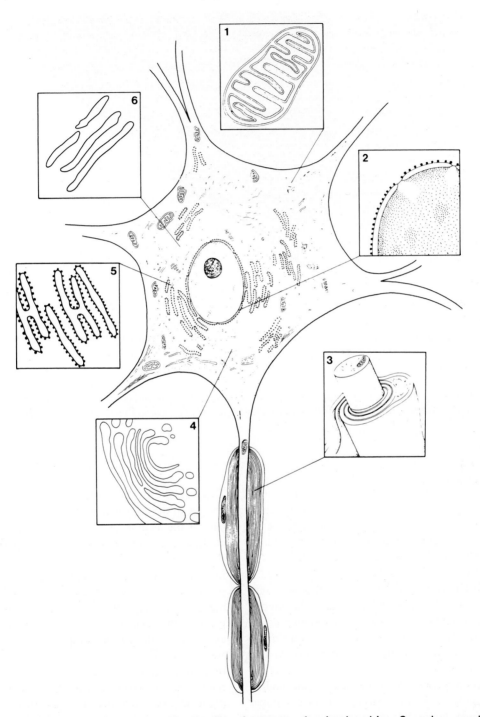

Fig. 2.1   General structural features and organelles of a neuron: 1, mitochondrion; 2, nuclear membrane; 3, myelin sheath; 4, Golgi apparatus; 5, rough endoplasmic reticulum; 6, smooth endoplasmic reticulum.

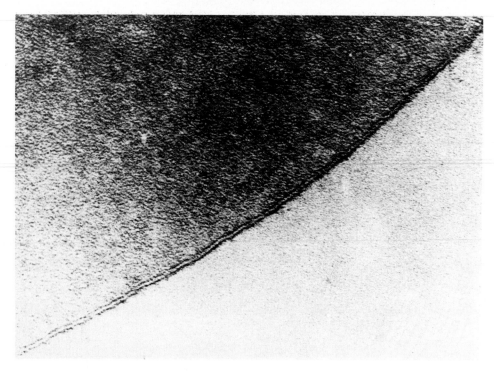

Fig. 2.2　Electron micrograph of the cell membrane (human red cell). (From Robertson, in M. Locked (ed.), *Cellular Membrane in Development*, Academic Press, New York, 1964.)

It would thus appear that to build up the membrane the cell would only have to synthesise phospholipids, which by virtue of their physical characteristics spontaneously form a membrane to which protein would then be added on each side.

The model that Danielli proposed envisaged a rigid orderly arrangement of the membrane components, which newer findings refute. The interior of the membrane is actually in an almost liquid state, because the phospholipid molecules are highly mobile, and the proteins seemingly float in this liquid layer. The earlier rigid membrane model has therefore been replaced by the 'fluid mosaic model', which proposes that cell membranes are composed of a fluid liquid bilayer matrix which permits lateral movements of the membrane's components.

This model differs from the earlier rigid one with respect to the arrangement of the protein components of the membrane. Rather than constituting a continuous layer on either side of the lipid bilayer, the proteins form globular units inserted into the membrane (Fig. 2.3). Such integral membrane proteins may extend all the way through the membrane or lie only on one side or the other. The proteins that penetrate the membrane may act as channels for the passage of ions (such as sodium and potassium). These protein molecules are thought to exist in either of two conformational states, one of which provides a channel through the membrane while the other is closed. Normally the majority of these protein molecules are maintained in the closed state by the resting membrane

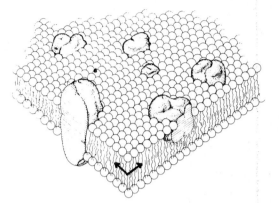

Fig. 2.3 Fluid mosaic model of the cell membrane. The large elliptical bodies represent globular protein complexes embedded in the core of the phospholipid matrix in a more or less random fashion. The phospholipid molecules are oriented with their non-polar fatty acid chains towards the interior of the bilayer and with their polar ends towards the cytoplasmic or extracellular surface of the membrane. The lateral adhesion between neighbouring phospholipid molecules is relatively weak and the whole ensemble of lipids and proteins is a fluid mosaic. The membrane is therefore highly labile and can alter its structure, for instance, in response to stimulation. (From Singer and Nicolson, *Science*, 175, 1972.)

potential. Under the influence of changes in the external ionic environment, changes in membrane potential, etc., these molecules may shift to the open state and thus allow the movement of ions across the membrane. The walls of the channels may have different properties; some appear to carry negative charges and therefore only allow cations to pass through, while others are open only to anions. Molecules which are larger than the tubular diameter are unable to cross the membrane through these channels. Large molecules may, however, pass directly through the lipid portions of the membrane; in this case their rate of entry is determined by their solubility in the lipids. Other molecules like amino acids, which are also too large to pass through the channels, are bound to specific sites on the membrane surface which appear to facilitate their movement through the membrane. The specific molecules of these sites

are generally referred to as carriers. It is supposed that a carrier molecule is able to combine with a molecule at the outer surface of the membrane, and this complex then moves through the membrane to the inner side where the complex dissociates, and the carrier releases the molecule in question. The carrier thereafter returns to the outer surface, and the cycle is repeated.

Recent progress in membrane research indicates that the membrane structure is more complex than has previously been assumed. It has been found with special staining techniques that there is a thin layer of material attached to the outer surface of the free cell membrane and to synaptic membranes. A similar membrane component is present on the cytoplasmic surface of the membrane. This cytoplasmic coat is modified in synaptic regions, as will be described below. The distribution of membrane proteins is asymmetric, with a higher concentration on the inner surface than on the outer; furthermore, the proteins are not all identical. This asymmetry may explain the different functional behaviours of the inner and outer sides of the cell membrane. Many of the membrane proteins include carbohydrates and are known as glycoproteins. They extend part of their peptide chain and probably all of their carbohydrate part into the extracellular space (see Fig. 2.4). It has been found that the outer cell surface has a negative charge; most probably this is due to the glycoproteins and glycolipids incorporated in the membrane. This negative charge is an important factor in providing for a mechanism by which cellular structures may repel each other. If for instance the negative charge is eliminated in ciliated cells, the cilia fuse together and lose their mobility. Furthermore the glycoproteins represent the binding sites for various substances, including hormones; they appear, in addition, to be responsible for the recognition of foreign cells and viruses.

Freeze–fracturing studies

Important insight into membrane structure, and in particular the topography of cell junctions, has been obtained by the freeze–fracturing technique.

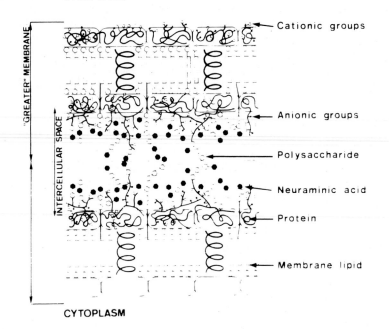

CYTOPLASM

← Cationic groups

← Anionic groups

← Polysaccharide

← Neuraminic acid

← Protein

← Membrane lipid

CYTOPLASM

Fig. 2.4 Schematic diagram illustrating current concepts of molecular structure of the cell membrane. The drawing shows the membranes of two cells in close apposition (From Pfenninger, in *Progr. Histochem. Cytochem.*, 1973.)

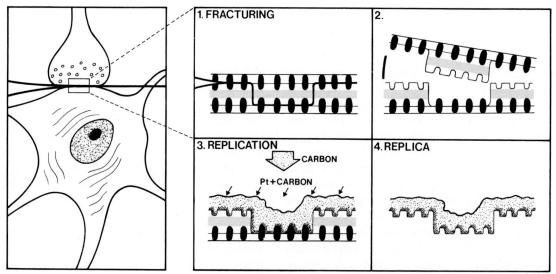

Fig. 2.5 Schematic illustration of freeze—fracturing technique. The frozen specimen is fractured either by cut-cleaving (as shown in 1) or by placing it sandwiched between two cold carriers which are then broken apart at −150°C to −100°C. The plane of fracture follows cellular membranes in the frozen tissue. The next step involves making a replica of the specimen by evaporating a thin layer of platinum and carbon on the fractured tissue surface at a fixed angle to the surface. This accounts for the shadowing effect and enhancement of relief differences of the final electron micrograph. The platinum—carbon replica is reinforced with a layer of carbon evaporated perpendicularly. The specimen is thereafter dissolved and the cleaned replica mounted for observation in the electron microscope.

In this technique a small piece of tissue is rapidly frozen at −210°C and thereafter fractured by cleavage. The surface thus exposed can be prepared by special techniques for examination in the electron microscope (Fig. 2.5).

The freeze—fracturing technique allows the examination of tissue specimens without dehydration and embedding, and the ultrastructural organisation of cells and cell organelles may be visualised in a three-dimensional fashion (Fig. 2.6). The fracture plane may occur at random, or it may follow natural boundary lines such as the outer membrane of the cell. It is the fracture occurring along natural membranes that provides the main information since it allows detailed study of the macromolecular organisation of cell membranes and of profiles and surfaces of cell organelles. It

was at first believed that the fracture followed the interface between the extracellular space and the outer leaflet of the cell membrane or the inner leaflet and the cytoplasmic matrix of the cell. Later studies have shown that the cell membrane splits along the middle of the double layer of lipids so that half of the membrane remains attached to the cell and half to adjacent extracellular structures. This implies that the freeze—fracture process exposes either the inner leaflet associated with the cytoplasm or the outer leaflet associated with the extracellular space.

It has been found in freeze—fracturing studies that all cell membranes have a common basic appearance: a smooth surface from which the globular proteins protrude as small bumps 6—19 nm in diameter. These so-called intramembranous

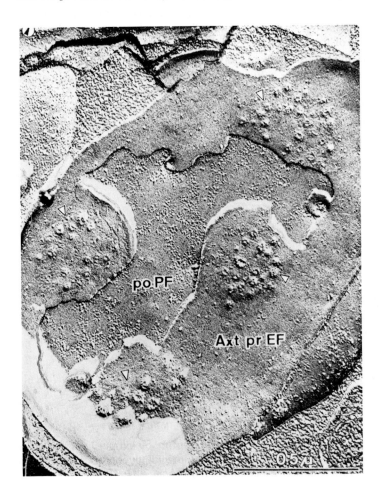

Fig. 2.6   Freeze—etch replica of axon terminal (Axt prEF) showing multiple active zones. In the centre the post-synaptic membrane (poPF) is exposed. Specimen from rat spinal cord. (From Sandri, Van Buren and Akert, *Prog. Brain Res.*, 46, 1977.)

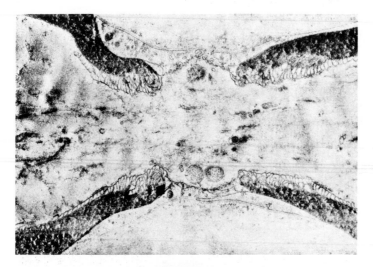

Fig. 2.17 Electron micrograph of a longitudinal section through a node of Ranvier in a frog sciatic nerve fibre. Within the node area the axon is surrounded loosely by processes of the Schwann cell. The current flow between the axoplasm and the exterior of the axon during propagation of the action potential takes place at the node of Ranvier. (From Robertson, in Bell, Davidson and Scarborough, *Textbook of Physiology and Biochemistry*, Livingstone, 1965.)

and of peripheral nerves. Unmyelinated nerve fibres are responsible for signalling pain and olfactory sensations and are numerous in the autonomic nervous system. In the central nervous system they are partially covered by glial cells; in peripheral nerves they are engulfed either singly or in small

bundles in invaginations of membranes of Schwann cells. Functionally the unmyelinated fibres are characterised by slow conduction, high thresholds and long refractory periods.

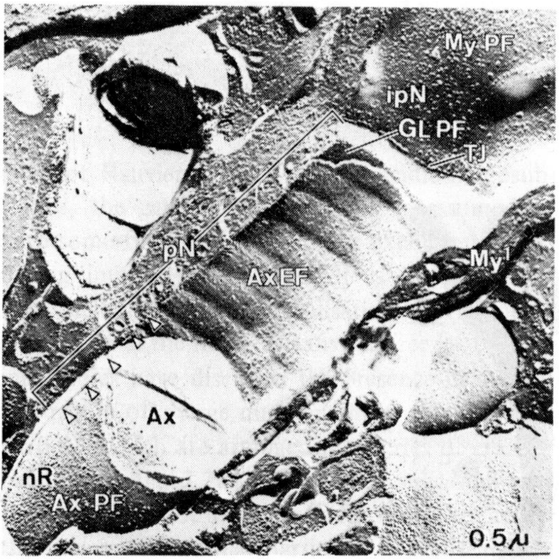

Fig. 2.18 Electron micrograph of freeze—etching replica of the Ranvier's node. Ax, axon; nR, node of Ranvier; pN, paranodal zone; ipN, interparanodal region; GL, glial loop; TJ, tight junction; My, myelin; MyPF, protoplasmic face of myelin. (From Sandri, Van Buren and Akert, *Prog. Brain Res.*, 46, 1977.)

Dendrites

As indicated earlier, the number and branching pattern of dendrites vary greatly throughout the nervous system (Fig. 2.20). In some cells the dendrites extend equally in all directions from the cell body. This kind of cell, termed stellate cell, is common in the cerebral cortex and in the spinal cord. In other cells, like the pyramidal cells, an apical dendrite emerges from the apex of the cell and basal dendrites emerge from the basal part of the cell body. In spindle-shaped cells, such as the fusiform cells of the cerebral cortex, the dendrites emerge from each end of the cell body. Still another type of branching pattern is that of the mitral cell of the olfactory bulb. These cells have only a few dendrites which branch profusely at their tips in spherical structures called synaptic glomeruli. The most conspicuous dendritic tree is that of the Purkinje cells (see p. 268). The functional role of the dendrites is to provide for an increase in the surface area and thereby in the receptive area of the neuron. It has been estimated that in spinal motoneurons the dendrites represent up to 80% of

Fig. 2.19   The myelin sheath. Freeze—fracture preparation of the Pacinian corpuscle showing the lamellar structure of the myelin sheath of the nerve at its entry into the corpuscle. (From Ottoson and Zelena, unpublished observations.)

the total neuronal surface area. The branching pattern displayed by the dendrites seems to relate closely to the specific functions of the cell. Another important feature is the distribution of incoming synapses. The efficacy of inhibitory or excitatory action of synapses must vary with their distance from the cell body and the initial segment of the axon. It should be noted that, although the dendrites represent the main afferent component of the neurons, recent evidence suggests that they may also provide for efferent transmission of activity from one cell to another (see below).

Synapses

As indicated above, the neurons are anatomically distinct units and there is no direct structural connection between their cytoplasms, except at gap junctions (see below). This raises the question of how nerve cells communicate with each other. Early light microscope studies revealed that the branches of the terminal axon end in small knobs which lie in close contact with the dendrites or soma of other neurons. At the turn of the century, Sherrington advanced the idea that the knobs

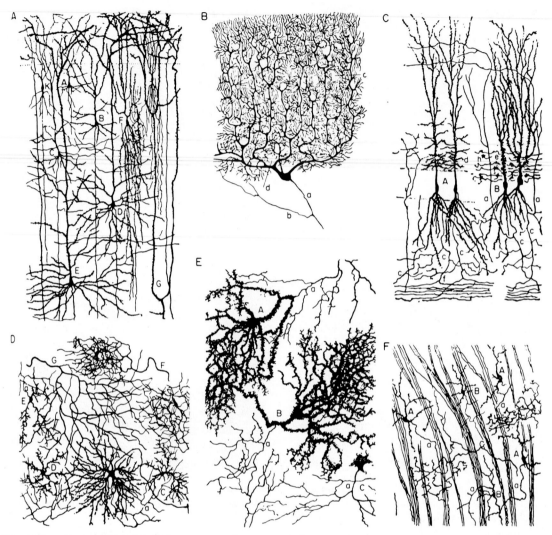

Fig. 2.20   Examples of dendritic patterns of neurons. (A) Dendritic patterns of neurons of the outermost three layers of frontal cortex. (B) Dendritic tree of a Purkinje cell. (C) Dendritic trees of pyramidal cells of hippocampus. (D) Dendritic trees of neurons of the somatic sensory nucleus of the thalamus. (E) Dendritic trees of neurons of the pons. (F) Axon and dendrites of neurons in the caudate nucleus.

represented specialised sites for transmission of signals from one neuron to another, and he introduced the term *synapse* for these functional connections.

As seen in the light microscope, there is a great variety of synaptic contacts between axons and nerve cells in the central nervous system. A typical motoneuron in the spinal cord may have its soma and dendrites covered with synaptic knobs (Fig. 2.21). The only region of the neuron relatively devoid of synaptic contacts is the axon hillock portion from which the axon emerges. In other cells the synaptic contact may take the form of a cup that covers a great proportion of the cell surface (Fig. 2.22). In regions receiving a major sensory input, such as the thalamic nuclei or the substantia

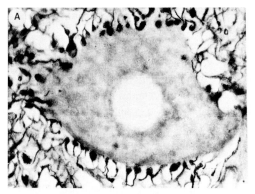 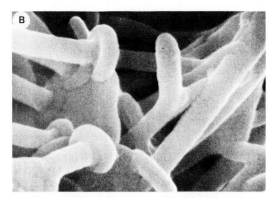

Fig. 2.21 (A) Synaptic terminals of axons in contact with a spinal motoneuron. (B) Scanning electron micrograph of button-like synaptic terminals in the nervous system of the 'sea hare', *Aplysia*. ((A) From Ormea, 1961; (B) from Lewis *et al.*, 1972, in G. S. Stent, *Scient. Am.*, 227(3), 43–51.)

gelatinosa of the spinal cord, the synaptic contacts are aggregated in clusters called *glomeruli* (Fig. 2.23).

The incoming neuron at the synaptic contact is called presynaptic (Fig. 2.24), and the neuron to which the activity is transmitted is postsynaptic. The majority of presynaptic fibres forming the synapses are unmyelinated axon branches. When approaching the terminal knob, myelinated fibres lose their meylin sheath gradually layer by layer; sometimes the myelin sheath is not entirely lost until about 1 μm from the synaptic knob. Depending on which cellular components are involved, synapses can be divided into axosomatic (an axon terminal contacting a cell body), axodendritic (axon terminal in contact with a dendrite), axo-axonic (two axon terminals in contact) or dendro-dendritic (contacts between two dendrites) (Fig. 2.25).

With the advent of electron microscopy, a study of the fine structure of the synapse became possible. It became clear that the presynaptic terminal knob is separated from the membrane of the postsynaptic neuron by a space, the 'synaptic cleft', with a width of about 20 nm. Another characteristic feature of synapses revealed in the electron microscope studies is the presence of a large number of small vesicles in the presynaptic terminals (Fig. 2.26). Furthermore, at the site of the synaptic junction there is an asymmetric thickening of the cell membranes. For a number of years it was

thought that this type of synapse was the only one present in the central nervous system. Subsequent studies disclosed, however, that there also exist synaptic junctions, so-called gap junctions, which are characterised by a structural symmetry and lack of synaptic cleft. There are thus two main anatomical classes of synapse. As we shall see later, the two types of synapse are also functionally different; transmission is mediated chemically in the first type and electrically in the second. Sometimes a chemical synapse and an electrical one are present in the same terminal; this is referred to as a mixed synapse. At a chemical synapse the activity passes in only one direction because only the presynaptic element releases transmitter, whereas at most electrical synapses activity passes in either direction.

The geometry of synaptic connections is another criterion for classifying synapses (Fig. 2.27). The simplest synaptic arrangement has a single presynaptic component, such as an axon terminal apposed to the postsynaptic membrane; most synapses in the brain are of this type. More complicated synaptic arrangements of several interacting structures are also possible. An example of such a synaptic complex is one presynaptic component in contact with two postsynaptic structures. The terminals of visual receptor cells in the retina make this kind of synaptic contact with processes of horizontal and bipolar cells. Another type of complex connection involves *serial synapses*. Here three structures are

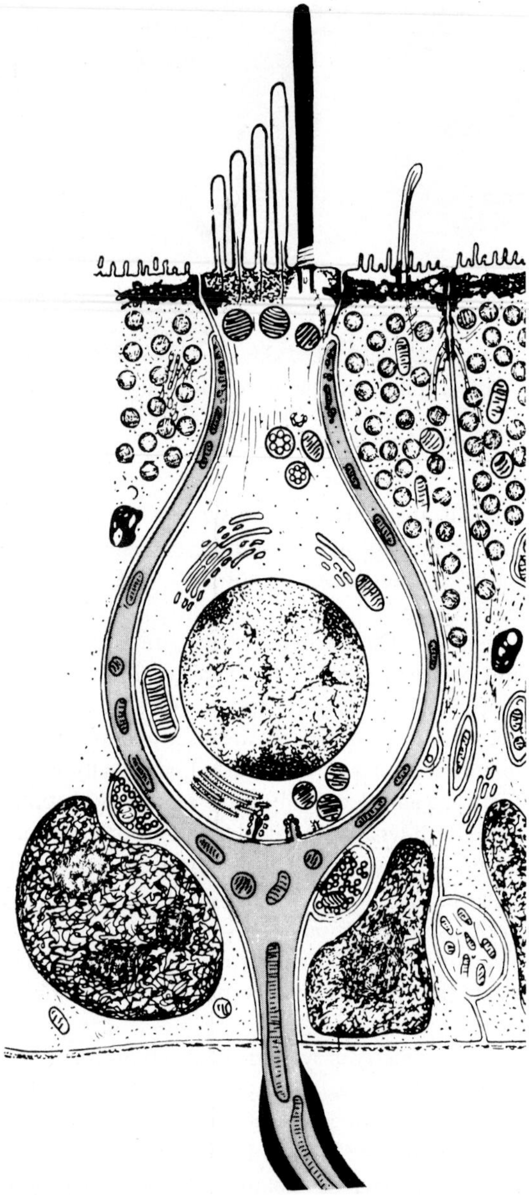

Fig. 2.22 Chalice-like nerve terminal enclosing a flask-shaped hair cell. (From Engström *et al., Acta Otolaryngol., Suppl.* 301, 1972.)

arranged in series with the activity being conducted from the first component to the second and thence to the third. A still more complicated pattern is the reciprocal synapse. In this case activity passes from one cell to a second and from this cell back to the first one; the second cell thus has pre- and postsynaptic functions side by side.

Chemical synapses

This type of cellular junction, which constitutes the classical synapse, exhibits considerable morphological variation. The most common type is represented by the synapse found between the afferent axon terminals and the soma of spinal motoneurons. Here the endings of the presynaptic fibre form bulbous *boutons terminaux* which closely approach the postsynaptic cell membrane. Electron microscopy shows a structural asymmetry in the contact region, with respect to the distribution of organelles in the presynaptic and postsynaptic components and with respect to the distribution of electrodense material near the two apposed membranes. The presynaptic part of the synapse usually contains clear synaptic vesicles and a varying number of mitochondria; in some cases, the vesicles are not randomly distributed but congregate near structures known as presynaptic dense projections, which may take various forms (see below). The postsynaptic component, in contrast, lacks vesicles. Its synaptic membrane is thickened in what is called the subsynaptic web. The synaptic cleft between the presynaptic and the postsynaptic membranes contains a material of intermediate density, the so-called *synaptic gap substance*. It has been proposed that the gap substance plays a role in the movement of transmitter substance across the cleft and impedes the diffusion of the transmitter away from the junctional area. It has also been suggested that the gap substance plays a role in the development of the synapses by forming recognition sites.

An outstanding morphological feature of chemical synapses is the accumulation of vesicles in the presynaptic ending. It is generally assumed that the vesicles contain the transmitter which is released in discrete quantal units. The first electron microscope studies of synapses suggested that there was only one type of vesicle; these were spherical in shape and had a mean diameter of 50 nm. With the development of new fixation techniques, it

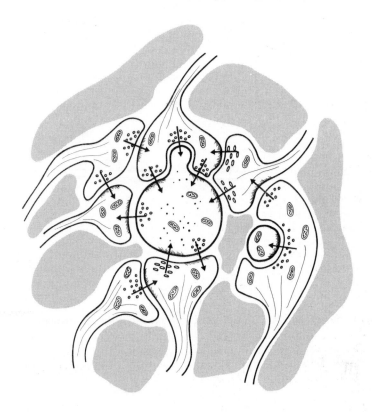

Fig. 2.23 Synaptic glomerulus. The synapses are grouped around a central dendrite shown in cross-section. Excitatory and inhibitory synapses are indicated by rounded and ellipsoidal vesicles respectively. The whole synaptic complex is enclosed by glial cells.

was reported that the vesicles at some synapses were flat or ellipsoidal (Fig. 2.28). From a correlation of morphological and neurophysiological observations, it was suggested that the round vesicles contain excitatory transmitter while the flat vesicles are inhibitory in nature. It now seems clear that the difference in shape between the two types of vesicles may be dependent on the fixatives and that the presence of flat vesicles is no direct evidence that a given synapse is inhibitory. Freeze–etching studies suggest that the spherical shape is the natural form of the vesicles. However, it is generally agreed that the appearance of the two types of vesicles with certain

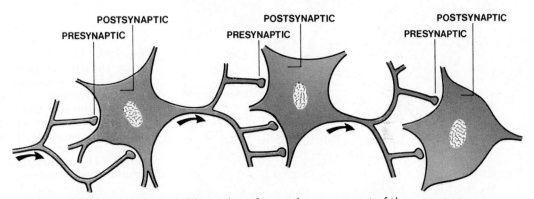

Fig. 2.24   Schematic illustration of synaptic arrangement of three neurons.

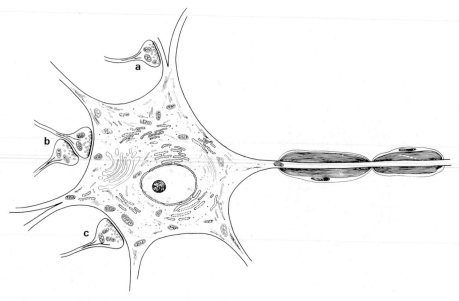

Fig. 2.25 Schematic illustration of variations of synaptic organisation: (a) axodendritic; (b) axoaxonic; (c) axosomatic.

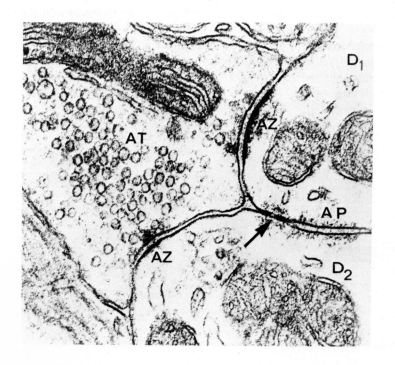

Fig. 2.26 Electron micrograph showing an axon terminal (AT) establishing a chemical synapse (AZ) on two dendrites (D_1, D_2) and a gap junction (arrow) and attachment plaque (AP) between the two dendrites. (From *The Neurosciences, Fourth Study Program*, eds F. O. Schmitt and F. G. Worden, MIT Press, 1979.)

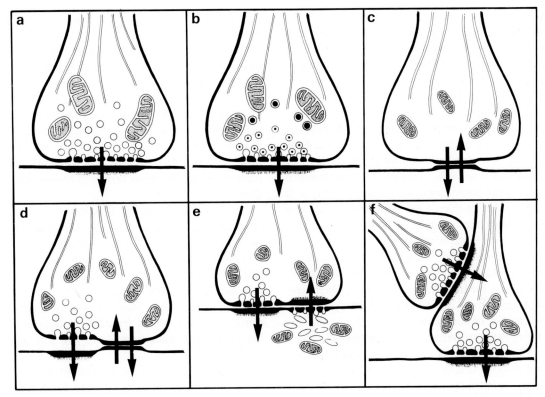

Fig. 2.27 Schematic representation of different types of synaptic junctions: (a) synaptic bouton characteristic of most central excitatory synapses; (b) dense-core type of synaptic bouton characteristic of peripheral adrenergic axon terminals; (c) gap junction; (d) mixed synapse, composed of chemical and gap junctions; (e) reciprocal synapse; (f) serial synapse.

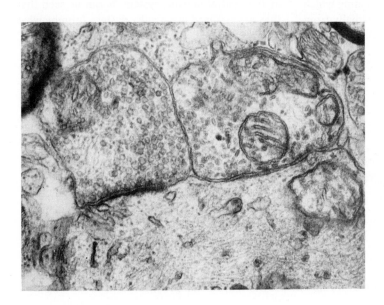

Fig. 2.28 Electron micrograph of two synaptic terminals in contact with a dendrite of a spinal motor neuron. In the terminal to the left the postsynaptic membrane is thickened and the vesicles are round. In the terminal to the right the vesicles have a more elongated form and the typical thickening in the postsynaptic membrane is lacking. It is likely that the terminal to the left is excitatory, and that to the right is inhibitory. (From Gray, *Sci. J.*, 3, 1967.)

fixation procedures indicates functional differences. This notion is supported by the finding that the presence of the two types of vesicles is generally associated with differences in other structural features of the synapses. On the basis of various criteria such as vesicle shape, the area of the synaptic membrane, the width of the cleft and the appearance of membrane thickenings, two types of chemical synapses may thus be distinguished. Type I is characterised by spheroidal vesicles, a wide synaptic cleft and an accumulation of dense material close to the postsynaptic membrane, while type II has elliptical vesicles, a narrow synaptic cleft and little or no accumulation of dense material next to the postsynaptic membrane.

In addition to the clear agranular vesicles, several other types of vesicles have been demonstrated. One type is the *large dense core vesicles* which have been found in a large variety of adrenergic and cholinergic terminals in the peripheral and the central nervous system. These vesicles have a size of 90 to 120 nm and a dense core which is separated from the vesicular membrane by a narrow gap. Within monoaminergic nerve terminals these vesicles accumulate biogenic monoamines. Still another type of vesicle is the *coated vesicle*, which appears together with empty vesicles in some synapses. The most characteristic feature of the coated vesicles is that they are wrapped in a coating which consists of an array of bars extending radially from the outer surface of the vesicular membrane, form-

ing what with special staining techniques looks like basketwork.

The mechanisms of formation of the vesicles is incompletely known. According to one hypothesis the vesicles are formed in the soma and transported to the nerve terminal (see Fig. 2.29). Another hypothesis envisages vesicle formation to occur in the nerve terminals. The generally accepted notion is that the major part of the synaptic vesicles is formed by the Golgi apparatus in the soma and is transported to the nerve terminals by axoplasmic flow.

As indicated above, the vesicles of a chemical synapse are always located on the presynaptic side. An apparent exception to this rule are the reciprocal synaptic endings. Here two synapses are side by side; at one site the vesicles are clustered on one side, at the other site on the opposite side of the junction (Fig. 2.30). However, the direction of synaptic transmission is according to the rule, i.e. the presence of vesicles indicates that this side is presynaptic.

A striking feature of the presynaptic membrane is the presence of diffusely outlined dense patches which protrude from the membrane into the cytoplasm of the synaptic knob. These local thickenings are usually known as presynaptic projections. In sections parallel to the synaptic cleft of synapses in the central nervous system, it can be seen that they are arranged in a regular pattern forming what has been called the 'presynaptic vesicular grid'

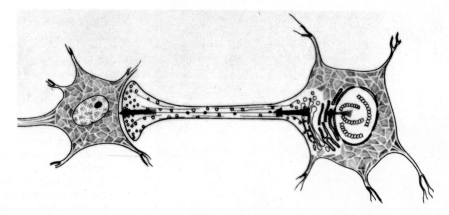

Fig. 2.29   Schematic representation of formation and transport of vesicles from soma to terminal.

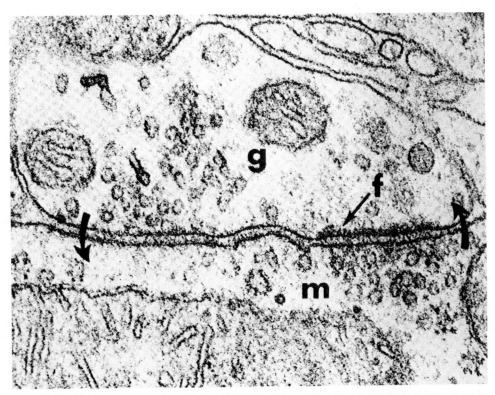

Fig. 2.30 Reciprocal synaptic ending of a gemmule (g) from a granule cell of the olfactory bulb on an accessory dendrite of a mitral cell (m). Polarity is deduced from the clustering of vesicles at the cell membrane of the presynaptic component and from the fuzz (f) on the cytoplasmic side of the membrane of the gemmule. ×100 000. (From Rall *et al., Exp. Neurol.*, 14, 1966.)

(Fig. 2.31), whereas in the motor endplate they are arranged in long rows (Fig. 2.32). In presynaptic endings of sensory receptor cells, such as the photo-receptors or the hair cells of the inner ear, the dense material is organised perpendicularly to the presynaptic membrane and is surrounded by vesicles; these structures are termed synaptic ribbons in the visual cells and synaptic bars in the hair cells (Fig. 2.33). These projections have been variously interpreted as diffusion pathways linking the vesicles to the presynaptic membrane, or as anchors which hold the vesicles at the site until their eventual release.

In the presynaptic vesicular grid the dense projections are often arranged so that they form what appears as a hexagonal sieve (Fig. 2.34). Generally there is a clustering of vesicles close to the dense projections. The interspaces between the dense

projections are of the same size as the vesicles which appear to fit into them. It has been thought that the dense projections form guiding pathways for synaptic vesicles to reach sites for the interaction between the presynaptic membrane and the vesicles. In freeze–etched preparations of presynaptic membranes, small circular pits or so-called *synaptopores* are seen which are arranged in a pattern resembling that formed by the dense projections. It has been suggested that the synaptopores represent channels for the release of the transmitter.

The postsynaptic membrane is characterised by the accumulation of cytoplasmic dense material which is often the most prominent feature of the synapse. This material, which in early electron microscope studies was called the *subsynaptic web*, may appear as a continuous bar; in synapses con-

Fig. 2.31   Schematic representation of presynaptic nerve terminal with vesicular grid, 'synaptopores' and synaptic vesicles. (From Pappas and Purpura, *Structure and Function of Synapses*, Raven Press, New York, 1972.)

taining spherical vesicles it has a considerable thickness, while in synapses with ellipsoidal vesicles it forms a very thin almost invisible band. In some synapses the dense material appears as a row of dense particles. Freeze—etching studies have revealed the presence of large particles embedded in the postsynaptic membrane; these particles have been thought to represent postsynaptic receptor sites.

Electrical synapses

The first electrophysiological studies showed that the chemically transmitting synapses described above were present throughout the organism. It was therefore concluded that chemical transmission was the only mode by which neurons communicate. It was therefore an unexpected finding that some synapses in *Crustacea* transmit signals electrically; these junctions have therefore been termed *electrotonic synapses*. It was at first thought that this type of synapse did not exist in the mammalian central

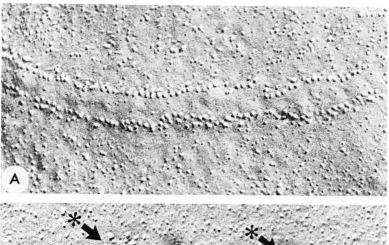

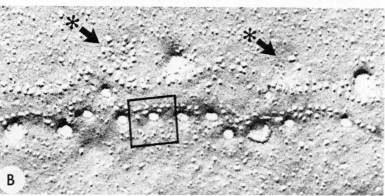

Fig. 2.32   Freeze—etching replica of resting (A) and active (B) motor endplate. Note membrane perturbations along the edges of the active zone. It is likely that these are exocytotic stomata, or openings into the underlying synaptic vesicles. The two areas marked by asterisks are probably vesicles that have collapsed flat after opening. The area in the square illustrates the characteristic domain of exocytosis. x143 000. (From Heuser *et al., J. Cell. Biol.*, 81, 1979.)

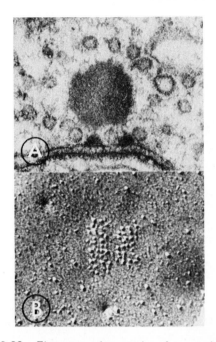

Fig. 2.33 Electron micrograph of synaptic arrangement in hair cell. (A) Synaptic bar in cross-section surrounded by vesicles and displaying synaptic (triangular) rodlets. (B) Freeze—etching replica showing particle array in the same synapse. (From Bagger-Sjöbäck and Flock, unpublished observations.)

nervous system. More recent studies have demonstrated that they are present in some regions such as in the mesencephalic trigeminal nucleus, in the lateral vestibular nucleus and in the primate retina. Although chemical transmission is the predominant mode of communication between neurons, it has become abundantly clear that both modes of transmission, chemical and electrical, operate in the mammalian nervous system.

The most characteristic morphological feature of the electrotonic synapse is the close apposition between the neuronal membranes. This kind of junction has also been termed a *gap junction* (Fig. 2.35). It may be axosomatic, axodendritic, axo-axonic, dendrodendritic or somatosomatic. In contrast to the chemical synapse, which is always asymmetric, the area of close membrane apposition of a gap junction appears symmetrical in electron micrographs. Usually there is no morphological feature by which the pre- and postsynaptic components can be distinguished. Vesicles may be present on one or both sides of gap junctions. Clear round or ellipsoidal vesicles as well as dense core vesicles have been found. In some synapses the vesicles are clustered close to the membrane at a distance from the area of close membrane apposition. These junctions which have the characteristics of both electrical and chemical synapses have been called 'mixed' synapses.

The two apposing plasma membranes of a gap junction sometimes appear to be fused so as to occlude the synaptic cleft. However, studies with marker substances have revealed that there is an intercellular space with a width of about 2 nm between the membranes. The cleft is bridged by small particles which are often arranged in a hexagonal pattern. These particles form intercellular pipes or channels which link the cytoplasm of the two cells (Fig. 2.35B). This has been demonstrated by iontophoretic injection of fluorescent dye into the cytoplasm of one of the cells; the dye spreads into the adjacent cell but none of the dye appears in the extracellular space. The intercellular channels allow the exchange of ions and molecules of small size but prevent the passage of large molecules.

Electrophysiological studies have demonstrated that the gap junctions represent low-resistance pathways for the direct conduction of electrical activity from one cell to another. Thereby they provide for a more rapid transmission of electrical signals between cells than at most chemical synapses. It is therefore interesting to note that gap junctions are present in tissues where either the speed of conduction of activity or the precise synchronisation of the activity of many cells is important. Thus gap junctions are found not only in the nervous system but also in cardiac muscle and in smooth muscle cells of the intestines. Their functional role in the central nervous system is not yet certain.

Junctional complexes

With the advent of thin-sectioning and freeze—fracturing techniques a variety of cellular connections have been disclosed which do not participate in transmission of activity from one cell to another.

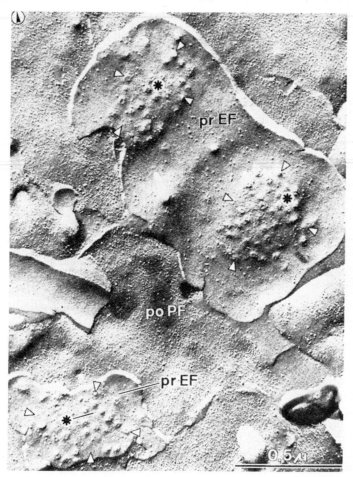

Fig. 2.34 Hexagonally ar-
ranged vesicle attachment sites
at two presynaptic membrane
faces (prEF) overlying the
postsynaptic membrane of a
neuron or a large dendrite
(poPF). Active zones are outlined by triangles. (From
Pfenninger *et al., J. Neurocytol.,* 1, 1972.)

Some of these junctions serve to prevent free passage of molecules in the intercellular spaces between
cells, whereas other junctions provide for mechanical coupling and adhesion between cells.

The category of junctions which provides for a
barrier against the free passage of molecules is
particularly important in epithelial tissue. These
so-called *tight junctions* are formed by what
appears to be a fusion of the plasma membranes of
two adjacent cells within a small region usually
located close to the surface of the cell layer.
Freeze—fracturing studies have revealed that the
plasma membranes are not cemented together but
rather are fused by a network of ridges of tightly
packed integral membrane proteins (Fig. 2.36).
These ridges hold the membranes close together

and block the passage of molecules across the cell
layer and thereby enable the cells to maintain an
intercellular environment that is different from the
external one to which their outer ends are exposed.
Tight junctions are for example present in the
olfactory epithelium where they provide for a
barrier against the diffusion of substances from the
mucus into the intercellular spaces in the sensory
epithelium.

The second category of cell junctions, which are
supposed to provide for mechanical coupling between cells, the so-called *desmosomes.* can be classified into two main types, belt desmosomes and
spot desmosomes. The belt desmosomes are usually
found in connection with tight junctions. They
form a belt or a band around the cells and within

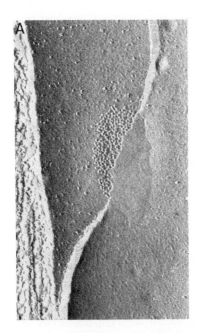

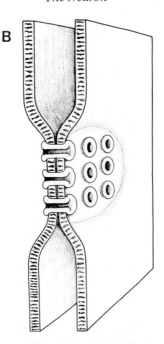

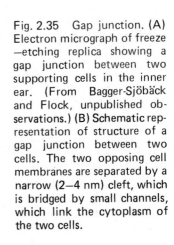

Fig. 2.35 Gap junction. (A) Electron micrograph of freeze—etching replica showing a gap junction between two supporting cells in the inner ear. (From Bagger-Sjöbäck and Flock, unpublished observations.) (B) Schematic representation of structure of a gap junction between two cells. The two opposing cell membranes are separated by a narrow (2—4 nm) cleft, which is bridged by small channels, which link the cytoplasm of the two cells.

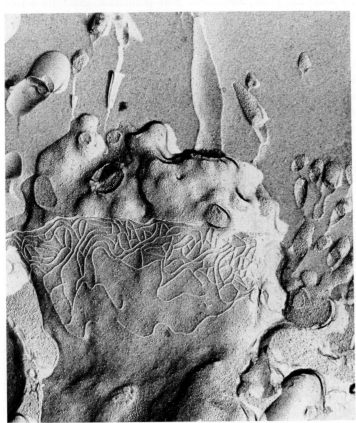

Fig. 2.36 Tight junctions around the neck of the olfactory vesicle of an olfactory receptor cell. The tight junctions extend around the circumference of the olfactory vesicles and link the vesicle to surrounding supporting cells. The tight junctions hold the cells together and seal the passageway from the mucus layer to the intercellular spaces between the olfactory cells and the receptor cells. (From Ottoson, unpublished.)

this region the intercellular space is filled with fine filamentous material. Inside the cell there is a system of filaments of actin which appear to be connected to the desmosome region. It has been suggested that the filaments would provide for contraction of the belt desmosome and for movements and changes in the shape of the epithelial cell sheet. The spot desmosomes have the same structure as the belt desmosomes but occupy only a small region of the cell membrane.

2.2   Nerve regeneration

The cell body is the trophic centre of the cell; it is here that essential materials are synthesised before being transported out into the dendrites and the axon. If a nerve fibre is transected, its distal part, deprived of this supply, undergoes a process of structural disintegration, known as *Wallerian degeneration* (Fig. 2.37). Its proximal part may also undergo degenerative changes (retrograde degeneration) which usually occur both at the region close to the transection and at the cell body, which grows pale, swells and shows signs of chromatolysis. In cat motoneurons the chromatolysis begins four or five days after transection and reaches a maximum in two weeks. The nearer the cell body is to the site of injury, the stronger and earlier is the

degenerative effect. Various hypotheses have been suggested to account for the retrograde degenerative changes in the cell body. The most likely explanation appears to be that transection of the fibre deprives the cell body of some signal substance which is normally carried by retrograde transport from the endings and serves to control the protein synthesis of the cell.

The first indication of degeneration in the part of the nerve distal to the place of transection, which usually appears within 12 hours, is a swelling of the axon. After 24 hours the myelin lamellae begin to break up, the axoplasm becomes granulated and seems to pull away from the myelin sheath; after two weeks the myelin sheath has almost totally disintegrated by phagocytic action of Schwann cells. About 5–7 days after transection the peripheral part of the nerve loses its ability to conduct impulses.

The Schwann sheath does not degenerate but its constituent cells proliferate and form a tube that may remain for months after the disappearance of the myelin and the axis cylinder. This endoneurial tube serves an important function in guiding the outgrowing fibres during regeneration. The first sign of regeneration is the outgrowth of small sprouts from the distal end of the central stump of the cut nerve. Some of these sprouts, which have the appearance of thin unmyelinated nerve

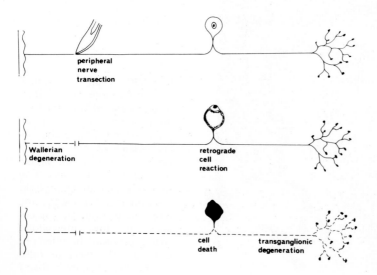

Fig. 2.37 Diagrammatic representation of the changes in a neuron of the dorsal root ganglion following transection of its axon. Peripheral to the cut the axon degenerates (Wallerian degeneration) and central to it the proximal part of the axon and the cell body undergoes retrograde degenerative changes which may spread to the central terminals. (By courtesy of G. Grant.)

fibres, may find their way successfully across the scar tissue and enter the endoneurial tubes in the distal stump while others may turn back into the central stump (Fig. 2.38). For the outgrowing fibres to reach the distal stump and find their way into the endoneurial tubes, the cut ends of the nerve must remain in close apposition. If not, the outgrowing sprouts may form a tangle called a *neuroma* which may become extremely painful. If, however, the outgrowing fibres find their way into the sheath of the degenerated distal part of the nerve, they undergo myelinisation. The regenerating fibre grows out at a rate of 1—4 mm per day and follows the course of the original nerve. Since a peripheral nerve trunk usually contains both motor and sensory fibres, it would appear that a regenerating motor fibre could pursue the path of a degenerated sensory fibre, thus terminating in a sensory organ instead of in its muscle; similarly, a sensory fibre might mistakenly end up in a muscle. However, no such confusion occurs; a motor fibre always returns to its muscle and a sensory fibre to its sensory organ. It has been thought that the outgrowing nerve fibre is directed by some unknown neurotropic guiding substance which is produced by the Schwann cell material left after degeneration of the distal part of the nerve.

In the adult mammalian central nervous system, regeneration following injury takes place only to a limited extent. This is mainly because glial cells grow in, usurping the place of the dead neurons and form a barrier to regeneration. However, it has been known since the pioneering work of Cajal and confirmed in many subsequent studies that severed central axons exhibit regenerative sprouting. More recent studies suggest that the adult mammalian brain in many instances is actually able to rebuild its circuitries and form new functional connections following a lesion. It has for instance been demonstrated that embryonic central nervous tissue can be made to survive transplantations to the brains of adult animals and to form connections. There are also observations suggesting that implants of peripheral nerve can serve as bridges for regeneration of axons across a spinal cord transection.

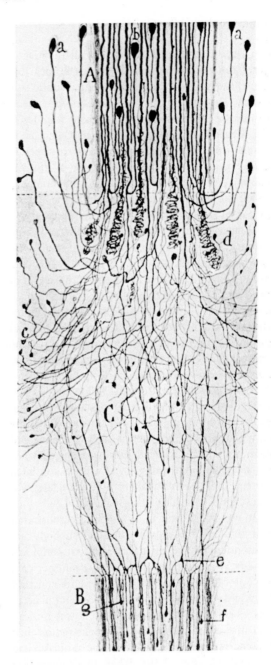

Fig. 2.38 Neuroma formation of a regeneration nerve: A, central stump; B, distal stump; C, sprouts of regenerating nerve fibres. (From Cajal, *Degeneration and Regeneration of the Nervous System*, Oxford University Press, 1928.)

2.3   Axoplasmic flow

Until the late eighteenth century all theories of nerve function were dominated by the idea that nerves are hollow tubes transmitting a subtle substance. The first to advance this concept appears to have been Erasistratos, the famous founder of the Alexandrian School of Medicine. Galen incorporated this idea in his theory of nerve function and suggested that nerves contain a *'pyschic pneuma'*, or the Latin equivalent, 'animal spirit', which is transmitted from the brain to the muscles or carries sensory messages from the periphery to the brain. Descartes, who considered the body constructed like a machine, was in agreement with Galen's general theory of nerve action. In his famous discourse, *The Senses in General*, he says that the 'animal spirits, flowing through the nerves into the muscles . . . cause the movements of the limbs; and that the little threads of which the internal substances of the nerves is composed serve the senses'. Willis, the author of *Cerebri Anatome* (London, 1664), also relied heavily upon Galen's ideas, as may appear from the following passages from the chapter 'On the nervous system in general': 'Indeed the animal spirits flowing within the nerves are like a river from a lively, bubbling and perennial source; they are in nowise stagnant nor remain still, but flowing down with a continual current. . . . ' Not until almost 250 years later was this concept proven to be correct.

It was Weiss who in 1948 first demonstrated that substances originating in the cell body are transported in the axon towards its peripheral endings at a constant rate of 1 or 2 mm per day. The procedure used by Weiss was to constrict surgically the sciatic nerve in rats. When the nerve was examined several weeks later it was noticed that the axon just above the constriction had become swollen, indicating that the axoplasm had accumulated (Fig. 2.39). When the constriction was removed the accumulated axoplasm was found to progress into the distal portion of the nerve fibres at a rate of 1–2 mm per day. It was at first thought that the transport occurred by some peristaltic movements of the axon, but later studies provided evidence that the transport was compar-

able to that of protoplasmic streaming. The function of the slow transport is to renew the axoplasm continuously; in growing or regenerating nerves it serves to supply the needed new axoplasm. In growing, as well as in mature, axons it depends on the continuous synthesis of material in the cell body.

In the early 1960s it was discovered that in addition to the slow transport there was a fast flow of material down the axon. This flow was demonstrated by injecting labelled amino acids into the eye. The labelled amino acid becomes incorporated into proteins in the cell bodies of the ganglion cells of the retina and transported out in the optic nerve fibres. By studying the appearance of the labelled proteins along the nerves (Fig. 2.40) it was demonstrated that the amino acid was transported down the axons at a rate of about 50 mm per day. The same experimental procedure has since been applied to dorsal root ganglion neurons of cats. These studies have provided evidence that the rate of flow is actually much higher; the injected labelled amino acid is transported at a rate of about 400 mm per day at normal body temperature. The flow rate is the same in sensory and motor nerves and is independent of the activity of the nerves. Inhibition of the fast axonal transport has no significant effect on impulse conduction but causes severe depression of synaptic transmission.

The material transported by the fast transport system is associated with particulate rather than soluble fractions of proteins, glycoproteins, phospholipids and membrane-bound enzymes. The fast transport is an active process and depends on an adequate supply of oxygen.

What is the driving mechanism responsible for the fast intra-axonal transport of material? Observations indicating that ATP is involved in the process and the finding of actin in various kinds of cells have led to the hypothesis that the fast transport is produced by sliding movements of the filaments, in analogy with the sliding filament hypothesis of muscle contraction (see p. 91). It has been suggested that the organelle to be transported is attached at one end of a filament, which at its other end is attached to a microtubule that runs for a long distance along the axon. The transloca-

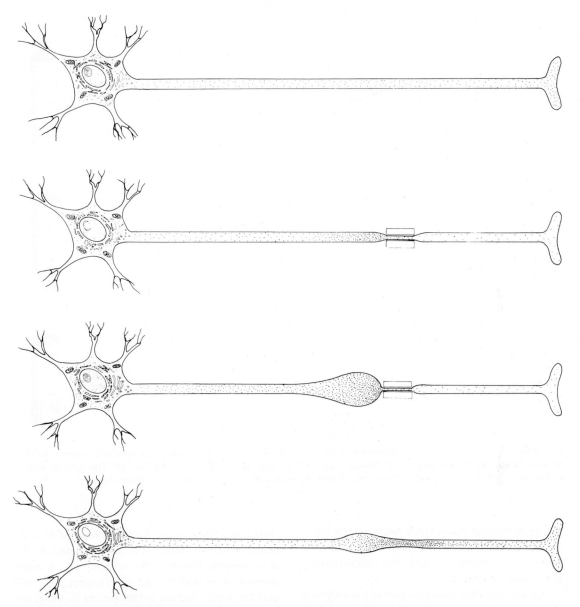

Fig. 2.39 Slow axoplasmic transport demonstrated by surgical constriction of a nerve fibre. After removal of constriction the axoplasm can be shown to flow down the distal portion of the nerve fibre.

tion of the organelle would in this model occur by a sliding movement of the filament along the micro-tubule. That actin is involved in the transport is indicated by the finding that substances which are known to depolymerise actin filaments and micro-tubules inhibit the fast axonal transport. There is a large body of experimental evidence suggesting that the system of tubules of the smooth endoplas-mic reticulum (Fig. 2.41) which run along the axon plays an important role in the fast axonal transport. It has been suggested that the rapid translocation of material from the perikaryon to

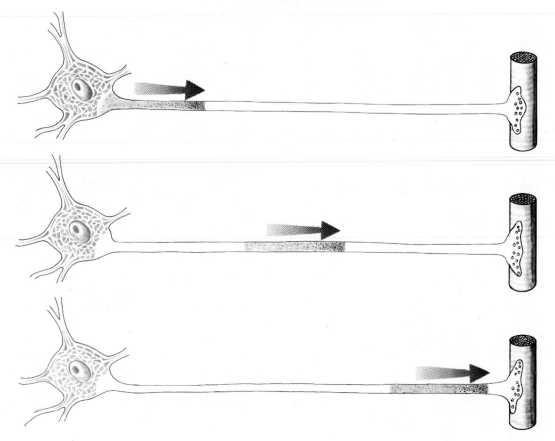

Fig. 2.40 Schematic drawing illustrating fast axoplasmic flow. Radioactively labelled amino acid is incorporated by the neurons and transported out in the axons. The distribution of the amino acid is determined by cutting the nerve into pieces and analysing their content of radioactive material.

the nerve endings would result from an interaction of the intra-axoplasmic channels of the smooth endoplasmic reticulum and the microtubule—neurofilament system.

Axoplasmic flow seems to proceed mainly in a proximodistal direction, but several lines of evidence suggest that some material is transported in the opposite direction as well (Fig. 2.42). This is the route, for example, by which viruses and some toxins may pass along the nerve fibres towards the brain. It has been demonstrated that polio, herpes and rabies viruses, reach the central nervous system by retrograde transport and the same is true for tetanus toxin. A given material can be transported in both directions, and by the fast as well as by the

slow transport systems. Acetylcholine (ACh) is an example of this. Most ACh is transported by the slow system towards the muscle, but a small amount is moved by the fast system, and still another small fraction is transported in the retrograde direction. Normally retrograde transport serves to return membrane constituents and proteins to the cell body. It is likely that this transport represents a negative-feedback mechanism for controlling the protein synthesis of the cell. It is also likely that retrograde transport plays an important role in the recycling process of synaptic vesicles (Fig. 2.43). As we shall see later (p. 202), following release of synaptic transmitter substance, the vesicle membrane is recaptured by a process similar

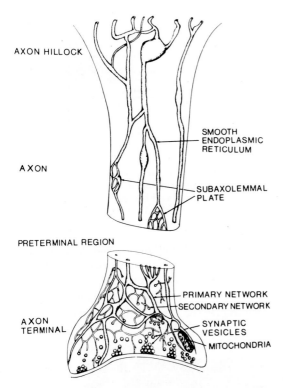

AXON HILLOCK

AXON

SMOOTH
ENDOPLASMIC
RETICULUM

SUBAXOLEMMAL
PLATE

PRETERMINAL REGION

AXON
TERMINAL

PRIMARY NETWORK
SECONDARY NETWORK
SYNAPTIC
VESICLES
MITOCHONDRIA

Fig. 2.41   The axonal smooth endoplasmic reticulum forms a continuous system of channels extending from the cell body to the axon terminals. It is postulated that the tubules of the smooth endoplasmic reticulum participate in the fast axonal transport of macromolecules. (From Droz *et al.*, *Brain Res.*, 93, 1–13, 1975.)

to *endocytosis*. The presynaptic membrane becomes invaginated and the pocket is pinched off. In this way a new vesicle is formed. In the course of this process some vesicles appear to be taken up by lysosomes and transported back to the cell body. Light microscope observations of living axons have demonstrated that intra-axonal particles, which are probably lysosomes, move by irregular saltatory movements and predominantly in the retrograde direction.

If there is a recycling process it is conceivable that a small amount of extracellular material in the synaptic cleft is taken up when the presynaptic membrane becomes invaginated and the pocket is pinched off. That this actually occurs is shown by the fact that the enzyme, horseradish peroxidase, is taken up at synaptic terminals and transported in the retrograde direction at a rate of about 80 mm a day. This enzyme can be detected by a histochemical technique and identified in electron micrographs. By injecting horseradish peroxidase into a region of the brain, the axons may thus be traced from their terminals to the cell body. This technique has become an important new tool in tracing neuronal pathways and synaptic connections in the central nervous system (Fig. 2.44).

It would thus appear that, although the material transported in the nerves is not a 'psychic pneuma', the axoplasmic transport system has a functional significance not remote from that proposed almost 2000 years ago by Galen.

2.4   The origin of the membrane potential

Ionic distribution and the resting potential

Bernstein's theory

By the middle of the nineteenth century, Matteucci and Du Bois-Reymond had demonstrated that a potential difference exists between the surface and the interior of a muscle and that during activity

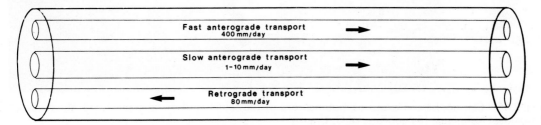

Fast anterograde transport
400 mm/day

Slow anterograde transport
1–10 mm/day

Retrograde transport
80 mm/day

Fig. 2.42   Summarising diagram illustrating the three major transport systems of nerve fibres.

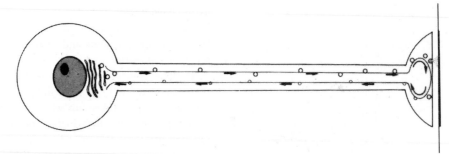

Fig. 2.43   Recycling of vesicles and other membranous organelles. The vesicles are transported by fast axonal transport to the nerve terminal. Following release of transmitter substance the vesicle membrane is recaptured and taken up by lysosomes which are transported back to the cell body.

this potential difference decreases giving rise to what Matteucci called the 'negative variation'. In the resting muscle the interior is always negative in relation to the exterior. Du Bois-Reymond suggested that this polarisation of the muscle was due to an uneven distribution of 'charged particles'. It should be noted that the dissociation of electrolytes was unknown at this time. In 1887 Arrhenius put forward the theory of electrolyte dissociation which formed the basis for the subsequent work of

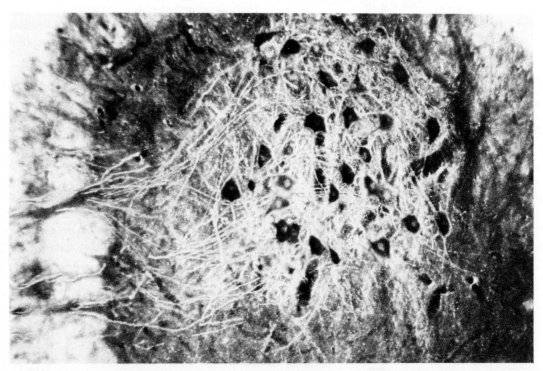

Fig. 2.44   Cell bodies and axons of motoneurons of the spinal cord of rat stained with the horseradish peroxidase technique. (By courtesy of G. Grant.)

Nernst on the potential gradients which arise at the boundaries of two solutions whose positive and negative ions diffuse at different rates. For instance, if two solutions of sodium chloride of different concentrations are brought into contact through a porous filter that allows free diffusion of both sodium and chloride ions, a liquid junction potential will develop, the more diluted solution becoming electronegative with respect to the more concentrated solution (Fig. 2.45A). This is explained by the following: as the two solutions are brought into contact, both sodium and chloride ions in the more concentrated solution will begin to diffuse down their concentration gradient into the more dilute solution. However, the chloride ions have a higher mobility than sodium ions and

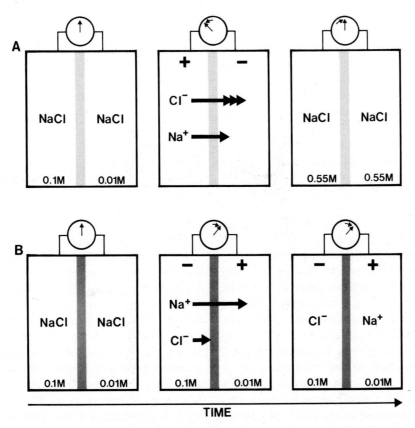

Fig. 2.45 (A) Development of diffusion potential as a result of the greater mobility of the chloride ions. The potential developed in this way disappears over time as the concentrations of sodium and chloride become equal in the solution. (B) Generation of transmembrane potential across a membrane permeable only to sodium ions. The sodium ions of the more concentrated side will diffuse down their concentration gradient into the less concentrated solution which will become increasingly positive. The potential difference created in this way counteracts the movements of the positive sodium ions until finally the potential difference prevents further movements of sodium ions. The transmembrane potential at which this occurs is called the *equilibrium potential*. In contrast to the example in (A) this potential will not decay with time but remains unchanged as long as the concentrations of the solutions on each side of the membrane remain constant.

the more dilute solution will therefore become negatively charged until the concentration gradient has run down. The potential difference developed depends on the relative mobilities of the ions involved and on the difference in concentration on either side of the boundary, and can be calculated from the equation

$$E = \frac{u - v}{u + v} \frac{RT}{F} \ln\left(\frac{C_1}{C_2}\right)$$

where u and v are the mobilities of the positive and negative ions respectively and C_1 and C_2 are the concentrations on either side of the boundary. R is the universal gas constant, T is absolute temperature and F is the Faraday. As the concentrations on both sides become equal, the potential difference gradually diminishes and finally disappears.

When the two solutions are separated by a membrane that only allows the sodium ions to pass, a quite different situation arises (Fig. 2.45B). The sodium ions will diffuse down their concentration gradient from the more concentrated to the more dilute solution which therefore becomes positively charged. However, as the dilute solution becomes increasingly more positive the potential gradient created begins to oppose the movement of the positively charged sodium ions; they are held back by the electrostatic force of the negatively charged chloride ions which are not able to pass the membrane. The diffusion of the sodium ions can therefore only continue as long as the concentration force is greater than the electrostatic force. Note that the amount of Na^+ that must move to set up the potential is too small to be detected chemically. Finally an equilibrium is reached when the electrostatic force is equal and opposite to the concentration force. Nernst demonstrated that the magnitude of the potential at which this occurs can be calculated from the equation

$$E = \frac{RT}{zF} \ln\left(\frac{[Na]_1}{[Na]_2}\right)$$

where E is the equilibrium potential, R is the gas constant, T is absolute temperature, F is the Fara-

day, z is the valence of Na^+ and $[Na]_1$ and $[Na]_2$ are the concentrations of sodium ions on the more concentrated and diluted sides respectively. Once equilibrium is established the potential will be maintained without any expenditure of energy, provided that the membrane properties remain unchanged. A similar equilibrium potential can be calculated from this equation for any other permeant ion if the concentration gradient across the membrane is known.

At the turn of the century the German chemist, Ostwald, advanced the theory that the electric charge of muscles and nerves might be accounted for by the permeability properties of the cell membrane, in analogy with the potential differences in artificial membranes demonstrated by Nernst. Ostwald's theory remained almost unnoticed until Bernstein, one of the great pioneers in neurophysiology, brought it up and incorporated it in his membrane model published in 1902. According to Bernstein (1902), in its resting state the living nerve cell holds a potential, the 'resting potential', that is maintained 'with the help of an electrolyte pre-existing in the fiber, which for the most parts, consists of inorganic salts, with the assumption that the living plasma membranes of fibers or fibrils are not easily, or not at all, permeable for one of two ions'. Bernstein went on to postulate that a transient breakdown of the membrane barrier occurs during activity and that the membrane becomes selectively permeable to potassium ions which would move out. Electric current would then begin to flow across the membrane until the potential difference between the inside and the outside was eliminated. The breakdown of the ionic barrier would pass along the fibre giving rise to a wave of depolarisation, the nerve impulse. In this way, according to Bernstein, the resting potential would be changed into an action potential.

At the time when Bernstein advanced this theory it was known from biochemical analysis of muscles that the concentration of potassium ions inside the muscle fibres was higher than in the extracellular fluid and Bernstein concluded that this concentration difference accounted for the potential difference discovered by Matteucci and Du Bois-Reymond in nerve and muscle. The situation would thus be similar to that illustrated in Fig. 2.45 if sodium is replaced by potassium. Besides potassium, a number of other ions are present in the extracellular fluid as well as intracellularly in nerve and muscle, but provided that the cell membrane only allows potassium to pass the same principle would apply.

Intracellular recording

Bernstein based his hypothesis on experiments in which he compared the potentials recorded with an electrode placed at the surface of a muscle and another electrode in contact with the cut end of the muscle. The potential difference (the 'injury potential') measured in this way was assumed to represent the resting potential of the individual cells. At the time when Bernstein published his

theory it was not possible to measure the resting potential of individual cells. It was therefore not until the advent of the technique for intracellular recordings in the late 1940s that his idea could be subjected to direct experimental testing. The electrode used for such recordings is a glass capillary pulled out to a fine tip (about 0.1–1 μm in diameter) which can be inserted into a cell without causing serious damage. To establish electrical contact with the interior of the cell the microelectrode is filled with a potassium chloride solution. This technique was first applied to frog muscle fibres. When a cell was impaled a sudden potential jump was recorded, the inside of the fibre being negative. It could be predicted from the ratio of potassium concentrations in the extracellular and intracellular fluids that the resting potential would be about 90 mV negative inside. The values obtained in the first intracellular measurements turned

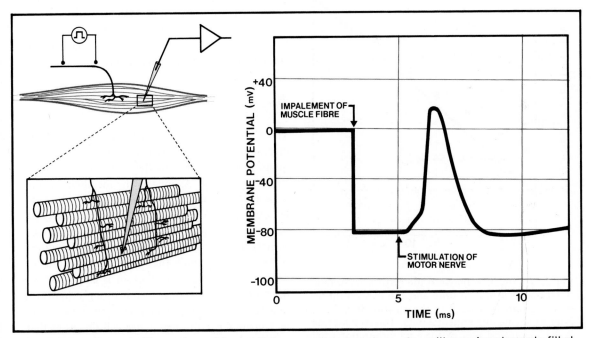

Fig. 2.46 Schematic illustration of intracellular recording technique. A capillary microelectrode filled with KCl solution is inserted into a muscle. At the moment of impalement of a muscle fibre there is a sudden potential jump as indicated by the sharp deflection of the trace of the oscilloscope. When the motor nerve is stimulated an action potential of the muscle fibre is induced. If the muscle fibre is impaled near the endplate a prepotential (the endplate potential) is also recorded.

out to be about −80 mV. Hence there was a surprisingly close correspondence between the predicted value and the actual measurements. Later studies have shown that the resting potential difference in many cells is considerably lower. In some cases this may be due to the fact that the cell is damaged by the recording electrode. On the other hand, several lines of evidence suggest that many cells actually have a low resting potential difference, for instance the retinal receptors. In some tissues this may be accounted for by a relatively high concentration of potassium ions in the extracellular fluid.

If the resting potential arises from an uneven distribution of potassium ions between the inside and the outside of a cell, as suggested by Bernstein, it should change if the outside concentration of potassium changes. Early experiments on the giant axon of squid confirmed that this is the case. As the diagram in Fig. 2.47 shows, the measured values

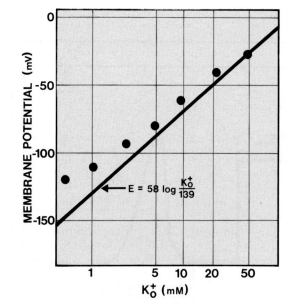

Fig. 2.47   Relation between the resting membrane potential in a muscle fibre and the concentration of potassium ions (K_o^+) in the surrounding fluid. Points indicate experimental data. The straight line is the theoretical plot of the equilibrium potential for potassium obtained from the equation in the diagram. Note the excellent agreement between the observed values and the calculated values except for low external concentrations of potassium.

lie close to those predicted by the Nernst equation. That the potassium ion is mainly responsible for the resting potential appears also from the fact that changes in the concentration of other ions in the outer solution have little or no effect on the membrane potential. For example, halving the sodium concentration or even removing sodium entirely from the outside solution affects the resting potential only insignificantly.

Sodium ions are present in higher concentrations in the extracellular medium than in the interior of the cell and therefore tend to diffuse into the cell. In the resting state the membrane is relatively impermeable to sodium ions. The resting potential is therefore largely independent of the concentration of sodium in the outer medium. The chloride ions are likewise more concentrated outside than inside the cell (Fig. 2.48). However, the situation is not the same for sodium and chloride since the electrical gradient opposes an increase in chloride ion concentration inside the cell. The equilibrium potential for chloride is close to the resting potential of the membrane. This suggests that the distribution of chloride ions is passive, that is determined only by the two opposing forces: the concentration gradient and the electrical gradient.

The sodium−potassium pump

The above interpretation of the generation of the membrane potential presumes that the cell membrane is impermeable to the large organic anions which are inside. As long as the membrane maintains these properties, the resting potential would be expected to persist, being purely a physical phenomenon quite independent of metabolic activity. It has been known, however, since the time of Du Bois-Reymond, that the resting potential of a muscle falls when metabolism is inhibited by a decrease in temperature. This strongly indicates that the membrane potential is, in the long run, in fact maintained through active cell processes that require a continuous expenditure of energy. In the early 1940s studies of the permeability properties of muscle cells yielded the puzzling finding that a muscle put in Ringer's solution loses potassium

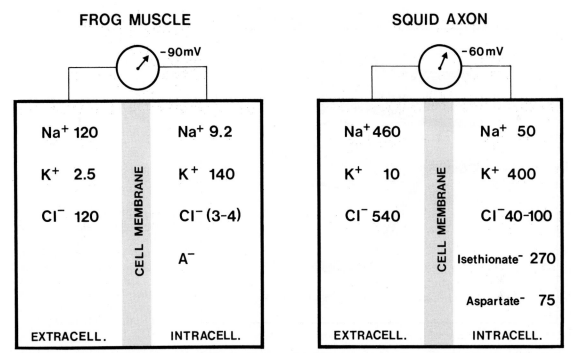

Fig. 2.48   The electrolyte concentration and potential difference across the cell membrane in the muscle fibre of the frog and the nerve fibre of the squid.

and takes up sodium. This was contrary to Bernstein's theory which anticipated that the membrane is impermeable to sodium. The observed sodium permeability would agree with Bernstein's original theory, however, if it was assumed that the membrane is somewhat permeable to sodium and that there exists a mechanism in the membrane that pumps sodium out as fast as it enters. Since the operation of such a pump requires energy supplied by metabolic processes, the sodium pump would presumably cease to function if the cell metabolism were stopped. This is in fact the case: substances known to block metabolic activity cause the resting potential difference to decrease. There is also evidence that the expulsion of sodium is coupled with an uptake of potassium. For this reason the pump has often been termed the sodium–potassium pump (Fig. 2.49). As much as 40% of the total energy produced by the 'resting' cell may be utilised for keeping the pump running. The actual pump is an enzyme, an Na^+–K^+ ATP-ase, which is found in high concentrations in cell membranes. This en-

zyme, which hydrolyses ATP in the presence of sodium and potassium ions, exists in two configurations. The transport of sodium outwards and of potassium inwards appears to be related to the molecule shifting from one conformational state to another.

It was at first thought that equal amounts of sodium and potassium were carried by the pump through the membrane. Hence the pump would not contribute to the resting potential, that is it would be electrically neutral. If, however, the amount of sodium pumped out were not the same as the amount of potassium pumped in, the pump would be *electrogenic*; that is, the potential across the membrane would depend on the activity of the pump. The assumption of a one-to-one relation was based on observations that both outflow and inflow decrease when the nerve is cooled, and that metabolic inhibitors affect both movements equally. Furthermore, when potassium is removed from the extracellular fluid the sodium outflow decreases. Later observations indicated, however, that there

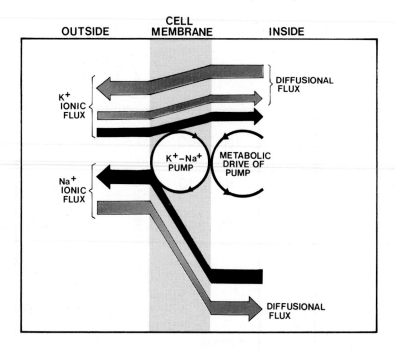

Fig. 2.49 The sodium–potassium pump. Schematic diagram showing potassium and sodium fluxes through the nerve cell membrane at rest. The steepness of the flows represents the electrochemical gradients of the ions. (Adapted from Eccles, 1957.)

is usually not a one-to-one relation between sodium outflow and potassium inflow; therefore, the pump might contribute to the resting potential in some cells. Just how much the pump contributes has been difficult to establish since the changes in the resting potential produced by variations in the activity of the pump are relatively small and therefore difficult to detect. The decisive factors are the rate at which the sodium ions are transported and how many sodium ions are carried out for each potassium ion taken in. The greater the ratio between sodium and potassium the more electrogenic is the sodium pump; in some cells it has been found that the relationship between sodium and potassium is 3:2, in other cells 3:1 and sometimes 2:1.

Ion passage through the membrane

The presence of lipid molecules in the membrane makes it difficult for water-bound ions to cross. Their passage takes place through pores represented by proteins that extend through the membrane from its inner to its outer surface. By testing the relative abilities of a number of substances to carry current through the membrane, it has been possible to estimate the dimensions and distribution of such channels. Sodium and potassium appear to have separate channels, those for sodium being about 0.3 nm x 0.5 nm, and the potassium channels being somewhat narrower and shorter. The number of channels per unit area of the membrane is surprisingly low; in the giant squid axon it has been calculated that there are not more than 100–500 channels per square micrometre (μm^2) in the membrane. Freeze–fracture studies indicate that the ionic channels may be grouped together in regular arrays. The total membrane area that they occupy seems to be relatively small, with groups of channels widely separated (of the order of tenths of a micrometre) from one another. Though relatively scarce, the channels are sufficient, however, since the number of ions which pass through the membrane during an impulse is very low.

Physical characteristics of the membrane

To understand the functions of the membrane it is imperative to know its physical properties. The membrane has a specific resistance roughly a million times greater than the surrounding solution, due to its lipid components. Since the potential difference between the outside of the cell and its inside is close to a tenth of a volt and the membrane is less than 10 nm thick, the potential gradient across the membrane is enormous (2×10^5 V cm^{-2}). Under such conditions, it is not surprising that a small change in permeability can produce large effects. Impedance measurements have shown that during the nerve impulse the resistance falls to a fraction of its value in the resting fibre. This is the direct expression of the permeability changes that attend the propagation of the impulse.

Given what we know about the permeability properties of the membrane, the ionic composition of the cytoplasm and the extracellular fluid, the membrane can be represented by an electric circuit diagram (Fig. 2.50). The diagram contains three separate conducting channels corresponding to the major ions. (In some cells, e.g. cardiac and smooth muscle cells, calcium channels would also have to be represented.) Each channel has a characteristic electromotive force, which is represented by the equilibrium potential for that particular ion, and a leakage resistance. For potassium and chloride the polarity of the battery is the same, and it is opposite to that of the sodium battery.

As indicated by C_m in Fig. 2.50, the cell membrane is also a capacitor and so can store electrical charge. This is due to the electrical property of the lipid bilayer portion of the membrane. To understand the functional importance of the membrane capacity, it is necessary to know that charge is transferred across it only when the membrane potential is changing; furthermore, the capacitative current is independent of the membrane permeability since it is carried by ions which move onto or off the capacitor but do not pass through the membrane. The net result of their movements is that the distribution of charges across the membrane is altered. There are thus two main routes whereby current may flow across the membrane: (1) the ionic channels, and (2) the membrane capacity.

The first thing that happens when current flows through the membrane is that the capacitor becomes charged, or discharged; meanwhile current will begin to flow through the ionic channels. The electrical capacity of the membrane therefore plays an important role in impulse generation and conduction, as will be described in detail below.

At this point it may be appropriate to introduce the reader to the terminology generally used. Thus a negative-going change of the resting membrane potential from, for instance, -70 mV to -80 mV is called a hyperpolarisation and a positive-going change from, for instance, -70 mV to -50 mV is a depolarisation (Fig. 2.51). A hyperpolarisation is often referred to as an increase of membrane potential and a depolarisation as a decrease.

Metabolism and maintenance of membrane potential

As we have seen, the nerve cell must expend energy continuously to keep the internal sodium concen-

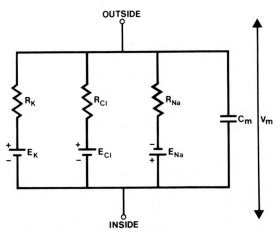

Fig. 2.50 Equivalent circuit for the excitable membrane. C_m is the membrane capacity, E_K, E_{Na} and E_{Cl} are potassium, sodium and chloride batteries. The potentials of these batteries depend upon the concentration gradients of the respective ions. Each battery also has an equilibrium potential which is the potential across the membrane which just balances the ion flow in the direction of the concentration gradient. Note that the polarity of the sodium battery is opposite to that of the potassium and chloride batteries.

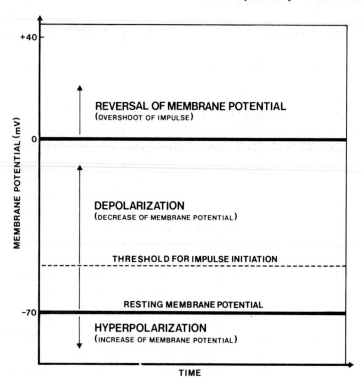

Fig. 2.51 Diagram illustrating the terminology commonly used for designation of changes of membrane potential. When the potential becomes more positive inside the cell than the normal resting potential, the cell is said to be depolarised; when it becomes more negative than the resting potential, the cell is said to be hyperpolarised. Depolarisation and hyperpolarisation are often denoted in the literature as a decrease and increase respectively of the membrane potential.

tration at a low level and to reabsorb potassium ions. The transport mechanism responsible for maintenance of the concentration difference between the interior of the cell and its exterior has been studied in experiments on the giant axon. Several lines of evidence suggest that the activity of the pump is directly proportional to the amount of ATP present in the nerve. It has been shown in these studies that the activity of the pump ceases when the energy-rich phosphate compounds in the cytoplasm are removed. If the sodium pump is inhibited by lowering the temperature or by treating the axon with substances that block the oxidative metabolism, the pumping machinery ceases to function as indicated by a rapid decline of the amount of sodium pumped out from the axon (Fig. 2.52). However, after blocking of the pump the nerve fibre is still able to conduct impulses (until the sodium gradient has appreciably run down) and neither the resting potential nor the action potential changes. Presumably, the volume of the squid axon is so large that blocking the

sodium pump causes relatively slow changes in the internal ionic concentration. In fine, unmyelinated fibres, however, inhibition of the metabolic processes soon causes a depolarisation of the resting potential and blockage of impulse conduction. In the giant axon of squid, stimulation at 200 Hz increases oxygen consumption by about 10%, while in thin nerve fibres even low-frequency activity may increase the oxygen consumption by as much as 50%. The thinner the nerve fibre, the more sensitive it is to lack of oxygen. This is important functionally, because a high percentage of the nerve fibres in the nervous system are very thin fibres. Dendrites are likewise sensitive to lack of oxygen and rapidly lose their excitability when deprived of oxygen. When the cortex of a cat is perfused with agents that block oxidative processes, dendritic function ceases in about 4 min. It is well known that a few minutes deprivation of oxygen seriously affects cortical activity in humans; this is probably due to the effect on the dendrites and the subsequent blocking of synaptic transmission.

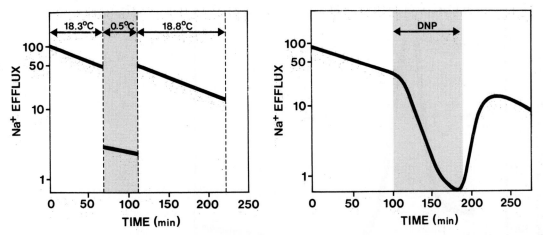

Fig. 2.52 Effects on the sodium pump of the giant axon of temperature (*left diagram*) and the metabolic inhibitor DNP (*right diagram*). Reduction of temperature from 18°C to 0.5°C immediately reduces the sodium efflux to near zero; DNP has a similar but more gradual effect. (From Hodgkin and Keynes, 1955.)

2.5 The action potential

Bernstein's original hypothesis stated that the nerve action potential arises when the permeability properties of the cell membrane suddenly change, permitting the free passage of all small ions. The result of this would be that the potential difference between the inside and the outside of the cell would disappear, that is the resting potential would go to zero. This change and the following restitution of the resting potential were thought to account for the ability of nerve fibres to transmit electrical signals. Bernstein's theory predicted that the magnitude of the action potential of a single nerve cell should not exceed that of the resting potential. It therefore came as a surprise when the first intracellular measurements on giant axons showed that excitation did not lead to a simple abolition of the resting potential, but actually involved a transient reversal, the inside of the cell becoming for a short time positive in relation to the extracellular medium (Fig. 2.53). This observation clearly showed that the generation of the nerve impulse could not be explained by a general breakdown of the permeability properties of the membrane as suggested by Bernstein. That sodium ions played a key role in the development of the positive overshoot of the action potential was indicated by

experiments showing that the magnitude of the membrane potential at the peak of the action potential, i.e. the overshoot, decreased when the concentration of sodium ions in the extracellular fluid was reduced (Fig. 2.54). Furthermore, when the extracellular sodium was removed, the generation of the action potential was completely blocked. These findings clearly showed that the production of the action potential was dependent on the presence of sodium ions.

From the positive value at the peak of the action potential, the membrane potential returns to its resting value. The most obvious explanation of this repolarisation would appear to be an outflow of some positive ions when the sodium influx ceases. The nature of the outward current has been elucidated in voltage clamp experiments (see below) which have provided evidence that the recharging of the membrane is associated with an accelerated efflux of potassium ions from the cytoplasm. This leads to a rapid repolarisation of the membrane and is accompanied by a restoration of its original ion permeabilities. The impulse thus leaves in its wake an addition of sodium ions to the cell and a loss of potassium ions. Quantitative measurements with radioactive tracers have shown that in the squid's giant axon the increase in sodium amounts to $(3–4) \times 10^{-12}$ mol cm^{-2}; an approximately

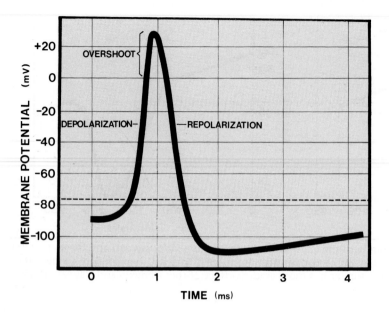

Fig. 2.53 Changes in membrane potential associated with the generation of an action potential.

equal amount of potassium is lost. These changes are negligible. The amount of potassium ions lost is less than a millionth of the total potassium in the cell, and subsequent metabolic processes restore the ion content of the cell to the initial levels. Thus, even if the metabolism of the cell is inhibited, the nerve can still conduct millions of impulses

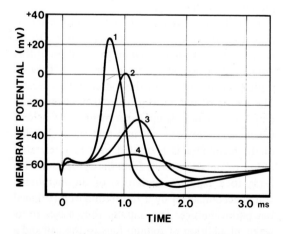

Fig. 2.54 Effect of removal of sodium from external solution on the action potential: record 1, in normal saline; records 2–4, after removal of 50% (2), 65% (3) and 90% (4) of external sodium (replaced by dextrose).

before the overall changes in the ionic concentration become large enough to affect its function. In the giant axon of the squid, the intracellular sodium concentration increases by only about 10% after 30 000 impulses, even when the metabolic pump is not functioning. The size of the cell is an important factor, however, because the ionic changes are relatively greater for a small cell than for a large one. The smaller the nerve fibre, the more it depends on metabolic processes and the more time is required for restoration. In a nerve fibre with a diameter of 0.1 μm, a single impulse causes an increase in sodium concentration estimated at 10%.

Changes in ionic conductance during action potential

Studies with radioactive tracers permit a quantitative analysis of the overall ionic changes during activity, but provide little information about the actual ionic flow through the membrane in the course of a single impulse. Considering that the impulse lasts at most a few thousandths of a second, measuring the flow of the ions would seem to involve insurmountable problems. However, by means of a special method, the *voltage clamp technique* (Fig. 2.55), Hodgkin and Huxley succeeded

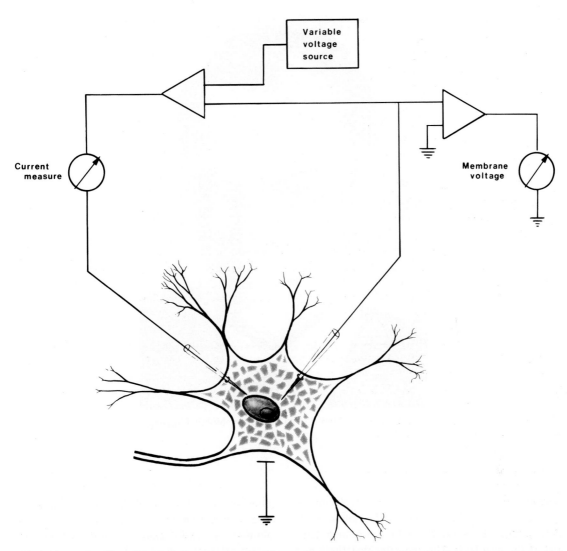

Fig. 2.55 Schematic diagram of voltage clamp technique. One electrode measures the membrane potential, the recording amplifier being connected to another amplifier by which the voltage of the cell can be set by the experimenter while the current flowing across the membrane is measured.

in the early 1950s in measuring with remarkable precision the ion flows in the membrane of the giant squid axon, and on the basis of these data they calculated the ion flow during the impulse. Their achievements, which form the basis of our current concept of the ionic mechanisms of the nerve impulse, were recognised with the Nobel Prize in 1963 (Figs 2.56 and 2.57).

The voltage clamp technique involves maintaining the membrane potential at a given value, using one electrode inside the cell and another on the outside, and simultaneously measuring how much current it takes to keep the potential constant. If, for instance, the membrane potential is hyperpolarised, little current is required to sustain this potential; in other words, the cell membrane be-

Fig. 2.56 Sir Alan Lloyd Hodgkin, Nobel Laureate in 1963.

haves as a passive structure. If, however, the membrane is depolarised, a considerable amount of current must be fed into the cell to keep the potential at the new level. This indicates that the ionic channels open up when the membrane is depolarised. The amount of current necessary to hold the potential constant is the same as that carried by the ionic flux through the membrane.

With this technique it has been possible to demonstrate that the current flowing across the membrane during depolarisation of the membrane consists of three components (Fig. 2.58). Immediately after a sudden depolarisation, there is a very brief surge of outward current lasting only while the membrane potential is changing: this is the capacitative current, which flows across the membrane capacitor. The second phase of the membrane current is a transient, inward current, which is followed by a third phase of prolonged outward current. If the sodium gradient is removed, the inward current disappears but the later outward current remains unchanged; the implication is that the inward current represents a flow of sodium into the cell. If the membrane potential is shifted to positive values, the sodium current reverses direction at a certain potential level, and flows outwards. The potential at which the sodium current reverses, or the *reversal potential*, provides a measure of the potential necessary to counterbalance the inflow of sodium; in other words, it equals the Nernst potential for sodium. It might be expected that the potential at the peak of the impulse

Fig. 2.57 Sir Andrew Fielding Huxley, Nobel Laureate in 1963.

would reach this value, but in fact the recorded amplitude is lower. This is because by the time the sodium inflow reaches its maximum, the outflow of potassium is already appreciable. The sodium current is very brief; it reaches its maximum within 0.5 ms and ceases about 0.5 ms later. The potassium current starts about 0.5 ms later than the sodium current, increases more slowly, and has a slower time course. By the time it attains its maximum, the sodium current has nearly ceased.

On the basis of the results obtained by the voltage clamp technique, Hodgkin and Huxley were able to construct a model of the nerve impulse. They proposed that the events that unfold in the course of an impulse may be described as a sequence of opening and closing of ionic channels in the nerve membrane. The initial event is a rapid opening of the sodium gates. This leads to an influx of sodium ions from the extracellular fluid and a depolarisation of the cell. This influx causes the rising phase of the impulse (Fig. 2.59). As the flow of sodium ions into the cell proceeds, the membrane potential reverses and the action potential approaches its peak amplitude. At this time the sodium gates begin to close; meanwhile the potassium gates open up, but more slowly, and potassium ions flow out of the cell in increasing numbers. This outflux makes the interior of the cell more negative and causes the falling phase of the impulse. As the membrane potential approaches its resting value, the potassium gates are slowly closed. Finally the Na^+-K^+ pump restores the

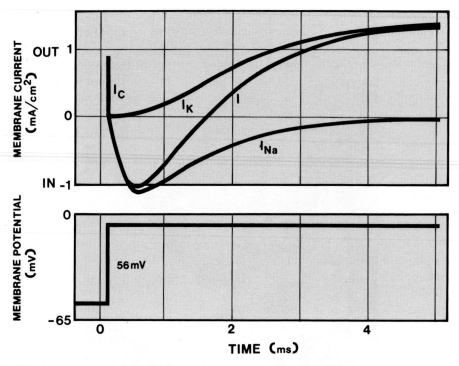

Fig. 2.58 Membrane currents (*upper diagram*) during step-like 56 mV depolarisation (*lower diagram*) of a squid axon. The currents consist of a brief outward capacitative current (I_C) which is followed by a transient phase of inward current and a more prolonged phase of outward current flow. The sodium and potassium components of the membrane current (I) can be separated by removing sodium from the outside solution; after this, only the outward potassium current (I_K) remains. The sodium current (I_{Na}) is obtained from the difference between the total current (I) and the potassium current (I_K). (After Hodgkin and Huxley, 1952.)

original ionic concentrations in the cell. It should be noted that the movements of ions during the action potential are down pre-existing concentration gradients, i.e. no metabolic energy is required to move the ions during the impulse itself.

There is an interesting difference between the behaviour of the sodium and the potassium currents. When the axon is kept depolarised at a certain level, the sodium current gradually declines while the potassium current continues to flow. The decline in the sodium current has been called sodium inactivation. This process has an important functional role, for the sodium channels can be opened again only after they have recovered from inactivation, and this recovery process controls the ability of the axon to be reactivated. It is therefore

not surprising that the mechanisms underlying sodium inactivation have excited considerable interest and study. Of particular interest is the finding that sodium inactivation is abolished by application of the proteolytic enzyme, pronase, to the inside of the membrane of the giant axon. This has led to the conclusion that the molecules that mediate sodium inactivation are exposed on the inside of the cell membrane.

The theory that Hodgkin and Huxley developed to explain the nerve impulse was based on results from the squid nerves. Later studies on frog myelinated nerve fibres strongly indicate a basic similarity in the ionic events of vertebrate axons and the squid axon.

In their measurements of the ionic currents,

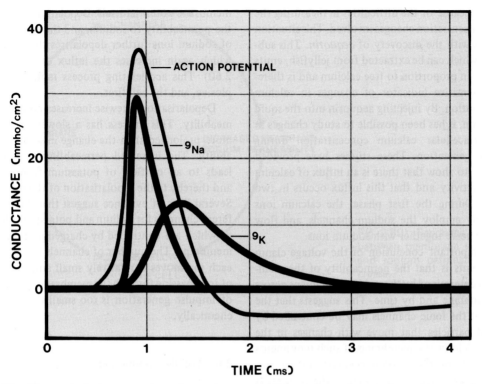

Fig. 2.59   Theoretical reconstruction of an action potential from the sodium and potassium conductances measured with voltage clamp technique in a squid axon. (After Hodgkin and Huxley, 1952.)

Hodgkin and Huxley had to limit themselves to effects obtainable by changing the external ionic environment. In later experiments on the giant axon it was found that the cytoplasm in the nerve could be squeezed out, without loss of the excitability of the axon. Since the nerve fibre could then be perfused with different solutions, it became possible to study the influence of different ions on the inside of the nerve membrane. The observations made with this technique have largely confirmed earlier findings and conclusions.

It has long been known that changes in the external concentration of calcium influence the excitability of nerves and muscles. Reduction in external calcium concentration lowers the threshold for excitation, while an increase acts in the opposite direction. It has been demonstrated in voltage clamp experiments that lowering of the external

calcium concentration causes a large increase in the sodium and potassium currents when the nerve is depolarised. This implies that the calcium ions have a crucial role in regulating the amount of ionic flow through the membrane and thereby the excitability. Calcium ions act as stabilisers of the membrane by increasing the amount of depolarisation needed for the generation of activity. In this context it is important to know that the intracellular concentration of calcium is low and closely related to the activity of the mitochondria, which are able to take up and release large amounts of calcium. There are indications that the mitochondrial regulation of intracellular calcium concentration is closely linked to the flow of calcium through the cell membrane.

Whether the calcium ions actually enter the nerve during activity was unclear until recently,

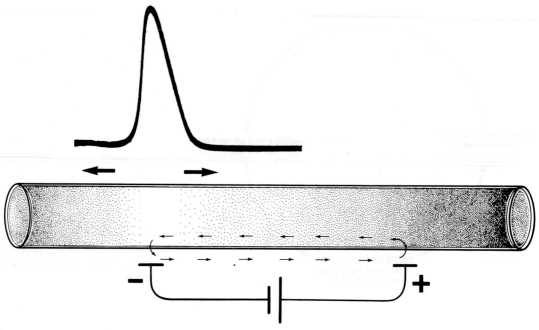

Fig. 2.61 Impulse initiation by electric stimulation of an axon. Current flowing through the nerve membrane causes hyperpolarisation at the anode and depolarisation at the cathode. When depolarisation reaches the threshold level for activation, the impulse is generated at the cathode; from here it propagates in both directions along the nerve.

sodium increases as described above, but if there is only a small change in resting potential, the sodium current will be counterbalanced by the potassium current. The threshold level for the impulse is thus the potential level at which the potassium current is no longer able to maintain this balance. The sodium influx then increases rapidly and, as we saw above, ultimately the process becomes explosive.

It is appropriate at this point to consider the phenomenon of accommodation, that is the ability of an axon to adapt to an electrical current. This property can be demonstrated most simply by depolarising a nerve with currents of gradually increasing intensity. If the increase in depolarisation occurs very slowly, no impulse may arise, even when the original threshold has been surpassed. An alternating current of low frequency, for example, will therefore not excite the nerve. Moreover, an alternating current of high frequency will also be ineffective because each period of depolarisation is

too short to allow for the nerve to respond. Thus, there is a limited frequency range over which an alternating current is effective as a stimulus for the nerve. The optimal frequency is around 50–60 Hz. Coincidentally, that turns out to be the frequency of the current ordinarily supplied to households and industry.

Impulse propagation

Thus an impulse is evoked when the membrane is depolarised at a certain rate to a certain threshold level. At this level the membrane permeability properties are such that sodium ions flow into the cell faster than potassium ions flow out. From the site where the impulse starts, it spreads rapidly along the nerve fibre like a wave, needing no further stimulus. The propagation of the impulse has often been compared to lighting a fuse. The stimulus is like the heat of the lit match. Like the axon, the fuse has a threshold; it takes a certain amount of heat to ignite it but, once the fire has caught, it spreads quickly by igniting neighbouring parts. There is, however, a significant difference between the nerve fibre and the fuse. In the nerve, a restitution of the resting potential occurs immediately after the impulse response, and the axon is ready to respond to a second stimulus.

To understand the mechanisms underlying impulse propagation in a nerve, let us now consider what happens in a resting region of the nerve when an impulse invades it. As the impulse approaches the inactive region the membrane capacity begins to discharge, the ionic channels being still in their resting state at this time. The capacitative current flows outwards, producing a depolarisation of the membrane. As this depolarisation approaches the threshold level for activation, the sodium channels swing open, and there is now an inward current carried by sodium ions. This influx causes a rapid depolarisation towards the sodium equilibrium potential, and beyond to a reversal of the membrane potential (the overshoot of the impulse). As the membrane potential approaches the sodium equilibrium potential, the influx of sodium ions slows down, since the electrical gradient to move the ions into the cell is much reduced and since the channels start to close (sodium inactivation). The membrane then begins to repolarise as a result of the increased outflux of potassium ions. These are the main events when an impulse passes through a region of the nerve. Let us now freeze the image at a single moment in the course of the impulse's passage (Fig. 2.62). In the region ahead of the impulse, a capacitative current has begun to flow out of the nerve; in the next region, which is occupied by the rising phase of the potential, the inward sodium current dominates. Finally, in the region of the tail of the impulse, the current is

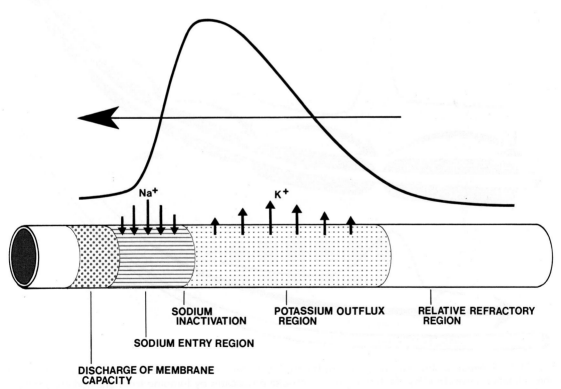

Fig. 2.62 Schematic illustration of changes in membrane potential and movement of sodium and potassium during the action potential. (After Eccles, 1953.)

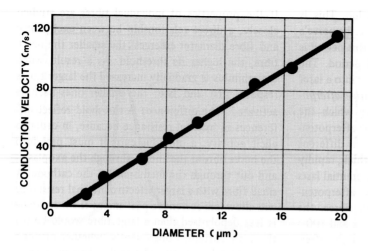

Fig. 2.67 Relation between fibre diameter and conduction velocity in myelinated mammalian nerves.

site, the conductance distance is too short to reveal the differences in conduction velocity between fibres, but if the recording is made further away, the compound action potential loses its monotonic appearance and instead consists of a series of waves. These waves represent the activity in groups of nerve fibres with different conduction velocities. Three main groups, termed A, B and C, have been distinguished in peripheral nerves of vertebrates. Group A contains several subgroups (α, β, γ and δ), ranging in conduction velocity from 120 m s^{-1} to about 10 m s^{-1} (Fig. 2.68). The Aα group includes sensory and motor fibres, the sensory fibres being concerned with proprioception, while the Aβ group consists of fibres which mediate sensations of touch and pressure. The Aγ group is purely motor and includes the small-diameter fibres innervating the intrafusal muscle fibres, whereas the Aδ group is

purely sensory and concerned with nociceptive sensations. The B fibres are autonomic preganglionic fibres: the postganglionic fibres belong to the C group which also includes slowly conducting pain fibres.

To classify the sensory fibres, another system has been introduced that divides afferent nerve fibres into four groups denoted I, II, III and IV. This classification and that described by lettered groups are not completely congruent and this has led to some confusion. In the numeral system group I is divided into two subgroups, Ia which includes afferents from primary endings in muscle spindles and Ib which includes fibres from tendon organs. Group II consists of fibres from cutaneous receptors and secondary endings in muscle spindles, group III pain and temperature afferents and group IV slowly conducting pain fibres. Table 2.1 shows

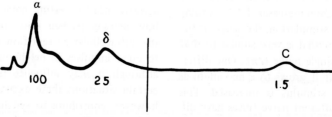

Fig. 2.68   The compound action potential of a human cutaneous nerve. The three peaks (α, δ and C) indicate that the nerve is composed of three major groups of fibres with different conduction velocities (indicated below the tracing). The picture illustrates one of the first recordings of action potentials in human peripheral nerves. (From Heinbecker *et al.*, *Arch. Neurol. Psychiatry*, 29, 1933.)

Table 2.1 Division of nerve fibre types according to the two systems.

Fibre	Type	Function		Diameter (μm)	Conduction velocity (m s^{-1})
Aα		motor	to skeletal muscle	15–20	70–120
Aα	Ia	sensory	muscle spindles (primaries)	15–20	70–120
Aα	Ib	sensory	tendon organs	15–20	70–120
Aβ	II	sensory	touch, pressure, muscle spindles (secondaries)	5–10	30–70
Aγ		motor	to intrafusal fibres	3–6	15–30
Aδ	III	sensory	pain, temperature	2–5	12–30
B		autonomic	preganglionic	3	3–15
C		autonomic	postganglionic	0.5–1	0.5–2
C	IV	sensory	pain	0.5–1	0.5–2

for comparison the division of nerve fibre types in the letter system and the numeral system.

Optical changes

In the early 1950s observations were made which suggested that the optical properties of nerves change during impulse activity. Newer techniques have revealed that these alterations are demonstrable either by measuring light scattering or optical polarisation. The changes are extremely small, and to measure them it is necessary to use relatively long-lasting stimulation and to sum the effects by means of a signal-averaging technique. That the variations observed are actually related to impulse activity is clear from the fact that, if conduction is blocked, no optical changes occur. It has been demonstrated in the giant axon that the alterations in light scattering appear somewhat after the impulse has begun and considerably outlast it (Fig. 2.69). The changes in optical polarisation are more prominent and seem to be directly dependent on the potential difference across the axon membrane.

More recently, optical recordings of impulses have been made in giant axons stained with a merocyanine dye. The generation of action potentials in such an axon is accompanied by a fluorescence increase, the time course of which is closely similar to that of the potential change. Voltage clamp studies have provided evidence that the change in fluorescence is related to the changes in membrane potential rather than to ionic current or membrane permeability. The same method has been successfully employed to record the activity in many cells simultaneously to obtain a map of their functional connections.

2.7 Non-conducted neuronal activity

The local response

For a long time it was generally accepted that the transition from resting state to the generation of

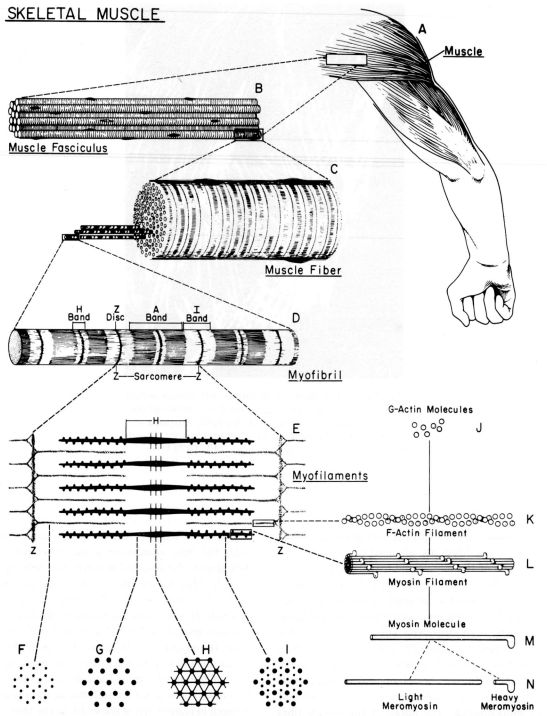

SKELETAL MUSCLE

A — Muscle

B — Muscle Fasciculus

C — Muscle Fiber

D — Myofibril

H Band   Z Disc   A Band   I Band

Z—Sarcomere—Z

E — Myofilaments

F   G   H   I

J — G-Actin Molecules

K — F-Actin Filament

L — Myosin Filament

M — Myosin Molecule

N — Light Meromyosin   Heavy Meromyosin

Fig. 3.2 Schematic representation of the structural organisation of a skeletal muscle from the level of the whole muscle to the molecular level. (From Bloom and Fawcett, *A Textbook of Histology*, W. B. Saunders, Philadelphia, 1968.)

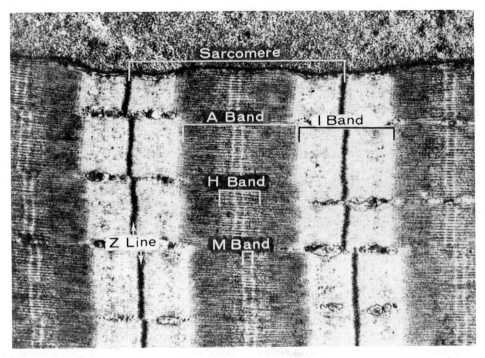

Fig. 3.3 Electron micrograph of muscle fibre showing typical pattern of cross-striations. (From Bloom and Fawcett, *A Textbook of Histology*, W. B. Saunders, 1968.)

elements, the myofilaments, which are of two types, thick filaments about 15 nm in diameter and 1.6 μm in length and thin filaments about 8 nm wide and 1.0 μm long (Fig. 3.4). The thick filaments are present only in the A-band where they are arranged alongside each other and anchored by a central structure, the *M-line*, in the middle of the H-band. The thin filaments extend from the Z-lines through the I-bands and into the A-band where they overlap with the thick filaments. The Z-line structure seems to hold the thin filaments in a regular spacing. The light H-zone marks the gap between the ends of the thin filaments in the middle region of the A-band. In transverse sections through the A-band where both thick and thin filaments are present, it can be seen that the thin filaments are arranged around the thick filaments in a regular hexagonal pattern. In longitudinal sections of the myofibrils at high magnifications, the thick filaments, except for a middle section, are seen to have short projections, cross-bridges, which appear to make contact

with the thin filaments in the overlap zone (Fig. 3.5). As we shall see later, the structure of the filaments reflects an orderly aggregation of the myosin molecules.

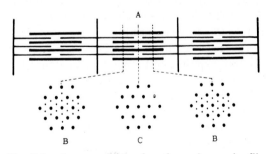

Fig. 3.4 Arrangement of actin and myosin filament in a skeletal muscle. In (A) are seen three sarcomeres in longitudinal section; (B) shows transverse sections through the A-band; (C) through the H-zone. (From Huxley and Hanson, in *The Structure and Function of Muscle*, ed. G. H. Bourne, Academic Press, New York, 1960.)

Fig. 3.5 Electron micrograph showing the cross-bridges between the coarse myosin filaments and the thin actin filaments. (From H. Huxley, *J. Biophys. Biochem. Cytol.*, 1957.)

Muscle proteins

At the time when the filaments were discovered it had long been known that there were two major protein components in the muscle, actin and myosin. It therefore appeared conceivable that the two types of filaments observed under the electron microscope represented these components. The problem of the distribution of the two proteins was solved when it was shown that if myosin was extracted from muscle without significantly affecting the actin component, thick filaments in the A-bands were absent. If the actin was then extracted the remaining material disappeared, and only the Z-bands were left. These findings clearly showed that the thicker filaments are composed of myosin and the thinner ones of actin.

The regular arrangement of the actin and myosin filaments explains why the myofibrils and therefore also the muscle fibres are cross-striated. The darker appearance of the A-band is due to the presence of both myosin and actin filaments in this zone. The I-zone is less dense, since there are only actin filaments in this region. The darker M-line is assumed to represent connections which stabilise the position of the myosin filaments within the fibril. Therefore this zone seems to fulfil the same function for the myosin filaments as the Z-band for the actin filaments.

The myosin molecules can be examined with a special technique under the electron microscope (Fig. 3.6). They appear as thin rods, 140–160 nm in length, each molecule having two globular heads attached to one end of a long tail. It has been found that the myosin molecule can be split by the use of specific enzymes into two major fragments composed of two kinds of proteins, *light* and *heavy meromyosin* (Fig. 3.7). In this way it has been demonstrated that the truncated tail is built up of light meromyosin; this part of the myosin molecule does not bind to actin and has no ATP-ase activity. The other fragment, which comprises the two globular heads and a part of the tail is heavy meromyosin. It binds to actin and has ATP-ase activity. The backbone of the myosin filament of the muscle fibre is made up of the tail portion corresponding to light meromyosin, while the heavy meromyosin part, i.e. the globular heads and the attached part of the tail, is free and functions as a cross-bridge reaching the thin filaments. The myosin molecules point in opposite directions in each half of the thick filament and this accounts for the fact that the middle of the myosin filament has no cross-bridges.

The thin filaments are composed of a double helix of globular subunits (Fig. 3.8). When actin is extracted from muscle it emerges in the form of globular molecules (G-actin); in the presence of ATP the molecules polymerise into long filaments

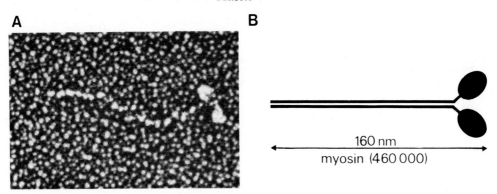

Fig. 3.6 (A) Electron micrograph of myosin molecules, visualised by the shadowing technique. (B) Schematic representation of the double-headed myosin molecule. (From *The Open University*, Open University Press, 1974.)

of F-actin, which resemble natural thin filaments. The thin filaments in living muscle contain two more proteins, *tropomyosin* and *troponin*, which form a complex. Tropomyosin is a rod-like molecule which forms fibrous strands which lie in the long-pitched helical grooves of the actin filament. The globular troponin molecules are bound to the tropomyosin strands at regular intervals. Thus the troponin molecules are not directly attached to the actin filament but linked to it through the tropomyosin molecules. X-ray diffraction studies suggest that the tropomyosin moves deeper into

the grooves of the actin filaments during contraction to expose sites to which the myosin heads can bind (see below). This movement of the tropomyosin is induced by a change in the configuration of the troponin molecules under the influence of calcium ions.

The motor unit

Contraction of skeletal muscles is controlled by the central nervous system through the motor nerve

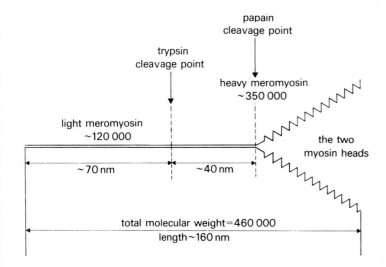

Fig. 3.7 Schematic representation of the myosin molecule showing its various fragments and their molecular weights. The myosin heads are indicated as zigzags but in reality form compact globular units. Points are also indicated at which the molecule can be cleaved by the enzymes, trypsin and papain. (From *The Open University*, Open University Press, 1974.)

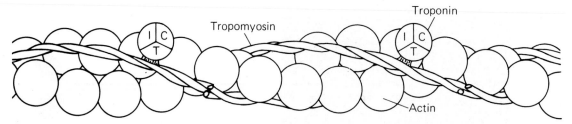

Fig. 3.8 Schematic representation of the structure of actin filaments showing the tropomyosin–troponin complex lying in the grooves of the actin double helix formed by globular units of actin. I, C and T indicate the three subunits of troponin.

fibres. Within the muscle each nerve fibre divides into a number of branches, each of which innervates a muscle fibre. A single motoneuron with the muscle fibres that it innervates forms a functional entity called the *motor unit* (Fig. 3.9). Once an impulse is generated in a motoneuron, it travels along the nerve fibre and its branches to all the muscle fibres in the unit. The number of muscle fibres in such a unit varies from one muscle to another. In eye muscles there are normally 3–10 muscle fibres per unit, in limb muscles about 150–500, and in postural muscles up to 800. The number of muscle fibres per motor unit is related to the function of the muscle; muscles with fine, precise movements have fewer muscle fibres per unit. The fewer fibres there are, the more precisely can the force of the muscle be controlled.

The force of contraction may be graded by varying the number of active units, as well as by changing the frequency of action potentials in each unit. Most muscles contain a range of motor unit sizes, so that the force of contraction also depends upon which motor units are activated. Recordings of the impulses in a contracting muscle by a needle electrode within the muscle (electromyogram) show that an increase in force of contraction is accomplished by both an increase in the frequency of impulses in single units and an increase in the number of motor units activated.

Fast and slow muscles

The characteristic colour of muscle varies in different muscles. For this reason muscles have long been classified into red and white muscles. The colour of red muscles is due to a relatively high content of myoglobin, a substance related to the blood pigment, haemoglobin. In most cases, but not in all, red muscles contract more slowly than white and have greater endurance. On the basis of these functional differences, it has been customary to divide muscle fibres into white fast and red slow. The differences between them are not quite distinct. It should be noted also that there exists no consistent relation between the colour of a muscle and its velocity of contraction. Furthermore, there are intermediate types which cannot be put into one or other group. In many muscles, both types of fibres are present, and the speed of contraction is therefore determined by their relative numbers. In the cat, for example, the *soleus muscle* consists mainly of slow muscle fibres, while *flexor digitorum longus* has almost entirely fast fibres; the *gastrocnemius muscle* has approximately an equal number of fast and slow fibres. If the nerve to the gastrocnemius muscle is stimulated so that all its fibres are activated, a relatively slow contraction results. If the nerve is stimulated relatively weakly, so that only the large nerve fibres are activated, a considerably faster contraction is induced because in this case mostly fast muscle fibres are activated.

The slow red fibres dominate in the postural musculature while the fast fibres are preponderant in muscles participating in fast movements. This latter category includes for example the muscles of the hand, jaw and eye. Slow muscle fibres are usually innervated by thin nerve fibres and fast muscle fibres by relatively large nerve fibres. These

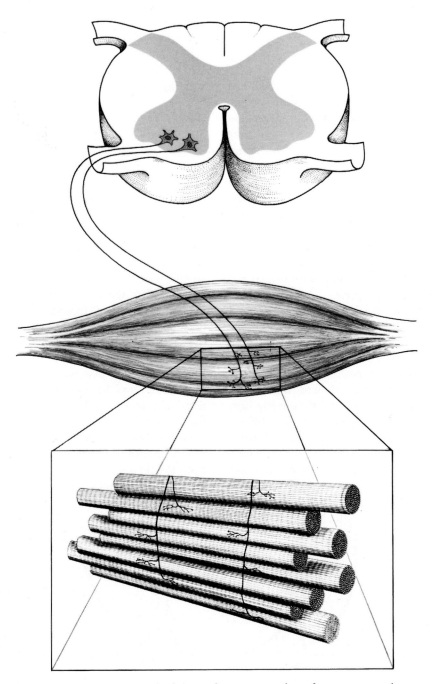

Fig. 3.9 The motor unit. Schematic representation of two motor units.

two types of nerve fibres in turn belong to two different types of motoneurons in the spinal cord, tonic and phasic cells respectively.

Cross-innervation

At birth, all muscle fibres contract at about the same speed. Then, during the first months of life, changes appear which lead to the differentiation into fast and slow fibres. Since the two types are innervated by phasic and tonic motoneurons, respectively, it has been thought that the differentiation might relate to some trophic factor. If the differentiation depends on the type of nerve fibre innervating the muscle, a fast muscle should presumably develop into a slow one if nerve fibres that normally go to a slow muscle were made to innervate it, and vice versa. Such a cross-innervation would have to be carried out before the normal differentiation has taken place.

Extensive studies of this type have been carried out in newborn kittens. The results show that the contraction properties of a muscle that has been invaded by 'foreign' fibres change but not always in a clearcut way. If nerve fibres that ordinarily innervate a slow muscle are allowed to grow into a fast muscle (i.e. one that would normally have developed into a fast muscle), it will later behave like a slow muscle (Fig. 3.10). When fast nerve fibres grow into a normally slow muscle, however, the contraction becomes faster but does not become as fast as in normally innervated fast muscle. These changes have been attributed to

the influence of some trophic factor carried to the muscle fibres by the axons. There is evidence that different patterns of activity in slow and fast nerve fibres may also contribute; slow nerve fibres are active tonically with firing frequencies of 10–20 Hz, while fast nerve fibres are active phasically with firing frequencies exceeding 100 Hz.

3.2 Muscle contraction

By simultaneously recording the electrical activity of a muscle and the force developed during contraction, it can be demonstrated that the electrical response not only precedes contraction but actually ends before contraction has started (Fig. 3.11). Since the electrical events in the muscle are faster than the contractile process, a second muscle impulse can be set up and propagated along the muscle before the tension change due to the first impulse has subsided. Indeed an individual muscle fibre may be invaded by several impulses before the contraction evoked by the first impulse is over. This raises the question of what effect these later impulses may have on the contractile process. The answer may be obtained by stimulating the nerve of a muscle at different intervals after contraction has been evoked by the first impulse. The tension will be seen to increase during the repetitive stimulation, the force developed being dependent upon the time interval between stimuli. It is greatest when the stimulus is applied so that the second contraction begins before the first contraction

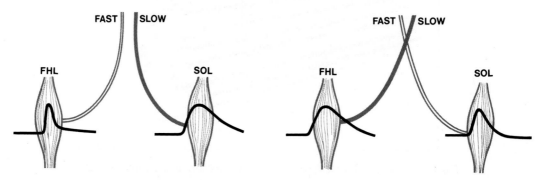

Fig. 3.10 The change in rate of contraction after cross-innervation. (After Buller and Lewis, *J. Physiol. (Lond.)*, 176, 1965.)

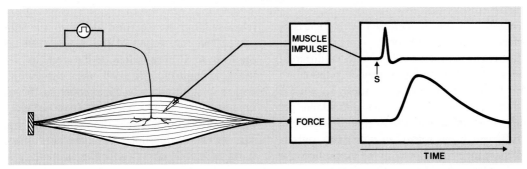

Fig. 3.11 Time relation of electrical and mechanical event in skeletal muscle, contraction being evoked by electric stimulation of the motor nerve. Note that the muscle impulse precedes contraction and is over before contraction starts.

reaches its maximum (Fig. 3.12). Repetitive stimuli repeated at short intervals will produce a prolonged contraction, the force of which may be as much as 2–3 times greater than that of a single muscle twitch. If the succession of stimuli is rapid enough, individual muscle twitches can no longer be observed; this state of continued contraction is called *complete* or *fused tetanus*. During fused contraction the muscle maintains a prolonged steady contraction. If the intervals between the stimuli are longer, the individual muscle twitches may appear as waves superimposed upon a sustained, steady tension; this type of contraction is called *incomplete tetanus*.

An important difference between the electrical and mechanical events in a single muscle fibre during contraction is that the mechanical process does not display refractoriness, and this is the basis for the summation of tension during a fused tetanus. The continuous smooth response seen in recordings from the muscle tendon during fused contraction corresponds to a similar summation of continuous smooth mechanical events in the individual muscle fibres. As we shall see later, the contractile process in the muscle fibres involves the release and diffusion of calcium ions in the interior of the muscle. The force of contraction therefore depends upon the level of calcium in the

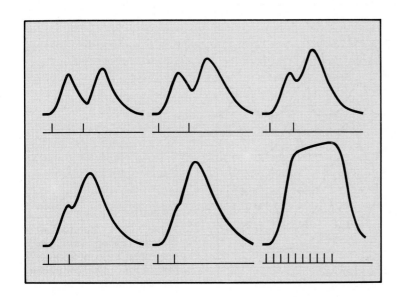

Fig. 3.12 Summation of muscle twitches. The muscle is stimulated with two electric shocks at successively shorter intervals. Fusion of muscle twitches to give a tetanus is indicated by bottom recording to the right.

sarcoplasm and this is increased with increasing frequency of impulse activity.

Just as the contraction time varies in different muscles, so the stimulus frequency required to evoke fused contraction also varies. To elicit a fused contraction in eye muscles, 300 stimuli per second are required, whereas 30 stimuli per second are sufficient in *m. soleus*. In voluntary contractions the impulse frequency in the motor nerves is considerably lower and for the flexors and extensors in the extremities it is usually not higher than 50 impulses per second. In postural muscles the corresponding impulse frequency is 5–25 per second. Despite this low discharge frequency of the motoneurons, muscle contractions during voluntary or reflex movements are usually smooth. This is because the discharge of different motor nerves is asynchronous: groups of motor units contract at irregular intervals, and the combined effect of their activity is a smooth development of force (Fig. 3.13).

Isotonic and isometric contractions

The time course of the contraction of a muscle can be studied most simply by recording the mechanical response after an electrical shock to the motor nerve. The contraction of the muscle then takes the form of a single twitch. If the strength of the shock is gradually increased, the contraction increases in strength up to a maximum, at the same time becoming more prolonged. These changes are explained by the fact that the motor nerve fibres have different thresholds and innervate different types of muscle fibres. Since the excitability of a nerve fibre is related to its diameter, the rapidly conducting thick fibres which generally innervate the fast muscle fibres are activated first. With increasing stimulus strength, the thinner axons which innervate slow muscle fibres also become activated. This explains why, in a muscle composed of slow and fast fibres, contraction is prolonged as the numbers of active muscle fibres grows.

The time course of contraction varies with the load of the muscle, and so it is convenient to study the development of force when the imposed load is so great that the muscle cannot shorten. The contraction under these conditions is called *isometric*, in contrast to an *isotonic* contraction, where the muscle is allowed to shorten. During isometric contraction, force is developed without

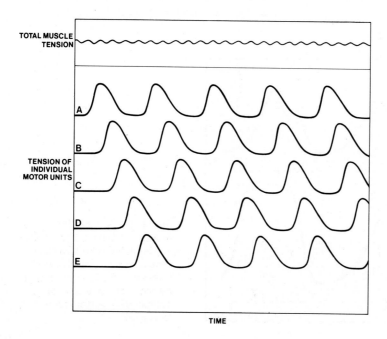

Fig. 3.13   Summation of muscle tension (*top trace*) developed by contractions of five motor units contracting asynchronously.

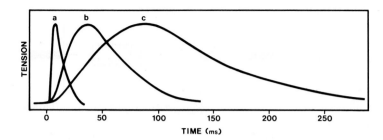

Fig. 3.14 Time course of isometric contraction and relaxation of three mammalian
muscles: a, lateral rectus of
the eye; b, gastrocnemius; c,
soleus.

any change in the external muscle length; however, the individual muscle fibres shorten and stretch the elastic tissue elements that transmit the tension to the tendon of the muscle. The tension developed during a muscle twitch rises rapidly and then decreases somewhat more slowly. The time from the start of increase in tension until maximum tension is reached is called the *contraction time*; the ensuing time for fall in tension is called the *relaxation time*. The contraction time is a measure of how fast the muscle fibres contract; it is therefore not surprising that it varies a great deal from one muscle to another (Fig. 3.14). Fast muscles such as the eye muscles have a contraction time of 7–8 ms; for most flexors and extensors in the extremities it is 20–40 ms, while in postural muscles it is about 100 ms. However, as we will see later, the time course of tension does not reflect the time course of the contractile process, because the elastic elements in the tendon introduce a delay in tension development.

Length–tension relationship

The amount of force developed when a muscle is stimulated to contract maximally depends on a number of factors, one of which is the length of the muscle prior to contraction. Experimentally this can be demonstrated by transecting the tendon and stretching the muscle to different lengths (Fig. 3.15). It will then be found that the muscle develops its greatest tension when it is set at the length that it assumes at rest in the body. If the length is increased or decreased beyond the rest length the force developed during maximal isometric contraction decreases. If the muscle is allowed to shorten against a load, that is during isotonic

contraction, the force developed decreases in relation to the shortening of the length of the muscle. Initially tension increases rapidly until the force developed is greater than the load. As shortening proceeds, tension begins to fall and, when the force becomes equal to the load, shortening ceases. At this moment, contraction becomes isometric and the force developed is the maximum tension that the muscle can exert at that length. From the isometric length–tension diagram it can be seen that the maximum force is reduced by 50% when the muscle shortens to about 85% of its rest length and if it shortens to 60% no tension can be developed. As we shall see later, this is due to the difference in filament overlap.

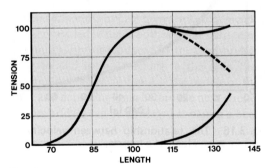

Fig. 3.15 The relationship between force and length of a muscle. Maximum force is developed at the rest length. The curve at lower right indicates the tension developed by passive stretch. The broken curve represents the tension obtained when the passive stretch tension is subtracted from the upper curve.

Force–velocity relationship

The velocity of contraction of a given muscle depends mainly on two factors, the load and the

which by cyclic motions 'row' the filaments past one another. X-ray diffraction studies indicate that the cross-bridges are attached to the backbone of the myosin filaments by a tail which makes it possible for the cross-bridges to move. The junction between the tail and the globular head of the cross-bridge constitutes another flexible part. The sliding force is developed by the heads, which attach to the actin filaments and exert a longitudinal force; the tail serves to sustain the tension thus developed; each individual cross-bridge is supposed to undergo cycles in which it attaches, generates force and detaches. For each cycle the thin filaments are pulled along the thick filaments for a maximum distance of about 10–12 nm. Because of the structural polarity of the thick filaments (see above), the thin filaments in both halves of the sarcomere are pulled towards the centre of the sarcomere.

The actual mechanisms underlying the generation of force are still unknown. According to one hypothesis, tilting of the globular heads of the cross-bridges would be responsible for the sliding of the filaments (Fig. 3.19). An alternative hypothesis is that the globular heads are formed by subunits which move in relation to one another. The cross-bridges are thus the force generators and the energy required for the sliding movements of the filaments is derived from the hydrolysis of ATP; splitting of one molecule of ATP appears to provide enough energy for one stroke of a cross-bridge.

It should be noted that tension may be developed with little or no sliding movements of the thin filaments. For instance, in an isolated muscle fibre, shortening may be minute during isometric contraction. The force generated is accounted for by the tension developed by the cross-bridges attaching to the thick filaments. In the whole muscle there is always a shortening of the contractile elements in isometric contraction, and this may allow for more attachments to be formed. The force developed thus is a function of the number of attachments at any moment and their degree of extension.

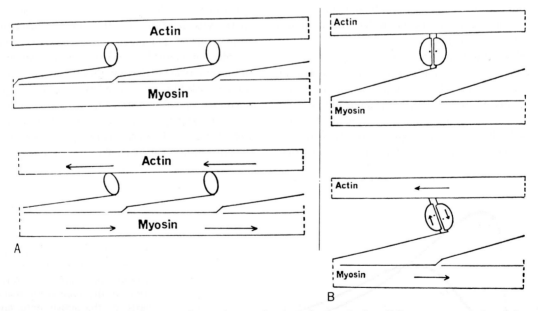

Fig. 3.19   Diagram illustrating two alternative mechanisms for producing sliding movements by tilting of cross-bridges. (A) In this model the sliding movement is produced by a change in the angle at which the head of the heavy meromyosin is attached to the actin filament. (B) In this model a small relative movement between two subunits of the myosin head gives rise to a change in tilt. (From Huxley, *Science*, 164, 1969.)

Length–tension relation in isolated muscle fibres

If the cross-bridges are the sites where tension is produced, it would follow that the force developed during contraction is proportional to the amount of overlap between the two sets of filaments. This is also borne out by the studies of A. F. Huxley and his colleagues who have demonstrated elegantly that the maximal force of a single muscle fibre is developed at a sarcomere length that allows for optimal utilisation of all the cross-bridges between the filaments. When the muscle is stretched, reducing the number of cross-bridges in the overlap region, the force decreases linearly with increasing sarcomere length (Fig. 3.20). With initial sarcomere lengths less than 2.0 μm, the force–length curve

shows a break; this corresponds to the length at which the actin filaments meet in the centre of the A-band. At this length the actin filaments of one half of the sarcomere begin to interfere with those of the other half and there is a 'double overlap' of filaments. A second break is present at a sarcomere length of 1.65 μm which corresponds to the length at which the thick filaments butt against the Z-line. In this context it is of interest to note that the curve for the force–length relation of a single muscle fibre shows a close resemblance to the corresponding curve for the whole muscle (see Fig. 3.15). This provides evidence that the force produced by a muscle during contraction is ultimately determined by the number of cross-bridges making contact with the actin filaments. The sliding

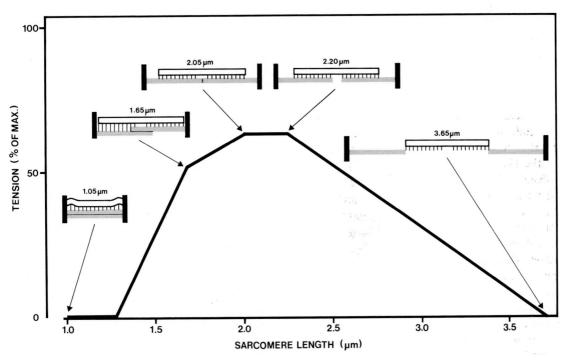

Fig. 3.20 Length–tension relation in an isolated frog muscle fibre. Insets show filament positions for five sarcomere lengths. Maximum tension is developed at a sarcomere length of 2.20 μm. At this length there is maximum overlap of thin filaments with bridges of thick filaments. At a sarcomere length of 2.05 μm, the ends of the thin filaments butt against each other and tension remains the same. With further decrease in sarcomere length, tension falls. At a sarcomere length of 1.65 μm, the thick filaments butt against the Z-line, and with further reduction in length they are compressed. At a sarcomere length of 1.05 μm, the tension has decreased near to zero. At sarcomere lengths longer than 2.20 μm, tension decreases linearly with increasing sarcomere length, and at a sarcomere length of 3.65 μm, where there is no overlap, tension is zero. (Modified from Gordon, Huxley and Julian, *J. Physiol.*, 171, 1964.)

filament hypothesis also appears to explain the
force–velocity relation of a muscle. When the
muscle is allowed to shorten against a small load,
relatively few attachments are required to develop
force, and the filaments are therefore able to slide
past one another rapidly. With greater force, more
attachments are necessary, and the sliding movement becomes slower.

Excitation–contraction coupling

The first step in the activation of a muscle fibre
following neuromuscular transmission is the propagation of the electrical impulse along the muscle
fibre. It was assumed for some time that the current
of the impulse somehow spread into the muscle
fibre to induce the contractile process. However,
several lines of evidence contradicted this idea. For
instance, the fibrils which lie centrally in the muscle
fibre may be 50 μm or more from the outer membrane and are thus unlikely to be reached by current produced in the surface membrane. A crucial
advance came in 1955 when Huxley and Taylor
stimulated an isolated muscle fibre with a microelectrode and demonstrated that a localised contraction occurred only if the stimulus was applied
to the I-band close to the Z-line, and not at the
A-band (Fig. 3.21). This hinted at some connection
between the exterior of the muscle membrane and
the interior of the fibre in the region of the Z-band.
At about the same time, a system of fine tubules
was demonstrated in the interior of the muscle
fibres. Originally discovered in the early 1900s,
this so-called *transverse tubule system* (Fig. 3.22)
had been largely forgotten for half a century.
Electron microscope studies now disclosed a set of
transversely oriented tubular structures which run
in the spaces between the myofibrils. In addition
there is the sarcoplasmic reticulum, which consists
of a longitudinal system of tubules and vesicle-
shaped formations. These run parallel to the myofibrils in the interstices between them; at regular
intervals they merge and form a girdle around each
fibril. In the frog the transverse tubules or the
T-system occurs at the level of the Z-lines. Here
the transverse tubules are in close contact with the

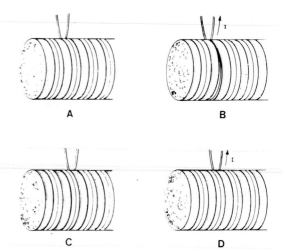

Fig. 3.21 Schematic diagram illustrating the experiment of Huxley and Taylor in which they
demonstrated the focal sensitivity of an isolated
muscle fibre to electrical stimulation. In (A) the
stimulating electrode is placed over the Z-line. (B)
When current is passed through the electrode, the
adjacent half sarcomeres contract. (C) and (D)
When the electrode is placed over an A-band, no
contraction is induced. (From Fawcett, in *The
Myocardium, Its Biochemistry and Biophysics*, ed.
Fishman, New York, 1961.)

vesicular girdles of the longitudinal tubular system
of the sarcoplasmic reticulum and form so-called
triads.

   With the discovery of the transverse tubules, it
was clear that there existed a system of tubular
structures that might subserve the inward spread
of activation. To do so, the tubules would have to
be open to the extracellular fluid. Despite intense
searching, no such openings could at first be found.
In 1964 Hill succeeded in demonstrating by radio-
autography that the transverse tubules are effectively open to the extracellular fluid and furthermore
that the openings are principally located near the
Z-line. Here was conclusive evidence that the T-
system provides continuity between the interior of
the fibre and the extracellular space. The question
remained whether the activity is conducted by
active propagation of the action potential or by
passive electrotonic spread from the surface membrane, and how this activity is transmitted to the
longitudinal tubular system. The experimental

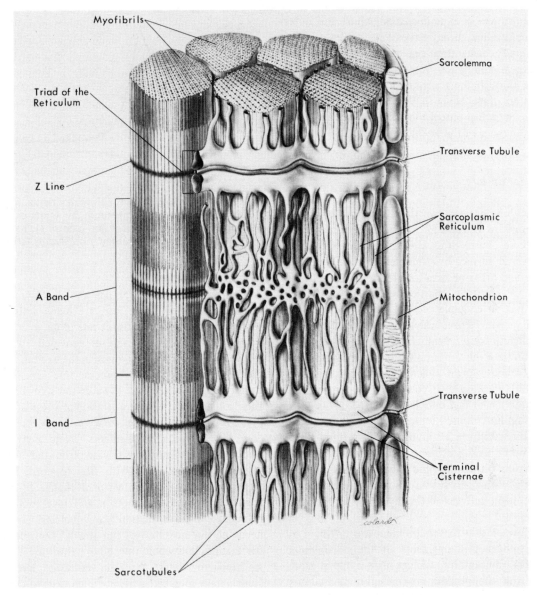

Fig. 3.22 Schematic representation of the sarcoplasmic reticulum in skeletal muscle. (From Fawcett and McNutt, in Bloom and Fawcett, *A Textbook of Histology*, W. B. Saunders, 1968.)

evidence suggested that the inward spread is an active process, and that the depolarisation of the transverse system is transmitted to the longitudinal system through special junctions at the triads. An interesting observation, which throws light upon the role of the T-system for the spread of activation into the muscle fibre, is that by treating the muscle fibre with glycerol it is possible to damage the T-system selectively. In muscle fibres so treated, the action potential is not followed by contraction since the inward spread of the impulse can no longer occur. The outer membrane, on the other hand, is not an absolute prerequisite for contraction, provided that the tubular system remains. This has been shown in experiments in which the outer membrane had been removed; in such a fibre, a localised contraction can be set up by direct electrical stimulation; activity still spreads into the fibre through the transverse tubule system but it does not travel along the fibre since the capability for longitudinal propagation of activity is abolished after removal of the sarcolemma.

Role of calcium

It has long been known that the injection of small amounts of calcium into a muscle fibre induces a localised contraction, whereas calcium applied to the outer surface of a muscle fibre has no effect. This and other observations led to the conclusion that calcium might participate in the excitation–contraction coupling process. It was thought that during contraction calcium ions would enter through the outer membrane, diffuse into the fibre and initiate the contractile process. Although such a mechanism might underlie contraction in slowly contracting muscle, it could not account for the contraction of fast muscles, since the diffusion of calcium ions would be too slow to induce activity simultaneously in all myofibrils of a fibre. If, on the other hand, calcium ions were stored in some structure within the fibre and then released more or less synchronously throughout the cross-section, they might activate all the myofibrils at the same time.

The solution to this problem was provided by the finding that fragments of the sarcoplasmic system concentrate calcium ions. This suggests that the sarcoplasmic system serves as a storage site for calcium ions, which are released by the invasion of the action potential into the T-system. Direct evidence showing that calcium ions are actually released from the sarcoplasmic system during contraction has been obtained in recent studies by using the photoprotein, *aequorin*, which forms a luminescent complex with free calcium ions. The release of calcium follows closely upon depolarisation of the muscle fibre and precedes initiation of contraction (Fig. 3.23). At the time when the tension reaches its peak the calcium

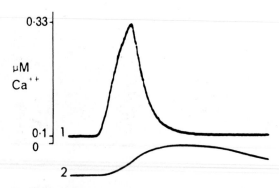

Fig. 3.23 Calcium release (1) in a muscle fibre during contraction (2), measured by injection of aequorin into the muscle fibre and recording change in light emission. (From Ashley, *Endeavour*, 1971.)

concentration in the fibre has already begun to decline and the calcium ions are being actively sequestered in the sarcoplasmic reticulum.

Although these observations provided strong evidence that calcium is involved in the excitation–contraction coupling, its precise role remained unresolved. A crucial step towards the solution of this problem was the demonstration of a regulatory system of proteins, the *troponin–tropomyosin complex*, in the actin filaments. There is strong evidence that calcium ions released from the sarcoplasmic reticulum react with the troponin. This seems to cause a conformational change of the troponin–tropomyosin complex and this is thought to uncover sites on the thin filaments to which the heads of the cross-bridges can attach. The role of the calcium ions would thus be to permit the myosin heads to contact the actin molecules. Recent studies have shown that troponin consists of three subunits, one of which (TnC) binds calcium strongly. Relaxation of the muscle is brought about by release of calcium from troponin and sequestration back in the sarcoplasmic reticulum, followed by a shifting of the troponin–tropomyosin complex to its original position and interruption of the actin–myosin interaction.

The role of the calcium ions in the contractile process is not limited to their binding to the troponin molecules. Since the end of the 1930s it has been known that myosin has ATP-ase activity, that is if myosin is added to ATP the ATP is broken down to ADP and energy is released. Actin does not have this effect. Later it was found that the ability of myosin to break down ATP in the muscle fibre requires the presence of calcium (Fig. 3.24). These findings suggested that the force generated during contraction might be related to the concentration of calcium. The role of calcium in the generation of tension has been disclosed by measuring the contractile force in bundles of myofibrils at different calcium concentrations. As illustrated in Fig. 3.24B the relation between the force and calcium concentration is similar to that between ATP-ase activity and calcium concentration. Therefore it is likely that tension production and ATP hydrolysis reflect the same reactions, i.e. the interaction between the thick and thin filaments. It has therefore been assumed that the difference in contraction speed between fast and slow muscle fibres is related to the amount of calcium stored in the sarcoplasmic reticulum, and that fast fibres should contain more calcium than slow fibres. Slow fibres would therefore be more dependent upon the inflow of calcium through the sarcolemma, and this would explain why the contractile process has a slower time course. However, recent observations suggest that the major cause for the difference in contraction speed is related to different ATP splitting rates of myosin in the two types of muscle.

Summary

In summary, the current concept of the processes underlying the contraction of a muscle fibre can be outlined as follows. The contractile process is initiated by the action potential which spreads along the muscle fibre. When the impulse passes the openings of the transverse tubules, the depolarisation travels into the muscle fibre interior. The depolarisation causes the release of calcium ions which are stored in the sarcoplasmic reticulum (Fig. 3.25). Calcium ions diffuse between the myofilaments and react with a protein complex (troponin—tropomyosin) in the thin filaments. As a result of this binding, active sites on the actin filaments are uncovered. This makes it possible for the heads of the myosin filaments to attach to the actin filaments and exert tension, pulling them in between the thick filaments. As the depolarisation of the sarcoplasmic reticulum subsides, calcium ions are released from the troponin—tropomyosin complex and actively pumped back into the sarcoplasmic reticulum. Following removal of the calcium ions, the tropomyosin molecules return to their original resting positions and cover the sites

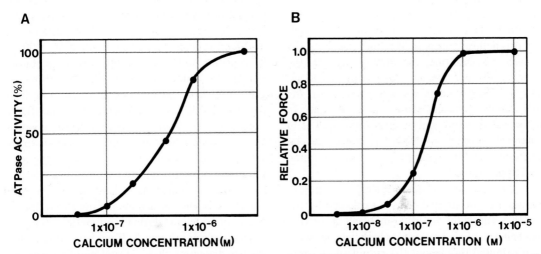

Fig. 3.24   Relation between calcium concentration and (A) ATP-ase activity and (B) force of contraction in an isolated bundle of myofibrils. (From Hellam and Podorsky, *J. Physiol.*, 200, 1969.)

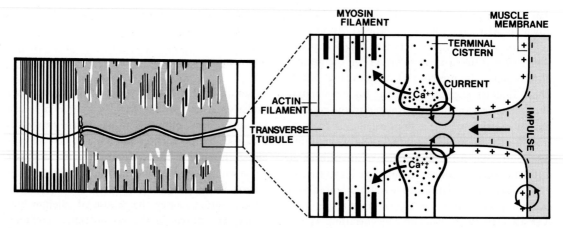

Fig. 3.25 Schematic diagram showing sequence of events in excitation–contraction coupling. The muscle impulse travelling along the muscle fibre invades the transverse tubules and induces the release of calcium ions from the cisternae into the sarcoplasm. The calcium ions released bind to troponin.

for the attachment of the cross-bridges to the thin filaments. Finally the return of the thin filaments to their resting position is provided by the tension exerted by the tendon elastic elements which have been extended during the contraction of the muscle fibres.

3.3 Smooth muscle

Functional anatomy

Smooth muscles form the main portion of the walls of most hollow organs in the body, such as the stomach, the intestine, the urinary bladder, the blood vessels and the air passages of the lungs. They are also found in the skin attached to the hairs. Smooth muscles show a great diversity in anatomical structure and innervation as well as in functional properties. However, some general structural and functional properties are common to all smooth muscles.

In contrast to skeletal muscles, the smooth muscles are not striated. This is explained by the fact that the actin and myosin filaments, rather than being regularly organised as in skeletal muscles, are distributed throughout the cytoplasm in parallel bundles. Between the filaments there are cross-

bridges as in skeletal muscle. There is, however, no anchoring of the filaments corresponding to, for instance, the anchoring of the actin filaments to the Z-bands in skeletal muscle. This appears to explain why smooth muscle fibres are able to develop tension over a wide range of muscle lengths. For example, as the bladder fills the smooth muscle fibres in the wall may be stretched considerably, yet still be able to exert force. In skeletal muscle a corresponding stretch would completely eliminate contraction.

The smooth muscle fibres generally lie in closely packed bundles surrounded by connective tissue. The cells are spindle-shaped, 5–200 μm long and 4–20 μm in diameter. Each bundle is 50–100 μm in diameter and is connected with neighbouring bundles by connective tissue. The smooth muscle cells differ from skeletal muscle fibres in having a less well developed sarcoplasmic reticulum. Below the plasma membrane is an accumulation of vesicular structures, which probably corresponds to the sarcoplasmic reticulum in skeletal fibres; the vesicles serve in the storage and release of calcium. It is likely that in addition, at least in some smooth muscle cells, the surface membrane allows for the entry of calcium during contraction. Since in general the smooth muscle fibres have considerably smaller diameters than skeletal muscle fibres, diffusion of ions from the surface membrane to the centre of the cell takes relatively little time. Contraction in smooth muscles is much slower than in skeletal muscle. This may be attributed partly to the lack of a well developed sarcoplasmic reticulum and partly to the fact that the amount of contractile material is only a tenth of that in skeletal fibres. In addition, the concentration of ATP is low.

Although smooth muscles vary widely in their structural and functional properties, they can be divided into two main groups. The first of these, the *unitary* type, is found in viscera, uterus, ureters and walls of small arteries and veins. The most characteristic functional feature of this type of muscle is that groups of cells show a synchronised activity and respond to stimulation as a single unit. The synchronised action is explained by the fact that the membranes of the cells in a functional unit are joined together by gap junctions, which provide for the passage of electrical signals from one cell to another. Typically, this type of muscle shows spontaneous rhythmical contractions which remain after the blocking of nerve activity. They arise in pacemaker areas and spread over the muscle in the same way as in cardiac muscle. The electrical activity of these cells has been examined with intracellular recordings. As the cell is usually spontaneously active, it is difficult to define its resting potential. On average the potential obtained is around -50 mV. The spontaneous contractions are usually preceded by slow depolarising waves; when the waves reach a given amplitude, they elicit an impulse discharge and thereby contraction of the muscle cells. Each spike is preceded by a prepotential known as the pacemaker potential (Fig. 3.26).

The pacemaker potential may also appear in the absence of the slow depolarising waves. This activity resembles pacemaker activity in the cardiac muscle, but rather than being limited to a specific region of the muscle cell it shifts from one site to another. Different pacemaker regions can be active concurrently and give rise to impulses which spread over the muscle fibres. Another characteristic property of smooth muscle cells of the unitary type is that they are depolarised by stretch. If the muscle is exposed to a constant stretch, it responds with a prolonged train of impulses and produces maintained tension. The function of the autonomic nerves is more to modulate by excitatory or inhibitory action the spontaneous activity and the activity evoked by stretch rather than to initiate and control activity in unitary smooth muscles.

The second group of smooth muscles, the *multi-unit* type, is found in the walls of the large arteries and in some regions of the intestinal tract. Their main functional characteristic is that the activity is initiated and controlled by autonomic nerves very much as in skeletal muscle. They are usually innervated by sympathetic nerves but may also have parasympathetic innervation; both have an excitatory action. The membrane of the muscle cell appears to have receptor sites over its entire surface, unlike the skeletal muscles, where the receptors are localised to the endplate region. A single nerve impulse usually produces only a subthreshold change; in order to generate contraction, multiple nerve impulses are required. Like the unitary smooth muscles, the multi-unit smooth muscles are sensitive to chemical substances and transmitters circulating in the blood.

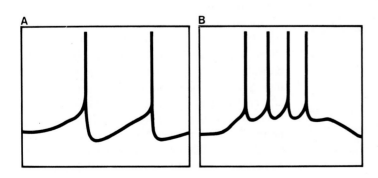

Fig. 3.26 Pacemaker potentials (A) and slow depolarisation wave (B) triggering action potentials in smooth muscle fibres.

Autonomic innervation

Smooth muscles receive their motor nerve supply via autonomic postganglionic nerve fibres. These fibres branch profusely within the muscle bundles to form networks of thin nerve fibres (see Fig. 3.27). At different points in their course, these fibres lose the Schwann sheath and occasionally lie in direct contact with the muscle cell. Within these regions of the nerve fibres there are vesicles resembling those at presynaptic terminals in the central nervous system. The release of transmitter substance at these points by a single nerve fibre may therefore affect a number of cells. Considering that the autonomic innervation of certain smooth muscles is relatively sparse, the question has been raised as to how the activity is controlled. It has been assumed that a widespread diffusion of the transmitter substance affects muscle cells lacking direct innervation, i.e. some fibres are directly activated by the transmitter released close by while others are activated by diffusion of the transmitter or by direct electrical coupling of the muscle cells.

The cholinergic as well as adrenergic nerve terminals in smooth muscle possess varicosities which contain synaptic vesicles. In adrenergic nerves three types of vesicles may be observed: small granular vesicles, small agranular vesicles and large granular vesicles. In cholinergic nerves only small agranular vesicles and large granular vesicles are

seen. The small granular vesicles in adrenergic nerves contain noradrenalin and the greater part of the transmitter in sympathetic nerves is stored in these vesicles. There is also evidence to suggest that the large granular vesicles found in the sympathetic axon of nerve trunks contain noradrenalin. The vesicles are manufactured in the neuron soma and transported along the axon to the nerve terminals. During this transport the large vesicles decrease in diameter and are transformed to the small granular vesicles found in the nerve terminals. Information about the manufacture and transport of synaptic vesicles in cholinergic nerves is more sparse due to the lack of histochemical methods for identification of the content of the synaptic vesicles. There is evidence to suggest that acetylcholine is located in two stores which may correspond to two different types of synaptic vesicles within the nerve varicosities. One type of vesicle is supposed to be close to the presynaptic membrane and readily released, while the other is more distant from the membrane and less readily released. The storage and release of noradrenalin in noradrenergic terminals is more difficult to study since the adrenergic terminals have the capacity to take up the noradrenalin that they release. There are observations that noradrenalin, like acetylcholine, is contained in two stores in the adrenergic nerve terminals, the noradrenalin being released more readily from one store than from the other.

Noradrenalin and most likely acetylcholine are released from the vesicles into the extracellular space by a process of exocytosis, which is triggered by the nerve impulse. The ionic requirements for the release are the same at adrenergic and cholinergic terminals and depend on the entry of calcium ions into the nerve terminals.

Stimulation of excitatory nerves to smooth muscle cells produces small potential fluctuations, called excitatory junction potentials (EJPs). The individual EJPs have long durations (100–1000 ms). Successive junction potentials may sum, and at a critical level an action potential is induced followed by contraction. Stimulation of the inhibitory nerves causes a transient hyperpolarisation, which is called the inhibitory junction potential (or IJP). The time courses of these potentials are dependent

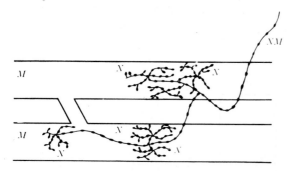

Fig. 3.27   Autonomic nerve terminals in a smooth muscle. A non-myelinated varicose nerve fibre (NM) subdivides within the muscle bundle to form systems of varicose nerve terminals. (From Olson and Malmfors, 1970.)

on the innervation pattern of the muscle, so that muscles that are innervated by close-contact varicosities have fast junction potentials whereas those innervated only by small axon bundles have slow junction potentials. In muscles having close-contact varicosities, spontaneous miniature potentials may be observed in the absence of nerve impulses. Thus the neuronal control of smooth muscle contraction depends on the potential change induced by the two types of nerves. The potential developed by activation of one or both sets of nerve fibres is dependent on the number of nerves activated and on the frequency of impulses in these nerves. The contraction of smooth muscle has a time course that is at least 10 times longer than the twitch of striated muscle. Calcium ions are carrying most of the inward current of the action potential in smooth muscle. It has therefore been suggested that the slow time course is due to either slow diffusion of calcium ions into the interior of the muscle fibres or to a slow rate of binding to contractile proteins.

It has long since been regarded as an experimentally well established fact that motility in the alimentary tract is regulated by an antagonistic interaction between cholinergic nerves and adrenergic nerves, the former causing excitation and the latter inhibition. Recent findings suggest that this view has to be modified partly because it appears that the adrenergic effect may not be exerted on the muscle directly as indicated by histochemical findings showing that there are intramural neurons which are neither cholinergic nor adrenergic. These cells receive terminals from preganglionic parasympathetic fibres in the vagus nerve. Activation of them by stimulating the vagus nerve produces inhibitory junction potentials in the smooth muscle cells of the gut. These junction potentials persist after the degeneration of sympathetic adrenergic nerves. It has been suggested that the transmitter released from these nerves is a purine nucleotide, and hence these neurons have been called *purinergic*.

A characteristic property of smooth muscles is their sensitivity to hormones circulating in the blood; this sensitivity is especially developed in the uterus, where the activity of the muscle cells is controlled by female sex hormones. It has been possible, by intracellular measurements in myo-metrial cells, to study changes during pregnancy, and it has been found that under the influence of increased oestrogen production the membrane gradually hyperpolarises to a maximum of $-60\,mV$. This value is reached in the middle of the pregnancy term and remains constant after that. Along with these changes, the potassium in the cell increases. Sodium concentration is relatively low throughout pregnancy but begins to increase just before parturition. Approximately 24 hours before delivery the membrane potential begins to depolarise, causing the contractile activity in the uterus to increase. When the potential level is reduced to about -50 mV, strong waves of contraction appear. Progesterone has the opposite effect, decreasing the activity and preventing contractions. The interaction between these two hormones is important: oestrogen prepares the uterus for the activity during delivery, while progesterone blocks activity until the pregnancy is ended.

3.4 Cardiac muscle

Structural characteristics

Cardiac muscle resembles skeletal muscle in certain aspects, smooth muscle in others. Cardiac muscle is striated like skeletal muscle, but the cells are arranged more like smooth muscle cells. In both smooth muscle and cardiac muscle there is an intrinsic rhythmic activity which is controlled by the autonomic nervous system and cardiac muscle cells form a functional syncytium (Fig. 3.28), as do the unitary smooth muscle cells.

The atria and ventricles of the heart may be considered as two separate functional units in which activity, once started, involves all cells. Electrically, the cardiac muscle fibres act as if they all were a single cell. This is explained by the fact that they are closely linked together through gap junctions. The ends of the individual fibres are joined together by an extensive series of membrane folds, called *intercalated discs* (Fig. 3.29), which are thought to provide for mechanical cohesion of the cells and to transmit the force developed by one unit to another. Cardiac muscle cells have a well developed

Fig. 3.28 Longitudinal section of human cardiac muscle. The dark transverse bands are the so-called intercalated discs. (From Bloom and Fawcett, *A Textbook of Histology*, W. B. Saunders, 1968.)

sarcoplasmic reticulum. Activation of the contractile system is induced by the release of calcium from the sarcoplasmic reticulum, as in skeletal muscle fibres, and the influx of calcium through the cell membrane. Since cardiac muscle cells are continually active, they depend greatly on the supply of oxygen. If deprived of oxygen for less than half a minute, cardiac cells may cease to contract and heart failure ensues.

Automaticity of heart

If the heart is removed from the body, it may continue to contract for several hours, provided that it is kept at an appropriate temperature and is well oxygenated. This ability to generate rhythmic

activity in the absence of signals from the central nervous system is accounted for by a built-in system which is responsible for the rhythmicity and other structures which distribute the impulses to all parts of the heart.

Anatomically, they consist of special cells and their branches which lie intermingled with the cardiac muscle fibres. The cells are assembled into two clusters, the sinoatrial (SA) node and the atrioventricular (AV) node (Fig. 3.30). The SA node is situated in the wall of the right atrium. Its cells are spindle-shaped and smaller than the usual cardiac muscle fibres; their branches extend and ramify among the muscle fibres of the atria. At the boundary between the atrium and the ventricle there is a similar formation, the AV node, whose cells are

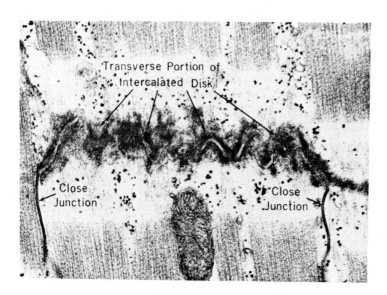

Fig. 3.29 Electron micrograph of an intercalated disc in cardiac muscle, showing the typical wavy appearance of the membranes. On each side of the intercalated discs are seen tight junctions which are assumed to represent connections of low electrical resistance between the cells. (From Bloom and Fawcett, *A Textbook of Histology*, W. B. Saunders, 1968.)

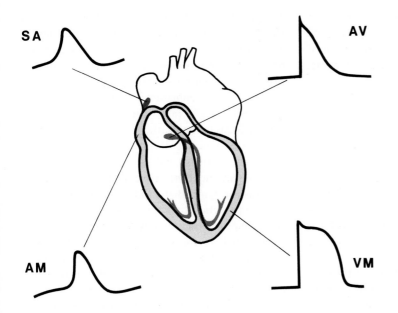

Fig. 3.30 Action potentials of various structures of the heart: SA, sinoatrial node; AM, atrial muscle cells; AV, atrioventricular node; VM, ventricular muscle cells.

like those of the SA node. Its branches are grouped together in a bundle (the atrioventricular bundle, or *bundle of His*), which runs in the ventricular septal wall. Here it divides into two branches, which pass along each side of the ventricular septum; they give rise to a network of fibres (the so-called Purkinje fibres), which intermingle with the ordinary muscle fibres in both ventricles. These fibres resemble both nerve and muscle fibres in various aspects.

The rhythmic activity of the heart starts in the sinoatrial node and spreads from there to the atrioventricular node. The rhythm of the SA node, the sinus rhythm, is normally 70–80 per minute. If the sinoatrial node is eliminated, the AV node becomes the pacemaker, and the heart goes over into a slower rhythm (40–60 per minute), the so-called junctional rhythm. Furthermore, the cardiac muscle itself is able to maintain rhythmic activity independent of the impulse conduction system (see below). For the atrial muscle this frequency is about 60 per minute, for the ventricular muscle it is 20–40 per minute. As the sinoatrial node has the highest frequency, it normally determines the rhythm for the heart. Under certain conditions, however, impulses may arise in other parts of the heart, from what are called *ectopic foci*. These foci can be sit-

uated anywhere in the heart, and their activity may interfere with the normal rhythm.

The wave of excitation travels from the SA node to adjacent muscle cells in the right atrium, and through a specialised bundle of fibres to the left atrium. Since the muscle cells are joined by gap junctions, the activity spreads rapidly through the two atria; in effect, they are simultaneously activated. The atrial muscle is separated from the muscle of the ventricles by a fibrous tissue ring, the *annulus fibrosus*. The only direct connection between the atria and the ventricles is the AV node and the bundle of His. It is by this pathway that the spread of activity takes place. The transmission of impulses from the atrial muscle to the AV node involves a delay of about 0.1 s. Therefore the atrial contraction is over before the ventricles begin to contract. Normally the AV junction allows only for spread of excitation in one direction, from the atrium to the ventricle. From the AV node the impulse travels through the bundle of His, conducted at 2–4 m s^{-1} and farther along the Purkinje network. From these fibres the impulse is transmitted to the cardiac muscle fibres through which the activity travels from cell to cell until the entire ventricular myocardium is activated. The ventricular septal wall is activated first and the papillary muscles thereafter.

Within 10–20 ms after activation of the ventricular septal wall, the impulse reaches the apex. From here the activity spreads through the side walls of the ventricles, activating the left ventricles somewhat later than the right.

Cardiac action potentials

Intracellular recordings have shown that the activity of the pacemaker cells in the sinoatrial node is characterised by a slowly developing depolarisation during diastole (Fig. 3.30). When this *pacemaker potential* reaches the threshold for the cell, an impulse is generated. The process of repolarisation is relatively slow and is followed by the progressive depolarisation leading to the generation of the next impulse. The pacemaker cells are thus inherently able to generate impulses in a self-sustained manner. Their rate of firing depends primarily on the slope of the pacemaker potential. As we shall see, this slope is under the control of the autonomic nerve fibres to the heart which can modulate the heart rate by their action on the pacemaker potential.

The impulses in cardiac muscle fibres are different from those of skeletal muscle or nerve fibres. In both skeletal muscle fibres and nerves, the membrane is rapidly repolarised and the potential returns to its resting level. In heart muscle, however, the depolarisation persists for 100–300 ms before the resting potential is re-established. The maintained depolarisation appears as a characteristic plateau which is somewhat briefer in atrial than in ventricular muscle fibres (see Fig. 3.30). The duration of the plateau varies with the heart rate, shortening as the frequency increases. The explanation for the sustained depolarisation is probably to be sought in an increase in calcium permeability and a delay of the increase in potassium permeability that normally accomplishes the repolarisation. This property of cardiac muscle is of essential functional importance. If an ordinary skeletal muscle is bombarded with an intense outflow of impulses in the motor nerve fibres, the muscle goes into a state of tetanus and it remains contracted as long as the nerve activity lasts. In the heart, the depolarisation of the muscle fibres lasts more than 100 times longer than in the skeletal muscle fibres, and during this time a second contraction cannot be set up. The heart muscle is therefore protected from entering into a state of tetanic contraction if exposed to a bombardment of impulses at an abnormally high rate, for instance from an ectopic focus in the heart.

The rhythmic activity of the heart is controlled by parasympathetic and sympathetic nerves. The parasympathetic fibres have an inhibitory effect, whereas the sympathetic fibres are excitatory. The parasympathetic fibres run in the vagus nerve and are arranged in such a way that the fibres in the right branch of the vagus end near the SA node, while most of the fibres in the left branch go to the AV node. Stimulation of the right vagus branch mainly affects the frequency of the heart through an action on the SA node; stimulation of the left branch largely influences the transmission of impulses from the AV node to the ventricles, increasing the nodal delay and eventually blocking activity. Parasympathetic activity therefore produces a slowing of the heart rate (Fig. 3.31). The vagal fibres exert their action by slowing the rate of rise of the pacemaker potential. This effect is induced by release of acetylcholine, causing a hyperpolarisation as a result of an increased permeability to potassium.

Activity of the sympathetic nerves increases the rate of rise of the pacemaker potential and thereby increases the heart rate (Fig. 3.31). Both the parasympathetic and the sympathetic system maintain a tonic activity under normal conditions. The sympathetic influence can be demonstrated by blocking the vagus nerve, whereupon the heart rate increases. Correspondingly, blocking the sympathetic fibres slows the heart rate. Variations in the balance between the sympathetic and the parasympathetic outflows may occur with physiological activities. Thus the heart rate increases during inspiration and slows during expiration as a result of reflex-controlled variations in vagal activity. During sleep, vagal activity normally increases, slowing the heart rate to around 50 beats per minute.

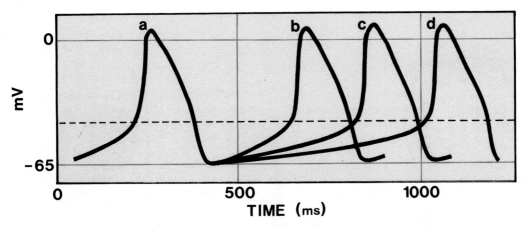

Fig. 3.31   Schematic diagram showing the mechanisms underlying changes in heart rate caused by alterations of the slope of depolarisation of the cells of the sinoatrial node: a and c show transmembrane potentials during normal resting activity of the heart; b and d under the influence of increased sympathetic and parasympathetic activity, respectively. Note change in slope of slow depolarisation preceding the action potential.

The electrocardiogram

Because the body fluids are good conductors, the electric currents of the heart spread throughout the body and may be recorded with electrodes placed on different regions of the body. The current of the heart can in this way be 'tapped' and correlated with the activity of the various parts of the heart. The record thus obtained, the *electrocardiogram*, is a valuable diagnostic tool since certain cardiac and vascular abnormalities alter the electrocardiogram in characteristic ways. This method for recording the activity of the heart was introduced in 1911 by Einthoven, who also introduced the three standard leads which are still generally used. These are as follows:

Lead I: from right and left arm
Lead II: from right arm and left leg
Lead III: from left arm and left leg

In addition, various chest leads are commonly used.

The electrocardiogram consists of a series of waves which Einthoven designated by the letters P, Q, R, S and T (Fig. 3.32). The P-, R- and T-waves are usually upward deflections and Q- and S- waves are downward deflections. The P-wave represents the spread of the excitation wave over the atria, followed by atrial contraction. Its duration is about 0.1 s and the electrical activity reaches the atrioventricular node at about the peak of the P-wave. The P-wave is followed by a brief isoelectric period after which the ventricular complex, or QRS complex, follows. The P–Q interval, that is the time elapsing between the beginning of the P-wave and the beginning of the QRS complex, varies in duration inversely with the heart rate; its normal duration is 0.15–0.20 s. The P–Q interval is a measure of the conduction time of the excitation wave from the atria to the ventricles; a value greater than 0.22 s indicates an abnormally slow conduction. The R-wave is the most conspicuous wave of the electrocardiogram; its upstroke signals the onset of the ventricular contraction. The QRS complex is followed by the S–T interval, lasting from the S-wave to the beginning of the T-wave. This period coincides with the maximal ejection of blood during the ventricular systole. It varies in duration from 0.10 to 0.25 s, depending on the heart rate. The T-wave represents the repolarisation of the ventricles; its average duration is 0.27 s. Sometimes there is a fourth wave, the U-wave, of unknown origin.

The electrocardiogram represents mainly the

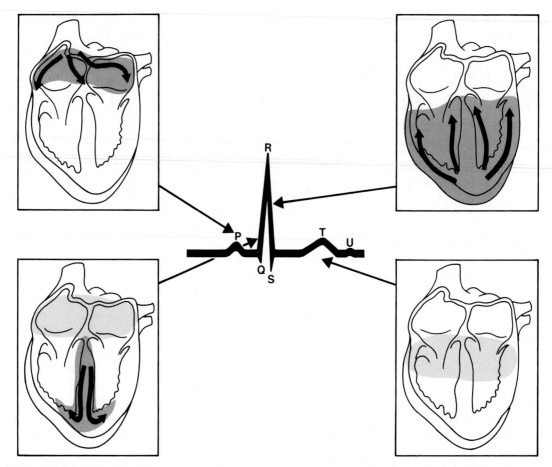

Fig. 3.32 Diagram indicating the spread of activation in the heart and the contributions of the activity of various parts of the heart to the electrocardiogram.

activity of the cardiac muscle fibres, since they make up the bulk of the heart. Of all the waves the R-wave of the QRS complex is by far the dominant one, because of the large total mass of the ventricular myocardium. Normally, ventricular activation results in a positive R-wave in all three standard leads; however, the magnitude of the R-wave is not the same in each lead.

To understand the features of the electrocardiogram in the various leads, the heart may be considered as a dipole or a rod-like battery with the positive pole at one end and the negative pole at the other end. The current from the battery passes from the positive pole through the surrounding tissues to the negative pole. The density of current

flow is greatest near both poles, diminishing with distance from the heart. The direction of the current flow depends upon the direction of the axis of the dipole, that is the lines connecting the positive and negative poles of the current source. Imagine the three standard leads as the sides of a triangle, the Einthoven triangle, with the heart in its centre and the electrical axis of the heart represented by an arrow (Fig. 3.33). The projections of the arrow upon the respective sides of the triangle may then be taken to correspond to the R-wave (minus the Q- and S-waves) in each of the three standard leads. The magnitude of this deflection recorded in each lead will consequently be proportional to the projection of the arrow upon the respective

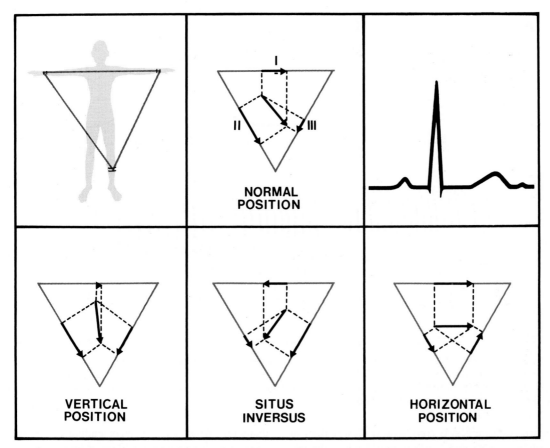

Fig. 3.33 Diagrammatic illustration of the changes in amplitude of the components of the electrocardiogram with changes of the electrical axis of the heart. Standard limb leads and Einthoven's triangle indicated by first diagram in the upper row. In the normal position of the heart, the vector of excitation is directed downwards and towards the left and deflection is greatest in lead II. With changes in direction of the axis and in *situs inversus,* the amplitudes of the deflections of the electrocardiogram change as indicated in the lower part of the diagram.

sides of the triangle. It thus follows that the magnitude and direction of the deflections in each lead depend primarily on the direction of the anatomical axis of the heart. This may normally be taken as being directed downwards, forwards and to the left. In the Einthoven triangle it may be imagined as being approximately parallel to the side represented by lead II. A change in the direction of the anatomical axis towards the left so that it becomes slightly more horizontal (left axis deviation) is accompanied by an increase of the R-wave in lead I and a diminishing of the same wave in lead III. A shift of the anatomical axis of the heart to

a more vertical position (right axis deviation) produces a reduction of the R-wave in lead I and an increased amplitude of the R-wave in lead III.

The difference between skeletal muscle, smooth muscle and cardiac muscle with regard to the relationship between electrical and mechanical events are illustrated in Fig. 3.34. In skeletal muscle (represented by a frog muscle fibre) the electrical impulse precedes contraction and is essentially over before contraction starts. The mechanical process is also rapid; within 30–40 ms the contraction has reached its peak. In cardiac muscle fibres, the time course is lengthened by the plateau phase. The

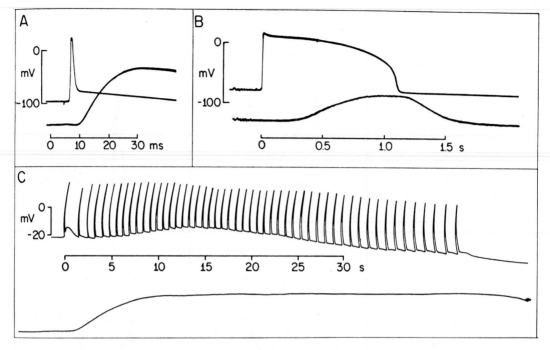

Fig. 3.34   Electrical (*upper trace*) and mechanical (*lower trace*) events during contraction in three types of muscle: (A) isolated frog skeletal muscle fibre; (B) frog ventricle muscle; (C) smooth uterus muscle (pregnant rat). (From Woodbury *et al.*, in *Muscle*, chapter 5, Physiology and Biophysics, eds T. C. Ruch and H. D. Patton, W. B. Saunders, 1965.)

contraction process is considerably slower than in skeletal muscle and is nearly ended when the impulse ends. During the whole plateau phase of the impulse, the cardiac muscle is protected against invasion by new signals. In smooth muscle (represented by the uterus of a pregnant rat) contraction starts with and is followed by a series of impulses. The duration and intensity of this activity determine the strength and the duration of the contraction. In some types of smooth muscle (the urethra, for example) the electrical events resemble those of cardiac muscle. Underlying all of these different functional properties are specific membrane properties, the nature of which is still under investigation.

3.5   Neuromuscular transmission

When entering a muscle, the motor axon divides into a number of branches which gradually become thinner until they are only a few micrometres in diameter. When such a nerve ending comes into contact with a frog muscle fibre, it loses its myelin sheath and splits into still finer branches, which run along the muscle fibre in grooves in the surface membrane (Fig. 3.35). The muscle membrane that lines the bottom of the grooves forms folds or ridges commonly termed junctional folds (Fig. 3.36).

In the late 1930s it was discovered that there was a relatively high concentration of acetylcholine (ACh) in the motor nerve fibres, and that ACh was released during contraction. Furthermore, it was found that application of ACh to a muscle induced contraction. These observations led to the conclusion that the transmission of activity from nerve to muscle was mediated chemically by the release of ACh from the nerve terminals. This notion was in itself not new. As early as 1904 Elliot had suggested that the transmission from sympathetic nerve fibres to smooth muscles was mediated chemically, and in 1921 Loewi had demonstrated the release

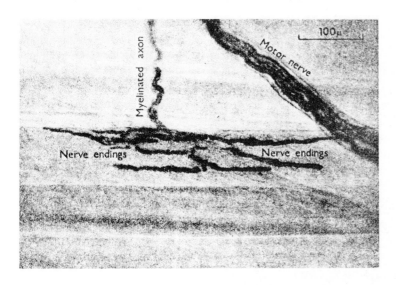

Fig. **3.35**   Neuromuscular
junction in frog muscle. (From
Katz, *The Release of Neural
Transmitter Substances*, Liverpool University Press, 1969.)

of ACh from the endings of the vagal nerve in the
heart. The field was therefore prepared for the
chemical theory, but nearly a decade would pass
before it won general acceptance.

The direct disproof of the electrical theory came
from electron microscope observations of motor
endplate structure and from electrophysiological
findings. The electron microscope studies showed
that there was a 50 nm wide cleft between the nerve
terminals and the muscle membrane. It was obvious
that the gap between the nerve terminals and the
muscle fibres was too wide to allow the currents
underlying the nerve impulse to generate impulses
in the muscle fibre electrically. Moreover, since the
nerve terminals are only a few micrometres in diameter, while the muscle fibre is about 100 μm
thick, it could be predicted that the current produced by the nerve terminals would be insufficient
to initiate impulses in the underlying muscle membrane; this was also later confirmed by direct
measurements. In addition, a delay of 0.5–0.8 ms
found between the arrival of the nerve impulse and
the onset of a muscle impulse was inconsistent
with the assumption of electrical transmission.

The endplate potential

Late in the 1930s it was found that the impulse in
the muscle fibre was preceded by a potential similar
to the local, graded response of the nerve (see p.
75). The local muscle potential could be obtained
in isolation by treating the muscle with curare;
stimulation of the motor nerve fibre after such
treatment produced a potential which was localised
to the endplate region (Fig. 3.37). This potential
was therefore called the *endplate potential*. Later
it was demonstrated that an almost identical response of the muscle fibre could be induced by
local application of ACh at the endplate; a few
millimetres away from the endplate ACh had no
effect.

The discovery of the endplate potential opened
new possibilities for studying the mechanisms of
synaptic transmission. Histochemical studies of the
endplate revealed in the so-called subneural apparatus a high concentration of an enzyme, acetylcholinesterase, which breaks down ACh rapidly into
choline and acetate. The surmise that the duration
of the endplate potential is determined by the
activity of this enzyme was confirmed by the
demonstration that substances known to block the
enzyme caused a considerable prolongation of the
endplate potential.

How does the release of a chemical transmitter
substance give rise to the endplate potential? The
answer was supplied by Katz, who showed that
ACh markedly increases the permeability of the
endplate membrane to small ions. This permeability

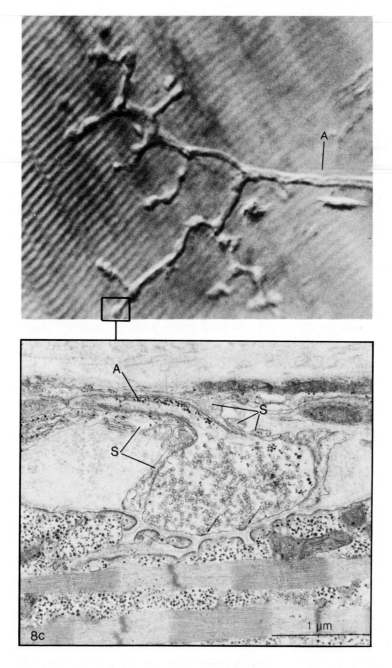

Fig. 3.36 Neuromuscular synapse. Upper figure shows live amphibian muscle seen with Nomarski optics. Lower figure is an electron micrograph of a bud-shaped motor terminal with a large number of vesicles. A, motor nerve fibre; S, Schwann cell. (From McMahan, Spitzer and Peper, *Proc. R. Soc. Lond.*, 181, 1972.)

change is clearly different from that underlying the generation of the propagated impulse since ACh renders the endplate membrane permeable to sodium, potassium and calcium, but not to chloride. Unlike the nerve membrane, which has separate sodium and potassium channels, the endplate has channels which permit sodium and potassium to move simultaneously. As a result, the endplate potential shows no overshoot as does the propagated impulse in nerve and muscle.

The next question is how the endplate potential gives rise to the propagated impulse in the muscle

Fig. 3.37 Isolation of end-plate potential by treating the neuromuscular junction with curare. (a) Recording obtained in normal saline; (b) separation of synaptic potential and action potential in the pres-

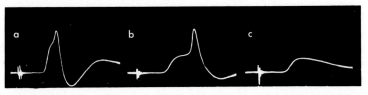

ence of curare; (c) blockage of nerve muscle conduction; only the synaptic potential is present. (From Kuffler, *J. Neurophysiol.*, 6, 1943.)

fibre. This problem has been solved by intracellular recordings showing that the muscle impulse is initiated electrically by the current generated at the endplate. From the endplate region the impulse travels along the muscle fibre.

Miniature endplate potentials

In studies of the endplate potential, Katz (Fig. 3.38) and colleagues made the important observation that when the frog muscle was at rest small spon-

Fig. 3.38 Sir Bernard Katz, Nobel Laureate in 1970.

taneous fluctuations of the membrane potential appeared in the endplate region. The fluctuations were less than 1 mV in amplitude and occurred with a mean frequency of about 1 per second (Fig. 3.39). Their time course was prolonged by substances inhibiting acetylcholinesterase, and their size reduced by curare. These and other observations strongly suggested that the small potentials, which were termed *miniature endplate potentials*, were associated with the release of ACh. At about the same time that the miniature endplate potentials were discovered, electron microscopy revealed that the motor nerve terminals were filled with small vesicles. This observation led to the conclusion that the vesicles contain ACh, and that the miniature potentials are induced by a spontaneous irregular release of ACh. To explain the miniature

potentials Katz postulated that the vesicles are in a state of random motion and collide intermittently with the membrane of the motor nerve terminal. Occasionally vesicles fuse with the nerve membrane and empty their contents into the synaptic cleft and thereby produce the miniature potentials.

Endplate potentials vary in size in a quantal manner, indicating that the endplate potential elicited by an action potential in the motor nerve represents the summation of many unitary potentials. When a nerve impulse invades the motor nerve terminals there is an enormous increase in the number of vesicles which fuse with the nerve membrane, and their synchronous release of transmitter produces the endplate potential. The original surmise was that each miniature potential was due to the release of one molecule of ACh, but later

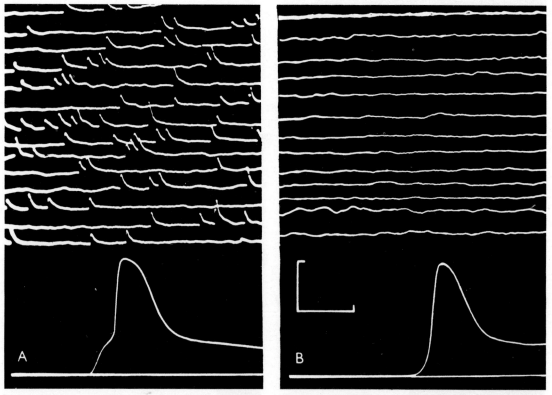

Fig. 3.39 Spontaneous miniature endplate potentials. (A) Intracellular recording near the endplate; (B) 2 mm away from the endplate. Lower records show the electric response to stimulation of the motor nerve: response in (A) shows endplate potential preceding the propagated action potential; in (B) only the action potential is obtained. (From Katz, *The Release of Neural Transmitter Substances*, Liverpool University Press, 1969.)

quantitative estimations have demonstrated that this is not so; each miniature potential is caused by release of several thousands of molecules of ACh, presumably the contents of a single vesicle.

The miniature potentials disappear if the motor nerve is cut and sufficient time is allowed for the fibres to degenerate. However, smaller miniature potentials may appear after some time even without regeneration of the nerve fibres. Electron microscope studies have shown that the Schwann cells still remain and that they contain vesicles similar to those seen in motor nerve terminals. Evidently after the nerve terminals degenerate, the Schwann cells begin to synthesise ACh and to store it in vesicles. A spontaneous release of ACh from these vesicles would explain the reappearance of the miniature potentials after nerve degeneration.

In a muscle subjected to long, repetitive activation via its motor nerve, the muscle contractions gradually weaken and finally cease. Yet, if the muscle is stimulated directly at this time, it will contract; its failure to respond when the nerve is stimulated must therefore be due to a transmission block at the endplate. Indeed, the endplate potential gradually becomes smaller during prolonged activity, apparently as the stores of ACh become depleted. If the muscle is allowed to rest, restitution takes place relatively quickly and the muscle is soon able to respond again when stimulated via its nerve.

The vesicular hypothesis

If the release of transmitter substance occurs because vesicles empty their contents into the synaptic cleft, it might be expected that electron micrographs would reveal vesicles opening into the synaptic cleft. In spite of intense searching, no such vesicle could at first be found. The explanation of this appears to be that the process of vesicle emptying is very rapid and therefore difficult to catch with the usual electron microscope technique. Only recently has the development of the freeze–etching technique overcome this difficulty and vesicles in different stages of emptying have been demonstrated.

The vesicular hypothesis has been questioned and it has been maintained that the vesicles which, in the freeze–etching micrographs, appear to open into the synaptic cleft do not represent vesicles in the process of emptying their contents but rather vesicles in the process of taking up material from the synaptic cleft. It has also been suggested that the transmitter is not released by exocytosis of synaptic vesicles but rather by opening of some sort of membrane gates and that the transmitter released derives from the presynaptic cytoplasm. According to this hypothesis the vesicles would serve as a reserve pool of transmitter.

Strong evidence suggesting that the vesicles which appear to open into the synaptic cleft are caught in the process of release of transmitter (in exocytosis) and not in the process of formation (endocytosis) has been obtained recently by a quick-freezing technique that allows vesicles to be captured at the moment of transmitter release. The freeze–fracture image obtained in this way shows a number of what look like holes or pores in the presynaptic membrane at the active zone of the nerve terminal (Fig. 3.40). After the vesicles have emptied their contents into the synaptic cleft, they collapse and flatten out. An interesting observation made in this study is that the vesicle openings occur close to double rows of particles which are a characteristic feature of the active zone. This suggests that vesicle emptying is associated with the particles. It has been suggested that the particles seen in the freeze–fracture image represent the channels through which calcium ions pass into the presynaptic endings.

It is now well established that calcium ions play an important role in the release of ACh. It has, for instance, been demonstrated that the amplitude of the endplate potential varies with the calcium concentration in the surrounding solution. As this concentration is lowered, the endplate potential is reduced; with sufficient lowering of the calcium concentration the endplate potential cannot reach the threshold level for the muscle impulse, and neuromuscular transmission is blocked. Recent studies have further clarified the role of calcium in the processes underlying the release of ACh from the vesicles. The local application of calcium near the motor nerve terminal increases the size of the

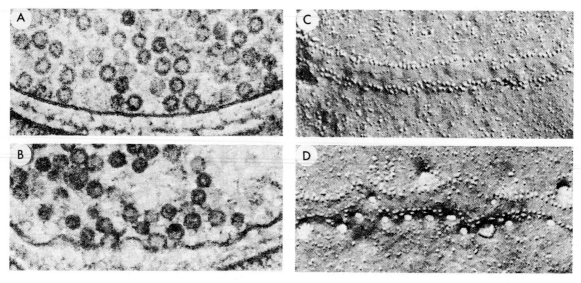

Fig. 3.40　Release of transmitter substance by vesicle emptying. Electron micrographs of frog neuro-muscular junctions in resting state (A) and immediately after stimulation (B). Note that, in the absence of stimulation, a number of synaptic vesicles lie close to the presynaptic membrane. After stimulation, a number of vesicles are seen in various stages of exocytosis. Electron micrographs in (C) and (D) show freeze—etch replicas of 'active zones' of neuromuscular junction in resting state and after stimulation. In (C) there is no exocytosis and the active zone can be identified by the presence of large intramembranous particles which presumably represent 'gates' in the presynaptic membrane. (D) shows an 'active zone' after stimulation of the motor nerve. Note presence of vesicle openings looking like depressions or dimples. (From Heuser, *Trends in Neurosci.*, 1(3), 1978.)

endplate potential, indicating an increased release of ACh. The calcium effect is limited to the initial phase of nerve depolarisation when the terminals are invaded by the nerve impulse. The current view is that during the impulse in the terminal, calcium channels open up and permit calcium inflow into the nerve terminals. The calcium ions, by some still unknown mechanism, cause the vesicles to empty their contents into the synaptic cleft. The release of the transmitter substance does not require the presence of sodium, for the end-plate potential may still be obtained when isotonic calcium solution is substituted for the normal external solution, and the nerve terminal is depolarised.

The interaction between ACh and cholinergic receptors

It is now widely assumed that the ACh molecules are recognised by and bound to highly specialised protein receptor molecules in the muscle membrane. The transmitter is thought to induce conformational changes in the receptor complex, resulting in an increase in the permeability of the membrane for certain ions. Recently the existence of ACh receptors in the endplate membrane has been demonstrated directly. This has been achieved owing to the discovery that some snake toxins bind specifically to the ACh receptors. If the toxin is labelled with radioactive tracers, the sites of the receptors can be detected by autoradiography (Fig. 3.41). The receptors seem strictly localised to the neuromuscular junction; a few millimetres away from the synaptic contact area practically no ACh receptors can be found in the muscle membrane. This agrees well with the finding that chemosensitivity drops sharply a short distance from the endplate. Chemically, the receptors are glycoproteins with a molecular weight of about 200 000. The density of the receptors is estimated to be as high as $2 \times 10^4 \ \mu m^{-2}$. As indicated by freeze—

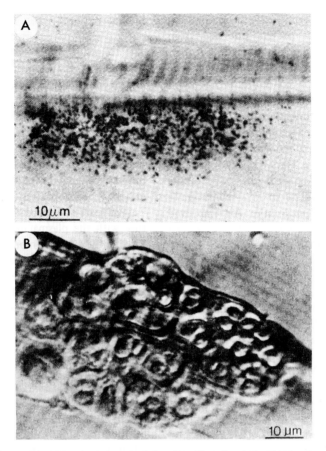

Fig. 3.41 Acetylcholine receptors at neuromuscular junction in skeletal muscle of snake. In (A) the receptors are labelled with radioactive α-bungarotoxin. (B) shows neuromuscular junctions in living muscle seen with Nomarski optics. ((A) From Burden *et al., Proc. Natl Acad. Sci. USA,* **72**, 1975; (B) from Kuffler and Nicholls, 1976.)

fracture the density is highest at the ridges of the folds in the endplate membrane, where the receptors are lined up in parallel rows (see Fig. 2.32).

Anything that interferes with the interaction between ACh and its receptors will block neuromuscular transmission. For instance, the ability of curare to block neuromuscular transmission is explained by the fact that the curare molecules occupy the sites in the muscle membrane to which ACh is normally bound. Thus curare does not affect the release of ACh, but rather prevents it from exerting its effect on the muscle fibre. While transmission is blocked, both the nerve fibre and the muscle fibre remain excitable; hence if the muscle is stimulated electrically, a muscle impulse

is produced and is followed by contraction. Another substance with an interesting effect is botulinus toxin. This poison blocks transmission by preventing the release of ACh.

In *myasthenia gravis*, a disorder characterised by muscular weakness and rapid tiring of muscles, the interaction between ACh and its receptor is prevented by antibodies in the serum. The antibodies bind to the ACh receptors and cause a destruction of the tips of the folds of the muscle membrane where the receptors are concentrated. The motor nerve endings contain a normal amount of vesicles which release their contents into the synaptic cleft but the muscle is less responsive to the transmitter. A similar muscular dysfunction

Huxley, H. E. (1969). The mechanism of muscular contraction, *Science*, **164**, 1356–1366

Huxley, H. E. and Hanson, J. (1960). The molecular basis of contraction in cross-striated muscles, in *The Structure and Function of Muscle*, ed. G. H. Bourne, Academic Press, New York, pp. 183–227

Iversen, L. L. (ed.) (1973). Catecholamines, *Br. Med. Bull.*, **29**, 91–178

Kandel, E. R. (1968). Dale's principle and the functional specificity of neurons, in *Electrophysiological Studies in Neuropharmacology*, ed. W. Koella, C. C. Thomas, Springfield

Karlin, A. (1975). The acetylcholine receptor: isolation and characterization, in *The Nervous System*, vol. 1, ed. D. B. Tower, Raven Press, New York, pp. 323–331

Katz, B. (1939). *Electric Excitation of Nerve*, Oxford University Press

Katz, B. (1966). *Nerve, Muscle and Synapse*, McGraw-Hill, New York

Katz, B. (1969). *The Release of Neural Transmitter Substances*, Liverpool University Press

Keynes, R. D. (1975). Organisation of the ionic channels in nerve membranes, in *The Nervous System*, vol. 1, ed. D. B. Tower, Raven Press, New York, pp. 165–175

Kristensson, K. and Olsson, Y. (1973). Diffusion pathways and retrograde axonal transport of protein tracers in peripheral nerves, *Prog. Neurobiol.*, **1**, 87–109

Lazarides, E. and Revel, J. P. (1979). The molecular basis of cell movement, *Scient. Am.*, **240** (5), 88–100

Levi-Montalcini, R. and Angeletti, P. U. (1968). Nerve growth factor, *Physiol. Rev.*, **48**, 534–569

Llinas, R. (1979). The role of calcium in neuronal function, in *The Neurosciences. Fourth Study Program*, eds F. O. Schmitt and F. G. Worden, MIT Press, Cambridge, MA, pp. 555–571

Mueller, P. and Rudin, D. O. (1968). Action potentials induced in biomolecular lipid membranes, *Nature*, **217**, 713–719

Ochs, S. (1975). Axoplasmic transport, in *The Nervous System*, vol. 1, ed. D. B. Tower, Raven Press, New York, pp. 137–146

Orci, L. and Perrelet, A. (1975). *Freeze–Etch Histology*, Springer-Verlag, Heidelberg

Ormea, F. (1961). *La Cute Organo di Senso*, Minerva Medica, Turin

Porter, K. R., Byers, H. R. and Ellisman, M. H. (1979). The cytoskeleton, in *The Neurosciences. Fourth Study Program*, eds F. O. Schmitt and F. G. Worden, MIT Press, Cambridge, MA, pp. 703–722

Robertson, J. D. (1970). The ultrastructure of synapses, in *The Neurosciences. Second Study Program*, ed. F. O. Schmitt, Rockefeller University Press, New York, pp. 715–728

Robertson, J. D. (1975). Membrane models: theoretical and real, in *The Nervous System*, vol. 1, ed. D. B. Tower, Raven Press, New York, pp. 43–58

Sandri, C., van Buren, J. M. and Akert, K. (1977). Membrane morphology of the vertebrate nervous system. A study with freeze–etch technique, *Prog. Brain Res.*, **46**, 1–381

Schmitt, F. O. and Samson, F. E. (1969). Neuronal fibrous proteins, *Neurosci. Res. Symp. Summ.*, **1969**, 301–403

Singer, S. J. and Nicolson, G. L. (1972). The fluid mosaic model of the structure of cell membranes, *Science*, **175**, 720–731

Synapse, The; Cold Spring Harbour Symp. Quant. Biol., **40** (1976)

Tasaki, I. (1975). Evolution of theories of nerve excitation, in *The Nervous System*, vol. 1, ed. D. B. Tower, Raven Press, New York, pp. 177–195

Thoenen, H. and Barde, Y. A. (1980). Physiology of nerve growth factor, *Physiol. Rev.*, **60**(4), 1284–1335

Thomas, R. C. (1972). Electrogenic sodium pump in nerve and muscle cells, *Physiol. Rev.*, **52**, 563–594

Trautwein, W. (1973). Membrane currents in cardiac fibers, *Physiol. Rev.*, **53**, 793–835

Weidmann, S. (1974). Heart: Electrophysiology, *Ann. Rev. Physiol.*, **36**, 155–169

Weiss, P. A. (1969). Neuronal dynamics and neuroplasmic ('axonal') flow, *Symp. Int. Soc. Cell. Biol.*, **8**, 3–34

Whittaker, V. P. (1970). The vesicle hypothesis, in *Excitatory Synaptic Mechanisms*, eds P. Andersen and J. K. S. Jansen, Universitetsförlaget, Oslo, pp. 67–76

Whittaker, V. P. and Gray, E. G. (1962). The synapse: biology and morphology, *Br. Med. Bull.,* **18**, 223–228

Woodbury, J. W., Gordon, A. M. and Conrad, J. T. (1965). Muscle, in *Physiology and Biophysics*, eds T. C. Ruch and H. D. Patton, W. B. Saunders, Philadelphia

Young, J. Z. (1951). *Doubt and Certainty in Science*, Clarendon Press, Oxford

Original Papers

Amstrong, C. M. and Bezanilla, F. (1974). Charge movement associated with the opening and closing of the activation gates of Na channels, *J. Gen. Physiol.,* **63**, 533–552

Baker, P. F., Hodgkin, A. L. and Shaw, T. I. (1962). Replacement of the axoplasm of giant nerve fibres with artificial solution, *J. Physiol. (Lond.),* **164**, 330–354

Baker, P. F., Hodgkin, A. L. and Shaw, T. I. (1962). The effects of changes in internal ionic concentrations on the electrical properties of perfused giant axons, *J. Physiol. (Lond.),* **164**, 355–374

Björklund, A., Stenevi, U. and Svendgaard, N. A. (1976). Growth of transplanted monoaminergic neurones into the adult hippocampus along the perforant path, *Nature,* **262**, 787–790

Brightman, M. W. and Reese, T. S. (1969). Junctions between intimately apposed cell membranes in the vertebrate brain, *J. Cell Biol.,* **40**, 648–677

Bülbring, E., Burnstock, G. and Homan, M. E. (1958). Excitation and conduction in the smooth muscle of the isolated taenia coli of the guinea pig, *J. Physiol. (Lond.),* **142**, 420–437

Buller, A. J., Eccles, J. C. and Eccles, R. M. (1960). Differentiation of fast and slow muscles in the cat hind limb, *J. Physiol. (Lond.),* **150**, 399–416

Buller, A. J. and Lewis, D. M. (1965). The rate of tension development in isometric tetanic contraction of mammalian fast and slow skeletal muscle, *J. Physiol. (Lond.),* **176**, 337–354

Burden, S., Hartzell, H. C. and Yoshikami, D. (1975). Acetylcholine receptors at neuromuscular synapses: phylogenetic differences detected by snake α-neurotoxins, *Proc. Natl Acad. Sci. USA,* **72**, 3245–3249

Burnstock, G. and Holman, M. E. (1961). The transmission of excitation from autonomic nerve to smooth muscle, *J. Physiol. (Lond.),* **155**, 115–133

Cohen, L. B., Keynes, R. D. and Hille, B. (1968). Light scattering and birefringence changes during nerve activity, *Nature,* **218**, 438–441

Cullheim, S. and Kellerth, J. O. (1976). Combined light and electron microscopic tracing of neurons, including axons and synaptic terminals, after intracellular injection of horseradish peroxidase, *Neurosci. Lett.,* **2**, 307–313

Dahlström, A. (1971). Axoplasmic transport (with particular respect to adrenergic neurons), *Phil. Trans. R. Soc. Lond. B,* **261**, 325–358

Del Castillo, J. and Katz, B. (1954). Quantal components of the end-plate potential, *J. Physiol. (Lond.),* **124**, 560–573

Droz, B., Rambourg, A. and Keoning, H. L. (1975). The smooth endoplasmic reticulum: structure and role in the renewal of axonal membrane and synaptic vesicles by fast axonal transport, *Brain Res.,* **93**, 1–13

Einthoven, W., Fahr, G. and de Waart, A. (1913). Uber die Richtung und die manifeste Grösse der Potentialschwangkungen im menschlichen Herzen und über den Einfluss der Herzlage auf die Form des Elektrokardiogramms, *Pflügers Arch.,* **150**, 275–315

Falck, B. (1962). Observations on the possibilities of the cellular localization of monoamines by a fluorescence method, *Acta Physiol. Scand.,* **56** (*Suppl.* 197), 1–25

Falck, B., Hillarp, N. Å., Thieme, G. and Torp, A. (1962). Fluorescence of catecholamines and related compounds condensed with formaldehyde, *J. Histochem. Cytochem.,* **10**, 348–354

Fatt, P. and Katz, B. (1951). An analysis of the end-plate potential recorded with an intracellular electrode, *J. Physiol. (Lond.),* **115**, 320–370

Fatt, P. and Katz, B. (1952). Spontaneous sub-threshold activity of motor nerve endings, *J. Physiol. (Lond.)*, **117**, 109–128

Franzini-Armstrong, C. (1976). Freeze–fracture of excitatory and inhibitory synapses in crayfish neuromuscular junctions, *J. Microsc. Biol. Cell.*, **25**, 217–222

Gasser, H. S. and Grundfest, H. (1939). Axon diameters in relation to the spike dimensions and the conduction velocity in mammalian A fibres, *Am. J. Physiol.*, **127**, 393–414

Gordon, A. M., Huxley, A. F. and Julian, F. J. (1966). The variation in isometric tension with sarcomere length in vertebrate muscle fibres, *J. Physiol. (Lond.)*, **184**, 170–192

Gray, E. G. (1975). Presynaptic microtubules and their association with synaptic vesicles, *Proc. R. Soc. Lond. B*, **190**, 369–372

Hellam, D. C. and Podolsky, R. J. (1969). Force measurements in skinned muscle fibres, *J. Physiol. (Lond.)*, **200**, 807–819

Heuser, J. E. and Reese, T. S. (1973). Evidence for recycling of synaptic vesicle membrane during transmitter release at the frog neuromuscular junction, *J. Cell Biol.*, **57**, 315–344

Heuser, J. E., Reese, T. S., Dennis, M. J., Jan, Y., Jan, L. and Evans, L. (1979). Synaptic vesicle exocytosis captured by quick freezing and correlated with quantal transmitter release, *J. Cell Biol.*, **81**, 275–300

Heuser, J. E., Reese, T. S. and Landis, D. M. D. (1974). Functional changes in frog neuromuscular junctions studied with freeze–fracture, *J. Neurocytol.*, **3**, 109–131

Heuser, J. E., Reese, T. S. and Landis, D. M. D. (1976). Preservation of synaptic structure by rapid freezing, *Cold. Spring Harbour Symp. Quant. Biol.*, **40**, 17–24

Hille, B. (1970). Ionic channels in nerve membranes, *Prog. Biophys. Mol. Biol.*, **21**, 1–32

Hodgkin, A. L. and Huxley, A. F. (1952). The components of membrane conductance in the giant axon of *Loligo*, *J. Physiol. (Lond.)*, **116**, 473–496

Hodgkin, A. L. and Huxley, A. F. (1952). A quantitative description of membrane current and its application to conduction and excitation in nerve, *J. Physiol. (Lond.)*, **117**, 500–544

Hodgkin, A. L., Huxley, A. F. and Katz, B. (1952). Measurement of current–voltage relations in the membrane of the giant axon of *Loligo*, *J. Physiol. (Lond.)*, **116**, 424–448

Hodgkin, A. L. and Keynes, R. D. (1955). Active transport of cations in giant axons from *Sepia* and *Loligo*, *J. Physiol. (Lond.)*, **128**, 28–60

Hodgkin, A. L. and Keynes, R. D. (1955). The potassium permeability of a giant nerve fibre, *J. Physiol. (Lond.)*, **128**, 61–88

Huxley, A. F. and Simmons, R. (1971). Proposed mechanism of force generation in striated muscle, *Nature*, **233**, 533–538

Huxley, A. F. and Taylor, R. E. (1958). Local activation of striated muscle fibres, *J. Physiol. (Lond.)*, **144**, 426–441

Huxley, H. E. (1957). The double array of filaments in cross-striated muscle, *J. Biophys. Biochem. Cytol.*, **3**, 631–648

Huxley, H. E. (1973). Structural changes in the actin and myosin containing filaments during contraction, *Cold Spring Harbour Symp. Quant. Biol.*, **37**, 361–376

Ito, Y. and Miledi, R. (1977). The effect of calcium-ionophores on acetylcholine release from Schwann cells, *Proc. R. Soc. Lond. B*, **196**, 51–58

Katz, B. (1971). Quantal mechanism of neural transmitter release, *Science*, **173**, 123–126

Katz, B. and Miledi, R. (1967). The release of acetylcholine from nerve endings by graded electric pulses, *Proc. R. Soc. Lond. B*, **167**, 23–38

Katz, B. and Miledi, R. (1967). The timing of calcium action during neuromuscular transmission, *J. Physiol. (Lond.)*, **189**, 535–544

Katz, B. and Miledi, R. (1972). The statistical nature of the acetylcholine potential and its molecular components, *J. Physiol. (Lond.)*, **244**, 665–699

Katz, B. and Miledi, R. (1973). The binding of acetylcholine to receptors and its removal from the synaptic cleft, *J. Physiol. (Lond.)*, **231**, 549–574

Kristensson, K. (1970). Morphological studies of the neural spread of *Herpes simplex* virus to the central nervous system, *Acta Neuropath. (Berl.)*, **16**, 54–63

Kuffler, S. W. (1943). Specific excitability of the endplate region in normal and denervated muscle, *J. Neurophysiol.*, **6**, 99–110

Levi-Montalcini, R. (1964). Growth-control of nerve cells by a protein factor and its antiserum, *Science*, **143**, 105–110

Ling, G. and Gerard, R. W. (1949). The normal membrane potential of frog sartorius fibres, *J. Cell. Comp. Physiol.*, **34**, 383–396

Loewi, O. (1921). Über humorale Übertragbarkeit der Herznervenwirkung, *Pflügers Arch. Physiol.*, **189**, 239–242

McMahan, U. J., Spitzer, N. C. and Peper, K. (1972). Visual identification of nerve terminals in living isolated skeletal muscle, *Proc. R. Soc. Lond. B*, **181**, 421–430

Miledi, R. (1960). The acetylcholine sensitivity of frog muscle fibres after complete or partial denervation, *J. Physiol.*, **151**, 1–23

Miledi, R. (1960). Junctional and extra-junctional acetylcholine receptors in skeletal muscle fibres, *J. Physiol.*, **151**, 24–30

Miledi, R. (1973). Transmitter release induced by injection of calcium ions into nerve terminals, *Proc. R. Soc. Lond. B*, **183**, 421–425

Miledi, R., Parker, I. and Schalow, G. (1980). Transmitter induced calcium entry across the postsynaptic membrane at frog end-plates measured using arsenazo III, *J. Physiol.*, **300**, 197–212

Nicolson, G. L. (1976). Transmembrane control of the receptors on normal and tumor cells. I. Cytoplasmic influence over cell surface components, *Biochim. Biophys. Acta*, **457**, 57–108

Ochs, S. (1972). Fast transport of materials in mammalian nerve fibres, *Science*, **176**, 252–260

Olson, L. and Malmfors, T. (1970). Growth characteristics of adrenergic nerves in the adult nerve, *Acta Physiol. Scand., Suppl.*, **348**, 1–142

Porter, K. R. and Palade, G. E. (1957). Studies on the endoplasmic reticulum. III. Its form and distribution in striated muscle cells, *J. Biophys. Biochem. Cytol.*, **3**, 269–300

Potter, L. T. (1970). Synthesis, storage and release of ^{14}C acetylcholine in isolated rat diaphragm muscle, *J. Physiol. (Lond.)*, **206**, 145–166

Reese, T. S. and Shepherd, G. M. (1972). Dendro-dendritic synapses in the central nervous system, in *Structure and Function of Synapses*, eds G. D. Pappas and D. P. Purpura, Raven Press, New York, pp. 121–136

Saltzberg, B. M., Davila, H. V. and Cohen, L. B. (1973). Optical recordings of impulses in individual neurones of an invertebrate central nervous system, *Nature*, **246**, 508–509

Schmitt, F. O. and Davison, P. F. (1961). Biologie moléculaire des neurofilaments, in *Actualités Neurophysiologiques*, ed. A. M. Monnier, Masson, Paris, third series, pp. 355–369

Singer, S. J. and Nicolson, G. L. (1972). The fluid mosaic model of the structure of cell membranes, *Science*, **175**, 720–731

Skou, J. C. (1964). Enzymatic aspects of active linked transport of Na^+ and K^+ through the cell membrane, *Prog. Biophys. Mol. Biol.*, **14**, 133–166

Whittaker, V. P. (1971). Origin and function of synaptic vesicles, *Ann. N.Y. Acad. Sci.*, **183**, 21

Section III: Sensory Receptors

4

Structural and Functional Features of Sensory End Organs

4.1 General properties of receptors

In sensory physiology, the term 'receptors' is used to designate a cell, or part of a cell, the function of which is to convert a stimulus into an electrical signal. Receptors thus function as transducers, translating the stimulus into a language comprehensible to the nervous system.

From the morphological point of view, no special structural feature identifies a receptor as such. In its simplest form, a receptor may consist of the terminals of a nerve fibre (Fig. 4.1), sometimes in close contact with special accessory tissues. The Pacinian corpuscle, for example, consists of a naked nerve ending surrounded by a number of concentric lamellae of connective tissue. As we shall see later, these accessory structures may have an important influence on the transmission of the stimulus to the receptor endings.

In general, the structure of a sensory receptor has no obvious relation to its specific functional properties. There are exceptions, however, such as the sensory cells of the vestibular organ in the inner ear, each of which has a number of fine hair-like processes (see below). Of these, one has the same structure as the motile cilia found in respiratory epithelium and is termed the *kinocilium*; all the others are non-motile and are called *stereocilia*. The cilia are arranged in a hexagonal pattern in which the kinocilium always occupies the same relative position (Fig. 4.2). This arrangement has

also been found in the lateral line organ of the fish, where the sensory cell is activated when the cilia are bent towards the kinocilium and inhibited when bent in the opposite direction. Evidently, the orientation of the cilia on the cell surface makes possible a directional sensitivity. The stereocilia are presumed to serve as levers; when bent, they deform the cell's outer membrane and thereby excite or inhibit the cell. Another hypothesis holds the stereocilia themselves to be the actual receptor elements; it is their own membrane that would be depolarised when they are bent. Recent observations suggest, however, that the kinocilium is not required for the transduction process. If the kinocilium is detached from the hair bundle by microdissection and deflected, no receptor potential is produced, while mechanical stimulation of the stereocilia still elicits responses of normal amplitude and sensitivity (Fig. 4.3). This suggests that transduction takes place by the bending of the stereocilia, whereas the kinocilium may serve primarily to provide for mechanical linkage, conveying the stimulus to the stereocilia. The kinocilium may also be necessary during ontogenesis for the polarisation of the hair bundle. It may be noted that in the mammalian cochlea the kinocilium is lost during development. This loss has been assumed to eliminate an elastic linkage and thereby to improve the responsiveness of the hair cells to high-frequency stimuli.

In several other types of receptors, sensory

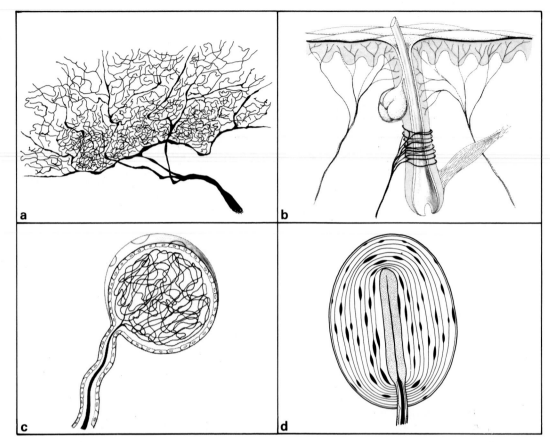

Fig. 4.1   Schematic representation of some of the principal sensory endings of hairless skin: (a) free naked endings; (b) free endings encircling a hair follicle; (c) Meissner's corpuscle; (d) Pacinian corpuscle.

transduction is associated with cilia or ciliary derivatives (Fig. 4.4). There is for instance considerable evidence that olfactory transduction takes place in the cilia of the olfactory receptor cells. Yet another example of receptor cells, whose sensory elements are formed by cilia-like processes, are the visual receptor cells in the retina. The outer segments of the rods and cones, where the primary excitation process takes place, are, phylogenetically speaking, modified cilia.

In most mechanosensitive systems in skin and muscle the receptor elements are the terminals of the primary afferent nerve fibres. The cell body in this case is situated in the dorsal root or cranial ganglion. In the olfactory mucosa, the situation is different. Here the cell body is located in the epithelium and sends a dendrite to the surface of the epithelium; the nerve fibre extends from the basal parts of the cell. In other systems the peripheral receptors lack axons, and the sensory information is transmitted via synapses from the sensory cells to the afferent fibre. Such an arrangement is found in the inner ear, where the receptors make synaptic contacts with the terminals of the afferent nerve fibres. Activity in these fibres is initiated chemically, as indicated by the accumulation of synaptic vesicles in the sensory cell near the contact sites of the terminals. A similar arrangement is present in the taste buds and in the retina.

Clearly, the various types of sensory receptor show a great diversity in their structural properties. Still, in general, the specific functional properties

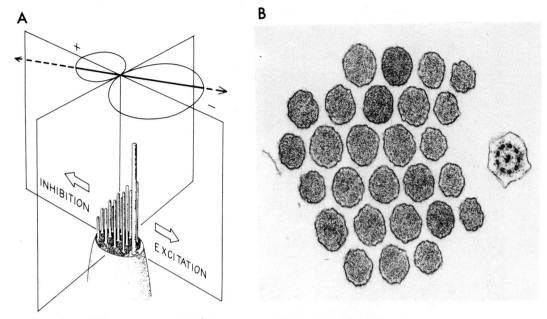

A

+

INHIBITION

EXCITATION

−

B

Fig. 4.2 Functional organisation of the sensory hairs of a hair cell in the lateral line canal of fish (*Lota vulgaris*). A bundle of sensory hairs protrudes from the top of the hair cell. The bundle is composed of several stereocilia and one kinocilium which is located in the periphery of the bundle. Displacement of the cilia (A) towards the kinocilium causes activation of the hair cell, and displacement in the opposite direction causes inhibition. The regular arrangement of the cilia is shown in the electron micrograph (B) of a cross-section through a sensory hair bundle. ((A) From Flock, *Cold Spring Harbour Symp. Quant. Biol.*, 30, 1965; (B) from Flock and Wersäll, *J. Cell Biol.*, 15, 1962.)

of a given receptor cannot be deduced from its structural characteristics. It is not known what makes the membrane of a mechanoreceptor specifically sensitive to mechanical stimulation; nor is it known why the olfactory sensory cell membrane is sensitive to chemical stimuli, or why heat and cold receptors are sensitive to thermal stimuli. The only exception is in the retina, where the presence of photopigments in the membranes of the discs (Fig. 4.5) indicates the relation between functional specificity and membrane structure. Other than this, the specific properties of a given type of receptors such as specific sensitivity can only be ascribed to as yet unknown factors.

It is a common feature of all sensory systems — whether the information reaches conscious perception or not — that the receptors of a given system are particularly sensitive to a specific kind of stimulation; this is termed the *adequate stimulus*. For the eye, the adequate stimulus is electromagnetic radiation within a given range of wavelengths; for the cells of the inner ear, as well as for many types of sensory endings in skin and muscles, the adequate stimulus is a mechanical deformation of the receptors. For smell and taste, the adequate stimulus is chemical in nature. On the basis of their specific sensitivities, the receptors can therefore be classified into four groups:

(1) *Mechanoreceptors*: to this group belong the receptors of the inner ear, touch and pressure receptors in the skin, stretch receptors in muscle and tendons, vibration receptors in connective tissue, pressure receptors in large blood vessels, etc.

(2) *Chemoreceptors*: this group includes olfactory sensory cells, taste buds, and some receptors in large vessels and in the central nervous system.

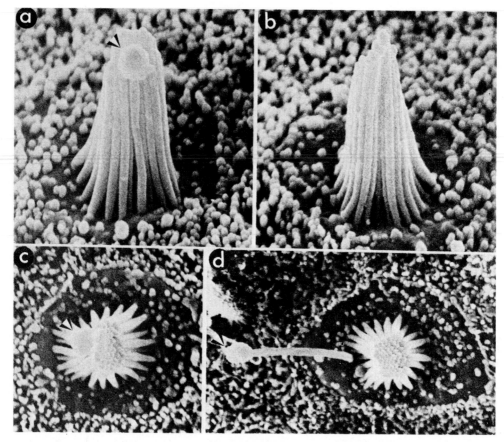

Fig. 4.3 Scanning electron micrographs of hair bundles from saccular hair cells. A normal hair bundle is shown in (a) and (c) in an oblique view and from directly above, respectively. The kinocilium is easily recognised since it has a bulbous swelling at its distal end. In (b) the kinocilium was removed during the experiment. In (d) the kinocilium was dissected free and held flat against the epithelial surface during recording. This cell responded normally to stimulation as did also cells whose kinocilia were removed by dissection. (From Hudspeth and Jacobs, *Proc. Natl Acad. Sci.*, **76**, 1979.)

(3) *Thermoreceptors*: the cold and heat receptors in the skin, and temperature-sensitive cells in the brain.

(4) *Photoreceptors*: the visual cells in the retina.

The specific sensitivity of the receptors implies that a sensory organ (under physiological conditions) conveys information about only one type of stimulus. This does not exclude the possibility that other stimuli may also produce excitation, but to do so they must be considerably stronger. Pressing on the eye causes a diffuse visual sensation due to mechanical stimulation of the cells in the retina. The inappropriate stimulus produces a sensation which is of the same nature as that of the adequate stimulus but lacks its detailed and precise quality. In whatever way the sensory cells of a system are stimulated, the type of sensation evoked remains the same; what determines the nature of the sensation is the central projection of the afferent fibres (the law of projection). Each sensory system has a discrete pathway from the receptors to the cortex, and no matter where along the pathway the afferent impulses are initiated the sensation evoked is the same. For instance, pressure on a nerve at the elbow gives a tingling sensation in arm and hand.

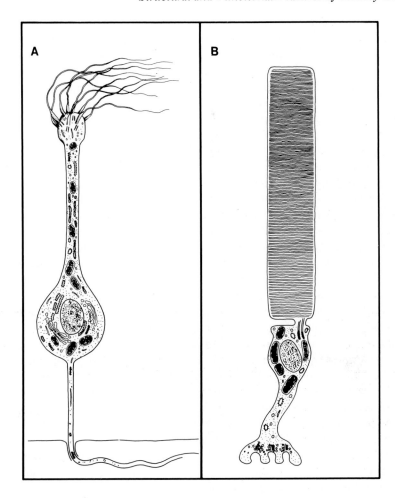

Fig. 4.4 The sensory elements of some types of receptors are cilia or derived from cilia as illustrated in this schematic drawing of an olfactory receptor cell and a rod of the retina. The olfactory cilia correspond to the outer segment of the rod.

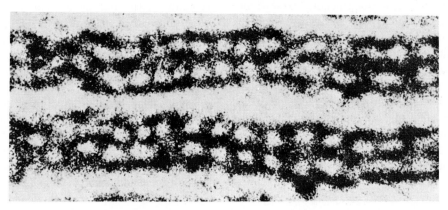

Fig. 4.5 High-resolution electron micrograph of the discs of a rod outer segment from the frog's retina. (From Nilson, *J. Ultrastruct. Res.*, 12, 1965.)

After amputation of a limb, pressure on the stump gives rise to sensations which are perceived as coming from the removed limb.

It is well known that the perceived intensity of a maintained stimulus is often strongest at the onset of stimulation and decreases thereafter. An odour sensed strongly at first may go unnoticed within a few minutes. Such an adaptation to a constant stimulus may arise in two ways. One mechanism for adaptation is that the afferent input from the receptors is reduced by inhibition at some relay station on the way to the cortex. This is most likely the mechanism underlying *habituation*, which is the phenomenon where a stimulus regularly repeated evokes weaker and weaker responses in the cortex. The other cause of adaptation is a gradual decrease in the activity of the receptor cells during stimulation, resulting in a reduced afferent impulse frequency. There is thus a central and a peripheral mechanism for adaptation, either of which leads to a decline in the perceived intensity of a given stimulus. The first of these is what operates when we grow oblivious of a clock's ticking; soon we no longer hear it, but by focusing our attention on the clock we can again perceive the sound. In contrast, peripheral adaptation is best illustrated by the short-lived sensation that a weak mechanical stimulus to the skin elicits. If we place a light object on the skin, the sensation rapidly fades and disappears entirely after a few minutes. In this case, we cannot revive the sensation by focusing attention on the stimulus.

Sensory end organs are generally classified into two main groups, rapidly and slowly adapting, with respect to their ability to respond to a constant stimulus. Receptors of the first group respond with a brief discharge at the onset of stimulation and then remain silent; with cessation of stimulation they usually discharge one or a few impulses. It is interesting to note that this group includes almost exclusively mechanoreceptors, such as the Pacinian corpuscle, sensory endings around hair follicles and rapidly adapting touch receptors in the skin.

The group of slowly adapting end organs is heterogeneous with respect to modality and includes visual receptors, chemoreceptors, thermo-receptors, pain receptors and various mechanoreceptors such as the muscle spindle and the tendon organ. Their response to a constant stimulus is characterised by an initial discharge of relatively high frequency at the onset of the stimulus and a later regular firing at lower rate during maintained stimulation. The functional importance of the different time courses of adaptation may lie in the fact that rapidly adapting receptors give information only about transients in stimulus intensity, while slowly adapting ones also transmit information about the steady-state level as well.

Why does the response of one type of receptor decline rapidly and that of another more slowly? Since the afferent impulses are generated by receptor current, two main sources of adaptation are possible. One possible source is that the afferent nerve fibre accommodates to the receptor current. Another source of adaptation would be that the receptor current decreases during constant stimulation. Both of these mechanisms appear to be responsible to a varying extent in the adaptation of different types of receptors. In the rapidly adapting stretch receptor in the crayfish (see p. 136), the relative rapid decline in impulse frequency appears to be explained by accommodation of the axon since the receptor potential does not show a corresponding fall. In other types of receptors, the rate of adaptation appears mainly to be determined by the decline of the receptor potential (see Fig. 4.6). This raises the question of the cause of this decline. In some types of mechanoreceptors, structural factors appear to play an important part in adaptation. In the Pacinian corpuscle, for example, the nerve terminal is surrounded by a number of concentric lamellae. Because of its size, the Pacinian corpuscle is relatively easy to isolate by dissection. Under constant pressure, the corpuscle gives only one impulse, when the pressure is first applied, and then remains silent although pressure is maintained constant. Photomicroscopical observations of the Pacinian corpuscle have disclosed that maintained pressure causes a constant displacement and deformation of the outer lamellae, whereas the lamellae close to the receptor terminal slide back to their resting positions; the nerve ending is thus released from

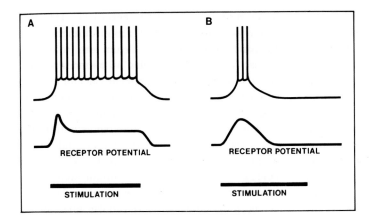

Fig. 4.6　Typical responses of slowly (A) and rapidly (B) adapting receptor.

the stimulus. Adaptation in the Pacinian corpuscle is therefore not a property of the receptor itself, but is due to the viscoelastic properties of the surrounding structures which transmit the stimulus to the nerve ending. Direct evidence of this has been obtained by removing the lamellae by microdissection (Fig. 4.7). Pressure applied to the naked nerve terminal evokes a response very like that of slowly adapting receptors such as the muscle spindle.

Adaptation of the muscle spindle has generally been attributed to mechanisms similar to those in the Pacinian corpuscle. It was assumed that application of stretch was followed by a sliding movement of the intrafusal fibres, whereby the sensory endings were partly released from the applied stretch. Photomicroscopical studies have disclosed that there is no such sliding movement in the early phase of stretch. This suggests that the early adaptive

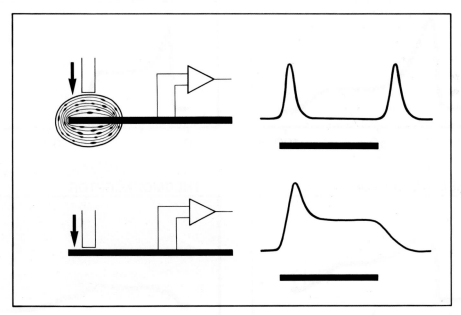

Fig. 4.7　Experiment demonstrating the influence of accessory structures on rate of adaptation. Upper part of the diagram shows typical receptor response of the Pacinian corpuscle to maintained stimulation (thick bar below recording). Lower part shows the response to the same stimulus after removal of the lamellae enclosing the sensory terminal of the afferent fibre.

Eledone : ERG   **A**   Frog : EOG   **B**

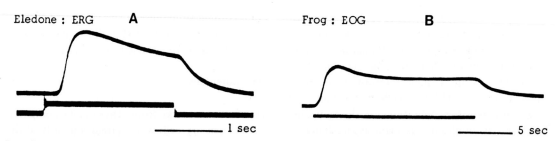

1 sec   5 sec

Fig. 4.10   Recordings illustrating the close similarity of receptor responses in two types of sense organs: (A) the response of the eye of *Eledone* to light; (B) the response of the olfactory organ of the frog to odour stimulation. ((A) From Fröhlich, 1914; (B) from Ottoson, *Acta Physiol. Scand.*, 35, 1956.)

second- or third-order neurons as in the eye. An electrode placed in contact with the mucosa will therefore record only the activity of the receptors. The response obtained by odour stimulation is like that of the simple eye of *Eledone* to a light stimulus (Fig. 4.10): it is graded in amplitude with the strength of the stimulus, and it adapts similarly when the stimulation is maintained.

The response of single receptors

The basic mechanism through which a receptor converts a stimulus into an electrical signal was disclosed by Katz in studies of frog muscle spindles isolated by microdissection from a toe muscle in the frog. This sense organ consists of a bundle of fine muscle fibres enclosed in a fluid-filled capsule (Fig. 4.11). A single sensory fibre penetrates into this space, and its endings spiral around the muscle fibres. These endings are extremely sensitive to mechanical stimulation and respond with a sustained discharge when the bundle of muscle fibres is stretched. In studying the discharge recorded

from the sensory fibre, Katz noticed that the impulses were superimposed upon a maintained depolarisation which remained even after impulse conduction in the nerve was blocked. Katz concluded that this depolarisation represented the response of the endings, which spreads electrotonically along the stem fibre.

The transducer activity of receptors remains unaffected by various substances, for instance local anaesthetics or poisons such as tetrodotoxin (TTX) which block impulse conduction in nerves (Fig. 4.12). This makes it possible to obtain the receptor response in isolation without the interference of impulse activity. In receptors such as the muscle spindle, the receptor potential spreads electrotonically in the afferent nerve and may be recorded with electrodes placed on the nerve at its exits from the spindle capsule. The spindle potential is graded in nature, and the dynamic as well as the static component increases in amplitude with lengthening of the spindle (see Fig. 4.13). The velocity characteristics of the stimulus are reflected in the rate of rise of the response; the spindle

SENSORY AXON

MOTOR AXON   MOTOR AXON

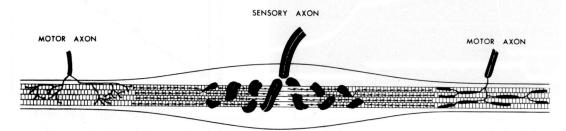

Fig. 4.11   Schematic representation of the muscle spindle of the frog. The myelinated sensory axon branches and gives rise to numerous beaded chains of unmyelinated endings.

A.

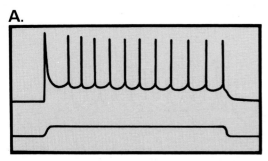

B.

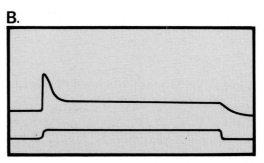

Fig. 4.12   Isolation of the receptor potential of the muscle spindle. Response before (*left*) and after (*right*) blocking of conducted activity. (From Ottoson and Shepherd, *Cold Spring Harbour Symp. Quant. Biol.*, 30, 1965.)

closely follows the changes in the stimulus. This property enables the spindle to reproduce the dynamic features of the stimulus with a high degree of precision.

Most receptor cells are extremely small and therefore difficult to record from intracellularly. Detailed studies of the membrane potential changes during activity have therefore been greatly hampered. However, a few types of receptors are large enough to permit intracellular recordings. One such receptor neuron is the crustacean stretch receptor, which from a functional point of view is analogous to the muscle spindle in vertebrates. This neuron is a large cell which bears a close resemblance to a motoneuron in the spinal cord. Its dendrites branch profusely in the connective tissue around a small muscle bundle, and when the muscle is stretched the cell discharges (Fig. 4.14). A microelectrode inserted into the cell will record a resting potential of about −65 mV. When the receptor muscle is stretched, a sustained depolarising potential appears, upon which there is superimposed a series of impulses. The sustained potential has the same general characteristics as the extracellularly recorded receptor potential of the muscle spindle. It is generated in the dendrites and spread electro-

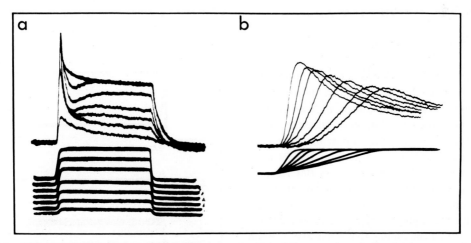

Fig. 4.13   Characteristic features of the receptor potential of the muscle spindle: (a) increase of dynamic and static components with increasing amounts of stretch; (b) dynamic phase of response to stretches at different velocities. Lower traces in (a) and (b) show stretch monitor. ((a) From Husmark and Ottoson, *J. Physiol.*, 212, 1971; (b) from Ottoson and Shepherd, *Acta Physiol. Scand.*, 82, 1971.)

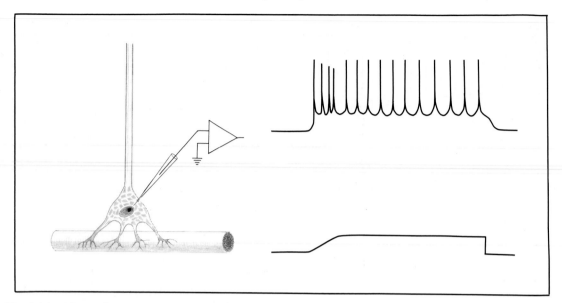

Fig. 4.14   The crustacean stretch receptor. The dendrites of the receptor neuron are embedded in the receptor muscle. Stretching the muscle deforms the dendrites where the transduction takes place and sets up the generator potential which in turn initiates the impulse discharge.

tonically via the neuron into the axon, and when threshold is reached action potentials are induced.

For a long time it was assumed that all receptors are depolarised during activity. It was therefore an unexpected finding that vertebrate photoreceptors hyperpolarise when exposed to light. The mechanisms underlying this kind of response will be discussed in the section on 'Vision' (see p. 347).

Ionic basis of receptor potential

While there is a considerable amount of information about the ionic flux across the nerve membrane during impulse generation, comparatively little is known about the contribution of different ions to the production of the receptor potential in sensory end organs. Early observations on the Pacinian corpuscle provided evidence that in this receptor sodium ions were responsible for the major part of the transport of charge across the membrane. However, other ions also appeared to be involved, as suggested by the finding that removal of sodium did not completely abolish the receptor response. Later studies on other types of receptors have confirmed these observations (Fig. 4.15). All evidence

so far obtained suggests that the receptor potential arises as a result of non-specific permeability changes to cations and that the driving forces are the actual concentration gradients for different ions across the receptor membrane. The contributions of different ions to the receptor current are therefore probably not the same for different types of receptors. Since most receptors are bathed in an intercellular fluid in which sodium ions are the

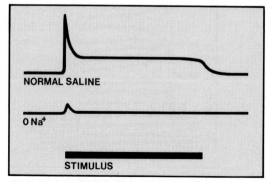

NORMAL SALINE

0 Na⁺

STIMULUS

Fig. 4.15   Schematic   diagram   illustrating   the effect of removal of sodium on the receptor response of the muscle spindle.

major cationic constituent, it is not surprising that sodium ions are responsible for carrying the main part of the receptor current during activity. The hair cells of the inner ear are an exception to this rule. Here the situation is different, since the fluid in the scala media contains potassium in high concentration. This suggests that potassium ions may participate in carrying the receptor current of the hair cells. This has actually been borne out by recent intracellular recordings from frog hair cells. However, the permeability changes induced by stimulation are non-specific and the ionic channels are also permeable to sodium, calcium and small organic cations.

Many attempts have been made to define the transducer actions of sensory receptors in mathematical terms, i.e. to determine their transfer functions. The usual method is to expose a single receptor to sinusoidal stimulation and to record the receptor potentials or the impulse responses evoked. The records in Fig. 4.16 illustrate such an experiment on the isolated frog spindle. It may be noted that the receptor potential does not have the same waveform as the stimulus, which indicates

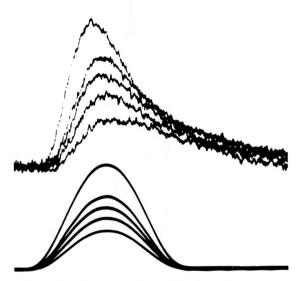

Fig. 4.16 Receptor potentials of the frog muscle spindle evoked by sinusoidal stretches (*lower trace*) of increasing amplitude. (From McReynolds, Ottoson and Shepherd, *Acta Physiol. Scand.*, 90, 1974.)

that the transfer function of the spindle is non-linear. This is probably true for most receptors. Definition of their transfer functions in mathematical terms is therefore extremely complex.

4.3 Impulse initiation

The transformation of the graded potential generated by the receptor membrane into the propagated impulse response occurs in different ways in various types of receptors; it depends on the actual anatomical relation between the receptive element and the afferent axon. In the Pacinian corpuscle and in the muscle spindle, the current spreads passively into the axon and the impulse is initiated by the outward-going current at the first node (Fig. 4.17). This is probably also the case in most peripheral receptors in skin and muscles.

Many types of receptor lack an axon of their own (Fig. 4.18); such is the case for the hair cells in the inner ear. At their base, these cells are in contact with endings of the eighth cranial nerve. The cells produce no propagated impulses; their activity is transmitted to the afferent nerves by synaptic action from the cell to the afferent nerve terminals. A similar mechanism underlies the transmission of activity from taste cells and visual cells.

In the olfactory system, the primary neuron is located in the periphery and the afferent axon emerges from the distal pole of the cell body. Here the transducer action probably involves an electrotonic spread of the receptor current from the cilia into the cell body. It would be reasonable to assume that the afferent impulses are initiated in the cell body and transmitted from here to the afferent nerve. There is, however, also the possibility that the impulses are initiated in the initial segment of the neuron. This assumption is supported by observations on another type of receptor neuron, the crayfish stretch receptor. This receptor cell is large and therefore allows for simultaneous recordings from different sites of the soma and the axon. In this way, it has been possible to follow the actual time course of events during impulse

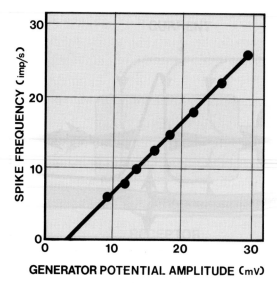

Fig. 4.20   Characteristic relationship between the amplitude of the receptor potential of a photo-receptor in the horseshoe crab (*Limulus*) and the impulse frequency of its afferent axon. (From Fuortes, *Am. J. Ophthal.*, 46, 1958.)

organ to the afferent nerve fibres involves a transition from amplitude modulation to frequency modulation of the afferent signals, no essential part of the information content in the message appears to be lost. There are reasons to assume that the same principle applies in subsequent steps of the transmission of the message to the brain. However, at these stages the transmission of the sensory message may be modulated by synaptic activity from other systems, so that the final message to the end station in the brain will not necessarily be an exact reproduction of the initial message in the primary afferent fibres. Hence, even if the message from our sensory organs provides relatively precise information about the outer world, the perceptual image ultimately formed in the brain is not by necessity an accurate representation of the input at the receptor level.

As we have seen, the nervous system uses two types of signal for transmitting information: (1) graded potentials which spread passively over short distances of the membrane and then die out, and

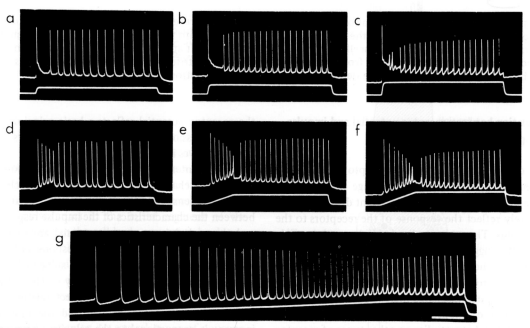

Fig. 4.21   Typical features of the response of the frog muscle spindle to increasing amplitudes of stretch at different velocities. Time bar: 50 ms. (From Shepherd and Ottoson, *Cold Spring Harbour Symp. Quant. Biol.*, 30, 1965.)

(2) all-or-nothing potentials which propagate without change in amplitude. The degree of activity is signalled by the amplitude of the first type of signal (amplitude modulation) and by the frequency of discharge of the second type of signal (frequency modulation). The graded local potentials are used to initiate impulses, to transmit activity from one neuron to another, or to suppress interactions between neurons, while the impulses are used for carrying messages over long distances. The alternation between these two modes of signalling may be

illustrated by the sequence of electrical events in the stretch reflex arc (Fig. 4.22). Here activity is initiated in the muscle spindle and transmitted by an afferent nerve to a motoneuron in the spinal cord. The nerve fibre of this motoneuron activates a group of muscle fibres. Stretch of the muscle gives rise to depolarisation of the sensory terminals in the spindle, resulting in the receptor potential, which faithfully reproduces the parameters of the stimulus. The receptor potential spreads passively into the afferent fibre and induces a burst of

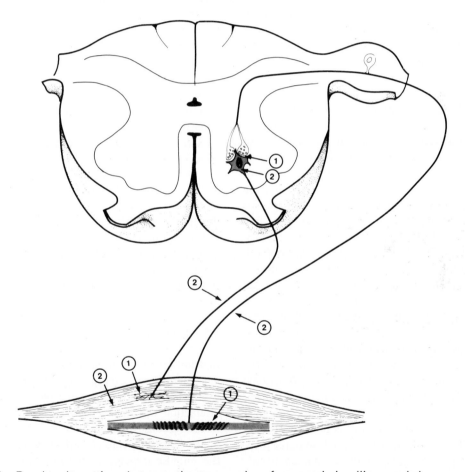

Fig. 4.22 Regular alternations between the two modes of neuronal signalling, graded non-propagated potentials (1) and all-or-nothing propagated action potentials (2), here illustrated by the events in the monosynaptic reflex arch. Activity is initiated in the muscle spindle by the receptor potential which spreads into the myelinated axon and induces the propagated impulses, which in turn set up an EPSP in the motoneuron. The EPSP causes the motoneuron to discharge and the impulses propagate to the endplate where a local non-propagated response, the endplate potential, is induced; this gives rise to the propagated muscle impulse.

impulses, the frequency of which reflects the depolarisation of the receptor endings. The afferent impulse volley, arriving at the nerve terminal, depolarises the motoneurons by releasing a transmitter substance. This depolarisation, the postsynaptic excitatory potential, spreads to the initial segment of the motoneuron axon and induces the discharge of the motor fibre. A similar sequence of events occurs at the motor endplate: the arrival of impulses in the motor nerve leads to a release of ACh and the generation of the endplate potential; this in turn initiates the impulses that travel along the muscle fibre and give rise to contraction. To transmit information and to activate effector organs, the nervous system thus regularly alternates between the two types of signal, graded and all-or-nothing.

4.4   Efferent modulation of receptor activity

Histological studies have shown that many sense organs receive efferent fibres whose terminal ramifications lie more or less close to the sensory cells. Once again the hair cells in the inner ear provide an example. At the basal part of this cell are two types of synaptic knobs. One type can be identified as the afferent terminal, since there is an accumulation of vesicles in the part of the receptor cell opposite the synaptic knob, which itself is devoid of vesicles. The other type of synaptic knob is filled with vesicles, while none are in the region of the receptor cell opposite to the synaptic ending. That such endings are efferent has been confirmed in recordings from the hair cells. Activity in the efferent fibres produces hyperpolarisation of the hair cells and thereby inhibition. The functional significance of this inhibitory action is not known. Owing to the small size of the hair cells, a detailed analysis of the action of the inhibitory fibres is technically very difficult. A more favourable preparation for such studies is the crustacean stretch receptor neuron. This cell receives two thin efferent fibres, the endings of which synapse upon its dendrites. If either of these nerves is stimulated, the discharge from the receptor declines or ceases (Fig. 4.23). Intracellular recordings have shown that each impulse in an efferent fibre causes a transient hyperpolarisation. Of particular interest is the regular way in which this inhibitory effect varies with the strength of sensory stimulation; the repolarising effect of the inhibitory nerve fibres increases linearly with the level of depolarisation produced by the stimulus. This means that when the receptor is activated more strongly, the inhibitory stimulus has a greater effect on the membrane potential than with weaker activation. If the cell is at rest, stimulation of the inhibitory fibre has little or no effect on the membrane potential. Similar results have been obtained in studies of motoneurons (see p. 192); here too the inhibitory impulses drive the potential of the cell towards its normal resting value. The inhibitory action on the crustacean stretch receptor is probably induced by the release of gamma-aminobutyric acid (GABA) from the endings of the efferent fibres; the hyperpolarisation of the receptor neuron results from an increased permeability, predominantly to chloride.

Still another type of efferent modulation of a sense organ is found in the muscle spindle. Here the modulatory influence is exerted not directly on the receptor element but indirectly through motor control of the intrafusal fibres. By controlling the length of the spindle through gamma fibres, the central nervous system can modulate the sensitivity of the spindle. This control is mainly exerted from the reticular formation and the cerebellum. It has a key role in controlling muscle tone and reflex functions (see p. 168).

4.5   Lateral inhibition

In addition to the modulation caused by activity in efferent fibres, a receptor may also be influenced by the activity of adjacent receptors. This kind of interaction was discovered by Hartline in studies of the response of single photoreceptors in the eye of the horseshoe crab (*Limulus*). He observed that the impulse response in the axon from a photoreceptor cell was reduced when neighbouring ommatidia were simultaneously illuminated (Fig. 4.24). Subsequent studies revealed that the inhibitory effect is mediated by a network of thin nerve fibres which connect each unit with neighbouring units. This kind of inhibition is therefore usually

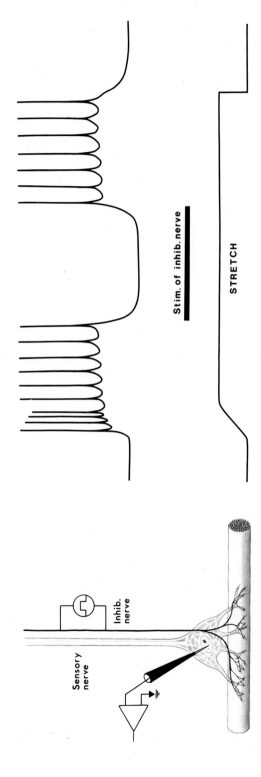

Fig. 4.23   Efferent control of a receptor organ. The discharge of the crustacean stretch receptor neuron induced by stretching its muscle is suppressed when the inhibitory nerve is stimulated. The inhibitory impulses tend to hyperpolarise the membrane potential and thereby bring the membrane potential below threshold for firing. (Adapted from Kuffler and Eyzaguirre, *J. Gen. Physiol.*, 39, 1955.)

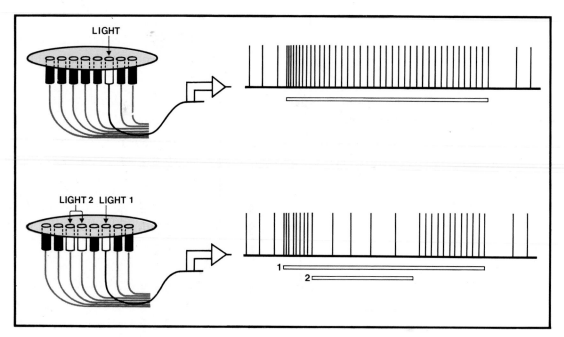

Fig. 4.24 Lateral inhibition in the eye of the horsehoe crab (*Limulus*). Upper part of the diagram shows response of a single ommatidium to steady illumination (open bar). Lower part shows inhibition of the response to the same illumination (1), during illumination of two nearby ommatidia (2). (Adapted from Hartline *et al., J. Gen. Physiol.*, 39, 1956.)

referred to as lateral inhibition. The degree of inhibition of a given unit depends on the activity of the neighbouring ommatidia; it increases the more they are illuminated, and also with the number of active ommatidia in the surround. For a given unit, the impulse response can be expressed by the equation

$$r = e - i$$

where r is the impulse response, e represents the stimulus (expressed as the frequency evoked in the absence of inhibition) and i signifies inhibition. If two units (r_1 and r_2) influence each other, their impulse responses can be expressed by

$$r_1 = e_1 - K_{1,2}(r_2 - r_{1,2}^0)$$
$$r_2 = e_2 - K_{2,1}(r_1 - r_{2,1}^0)$$

The inhibitory effect is given by the expression $K(r - r^0)$ where K is the inhibitory coefficient and r^0 characterises the threshold frequency at which a unit may exert an inhibitory effect. The term $r_{1,2}^0$

is the frequency at which unit 2 begins to inhibit unit 1, and the term $r_{2,1}^0$ is the opposite relationship. This quantitative description may be extended to include a population of elements, provided the inhibitory influence between different elements is known. This has been studied by illuminating different groups of photoreceptors, which are too far apart to have any mutual inhibitory effect, and evaluating their effect on a test unit. The inhibitory effects of these groups sum in a simple, additive way. Inhibition of any given ommatidium in the eye can therefore be expressed as the sum of the inhibitory influences from all other elements. For a system with n receptor elements which mutually influence each other, the following equation applies:

$$r_p = e_p - \sum_{j=1}^{n} K_{p,j}(r_j - r_{p,j}^0)$$

where r_p is the frequency response of a single receptor element inhibited by the other elements (j).

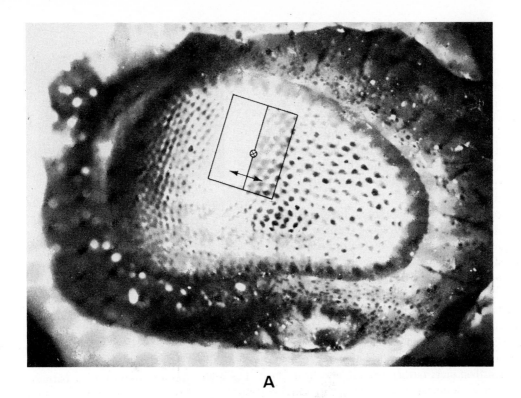

A

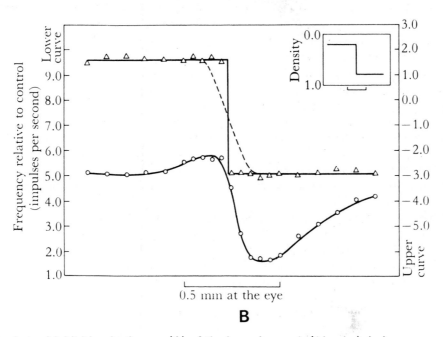

B

Fig. 4.25 Lateral inhibition in the eye (A) of the horseshoe crab (*Limulus*) during movement of a step pattern of illumination across the eye. (B) The response of a single ommatidium to illumination with lateral inhibition (*open circles*) and (using a special technique) without inhibition (*triangles*). The inset shows the relative density of the step pattern. (From Ratliff, in *Mach Bands*, Holden-Day, 1965; Ratliff and Hartline, *J. Gen. Physiol.*, 42, 1959.)

An interesting phenomenon is so-called disinhibition (i.e. the inhibition of inhibition) which is the direct result of the mutual inhibitory effect between different units. If a unit is situated between two groups of units which, in turn, may influence each other, their added inhibitory effect is less than the sum of their separate effects. This is because the two groups mutually inhibit each other's activity, curbing their effect on the test element.

Since the degree of inhibition is directly related to the level of activity, it follows that the mutual influence of different parts of the retina on each other depends upon the intensity of the illumination in different areas. To take the simplest case, if one half of the eye is strongly illuminated and the other half weakly illuminated, an interesting effect appears at the border between these two fields (Fig. 4.25). In the border zone, the units on the weakly illuminated side will be more strongly inhibited than units farther away in that field. On the strongly illuminated side, the cells near the border will be inhibited relatively less than those situated farther away, on the same side of the borderline, since the units close to the border receive part of their inhibitory inflow from the cells in the adjacent, weakly illuminated zone. Because the impulse frequency in each fibre signals the intensity of illumination, the effect of the lateral inhibition in the border zone is as follows. The nerve fibres from the border zone receptors on the dimmer side will have a lower impulse frequency than the fibres elsewhere on the same side, and the border will therefore be signalled as relatively darker. On the more strongly illuminated side, the relationship will be the opposite: the border units, being inhibited relatively less than other elements in this field, discharge with a higher frequency and thus signal a stronger illumination. The final result is a contrast sharpening of the borderline between the two areas.

That the same interaction actually occurs in

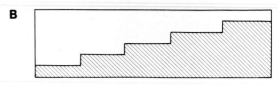

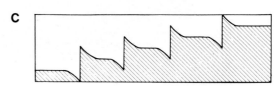

Fig. 4.26 Border contrast in a pattern of grey strips (A). Each individual strip has the same greyness across its whole width as indicated by the luminance diagram (B). This can also be demonstrated by covering the adjacent strips with two pieces of paper along the borderlines of a strip. The perceived lightness profile of the pattern of bands is shown in the lower diagram (C).

our own eyes can easily be demonstrated by looking at Fig. 4.26. It will be noticed that in any given strip the greyness is not even. At its border with an adjacent darker strip, a given field appears relatively lighter, while near a lighter strip it appears darker. This contrast illusion was described as early as 1865 by the Austrian physicist, Mach, and is therefore usually called 'Mach bands'. If you think that the effect as seen in Fig. 4.26 is due to the print itself, cover everything except one strip and you will see that within that strip the field is uniform. Thus the eye sacrifices accuracy for the sake of what is significant in the image.

BIBLIOGRAPHY FOR SECTION III

Suggested Reading and Reviews

Adrian, E. D. (1928). *The Basis of Sensation*, Christophers, London

Adrian, E. D. (1931). The message in sensory nerve fibres and their interpretation, *Proc. R. Soc. B*, **109**, 1–18

Flock, Å. (1971). Sensory transduction in hair cells, in *Principles of Receptor Physiology, Handbook of Sensory Physiology*, vol. I, ed. W. R. Loewenstein, Springer-Verlag, Heidelberg, pp. 396–441

Fuortes, M. G. F. (1971). Generation of responses in receptor, in *Principles of Receptor Physiology, Handbook of Sensory Physiology*, vol. I, ed. W. R. Loewenstein, Springer-Verlag, Heidelberg, pp. 243–268

Kuffler, S. W. (1960). Excitation and inhibition in single nerve cells, *Harvey Lecture*, Academic Press, New York, pp. 176–218

Loewenstein, W. R. (1971). Mechano-electric transduction in the Pacinian corpuscle. Initiation of sensory impulses in mechanoreceptors, in *Principles of Receptor Physiology, Handbook of Sensory Physiology*, vol. I, ed. W. R. Loewenstein, Springer-Verlag, Heidelberg, pp. 269–290

MacNichol, E. F., Jr (1956). Visual receptors as biological transducers, in *Molecular Structure and Functional Activity of Nerve Cells*, eds R. G. Grenell and L. J. Mullins, American Institute of Biological Sciences, Washington, pp. 34–52

Matthews, B. H. C. (1931). The response of a single end organ, *J. Physiol. (Lond.)*, **71**, 64–110

Munger, B. L. (1971). Patterns of organization of peripheral sensory receptors, in *Principles of Receptor Physiology*, vol. 1, ed. W. R. Loewenstein, Springer-Verlag, New York, pp. 523–556

Ottoson, D. (1974). Generator potentials, in *Transduction Mechanisms in Chemoreception*, eds T. M. Poynder, L. H. Bannister, H. Bostock and G. H. Dodd, IRL, London, pp. 231–239

Ottoson, D. and Shepherd, G. M. (1971). Transducer properties and integrative mechanisms in the frog's muscle spindle, in *Principles of Receptor Physiology, Handbook of Sensory Physiology*, vol. I, ed. W. R. Loewenstein, Springer-Verlag, Heidelberg, pp. 443–499

Perkel, D. H. and Bullock, T. H. (1968). Neural coding, *Neurosci. Res. Prog. Bull.*, **6**, 221–347

Tomita, T. (1970). Electrical activity of vertebrate photoreceptors, *Q. Rev. Biophys.*, **3**, 179–222

Original Papers

Adrian, E. D. and Zotterman, Y. (1926). The impulses produced by sensory nerve endings. II. The response of a single end-organ, *J. Physiol. (Lond.)*, **61**, 151–171

Alexandrowicz, J. S. (1951). Muscle receptor organs in the abdomen of *Homarus vulgaris* and *Palinurus vulgaris*, *Q. J. Microsc. Sci.*, **92**, 163–199

Baylor, D. A. and Fuortes, M. G. F. (1970). Electrical responses of single cones in the retina of the turtle, *J. Physiol. (Lond.)*, **207**, 77–92

Boeckh, J., Kaissling, K. E. and Schneider, D. (1965). Insect olfactory receptors, *Cold Spring Harbour Symp. Quant. Biol.*, **30**, 263–280

Brown, H. M. and Ottoson, D. (1976). Dual role for K^+ in *Balanus* photoreceptor: antagonist of Ca^{++} and suppression of light induced current, *J. Physiol. (Lond.)*, **257**, 355–378

Brown, H. M., Ottoson, D. and Rydqvist, B. (1978). Crayfish stretch receptor: An investigation with voltage-clamp and ion-sensitive electrodes, *J. Physiol. (Lond.)*, **284**, 155–179

Edwards, C. and Ottoson, D. (1958). The site of

Section IV: The Spinal Cord

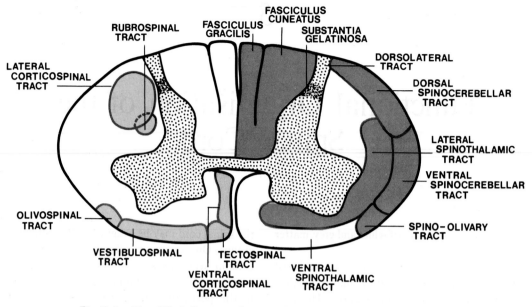

Fig. 5.1 Simplified diagram of some of the major tracts of the spinal cord.

synapses situated near the cell body can directly excite or inhibit a neuron, whereas synapses further out on the dendrites are more involved in modulations of excitability.

The large *alpha-neurons* which innervate the extrafusal muscles may be divided into two functional groups, phasic and tonic alpha-neurons. The former have a higher rate of impulse firing and higher conduction velocity than the latter, the activity of which is characterised by a sustained discharge at low frequency. In addition to the large alpha-neurons, there are in the ventral horn two types of functionally distinct *gamma-motoneurons*, which innervate the intrafusal fibres of the muscle spindles (see p. 166).

The neurons of the spinal cord are not distributed at random but are gathered together into larger or smaller groups. Usually, the cells within such a

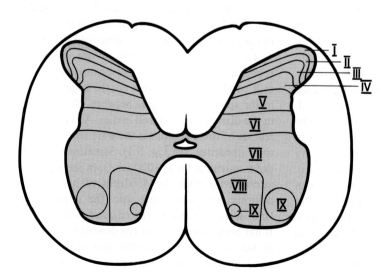

Fig. 5.2 Laminar organisation of the spinal cord.

group are involved in some common function. The topographical grouping of cells is particularly apparent in the ventral horn. Here the motoneurons are arranged longitudinally in columns (see Fig. 16.5), the cells in a given column innervating a particular group of muscles involved in the movement of a joint. It thus appears that there is not a representation of discrete motor pools for individual muscles but rather a functional grouping of muscles acting on a common joint.

An afferent volley of nerve impulses invading the spinal cord is distributed either directly or via interneurons to a population of motoneurons. The reflex evoked by direct transmission is said to be *monosynaptic* and that conducted via interneurons *multisynaptic* (Fig. 5.4). Typically the monosynaptic reflex has a shorter latency than the multisynaptic, the central delay for the monosynaptic reflex being about 0.5 ms while that for the multisynaptic reflex is of the order of 3–5 ms. Only some of the motoneurons that receive afferent input will respond with action potentials. These neurons are said to represent the *discharge zone* of the motoneuron pool to which the afferent impulses are conveyed. The affected neurons which remain silent are said to belong to the *subliminal fringe*. Presumably these neurons receive fewer synaptic inputs than the cells in the discharge zone and are therefore not activated. However, their excitability is increased, and they may become active if stimulated by an input from another afferent source. Neurons which are activated in this way from two afferent sources may lie in a

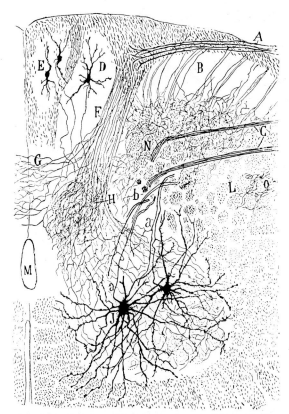

Fig. 5.3 Golgi-stained transverse section of the spinal cord of cat foetus showing the arrangement of dorsal root afferents and their interconnections with the dendritic trees of two motoneurons. (From Cajal, *Histologie du Système Nerveux de l'Homme et des Vertébrés*, Madrid, 1955.)

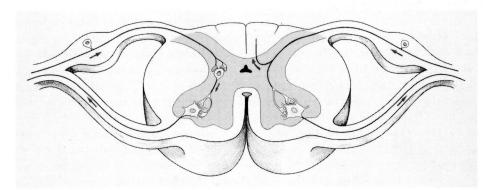

Fig. 5.4 Schematic diagram showing monosynaptic and disynaptic reflex arcs in the spinal cord.

region where the two pools overlap; the afferent fibres are said to converge upon these neurons. Neurons in the subliminal fringe zone may also be activated if the stimulus is prolonged; in this case the activity spreads from the initial discharge zone by *recruitment* of neurons in the subliminal fringe zone. Such spread of activity in the central nervous system occurs in many situations. When, for instance, pain arising from a localised region of the body becomes more intense and appears to spread to surrounding regions or organs, this may be due to spread of synaptic activity in synaptic relay stations.

In a monosynaptic reflex arc the response ceases immediately after the stimulus terminates. In contrast, the reflex action in a multisynaptic reflex persists for a considerable time after the afferent input has ended. In part, this persistent activity reflects the delay at successive synaptic relays, but it may also represent activity in reverberating circuits. Such a circuit consists of a number of neurons coupled in a closed system, where the entering activity may for a time be self-sustaining. Consider a series of neurons, A, B, C, D, E and F, with A activating B, B activating C, and so on, and F finally being in synaptic contact with A (Fig. 5.5). It is possible that A may again be activated when it is reached by the impulses from F. If A is also in contact with a motoneuron, it follows that its activity may outlast the incoming impulse volley that started the activity in the circuit.

5.2   The sensory input to the spinal cord

The fibres carrying the sensory message to the spinal cord have their cell bodies located in the dorsal root ganglia. Most of the cells are of the simple unipolar type (see p. 13). They can be subdivided into two groups: large cells with diameters ranging from 60 to 120 μm and small cells with diameters of 15–30 μm. About 60–70% of the total population of dorsal root ganglion cells are of the small type. The large cells give rise to large-diameter myelinated nerve fibres and the small cells to small myelinated and unmyelinated axons. Since the majority of the dorsal root ganglion cells

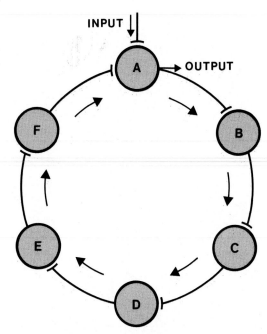

Fig. 5.5   Schematic diagram of a reverberating neuronal circuit. The dorsal root afferent activates A which is connected to five interneurons (B to F), the last neuron in the circuit feeding back to A.

are small, this implies that there is a preponderance of sensory modalities carried by fine fibres to the spinal cord. From the site of bifurcation of the axon in the dorsal root ganglion, the two processes travel in opposite directions; one enters the spinal cord through the dorsal root and one projects peripherally in spinal nerves to terminate in sensory end structures such as free nerve endings, muscle spindles, Pacinian corpuscles, etc. In the dorsal root the large and small fibres are segregated, the thin fibres being congregated on the lateral side and the large fibres on the medial side. When entering the spinal cord the small fibres pass into the Lissauer tract and towards the apex of the dorsal horn, whereas the large fibres pass medially and travel in the dorsal columns.

The cutaneous afferents in a dorsal root all come from the same body segment or *dermatome* (Fig. 5.6). Mapping of the dermatomes has shown that there is a considerable amount of overlapping between the dermatomes of adjacent roots. A single point in the skin may thus be supplied by terminals

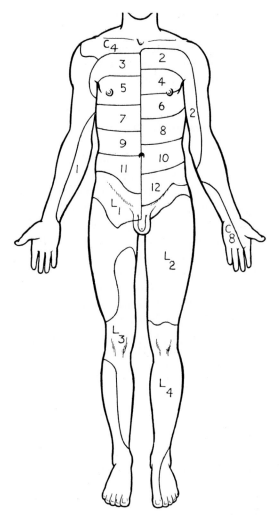

Fig. 5.6 The dermatomes of the thoracic and upper four lumbar nerves. (From *Gray's Anatomy*, Longman, 1973.)

reasons why pain arising in muscles is often perceived as coming from more or less distant skin areas.

The recent development of techniques for intracellular injection of the enzyme, horseradish peroxidase, has made it possible to map the terminations of cutaneous nerve fibres in the dorsal horn of the spinal cord. These studies have clearly established that each type of cutaneous mechanoreceptive afferent fibre has a highly specific distribution not only in terms of the orientation of its terminals but also with respect to the density and arrangement of synaptic contacts. Fig. 5.7 illustrates schematically the organisation of the five main types of cutaneous afferents studied. The arborisations of hair follicle afferent fibres form longitudinally running columns of terminals in lamina

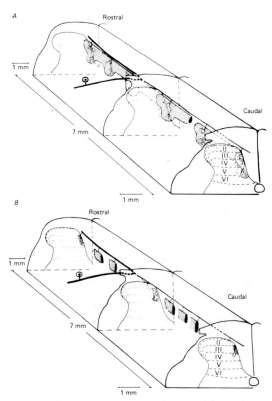

Fig. 5.7 Schematic representation of the organisation of terminal endings of (A) Pacinian corpuscle and (B) rapidly adapting (Krause) mechanoreceptor fibre from glabrous skin. (From Brown *et al., J. Physiol. (Lond.)*, 307, 1980.)

from three roots. Lesion of a single root is therefore in general not followed by sensory loss. It is important to note that the dermatomes for different skin sensations are not identical, the dermatomes for touch being larger than those for pain and temperature. The threshold to various stimuli is always lowest in the central part of the dermatomal field. A segmental distribution also exists for visceral and proprioceptive afferents. The muscular dermatomes, the *myotomes*, may be more or less distinct in their distribution from the corresponding cutaneous dermatomes. This may be one of the

III whereas the axons of Krause's receptors terminate in arborisations which form thin slabs of endings in lamina III but also in lamina IV. The endings of Pacinian corpuscle afferent fibres produce extensive aborisations in laminae II to VI, while the axons of slowly adapting receptors such as Merkel's receptors have endings which form spherical volumes of arborisations in lamina IV. Slowly adapting receptors such as the Ruffini corpuscle axons have endings that form thin transversely oriented slabs of endings in laminae III to VI. These observations show that the axons of different kinds of receptors are arranged in specific patterns of synaptic connections with second-order neurons in the dorsal horn. Furthermore there is a precise somatotopic organisation of the dorsal horn neurons such that their receptive fields form a map of the body surface. Thus within the lumbosacral cord the toes are represented medially and this area is surrounded by neurons receiving the afferents from the foot, the leg and most laterally the thigh.

The ventral roots have generally been thought to have efferent fibres only. However, in recent years it has become clear that certain ventral roots have a large number of small afferent fibres. These fibres may have relevance to observations suggesting that pain impulses may enter the spinal cord via ventral roots (see p. 469).

5.3 Structural organisation of the dorsal horn

In structural organisation, the dorsal horn strikingly resembles the cerebral cortex. Like the cortex, the dorsal horn has six layers or laminae, each with characteristic structural features (see Fig. 5.8).

Lamina I is a thin layer of grey substance at the dorsal-most part of the spinal grey matter. Its most characteristic feature is the presence of large marginal cells with long poorly branched dendrites which closely follow the contours of the dorsal horn. Some of the dendritic branches enter into the lamina II. Here they are densely covered with presynaptic terminals which derive mainly from small afferent fibres. The axons of the marginal cells pass through the anterior commissure to the contralateral region of the spinal cord where they

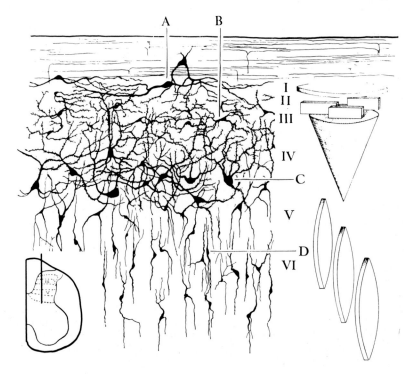

Fig. 5.8 Sagittal section through the dorsal horn showing typical patterns of dendritic branching of neurons in the first six laminae: A, marginal cell; B, small gelatinosa neuron; C, lamina IV neuron; D, lamina V neuron. The dendritic domains of the neurons in the various layers are outlined in the geometrical figures on the right. (From Scheibel and Scheibel, *Brain Res.*, 9, 1968.)

join the ascending pain pathway, the spinothalamic tract; their end station appears to be the intralaminar nuclei of the thalamus. On their way to the thalamus the fibres send collaterals to cells within the periaqueductal grey matter. Electron microscope studies indicate that, besides the excitatory nociceptive afferent input, the marginal cells also receive inhibitory input from gelatinosa neurons. In contrast to the neurons in laminae IV–V the marginal neurons appear not to be under inhibitory control from supraspinal centres.

The *substantia gelatinosa*, which comprises lamina II, is characterised structurally by a dense network of cell bodies of small cells, nerve termin-

als and synaptic endings. Its complete anatomical and functional organisation is still unknown, but recent studies indicate that its cells play a significant part in controlling the transmission of pain impulse to higher centres. A characteristic structural feature of these cells is that they have a profusely branching dendritic tree and that their main dendrites are orientated towards Lissauer's tract and towards the cells in laminae IV and V with very little lateral extension (Fig. 5.9). The dendritic trees of the substantia gelatinosa cells closely resemble those of Purkinje cells of the cerebellar cortex and can be depicted as forming thin radially oriented sheets. Their axons have a

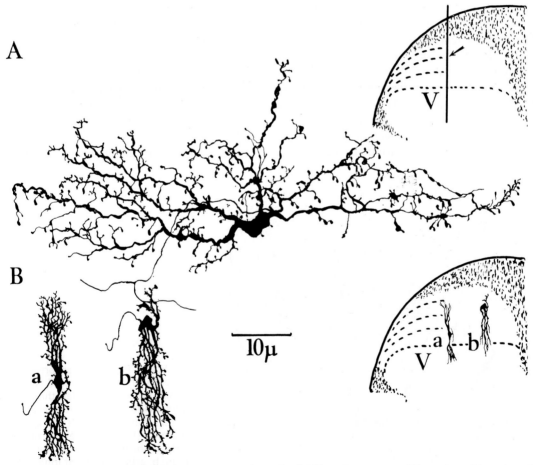

Fig. 5.9   Typical features of gelatinosa neurons in sagittal (A) and transverse (B) sections. Note that the dendritic pattern is spreading out along the longitudinal axis of the spinal cord and that the dendrites are covered with numerous spines. (From Scheibel and Scheibel, *Brain Res.*, 9, 1968.)

which are in synaptic contact with the central terminal. There is evidence that the central terminal arises from a primary afferent fibre. The origins of the peripheral processes remain obscure. It has been suggested that the inhibitory effect of large fibre activity on transmission of pain impulses takes place in the glomeruli (see p. 468).

Laminae IV, V and VI represent the greater portion of the dorsal horn deep to the substantia gelatinosa. The nerve cells of lamina IV are of various sizes, ranging from small cells to relatively large cells. Their dendritic trees radiate medially, laterally and dorsally. The lateral dendrites receive high-density innervation from corticospinal fibres; through this pathway the activity of the lamina IV cells is under the control of descending systems. The dorsal dendrites receive their input from substantia gelatinosa cells. Many cells in lamina IV respond exclusively to tactile stimulation. Other cells are activated both by mechanical and noxious stimuli; these cells have been denoted 'wide dynamic range cells'.

When passing from lamina IV to laminae V and VI, there is a dramatic change in the orientation of the dendritic systems. The dendrites of the cells in laminae V and VI have little or no extension along the longitudinal axis of the spinal cord and radiate almost exclusively in the dorsoventral and mediolateral planes. As is illustrated in Fig. 5.13 the receptive domains of the neurons in lamina IV have topographical patterns related to the orientation and distribution of their dendritic branches.

It is supposed that the cells in lamina V are activated by the input from lamina IV and in turn excite the neurons in lamina VI. The axons of laminae IV–VI project to the thalamus via the spinothalamic tract, to the lateral cervical nucleus via the spinocervical system and to the grey matter of the spinal cord.

5.4 Descending control systems

It has been known for a long time that some axons in the pyramidal tract terminate in the dorsal horn in laminae III–VI. No projections have been traced to laminae I and II. Activation of the pyramidal tract produces inhibition of many cells in lamina IV, whereas most cells in lamina V and VI are either inhibited or excited. Recent studies have demonstrated that in addition to the pyramidal tract there are several other descending projections

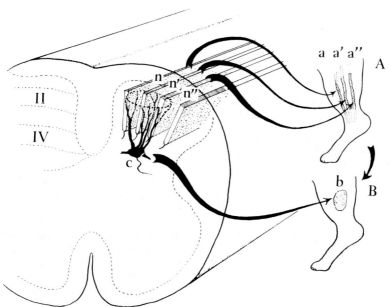

Fig. 5.13   Receptive field representation at different levels in the dorsal horn. The peripheral cutaneous strip areas a, a′ and a″ are believed to be represented in the dorsal horn by sheets n, n′ and n″. The cells (c) of the lamina IV assemble the patterns of activity in the sheets and, because the sampling area is circular, their peripheral receptive field is of that configuration. (From Scheibel and Scheibel, *Brain Res.*, 9, 1968.)

through which the activity of dorsal horn neurons can be influenced. Thus there is a projection of the lower brain stem through the dorsolateral funiculus (DLF). This pathway forms part of a descending inhibitory system which is involved in the control of pain. Many other descending projections are capable of modifying the activity of dorsal horn neurons. For instance, stimulation of the reticular formation has been shown to modulate transmission of afferent input to the spinal cord. Furthermore, the activity of dorsal horn neurons is influenced by descending vestibular projections.

6

Spinal Reflexes

The concept of 'reflex' first appeared in physiological literature with Descartes, who referred to 'esprits réfléchis' in describing reactions to pain. Descartes thought that nerves are like strings which by their tension on the brain elicit pain reflexes. A similar idea is met in the work of Willis, who used the term 'motus reflexus' to describe muscle movements elicited by a painful stimulus. As did Descartes, Willis thought that the input–output coupling occurred in the brain. But in the middle of the eighteenth century, Whyatt demonstrated that reflexes could also be elicited in decapitated animals. That the brain's participation is not a prerequisite for muscle movements was common knowledge: a chicken can run a long way with its head cut off. What Whyatt established was that the reflexes that remain after decapitation are transmitted by the spinal cord; its destruction eliminates them. The understanding of the neurophysiological basis for these reflexes was advanced again with the discovery that the dorsal roots conduct impulses towards the spinal cord, while the ventral roots carry outgoing motor signals. What inspired interest and a flurry of speculations was the purposefulness of many of the spinal cord reflexes. It was found, for example, that a decapitated frog could scrape away with great precision bits of paper soaked in acetic acid from different points on the body. If such a piece was placed on the right side of the abdomen the right leg was used to remove the paper; on the left side, the left leg; and if the paper was placed in the midline, reflex scratching movements were elicited in both legs alternately.

The neuronal processes underlying reflexes remained obscure until Sherrington's work around 1900. In order to eliminate the influence of higher centres on spinal functions, Sherrington used animals in which the connections between the brain and the spinal cord had been interrupted by a transection of the spinal cord. Sherrington's classical studies provided insight into the basic properties of spinal reflex mechanisms and laid the basis for our present knowledge of reflex functions.

6.1 The stretch reflex

General properties

No other reflex has been studied more intensely than the stretch reflex. The interest focused on this reflex is explained by the fact that the reflex arc is composed of only two components: an afferent limb represented by the input from the muscle spindle and an efferent limb represented by the motoneuron and its muscle. Furthermore, the stretch reflex may easily be elicited and measured under well controlled experimental conditions. Sherrington became interested in this reflex when he noted that there was often a considerable resistance to passive movements of the limbs in the experimental animals and that this resistance was particularly marked in the antigravity muscles. He noticed that stretching the quadriceps muscle in the decerebrate cat by only a few millimetres induced a considerable increase in tension of the muscle and that this effect disappeared when the dorsal or ventral roots were cut. These observations clearly showed that the increase in tension could not be attributed to the elasticity of the muscle but rather was the result of active contraction of the muscle induced by afferent input.

Sherrington also demonstrated that, although the stretch reflex was best developed in extensor muscles, it is present in all skeletal muscles. The reflex is induced by stretch; in extensor muscles this evokes a reflex contraction that lasts as long as the muscle is stretched, while flexor muscles generally only respond with a brief transient contraction. The reflex is strictly localised in the sense that only the muscle that is stretched contracts; moreover, if one head of a two-headed muscle is stret-

ched, only this portion of the muscle will contract. The fact that only the muscle that is subjected to stretch contracts indicates that the sensory input goes mainly to the motoneurons that innervate the muscle from which the sensory input derives. In addition, some of the afferent inflow is distributed to the motoneurons of synergistic muscles. This inflow is insufficient to elicit activity in these cells, but may contribute to raising the level of their excitability (see facilitation on p. 190).

The prototype of stretch reflexes is the patellar reflex or the knee jerk (Fig. 6.1). This reflex can be elicited by a sharp tap on the patellar tendon with a small hammer. If one hand is laid on the surface of the thigh, over the quadriceps muscle, it is easy to determine that the movement of the leg is due to a quick contraction in this muscle, while

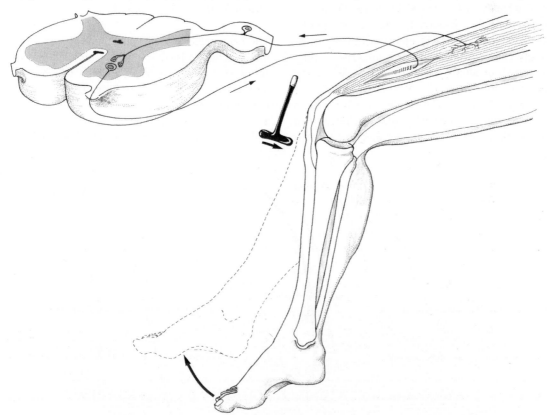

Fig. 6.1 The spinal pathways for the patellar (stretch) reflex. Tapping the patellar tendon causes a brief stretch of the quadriceps femoris muscle and of the muscle spindles in this muscle. The primary endings of the spindles respond with a brief discharge that is monosynaptically transmitted to the motoneurons of the quadriceps muscle and elicits the knee jerk.

other thigh muscles remain inactive. Early investigators arrived at the conclusion that the contraction could not be a reflex since it appears with such a short delay. It was Sherrington who first established that the contraction is evoked by an afferent input to the spinal cord by demonstrating that the muscle twitch disappeared when the dorsal roots were cut. This raised the question of which end organs are the source of the input. It was natural to assume that the tap on a muscle tendon stimulated receptors in the tendon or in the overlying skin. However, the reflex remains after the tendon and the skin are anaesthetised. This suggested that receptors within the muscle must be responsible for the afferent input to the spinal cord. The muscle contains a variety of receptors, such as free nerve endings, Pacinian corpuscles and muscle spindles, all of which at first seemed likely candidates for the stretch reflex. Eventually, the muscle spindles were identified as the receptors, which by their activity elicit the muscle contraction. The spindles are found in almost all striated muscles in the body and are particularly numerous in the small muscles of the hand. They are extremely sensitive to stretch and respond with a brisk discharge when the muscle is stretched, for instance, by tapping

its tendon. If a muscle is kept stretched, the spindles deliver a sustained discharge. There are thus two types of response to stretching, the phasic response to a brief stretch and the tonic response to continuing stretch. The latter component of the stretch reflex is particularly important in maintaining posture.

The key to understanding the functional significance of the stretch reflex in various muscle functions is the muscle spindle. Early on, the spindle was considered to be a device for measuring the length of a muscle. Later studies revealed a considerably more complex functional role and also disclosed that the structure of the spindle is more intricate than originally thought.

Structure of the muscle spindle

The mammalian muscle spindle is only a few millimetres long and is composed of a bundle of muscle fibres, the so-called *intrafusal* fibres, which are innervated by gamma motor fibres (Fig. 6.2). The muscle bundle, whose central region is enclosed in a fluid-filled fusiform capsule, is attached at each end to the connective tissue surrounding the ordin-

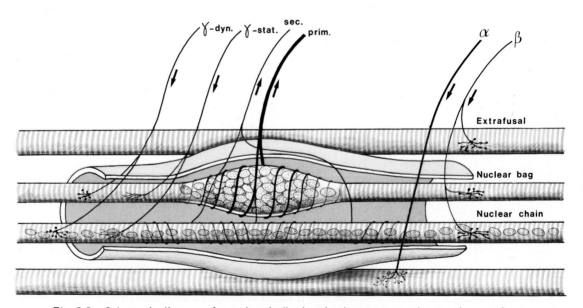

Fig. 6.2　Schematic diagram of muscle spindle showing its sensory and motor innervation.

ary *extrafusal* or ordinary muscle fibres. The spindles are therefore said to lie in parallel with the extrafusal fibres. Contraction of the extrafusal fibres relieves tension on the spindles, and stretching of the muscle lengthens the spindles.

The intrafusal muscle fibres of the spindle are of two types: *nuclear bag* and *nuclear chain*. The former are characterised by an accumulation of nuclei in the equatorial zone, which appears swollen; in the chain fibres, the nuclei are evenly distributed and arranged in series like links in a chain. Nuclear bag fibres are usually somewhat longer and thicker than chain fibres. The ultrastructural differences between the two types are even more pronounced. A bag fibre has regularly arranged myofilaments, relatively little cytoplasm, a few mitochondria and a poorly developed sarcoplasmic reticulum. A chain fibre has a less regular arrangement of filaments, a greater amount of cytoplasm, and a well developed sarcoplasmic reticulum. These ultrastructural differences suggest that the chain fibres may contract more rapidly than the bag fibres. Both are innervated by gamma motor fibres, which travel with the sensory fibres and enter the spindle in its equatorial region. The motor axons are distributed to the polar regions of the intracapsular portions of the muscle fibres. There are two types of endings of the gamma fibres, endplate (designated as the p_2 type) and trail endings. The plate endings, which are similar to the motor endplate of extrafusal muscles, are mainly located on the nuclear bag muscle fibres. The trail endings, which have a more widespread and diffuse appearance, are distributed to both the bag and chain fibres.

Until quite recently, it was generally thought that all the motor terminals of the intrafusal fibres came from gamma fibres. Recent studies have provided evidence that the intrafusal muscle fibres also receive endings from axons that innervate the extrafusal muscle fibres as well. The terminals of these so-called beta fibres form plate endings (termed p_1 type). Information about the relative distribution of gamma and beta fibres in various types of muscle is still fragmentary. It appears, however, that beta fibres are more common in some muscle than in others. Functionally, the presence of beta fibre innervation implies coordination of the intrafusal and the extrafusal muscle fibres.

Most mammalian spindles receive at least two sensory axons. One is relatively coarse and rapidly conducting, with a terminal that coils around the central zone of the intrafusal muscle fibres. This is the primary sensory fibre, which is mainly responsible for the stretch reflex. The secondary sensory fibre is thinner and its terminals usually lie in the polar areas of the chain fibres, and sometimes of the bag fibres. On the chain fibres they end in spirals, and on the bag fibres in clustered ramifications, called *flower-spray endings*. The nerve fibres that give rise to the primary terminals are $6-18\ \mu m$ in diameter at their entrance to the spindle, while the fibres to the secondary terminals are $4-10\ \mu m$ thick.

The anatomical differences between primary and secondary terminals, such as their preferential distribution to the bag or chain type of intrafusal muscle fibre respectively, suggest that their functions may differ as well. Studies of the activity of the terminals during muscle stretch have shown that in general the primary terminals are characterised by higher dynamic sensitivity than the secondaries. This can be observed when a muscle is stretched to a given length and maintained there. The primary terminals respond strongly during the lengthening of the muscle (Fig. 6.3) and at a lower frequency during maintained stretch. The secondary terminals show a relatively smaller increase in frequency during stretch and a smaller decline at the transition to maintained stretch. Thus the primary terminals are more sensitive to the dynamic component of stretch than are the secondary terminals, but both types are about equally sensitive to maintained stretch. These differences may be accounted for by the transducer properties of the sensory endings, as is indicated by recordings of the receptor potentials of single primary and secondary fibres (see Fig. 6.2). The dynamic sensitivity of the primary terminals is also reflected in the fact that they respond to vibratory stimulation or to a brief small stretch (such as a tendon tap) (Fig. 6.4), while the secondary terminals do not. Another difference is their behaviour after stretch. The primary terminals are silent for a short

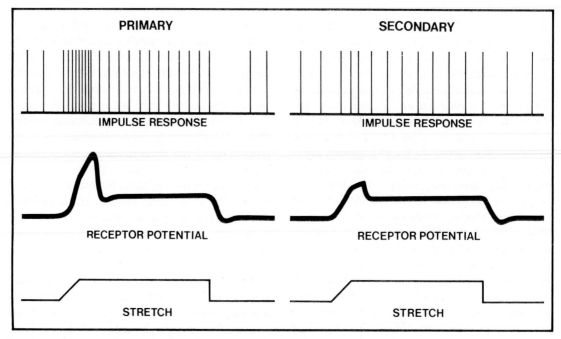

Fig. 6.3   Response characteristics of primary and secondary endings of mammalian muscle spindle. Note the close correlation between the features of the impulse discharge and those of the receptor potential for the two types of endings. (Adapted from Hunt and Ottoson, *J. Physiol.*, 252, 1975.)

period, while the normal spontaneous activity of the secondaries rapidly returns.

Despite these general behavioural distinctions between the primary and secondary terminals, no terminal always responds in the same way to a given stimulus. Their properties are highly dependent upon the prevailing activity in the gamma motor system. For example, under the influence of increased gamma fibre activity, a primary terminal may behave like a secondary terminal.

The role of the gamma fibres

The functional importance of the gamma fibres was discovered in 1945 by Leksell. In studying the effect of ventral root stimulation, he found that

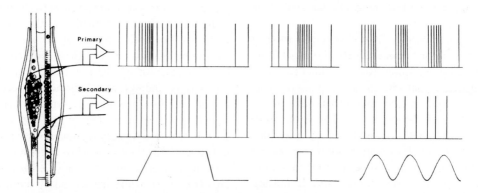

Fig. 6.4   Responsiveness of primary and secondary endings to different types of stretches in the absence of fusimotor activity. (Adapted from Matthews, 1964.)

selective activation of the small fibres produced no noticeable contraction of the innervated muscle but caused a vigorous discharge in the spindle afferents from the muscle. From this finding he concluded that the small motor axons must selectively innervate the intrafusal muscle fibres and that the spindle discharge was due to contraction of these fibres without concomitant activation of the extrafusal muscle fibres. Because the intrafusal fibres are so few relative to the total mass of the muscle, their contraction had no significant effect on muscle tension.

Gamma activation, in principle, has the same effect as stretching the muscle (Fig. 6.5), for in both cases the spindle terminals are exposed to tension. That the spindle is stretched rather than shortened during contraction of the intrafusal fibres may at first seem paradoxical. The effect is explained by the structure of the spindle. The intrafusal fibres consist of a central non-contractile region and two contractile polar regions, each with its motor innervation. The shortening of the polar parts during contraction extends the equatorial region where the primary terminals are situated. To understand the function of the spindle, it is also important to know that the gamma fibres are normally activated in parallel with the motor nerves

to the extrafusal fibres. During muscle contraction, the intrafusal muscle fibres therefore shorten, as does the whole muscle. Thus the activity of the gamma fibres adjusts the length of the intrafusal fibres to that of the muscle as a whole and the spindle is therefore always ready to respond to length changes of the muscle.

When it was discovered that there are two types of intrafusal muscle fibre, and that the motor innervation is mediated by two types of gamma fibre, the natural assumption was that this anatomical arrangement enables the length of each type of intrafusal fibre to be regulated independently of the other. Support for this came from studies indicating that each type of intrafusal fibre receives mainly either one or the other type of motor supply. In experiments where individual gamma fibres were stimulated in ventral roots and afferent response recorded from the muscle spindle, two types of effect on the primary terminals emerge (Fig. 6.6). In some cases the dynamic sensitivity is increased, and in others it is reduced. The gamma fibres are therefore classified from a functional viewpoint as dynamic or static according to whether they augment or suppress the dynamic sensitivity of the primary terminals. The secondary terminals in the spindle seem to be influenced only by static

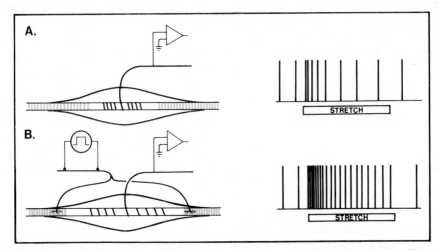

Fig. 6.5   Effect of intrafusal muscle activation on responsiveness of muscle spindle afferent. In (A) is shown the response to stretch when the intrafusal fibres are relaxed; in (B) the same stretch induces a considerably more intense response when the intrafusal fibres are activated by stimulation of the gamma fibres.

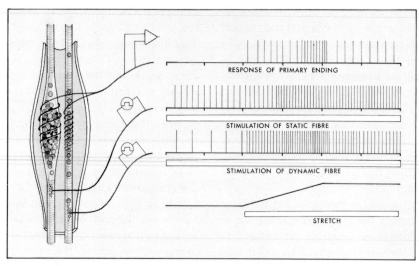

Fig. 6.6   Effects of stimulation of static and dynamic fusimotor stimulation on the response of a primary ending to stretching. (Adapted from Crowe and Matthews, 1964.)

gamma fibres. They increase the sensitivity of the secondary terminals during maintained steady stretch but not during the actual increase in length.

As mentioned, the stretch reflex is present in nearly all muscles, but is particularly well developed in extensor muscles. This gives an indication of its main functional task. The stretch reflex has a stabilising effect on the joints of the extremities and the vertebral column, and thus plays an important role in postural reactions. This may be illustrated by considering the quadriceps muscle of the thigh. In a standing position, the knee tends to bend because of body weight. This bending is counteracted by the reflex contraction of the muscle. The same reflex mechanism is active in all muscles participating in the maintenance of posture or attitude.

Muscle tone

In studies of gamma nerve fibres, an almost constant outflow of tonic impulses has been observed. This suggests that the muscle spindles are continually under some tension, with consequent afferent discharge. Such a continuous influx to the spinal cord also indicates that the alpha motoneurons are more or less constantly active. Muscles that have

been studied by electromyography display a constant ongoing activity, even when no contraction is observable, but whether this is generally true for all muscles is disputed, for most such studies have been done on cats. Being a four-footed animal, the cat must maintain a certain degree of activity in the extensor musculature of the legs simply to stand. In humans, recordings from various muscles indicate that in the recumbant position there is normally little or no activity.

As we have seen above, movement always involves activation of the gamma motoneurons, which means that a certain background muscle tone accompanies contraction. The activity in gamma neurons is regulated from higher centres in the brain stem and the cerebellum. In addition, the gamma neurons are also affected by various sensory inputs. A particularly strong influence is stimulation of the skin, but light and sound stimuli can also be effective.

The gamma system as a servomechanism

Recordings from cells in the anterior horn of the spinal cord indicate that gamma neurons are sometimes activated before alpha neurons when the cerebral cortex is stimulated. This has given rise to the 'follow-up length servo-theory', according to which the initiation of a muscle movement occurs because cortical activation of the gamma neurons makes the spindle contract, producing a discharge of the primary terminals (Fig. 6.7). The afferent inflow from the spindles is then transmitted to the alpha neurons of the muscle. According to this theory, in each situation it is the muscle length that is adjusted to the length of the spindle, rather than vice versa. The muscle contraction would thus be controlled not through direct cortical regulation of the alpha neurons but rather by control of the length of the intrafusal muscle fibres of the spindle. This theory, which offers a sophistica-

ted alternative to the control of muscle movement, gained wide acceptance at first. Yet later studies have shown that it is possible to activate from the cortex either the alpha or the gamma neurons selectively. Furthermore, the theory has been difficult to reconcile with the discovery of the two types of gamma fibre. The existence of dynamic and static fibres indicates that the control of the intrafusal fibres is a more complex operation than was thought at first. Only the chain fibres would be fast enough for the postulated servo-system, so in theory they would be the only fibres participating in the control. To establish whether voluntary contraction is initiated and controlled by the

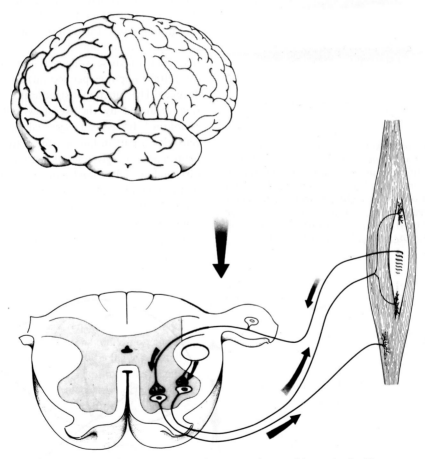

Fig. 6.7 Diagrammatic representation of the 'follow-up length servo' hypothesis. The gamma-neurons are activated from a higher centre and the output from these neurons causes intrafusal muscle contraction, which in turn induces a discharge in the spindle afferents. Muscle contraction is induced by monosynaptic activation of the alpha-neurons by the afferent spindle discharge.

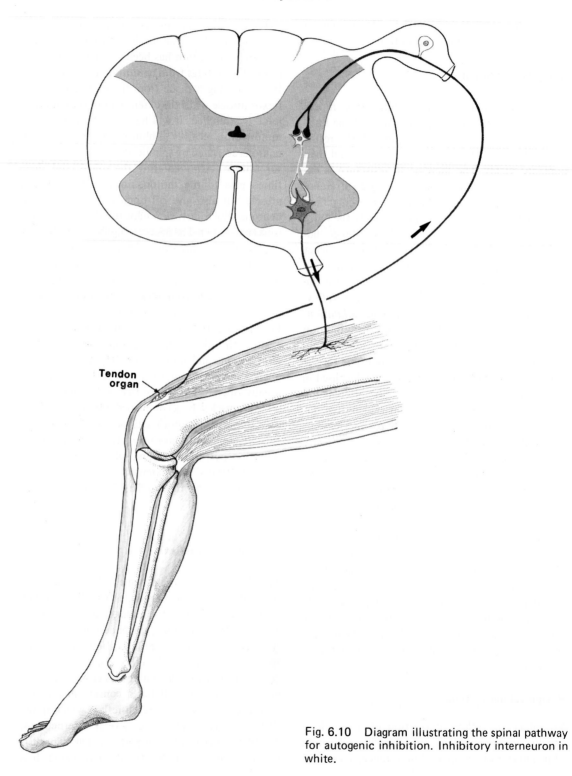

Tendon organ

Fig. 6.10   Diagram illustrating the spinal pathway for autogenic inhibition. Inhibitory interneuron in white.

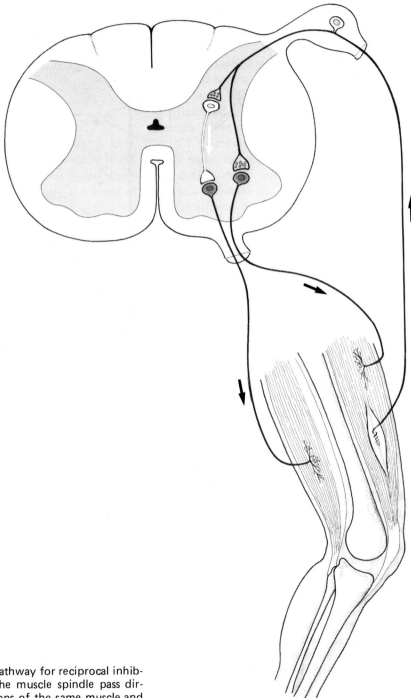

Fig. 6.11   The spinal pathway for reciprocal inhibition. Impulses from the muscle spindle pass directly to the motoneurons of the same muscle and
via collaterals to interneurons (white) which inhibit
the activity of the motoneurons of the antagonist
muscle.

supine and the head bent approximately 45° up-wards. Minimal extensor tone is obtained if the animal is placed in the prone position with its head bent approximately 45° forwards. In either case, the change in extensor tone is the same in all four limbs. The receptors responsible for these changes are situated in the otolith organs.

The statokinetic reflexes serve the function of restoring the body to a normal position. These reflexes depend not only on the labyrinth organs and the proprioceptors of the neck muscles but also on visual input and the input from muscle and skin receptors in the trunk and limbs. The stato-kinetic reflexes usually follow a regular pattern, the first step of which is to return the head to its normal orientation in space by means of righting reflexes mediated mainly by the labyrinths and the eyes. These movements bring the head into a posi-tion which increases the inputs from the proprio-ceptors in the neck muscles. Their inputs evoke a whole series of righting reflexes of the trunk musculature aimed at bringing the body to a normal position in relation to the head. This sequence of righting reflexes may be illustrated by holding a cat upside down and dropping it. Given a sufficient height, the cat is sure to land on all four feet. Photo-graphs of the course of events show that the first thing the cat does is to turn its head, a movement elicited by the input from the labyrinth and partly also from the eyes. The head turning elicits reflexes in the neck musculature, accompanied by successive reflexes in the body musculature. The result is a rotatory movement which spreads from the head in a strict segmental order to the body muscles and the limbs, so that the animal quickly regains a normal orientation in space before landing.

BIBLIOGRAPHY FOR SECTION IV

Suggested Reading and Reviews

Barker, D. (1974). The morphology of muscle receptors, in *Muscle Receptors, Handbook of Sensory Physiology*, vol. III/2, ed. C. C. Hunt, Springer-Verlag, Heidelberg, pp. 1–190

Burke, R. E. (1971). Control systems operating on spinal reflex mechanisms, in *Central Control of Movement*, ed. E. V. Evarts, *Neurosci. Res. Prog. Bull.*, **9**, 60–85

Eccles, J. C. (1952). The electrophysiological properties of the motoneurone, *Cold Spring Harbour Symp. Quant. Biol.*, **17**, 175–183

Eccles, J. C. (1964). *The Physiology of Nerve Cells*, Academic Press, New York

Eccles, J. C. and Schade, J. P. (eds) (1964). *Organization of the Spinal Cord*, Elsevier, Amsterdam

Henneman, E. (1974). Principles governing distribution of sensory input to motor neurons, in *The Neurosciences. Third Study Program*, eds F. O. Schmitt and F. G. Worden, MIT Press, Cambridge, MA, pp. 281–291

Henneman, E. (1974). Organization of the spinal cord, in *Medical Physiology*, vol. 1, ed. V. B. Mountcastle, C. V. Mosby, St Louis, pp. 636–650

Hunt, C. C. (1974). The physiology of muscle receptors, in *Muscle Receptors, Handbook of Sensory Physiology*, vol. III/2, ed. C. C. Hunt, Springer-Verlag, Heidelberg, pp. 191–234

Kostyuk, P. G. and Vasilenko, D. (1979). Spinal interneurons, *Ann. Rev. Physiol.*, **41**, 115–126

Liddell, E. G. T. (1960). *The Discovery of Reflexes*, Oxford University Press

Liddell, T. and Sherrington, C. S. (1932). *Reflex Activity of the Spinal Cord*, Oxford University Press, New York

Matthews, B. H. C. (1933). Nerve endings in a mammalian muscle, *J. Physiol. (Lond.)*, **78**, 1–53

Matthews, P. B. C. (1964). Muscle spindles and their motor control, *Physiol. Rev.*, **44**, 219–288

Matthews, P. B. C. (1972). *Mammalian Muscle Receptors and Their Central Actions*, Monographs of the Physiology Society, Edward Arnold, London

McIntyre, A. K. (1974). Central actions of impulses in muscle afferent fibres, in *Muscle Receptors, Handbook of Sensory Physiology*, vol. III/2, ed. C. C. Hunt, Springer-Verlag, Heidelberg, pp. 235–288

Ottoson, D. (1972). Mechanisms of spindle adaptation, in *Research in Muscle Development and the Muscle Spindle*, eds B. Q. Banker, R. J. Przybylski, J. P. Van Der Meulen and M. Victor, Excerpta Medica, Amsterdam, pp. 43–54

Ottoson, D. (1976). Muscle spindles. Morphology and physiology of muscle spindles, in *Frog Neurobiology*, eds R. Llinás and W. Precht, Springer-Verlag, Heidelberg, pp. 643–675

Peterson, B. W. (1979). Reticulospinal projections to spinal motor nuclei, *Ann. Rev. Physiol.*, **41**, 127–140

Rexed, B. (1954). A cytoarchitectonic atlas of the spinal cord in the cat, *J. Comp. Neurol.*, **100**, 297–380

Scheibel, M. E. and Scheibel, A. B. (1968). Terminal axonal patterns in cat spinal cord, II. The dorsal horn, *Brain Res.*, **9**, 32–58

Sherrington, C. S. (1906). *The Integrative Action of the Nervous System*, Yale University Press, New Haven

Szentagothai, J. and Rethelyi, M. (1973). Cyto- and neuropil architecture of the spinal cord, in *New Developments in Electromyography and Clinical Neurophysiology*, vol. 3, *Human*

Section V: Synaptic Transmission in the Central Nervous System

7

Synaptic Potentials

7.1   Excitatory and inhibitory synaptic potentials

Until the beginning of the 1950s, studies of the central nervous system were restricted to the analysis of potentials which could be recorded from the brain or the spinal cord by relatively coarse extracellular electrodes. Such recordings provided valuable information of the activity in groups of cells or bundles of nerve fibres, but not of the activity of individual cells. It was therefore a crucial advance when Eccles (Fig. 7.1) and his collaborators in 1951 succeeded in recording intracellularly from single motoneurons in the spinal cord. Their studies mark the beginning of a new era in neurophysiology and have greatly deepened our insight into the mechanisms of synaptic transmission in the central nervous system. Intrinsic to the technique developed by Eccles and collaborators is that a fine glass capillary filled with KCl is introduced into the spinal cord aiming at the motoneurons in the anterior horn (Fig. 7.2). The tip of the electrode has a diameter less than 1 μm and can therefore penetrate the cell membrane without seriously damaging the cell. Upon penetration of the membrane of a neuron a sudden potential shift in the potential occurs. The resting potential of the cell may range from -60 to -80 mV, with the inside of the cell being negative in relation to the outside. This potential remains stable except for small fluctuations as long as the cell is not activated. A convenient method of inducing activity in the cell is to stimulate peripheral muscle afferents. The arrival of the synchronous impulse volley produces a small transient depolarisation, which reflects the excitatory influence on the motoneuron of the action potentials in the afferent nerves. For this reason the transient potential is usually referred to as the *excitatory postsynaptic potential*, or the EPSP.

The EPSP arises approximately 0.5 ms after the arrival of the afferent volley at the motoneurons. It has a relatively fast rising phase and a slow

Fig. 7.1   Sir John C. Eccles, Nobel Laureate in 1963.

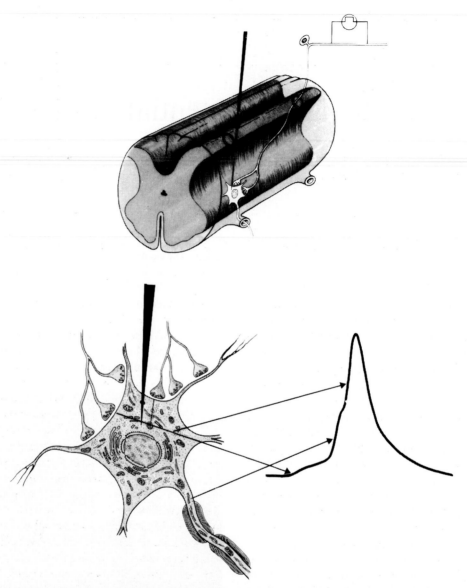

Fig. 7.2 Schematic diagram showing technique introduced by Eccles for intracellular recordings from spinal cord motoneurons. Upper diagram shows insertion of a microelectrode from the exposed dorsal side of the spinal cord until the electrode tip penetrates into a motoneuron in the anterior horn. Lower diagram shows the response recorded when the afferent nerves are stimulated. The potential evoked is made up of several components representing the activity in various parts of the neuron as indicated by arrows.

approximately exponential decline (Fig. 7.3); the total duration of the potential is about 15 ms.

The EPSP increases in amplitude as the afferent volley is increased in strength until a critical level of depolarisation is reached and an action potential is generated. Thus the EPSP is not an all-or-nothing phenomenon but is graded in amplitude in relation to the afferent input. Each afferent terminal can be envisaged to cause a small depolarisation of a restricted area of the cell membrane, and as more

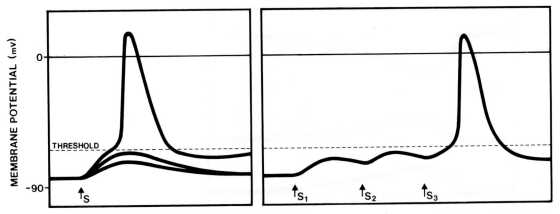

Fig. 7.3 The excitatory postsynaptic potential (EPSP). *Left diagram*: increase of EPSP with gradually increasing strength of afferent input. *Right diagram*: summation of subthreshold EPSPs by repetitive afferent input.

and more synaptic terminals are activated successively greater portions of the postsynaptic membrane are depolarised until the threshold for impulse initiation is reached. When two or more subliminal volleys are delivered in rapid succession, the EPSP produced by the second volley will sum with the first EPSP (Fig. 7.3). The functional implication of the summation is that the effect of impulses arriving closely in time may initiate a discharge. Summation of EPSPs is the electrophysiological basis at the level of a single neuron for the process of facilitation (see p. 190). Another important feature of the EPSP is that it varies in amplitude with the resting potential of the neuron. By injecting current into the cell, it can be shown that the amplitude of the EPSP decreases in direct relation to an imposed depolarisation of the membrane potential (Fig. 7.4). If the potential is lowered to zero, the postsynaptic potential disappears. If the cell's interior is made positive, synaptic activation causes the membrane potential to reverse polarity. In short, the EPSP always tends to move the membrane potential towards zero. Thus the presynaptic input seems to short-circuit the cell membrane, probably by making it permeable to small ions. It would thus appear that the postsynaptic potential arises as a result of a non-specific permeability increase, which allows small ions on both sides of the active membrane to cross it freely.

The EPSP is in many respects closely similar to the endplate potential. Since the terminals of the afferent fibres contain vesicles which are identical in appearance to the vesicles in the motor nerve terminals, it would be tempting to assume that the EPSP, like the endplate potential, results from the release of acetylcholine. Although it appears well established that the EPSP is induced by the action of a chemical transmitter on the postsynaptic membrane, the identity of this transmitter still remains unknown. Acetylcholine is a putative transmitter in some spinal synapses, but it is almost certain that acetylcholine is not the transmitter released at the terminals of muscle afferents. Several lines of evidence suggest that the amount of transmitter released is dependent on the amplitude of impulses invading the terminals and that transmission may be blocked when the presynaptic terminals are depolarised (see presynaptic inhibition on p. 193). The relation between the amount of transmitter released and the size of the impulses invading the terminals would also appear to account for the phenomenon of *post-tetanic potentiation*, that is the augmented monosynaptic response obtained after a brief period of strong stimulation of a dorsal root. There is indirect evidence to suggest that following intense activity the presynaptic terminals become transiently hyperpolarised. It can therefore be assumed that the impulses generated during the

indicate that under certain conditions impulses may invade the dendritic tree.

7.3   Functional characteristics of synaptic transmission

A synapse represents a structural discontinuity in the system by which neurons communicate with one another, and as a consequence synaptic transmission of signals is characterised by special properties.

One-way conduction

Normally a nerve fibre carries impulses in only one direction (orthodromic conduction). For motor nerves this is towards the muscles, and for sensory nerves towards the central nervous system. The nerve fibres are able to conduct an impulse in the direction opposite to what occurs normally (antidromic conduction) but the functional properties of the chemical synapses generally allow signal transmission in only one direction. For instance, if the ventral roots are stimulated, no response can be recorded from the dorsal roots, although it can be shown that activity is induced in the cell bodies and dendrites of the motoneurons. The current flow produced by the motoneurons is not in itself sufficient to activate the presynaptic terminals. The chemical synapse thus functions as a 'one-way valve' which allows transmission only in one direction. The reciprocal synapses (see p. 36) are an exception to this rule, since here activity may be transferred in both directions.

Delay

Measurements of the time course of synaptic transmission have shown that the depolarisation of spinal motoneurons does not begin until about 0.5 ms after the arrival of the impulses at the presynaptic terminals. This synaptic delay is accounted for by the chemical processes involved. In the simplest reflex arc with only one synaptic relay, the delay is relatively insignificant in relation to the total conduction time. In contrast, the total delay may be considerable in pathways involving several synapses such as flexor reflexes.

Fatigue

A characteristic feature of peripheral nerves is that they are able to conduct impulses for a considerable time without becoming fatigued. If, however, presynaptic fibres are stimulated at a high frequency (for instance 100–200 stimuli per second), the impulses in the postsynaptic neuron soon become irregular and may finally vanish completely. The transmission through the synapse will falter even though both the presynaptic fibre and the postsynaptic neuron remain fully capable of generating impulses. The failure is most likely to be attributed to depletion of the stores of transmitter in the nerve terminals during intense and sustained stimulation. Since the resynthesis of the transmitter substance is dependent on metabolic processes, the synapse is more sensitive than the nerve fibre to asphyxia and ischaemia. It is also more susceptible to the action of drugs and to general anaesthetic agents. The synapse therefore represents a region of low safety factor. The functional significance of this is that the transmission of impulses through a synapse may be altered under physiological conditions as well as under the action of drugs. In general, the more synapses that are involved, the more susceptible is the transmission process to the influence of such factors.

Summation

As described in the foregoing section, the EPSPs of different inputs may sum and produce a greater and more prolonged depolarisation of a postsynaptic cell. This characteristic of synaptic transmission provides the basis for *facilitation*. This phenomenon may be demonstrated by stimulating a sensory nerve from the skin with an electrical shock too weak to elicit a reflex action. If, however, two shocks are applied in rapid succession, the reflex is induced. By increasing the interval between the two shocks, it can be shown that the second stimulus gradually loses its effectiveness, and when the two stimuli are 15 ms apart the effect has disappeared. This experiment clearly shows that the effect of the two stimuli, each of which by itself is insufficient, may sum if applied successively within an interval of less than 15 ms. This is approximately the duration of the EPSP elicited in the postsynaptic neuron by a single afferent volley. If a second volley arrives before the EPSP induced by a preceding volley has subsided, the two depolarisations sum. Synaptic activation of a neuron can thus be facilitated by a stimulus applied either simultaneously or within a certain period before another stimulus. Neurons which are subliminally excited by afferent impulses may in this way be brought to threshold by the arrival of an additional afferent volley which in itself is too weak to bring the postsynaptic neuron to threshold. Facilitation is of considerable functional significance, particularly in sensory systems. For instance, a single stimulus to the skin that is too weak to be perceived may give rise to a sensation if followed within a short time interval by an identical stimulus. This type of summation is usually referred to as *temporal summation*. Similarly, two subthreshold stimuli delivered simultaneously to adjacent regions of the skin may be perceived although either alone fails; this is referred to as *spatial summation*. The high sensitivity of the eye in dim light is another example of spatial summation of rod activity.

Most neurons in the central nervous system are subjected to a more or less constant irregular bombardment of impulses in the presynaptic fibres and their excitability varies accordingly. The excitatory state of the central nervous system is thus set by the ongoing 'spontaneous' activity. To define this state, Sherrington introduced the concept of *central excitatory state* or CES. At that time the mechanisms underlying synaptic transmission were unknown and CES was generally attributed to the electrotonic properties of nerve membranes. Today we know that CES may be attributed to the characteristics of chemical synaptic transmission and the time course of the EPSPs and that of corresponding inhibitory potentials (IPSP).

7.4 Electrical transmission

The introduction of the technique for intracellular recording and the discovery of excitatory postsynaptic potentials led to the abandonment of the earlier generally accepted idea that synaptic transmission occurred by direct electrical contacts between neurons. It therefore came as a surprise when it was found that transmission in some invertebrate synapses does in fact occur by current spread. The recorded delay in conduction was negligible so that the postsynaptic potential was concurrent with the rising phase of the impulse in the presynaptic nerve fibre; this finding precluded a chemical link in the transmission. These observations demonstrated that there are specialised synapses for electrical coupling between neurons. An intensive search soon disclosed regions where the membrane of neighbouring neurons appeared to be fused. These so-called *gap junctions* apparently (see also p. 39) provided for low-resistance electrical contacts between cells. The structural gap junctions were first described in non-nervous tissues; they have since been demonstrated in various regions of the mammalian brain. These junctions allow electrical activity to be transmitted from one cell to another without the mediation of neurotransmitters. Some gap junctions allow current spread equally well in both directions while other gap junctions rectify, i.e. current passes more easily in one direction than in the other.

What is the functional role of electrical synapses? It is likely that they provide for a greater speed of synaptic transmission and participate in mediating rapid reflexes. In cardiac and smooth muscle and in certain gland cells, their role appears to be to synchronise the activity of a population of cells. An important functional feature of these synapses is that they are resistant to drugs that block chemical transmission. Interestingly, electrical synapses often may be closely associated with chemical synapses; these are known as mixed synapses (see p. 39).

It is interesting to see how the notion of synaptic transmission in the nervous system has changed in the past few decades. From a position of universal acceptance for almost a century, the electrical hypothesis was ousted in the early 1950s and the chemical hypothesis was greeted with great acclaim. Today, abundant evidence for both modes of transmission exists. The challenge for future research is to assess the relative incidence of the two modes of cellular intercommunication and their specific functional roles in the central nervous system.

7.5 Inhibitory neuronal interaction

For a long time, studies of the function of the nervous system focused mainly on excitatory processes. Little attention was paid to inhibition, which was generally explained as a lack of excitation. The first observation suggesting that inhibition is an active process and mediated by specific nerves comes from studies in the middle of the last century on the cardioinhibitory effect of stimulation of the vagal nerve. It was, however, not until in 1921 with Loewi's discovery of the vagal inhibitory transmitter, the *Vagusstoff*, that the humoral mechanism of inhibition was established. A similar mechanism for inhibition is found in the muscles of certain species of crustacea. Their muscles are supplied with two types of nerves, one excitatory and one inhibitory. Stimulation of the inhibitory axon stabilises the membrane of the muscle fibres near resting level, so that the depolarising effect of the motor fibres is reduced; the effect on the potential is accounted for by changes in membrane permeability. Skeletal muscles in vertebrates lack such inhibitory fibres. In vertebrates, inhibition is a property of the central nervous system and exerted by special interneurons which suppress the activity of other neurons.

Postsynaptic inhibition

In the early 1940s it was found that the inhibition of muscle reflexes is accompanied by slow potential changes in the spinal cord. Their origin and nature remained obscure until the advent of the intracellular recording technique introduced by Eccles and his collaborators, who demonstrated that inhibition is associated with hyperpolarisation of the motoneurons and suppression of the response to an excitatory volley. The hyperpolarising potential, termed the *inhibitory postsynaptic potential* (IPSP), is a mirror image of the excitatory postsynaptic potential (EPSP) described earlier. It differs,

however, from the EPSP in having a somewhat longer latency (1.5 ms). The long delay is due to the fact that an interneuron is interposed in the pathway between the afferent terminals and the motoneurons. The synapses made by sensory afferents always seem to be excitatory; for inhibition to occur, an inhibitory interneuron must be present. It is excited by the sensory afferents and its action on the motoneuron is hyperpolarisation.

Like EPSPs, the individual IPSPs sum if the motoneuron is exposed to inhibitory volleys in rapid succession. Furthermore, the magnitude of the IPSP varies with the resting potential of the neuron (Fig. 7.6). For a given inhibitory input, the hyperpolarising response is greater the more depolarised the membrane potential; thus, the closer the cell is to its firing level, the larger the IPSP. If, however, current is passed across the cell membrane to hyperpolarise the cell to potential values between -80 and -90 mV, the inhibitory stimulus causes depolarisation. This shows that the inhibitory potentials always drive the cell towards a membrane potential of about -80 mV. Such an effect could be produced by an influx of chloride ions, an outflow of potassium ions, or both of these events. The equilibrium potential for potassium is about -90 mV and for chloride about -70 mV. By injecting small amounts of different ions into the cell, it has been possible to obtain information about the permeability changes underlying the IPSPs. Of the various anions tested, some affect the amplitude of the IPSP while others have no effect. The critical factor appears to be the size of the ion. The inhibitory effect can be explained most simply by assuming that the membrane becomes permeable to ions which are the same size as or smaller than potassium. Potassium and chloride are the only ions normally present which fulfil this condition; the sodium ion is somewhat bigger than the potassium ion. It is now generally agreed that the inhibitory current is mainly carried by chloride ions. As for potassium, the experimental findings are equivocal. It has been estimated that the contribution of potassium ions is about 20% of the total inhibitory effect, but it might be less.

The hyperpolarisation caused by the IPSPs moves the membrane potential away from the firing

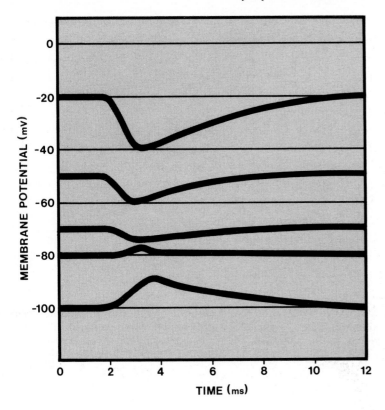

Fig. 7.6 Changes in amplitude and polarity of inhibitory postsynaptic potential with changes in membrane potential. Potentials recorded from motoneuron in response to stimulation of inhibitory afferent fibres, the membrane potential being preset at different voltages.

level and thereby reduces or inhibits the effect caused by a simultaneous arrival of excitatory impulses (Fig. 7.7). The inhibitory effect depends on the respective magnitudes of the IPSPs and the EPSPs, and their time course. At excitatory synapses the channels open to pass sodium and potassium, while at inhibitory synapses the channels open to pass chloride and possibly potassium. The final effect on the membrane potential is therefore dependent on the way these permeability changes interact.

Presynaptic inhibition

In the process of synaptic inhibition described, excitatory impulses reach the motoneuron but impulse generation is inhibited because of the hyperpolarisation of the cell. It was once thought that this was the only mechanism for inhibition in the central nervous system. It was found, however, that the response to an excitatory volley is some-

times inhibited without any simultaneous hyperpolarisation of the cell; in this case both the resting potential and the permeability properties of the neuron remained unchanged. The cell appeared to be completely at rest, yet it did not respond to an inflow of excitatory impulses.

An early speculation was that the inhibitory impulses were reaching the cell by way of synapses situated too far out on the dendrites for their hyperpolarising effect to be recorded by the microelectrode in the cell body. This may indeed be the case at times, but present recording techniques are still inadequate to prove it. Abundant experimental evidence suggests, however, that inhibition of this kind is not due to an effect on the motoneuron or its dendrites but rather to a direct inhibitory effect on the terminals of the excitatory nerve. The influx of excitatory activity is thus influenced before even reaching the synapse by the activity of inhibitory terminals that form axoaxonic synapses with the endings of the excitatory fibres (Fig. 7.8).

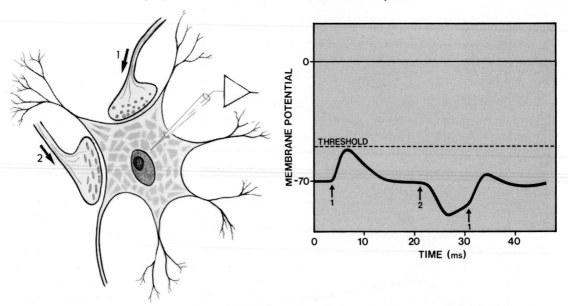

Fig. 7.7   Postsynaptic inhibition. The postsynaptic potentials are recorded with a microelectrode from within the motoneuron. Subthreshold stimulation of excitatory afferents (1) gives rise to an EPSP that approaches the threshold for a conducted action potential. When the excitatory volley is preceded by an inhibitory volley (2), the inhibitory postsynaptic potential decreases the depolarising action of the EPSP to far below the critical level for firing.

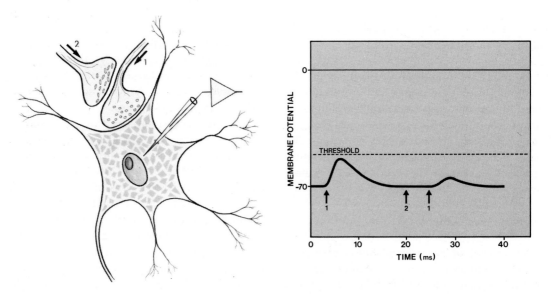

Fig. 7.8   Presynaptic inhibition. Intracellular recording from a motoneuron. The EPSP evoked by an excitatory volley (1) nearly reaches the threshold for firing, as indicated in the diagram to the right. Stimulation of the presynaptic inhibitory afferents (2) causes no change in membrane potential but decreases the amplitude of the EPSP (1) evoked by an excitatory volley.

Hence the term *presynaptic inhibition*. This differs from postsynaptic inhibition in having a considerably longer duration (100–150 ms), which is attributed to a prolonged action of the transmitter. The current concept of the mechanisms underlying presynaptic inhibition is that activity in the terminals of the inhibitory interneuron causes a depolarisation of the afferent excitatory terminals, thereby reducing the amplitude of the impulses arriving in these terminals. This reduction is thought to reduce the amount of excitatory transmitter released at the synapses. A sufficiently strong depolarisation of the excitatory terminals could conceivably prevent the impulse from reaching the synaptic endings and block synaptic transmission completely. Recent findings suggest that the main effect of the inhibitory input is to reduce the entry of calcium into the afferent terminals during the impulse and thereby reduce the amount of transmitter released.

The functional importance of presynaptic inhibition lies in the fact that the membrane potential, and consequently also the excitability of the postsynaptic neuron, is not affected; it is the afferent input in the excitatory terminals that is reduced or eliminated. Therefore presynaptic inhibition provides for a higher degree of selectivity than postsynaptic inhibition. There is strong reason to believe that inhibition in the central nervous system is to a great extent mediated by presynaptic inhibition. Several lines of evidence suggest that presynaptic inhibition is particularly important in some sensory systems; it may play an important role in signal processing in neurons that receive extensive input, such as the motoneurons in the spinal cord.

Electrical inhibition

If a weak electrical current is passed between a pair of electrodes in contact with a nerve, the excitability of the nerve is lowered at the anode, and impulses may be prevented from passing this region. A similar mechanism for inhibition has been found to occur in some neurons in the brain of the goldfish. Inhibition in these cells is accompanied by hyperpolarisation, but with no change in membrane conductance. This shows that the inhibition cannot be attributed to the release of a chemical transmitter. Yet the initial electrical effect is followed by a second phase of inhibition which has all the characteristics of being chemically mediated. It thus seems that in this cell there are two mechanisms for inhibition: a rapid, initial, electrical one and a slower, chemical one. Similar inhibitory mechanisms in the central nervous system of mammals have not yet been demonstrated, but may very well exist. Inhibition may also be mediated by still other mechanisms. There are, for instance, indications that inhibitory effects may be caused by changes in the activity of electrogenic pumps.

The general importance of inhibition may be illustrated by the effects caused by complete removal of inhibition in the central nervous system. This can be achieved by injecting substances that block transmission at inhibitory synapses. For example, only a few milligrams of strychnine injected into an animal will produce violent convulsions and death within a few minutes. The action of the nervous system thus relies on a delicate balance between excitatory and inhibitory synaptic processes.

8

Putative Transmitters

It is now generally agreed that most neurons in the central nervous system communicate with one another by releasing chemical transmitters. Despite arduous efforts, only a few compounds have been identified which can with various degrees of certainty be considered as neurotransmitters. To be identified as a transmitter, a substance should fulfil certain criteria. The main properties to be established are the presence of the substance in the presynaptic terminals and its release during presynaptic activity. Furthermore, there should be a correlation between its release and the amount of presynaptic activity; local administration of the compound should produce the same effect as presynaptic activity and substances antagonistic to the putative transmitter should block synaptic transmission. Actually, none of the compounds generally considered to be transmitters in the central nervous system fulfils all these criteria. Because of the complexity of the central nervous system, it is technically difficult to prove the release of a putative transmitter or to administer it locally at the synapse. The rigorous criteria which are applied to the peripheral system therefore cannot be easily satisfied within the central nervous system.

Until recently it was thought that all transmitters were comparatively small molecules such as amines or amino acids. Recent evidence suggests, however, that polypeptides may play a role as chemical messengers between neurons in the central nervous system. The substances which are at present considered as neurotransmitters in the central nervous system comprise three chemical groups: amines, amino acids and polypeptides. The amines include acetylcholine, dopamine, noradrenalin and serotonin; in the second group are glycine, gamma-aminobutyric acid (GABA), glutamate, aspartate and taurine; the third group comprises a number of polypeptides generally termed neuropeptides such as enkephalin and endorphins.

ACh is the transmitter at the motor nerve terminals in the neuromuscular junctions in vertebrates. Before leaving the spinal cord, the motor axon gives off collaterals which activate the Renshaw cells. In accordance with Dale's law, ACh would be the transmitter in the terminals of these collaterals, as is also strongly suggested by neurophysiological findings. In the rest of the central nervous system, however, the evidence for ACh as a transmitter is equivocal.

Dopaminergic neuronal tracts demonstrated in the limbic system and in the basal ganglia of the mammalian brain (Fig. 8.1) have been a focus of great interest because of their clinical importance in the pathophysiology of Parkinson's disease. The primary action of dopamine is inhibition. Neurophysiological data suggest that dopamine hyperpolarises the postsynaptic neuron by decreasing the sodium conductance. This effect appears to be mediated by an increased synthesis of cyclic AMP (see p. 203).

Neurochemical mapping of the brain has revealed the presence of noradrenalin in widespread regions of the brain and the spinal cord. The highest concentrations are in the hypothalamus and in the locus coeruleus. Noradrenalin is also found in the

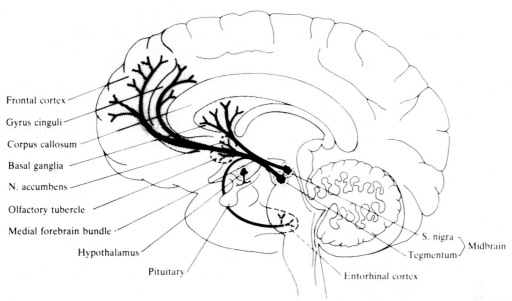

Frontal cortex

Gyrus cinguli

Corpus callosum

Basal ganglia

N. accumbens

Olfactory tubercle

Medial forebrain bundle

Hypothalamus

Pituitary

S. nigra

Tegmentum

Midbrain

Entorhinal cortex

Fig. 8.1 The principal dopamine pathways of the human brain. (From Baldessarini, *Trends in Neurosci.*, 2, 1979.)

midbrain and medulla oblongata, whereas the cerebral cortex contains relatively little of the substance. The noradrenalin cells in the locus coeruleus send processes widely in the brain and spinal cord. This system appears to have an important role in the regulation of sleep—wakefulness and attention. The neurons in the locus coeruleus have connections with Purkinje cells of the cerebellum. Stimulation of the locus coeruleus or local administration of noradrenalin to the Purkinje cells causes a hyperpolarisation, by the same ionic mechanism as dopamine (i.e. a decrease in sodium conductance).

Serotonin is widely distributed in all brain regions, but most densely in the hypothalamus. Serotonergic axons have been found to descend in the lateral columns of the spinal cord, and these pathways appear to mediate the central control of the spinal transmission of pain impulses (see p. 482). The serotonergic neurons of the raphe nuclei participate in the regulation of sleep and wakefulness; inhibition of serotonin synthesis or destruction of the raphe nuclei in cats produces insomnia. The highest concentration of serotonin in the central nervous system is found in the pineal gland, where its concentration undergoes diurnal fluctuations which are independent of changes in illumina-

tion. The ionic mechanisms for serotonergic transmission are not known. Like several other putative transmitters, serotonin binds not only to the postsynaptic membrane but also to the presynaptic membrane. This suggests that there is a direct auto-feedback which might regulate the release of the transmitter.

Glycine is evidently a major inhibitory neurotransmitter in the spinal cord and brain stem, while GABA plays that part in the cerebral cortex. Glycine mediates postsynaptic inhibition by increasing chloride permeability. GABA induces the same change in permeability, but the action of the two inhibitors can be distinguished, for glycine is potently antagonised by strychnine, which scarcely affects GABA inhibition. It has been estimated that glycine and GABA account for about half of the inhibitory action in the central nervous system, the remainder being mediated by serotonin, dopamine and noradrenalin. Another naturally occurring amino acid proposed as a transmitter is taurine. It may be the transmitter that mediates lateral inhibition in the retina. Taurine has been found in many regions of the brain and has a general suppressive action on spontaneous firing.

Except for ACh, all the substances described

above have inhibitory actions. Which, then, are the transmitters mediating excitatory action in the central nervous system? We still do not know. There are strong reasons for suspecting two dicarboxylic amino acids, glutamate and aspartate, but the evidence is much weaker than for the inhibitory transmitters. Glutamate and aspartate have a potent depolarising action on neurons throughout the central nervous system, which makes it difficult to discriminate between a non-specific action of these compounds and their possible role as transmitters.

Localisation of transmitters

Various methods for both light microscopy and electron microscopy have recently been developed for the identification and localisation of neurotransmitters in the central nervous system. Monoamines may for instance be visualised by the Falk—Hillarp fluorescence technique. This method is based on the finding that biologically active amines form strongly fluorescent compounds with formaldehyde which can be readily seen in a fluorescence microscope. With this method it is possible to identify cell bodies and axon terminals containing catecholamines. The method is less satisfactory for tracing of axonal pathways. However, the recently developed glyoxylic acid technique significantly increases the sensitivity of the method and makes it possible to visualise the relatively small amounts of amines present in axons. Different amines may be distinguished with these methods owing to slight differences in their fluorescence. Immunohistochemical methods may also be used for the identification of amine neurons by visualising carrier proteins or the enzymes involved in the biosynthesis of the transmitters. In this method, a fluorescence labelled antibody is used that binds specifically to a given enzyme. This technique was first applied successfully for the localisation of tyrosine hydroxylase (Fig. 8.2), which is involved in the synthesis of noradrenalin. The same method has since been applied for the localisation of GABA, substance P and serotonin.

Another method for visualising neurotransmitters is based on the finding that a particular transmitter is recaptured by the neuron from which it is released. The specificity of this uptake has been demonstrated with several biochemical techniques. By exposing neurons to a concentrated solution of a putative transmitter that has been labelled (for instance with tritium), the presence of the transmitter may be detected by autoradiography. This technique has been applied to localise neurons containing noradrenalin, dopamine, GABA and glycine. Autoradiography may also be used to localise neurotransmitters at the ultrastructural level.

Neuropeptides

It has been known for many years that certain neurons in the brain are able to synthesise and secrete small peptides. For example, hypothalamic neurons manufacture and secrete the peptide hormones, oxytocin and vasopressin, from their terminals. Until recently, the peptidergic neurons have been thought to represent a very small population with highly specialised neuroendocrine functions. However, it has become increasingly clear in the last few years that this is not the case. A dramatic explosion in this field came with the discovery of the enkephalins and the endorphins. To date, more than 20 active peptides or factors of suspected peptide nature have been demonstrated in the brain. The study of their neurophysiological actions is still in its infancy. A number of reports suggest that they are involved in diverse aspects of behaviour, for instance, pain, euphoria, thirst, sleep, learning and mental illness. In addition, a variety of peptides which have long been known to be present in the gastrointestinal system have been shown to exist also in the central nervous system. One of these gut peptides is substance P, which was discovered in 1931 by von Euler and Gaddum in tissue extracts. The idea that substance P might be a neurotransmitter was first advanced in 1953 by Lembeck, who suggested that substance P is the excitatory transmitter at the first sensory synapse in the spinal cord. Later studies proved that substance P is synthesised in the cell bodies of primary afferent neurons and transported towards the axonal terminals in the spinal cord. Its role as a neurotransmitter is supported by recent findings

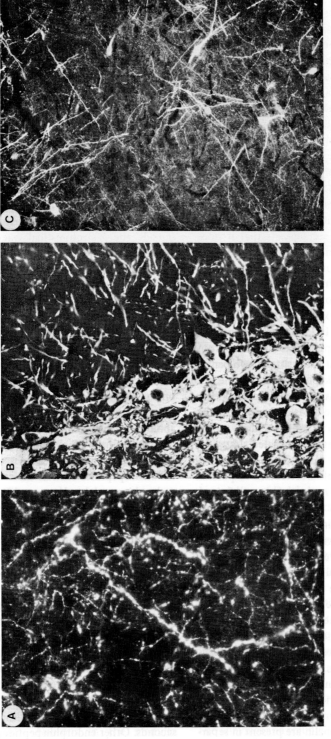

Fig. 8.2 Histochemical demonstration of central monoaminic neurons. (A) Network of catecholamine-containing nerve terminals in the pre-pyriform cortex of the rat. (B) Immunohistochemical visualisation of monoaminic neurons in the substantia nigra of the rat. (C) Dopaminergic neurons in the hypothalamus of the rat. (From Hökfelt *et al.*, *Med. Biol.*, 54, 1976 and 55, 1977.)

cell bodies along the axons by intracellular transport systems. To meet the demand during activity, an ample reserve of the transmitter must be maintained in the terminals, since the axoplasmic flow is too slow to keep up with the events which may take place in fractions of a second. Immediate replacement of the transmitter released during activity seems to occur in the terminals. However, the long-term supply of precursor material must occur by transport from the cell body. In order that the demands of the terminals should be met, there must be a two-way system by which the needs of the terminals are communicated to the cell. Studies of the axoplasmic flow indicate that a feedback system exists by which the cell body is informed about the actual demands of the terminals. The emptying of the vesicles containing the transmitter is supposed to occur by a fusion of the vesicular membrane with the plasma membrane. At the site of fusion, both membranes rupture, and the contents of the vesicles are extruded into the synaptic cleft. It has been suggested that extrusion (exocytosis) occurs by active contraction of microfilaments in the cytoplasm (see p. 23). The following step involves the vesicles being pinched off from the membrane and incorporated into the cytoplasm (Fig. 8.4). This process is called endocytosis.

Although this is the generally accepted concept of transmitter release, other mechanisms cannot be excluded. For instance, the apparent emptying of the vesicles might actually represent a pinocytotic uptake of material from the extracellular space. If so, the transmitter may come from the cytoplasmic pool rather than from the vesicles. Indeed, under some experimental conditions, transmission may occur in the absence of vesicles. All the same, there are strong reasons to believe that under physiological conditions transmission involves transmitter release by vesicular emptying.

To ensure a rapid reactivation of the synapse, the transmitter released must be removed rapidly. At the neuromuscular junctions, this occurs by enzymatic breakdown of the transmitter. In many other synapses, inactivation appears to be mediated by an uptake of the transmitter by the presynaptic

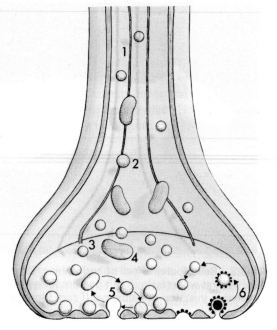

Fig. 8.4 Hypothetical mechanisms of vesicle formation: 1, microtubule; 2, transport of vesicles formed in the cell body; 3, formation from microtubules; 4, mitochondrion; 5, formation by endocytosis; 6, formation from dense core vesicles after release of their content. (Modified from Pfenninger, *Progr. Histochem. Cytochem.*, 5, 1973.)

terminals and by the glial cells which surround the synapse.

Neuro-'modulators'

There is evidence that the vesicles contain not only the transmitter substance but also substances which modulate the action of the transmitter on the postsynaptic membrane. It has been found that adenine nucleotides are released in some synaptic systems together with the specific transmitter substances. As already indicated, the non-transmitter substances may have long-term modulatory effects on neuronal activity.

It is known from studies of the action of hormones on their target cells that, when certain hormones bind to the cell membrane, catalytic subunits located at the inner surface of the membrane induce an increased production of cyclic AMP in the cell. Cyclic AMP has consequently been considered as a 'second messenger' that translates the extracellular message into an intracellular response. Furthermore, there is growing evidence that cyclic AMP is also involved in synaptic transmission. Preganglionic stimulation of sympathetic nerves seems to increase the content of cyclic AMP in the postsynaptic ganglion cells. Cyclic AMP induces a hyperpolarisation of cells in several regions of the brain; surprisingly, this effect is not associated with an increased membrane conductance but with a decrease in conductance to sodium and calcium.

In contrast to the membrane permeability changes induced by the direct action of a transmitter, the effects mediated by cyclic AMP are relatively long-lasting. Since the effects caused by the increased synthesis of cyclic AMP develop slowly, this mechanism probably does not operate in synapses where rapid transmission and recovery are important. Experimental data suggest that cyclic AMP is involved in the transmitter action of dopamine, noradrenalin and serotonin. Work in this field is still in its infancy and the extent to which cyclic AMP is involved in synaptic transmission in different synaptic systems remains an open question.

Curtis, D. R., Duggan, A. W., Felix, D. and Johnston, G. A. R. (1970). GABA, bicuculline and central inhibition, *Nature*, **226**, 1222–1224

Curtis, D. R. and Eccles, R. M. (1958). The excitation of Renshaw cells by pharmacological agents applied electrophoretically, *J. Physiol. (Lond.)*, **141**, 435–445

Curtis, D. R. and Eccles, J. C. (1959). The time courses of excitatory and inhibitory synaptic actions, *J. Physiol. (Lond.)*, **145**, 520–546

Curtis, D. R. and Eccles, J. C. (1960). Synaptic action during and after repetitive stimulation, *J. Physiol. (Lond.)*, **150**, 374–398

Curtis, D. R., Lodge, D. and Brand, S. J. (1977). GABA and spinal afferent terminal excitability in the cat, *Brain Res.*, **130**, 360–363

Curtis, D. R. and Ryall, R. W. (1966). The synaptic excitations of Renshaw cells, *Exp. Brain Res.*, **2**, 81–96

Dale, H. H. (1935). Pharmacology and nerve-endings, *Proc. R. Soc. B*, **28**, 319–322

Eccles, J. C. (1949). A review and restatement of the electrical hypothesis of synaptic excitatory and inhibitory action, *Arch. Sci. Physiol.*, **3**, 567–584

Eccles, J. C., Eccles, R. M. and Lundberg, A. (1957). Synaptic actions on motoneurones in relation to the two components of the group I muscle afferent volley, *J. Physiol. (Lond.)*, **136**, 527–546

Eccles, J. C., Eccles, R. M. and Magni, F. (1961). Central inhibitory action attributable to presynaptic depolarization produced by muscle afferent volleys, *J. Physiol. (Lond.)*, **159**, 147–166

Eccles, J. C., Schmidt, R. F. and Willis, W. D. (1963). Pharmacological studies on presynaptic inhibition, *J. Physiol. (Lond.)*, **168**, 500–530

Eccles, J. C., Schmidt, R. F. and Willis, W. D. (1963). The mode of operation of the synaptic mechanism producing presynaptic inhibition, *J. Neurophysiol.*, **26**, 523–536

Eccles, R. M., Shealy, C. N. and Willis, W. D. (1963). Patterns of innervation of kitten motoneurones, *J. Physiol. (Lond.)*, **165**, 392–402

Henneman, E., Somjen, G. and Carpenter, D. O. (1965). Functional significance of cell size in spinal motoneurons, *J. Neurophysiol.*, **28**, 560–580

Henneman, E., Somjen, G., and Carpenter, D. O. (1965). Excitability and inhibitibility of motoneurons of different sizes, *J. Neurophysiol.*, **28**, 599–620

Hökfelt, T. (1967). On the ultrastructural localization of noradrenaline in the central nervous system of the rat, *Z. Zellforsch.*, **79**, 110–117

Hökfelt, T., Johansson, O., Fuxe, K., Goldstein, M. and Park, D. (1976). Immunohistochemical studies on the localization and distribution of monoamine neuron systems in the rat brain. I. Tyrosine hydroxylase in the mes- and diencephalon, *Med. Biol.*, **54**, 427–453

Jankowska, E. and Roberts, W. J. (1972). Synaptic actions of single interneurons mediating reciprocal Ia inhibition of motoneurons, *J. Physiol. (Lond.)*, **222**, 623–642

Kravitz, E. A. (1967). Acetylcholine, γ-aminobutyric acid and glutamic acid: physiological and chemical studies related to their roles as neurotransmitter agents, in *The Neurosciences. A Third Study Program*, eds G. C. Quarton, T. Melnechuk and F. O. Schmitt, Rockefeller University Press, New York, pp. 433–444

Otsuka, M. and Konishi, S. (1976). Substance P and excitatory transmitter of primary sensory neurons, *Cold Spring Harbour Symp. Quant. Biol.*, **40**, 135–144

Section VI: The Cerebral Cortex: Development, Structure and General Functions

9

Historical Survey

That the brain is the highest organ of the body seems so obvious today that it would appear that this has always been known. However, throughout antiquity and to some extent up to the end of the eighteenth century, all higher functions were thought to have their centres in the heart. This concept also had currency among the Greeks. Aristotle, for instance, maintained vigorously that the heart is the body's main organ and the centre of thoughts and feelings, contending that sensations are transmitted via the blood vessels to the heart. According to Aristotle, the function of the brain was merely to cool the blood from the heart. But rival theories were emerging at this time. In a book probably written by a pupil of Socrates, we find the following statement: 'We know that pleasure, happiness, laughter and pain, as well as fear, sorrow and dissatisfaction are present only in the brain. It is only with the brain that we think, understand, see and hear, and that we can distinguish the plain from the beautiful, the pleasant from the unpleasant. For this reason I consider the brain the most important organ in the human body, for when it is healthy it is the interpreter that helps us to understand our sensations ...'. Plato's writings contain similar ideas: according to him, higher intellectual functions have their seat in the brain, while passion comes from the spinal cord, beneath the diaphragm.

We must bear in mind that anatomical dissection was as yet unknown and knowledge of body organs consequently scanty; Aristotle based his theory on observations of animals. The first dissections of human bodies were carried out about 300 BC by Erasistratos and Herophilos at the famous medical school in Alexandria. Erasistratos maintained that the brain is the seat of the soul and the centre of all higher intellectual functions. Among those who shared this idea was Galen. Originally a physician to the gladiators in Pergamon, Galen moved to Rome and became the Emperor's physician. He was probably one of the first to perform neurophysiological experiments, showing among other things that pressure applied to the brain renders an animal motionless, whereas pressure on the heart has no such effect. Galen in his writings attacked Aristotle, and held the brain to be the seat of intelligence, movement and sensation. In spite of this and in spite of the strong influence of Galen's view on scientific thoughts, the notion of the heart as the centre of higher functions persisted; it could still be found in medical textbooks into the seventeenth century.

After Galen there was little significant progress in medicine until the sixteenth century. During the Middle Ages it was thought that knowledge of body functions was best achieved by rational discourse. It was in the Arabic world that the ideas of the Greek and Alexandrian medical schools survived. A pillar of the Arabic school was Avicenna, who early in the eleventh century assembled the medical knowledge of the time in one massive work, which influenced medical concepts throughout the Orient for centuries.

At the beginning of the fourteenth century, several medical schools in Italy and France began studying the human body through the dissection of cadavers. Mondino's textbook, *Anatomia*, a landmark in medical history, dates from this period. In 1543 Vesalius's great work, *De humani corporis fabrica*, was published and a century later came Willis's work, *Cerebri anatome*, which contains one of the first detailed anatomical descriptions of the brain. However, more than two hundred years would pass before the fine structure of the brain was disclosed.

In the seventeenth century, Malpighi examined the brain using the primitive microscope then available. He is often credited with the discovery of the cells in the cerebral cortex, although he described the structures he saw as miniature glands.

The first histological studies of the cerebral cortical cells were not made until the middle of the nineteenth century. After that, progress became rapid with the development of new staining and fixation techniques. In 1875, Golgi's discovery of the silver impregnation method, now bearing his name, opened hitherto unsuspected possibilities for precise analysis of the structure of the brain. It now became possible to stain cells and nerve fibres so that they were distinctly outlined against background tissues (Fig. 9.1). New structures came to light and the pathways of the brain and the spinal cord were mapped out. In his studies, Golgi (Fig. 9.2) reached the conclusion that all nerve cells were

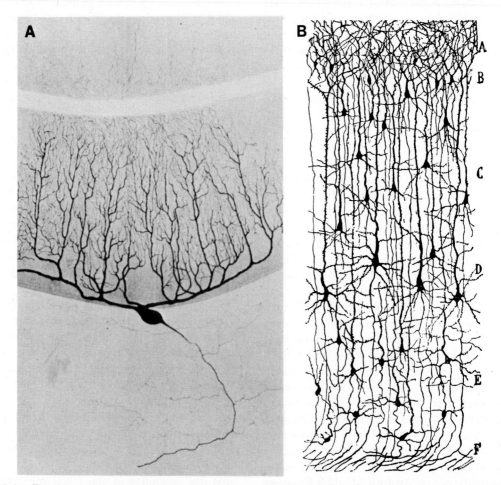

Fig. 9.1 Examples of the important contributions to the knowledge of the structure of nerve cells and their processes obtained with the silver-staining method. (A) Human Purkinje cell; (B) visual cortex of newborn rat. ((A) From Golgi, 1883; (B) from Cajal, 1911.)

Camillo Golgi

Fig. 9.2 Camillo Golgi (1843–1926), Italian histologist and Nobel Laureate, discoverer of the silver nitrate method for staining of nerve cells and fibres, a method that gave the key to the finer structure of the nervous system.

Fig. 9.3 Santiago Ramón y Cajal (1852–1934), Spanish histologist, whose acuity of observations and extensive investigations represent a landmark in research on the structure of the nervous system. One of his fundamental achievements was the demonstration that neurons were independent units that do not anastomose. By this he refuted Golgi's nerve net theory and replaced it with the doctrine of the neuron. In 1906, Cajal shared the Nobel Prize with his opponent, Golgi.

in direct continuity with one another. But Cajal (Fig. 9.3), in emphatic contradiction, maintained that each neuron was a separate anatomical entity. The ensuing combat was intense and lasted into the twentieth century; ultimately the verdict went to Cajal.

Interest in the localisation of higher functions in the brain was focused for a long time on the site of the soul. One of those intrigued by this problem was Descartes, who maintained that the soul resides in the pineal gland, the *corpus pineale*. Descartes assumed that sensory messages are transmitted to the pineal gland and hence passed to the muscles (Fig. 9.4); we may discern here the earliest outline of the concept of reflex. At about the same time an English anatomist, Willis, suggested that it is the cerebellum that controls movements in the heart and lungs, whereas the cerebrum controls voluntary movements and is the centre of memory.

Among the many scientists interested in the functional anatomy of the brain was the Swedish philosopher, Swedenborg. His magnum opus, *De cerebro*, finished in 1745, was not printed during his lifetime and was largely unknown until 1882, when published in an English translation. It is the brain, he wrote, that 'understands, coordinates, decides, has will-power, wishes, dreams, desires, sees, hears, discerns, senses, tastes and smells, speaks and acts'. He thought that higher intellectual functions were located in the frontal regions of the brain. In his own words: 'If the front region of the

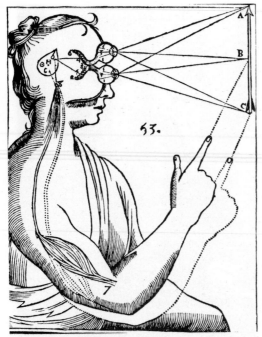

Fig. 9.4   Descartes' drawing illustrating his concept of reflex action. The retina is connected to the walls of the ventricle by the optic nerves, which Descartes thought were hollow tubes through which the animal spirit carried the message to the pineal body and the ventricles. From here, the animal spirit reached the muscle which it inflated and thereby produced motion. (From Descartes, *De Homine*, 1662.)

brain is wounded, the higher functions will suffer, the ability to imagine, remember and think, the will-power will diminish and the ability to decide will be weakened'.

Swedenborg thought that the cortex also controls movements and he referred to the cortex as the '*motorium commune voluntarium*'. He considered the region in front of the central fissure to be the centre for the control of movements. Swedenborg also saw the significance of reflex movements, realising that even though the brain controls the muscles, movements not elicited from the cortex can still occur. According to him, there are subordinate centres in the spinal cord, which participate in automatic and involuntary movements. In this, Swedenborg long anticipated the discussion in

recent years regarding the roles of the cortex and the spinal cord in the control of movement.

From the late eighteenth to the mid-nineteenth century, the concept of the localisation of higher functions in the brain was dominated by the ideas of Gall, which came to be known as phrenology. Gall maintained that the brain is composed of discrete organs or regions which represent different faculties or powers of the mind and that there are as many such organs as there are mental faculties (Fig. 9.5). Moreover, he suggested that the development of the cerebral cortex is associated with corresponding prominences of the skull. By measuring the dimensions of the skull it was possible, according to Gall, to disclose a person's intellectual abilities and inclinations (Fig. 9.6). Gall's doctrine was strongly contested by the French physiologist, Flourens, who maintained that higher brain functions were dependent upon the functions of the whole brain rather than being represented in discrete parts of the brain.

Gall's ideas stimulated clinical studies on the relations between lesions of the brain and the ensuing mental disorders. In 1861 Broca examined the brain of a person who earlier in life had lost the power of speech and found a lesion in the pos-

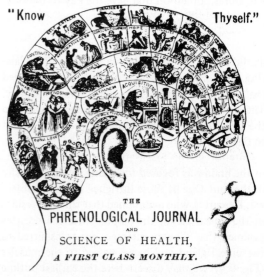

Fig. 9.5   Phrenological chart showing the localisations of various moral and intellectual qualities.

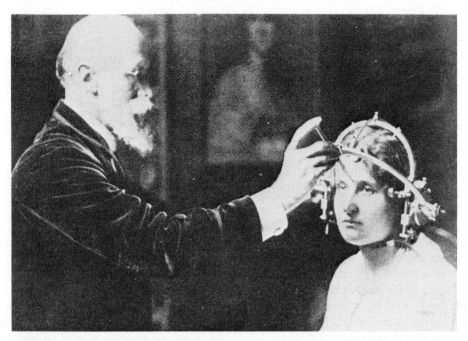

Fig. 9.6   Measurements of intellectual capacities according to the concept of phrenology introduced by Gall. (From Bilderdienst Süddeutscher Verlag.)

terior part of the left frontal lobe. Broca was very cautious in interpreting this finding and it was not until after having studied eight similar cases that he made his famous statement: 'We speak with the left hemisphere'. Shortly after Broca's first report, Wernicke demonstrated a case in which a lesion in the left temporal lobe was associated with a reduced ability in the comprehension of speech. Broca's and Wernicke's findings stimulated the search for other centres for mental functions, and in the following years numerous reports were published of discoveries of 'centres' for various mental functions. Many of these reports were highly speculative and the cortical maps which appeared in the literature at this time are somewhat reminiscent of the phrenological maps. It was not until the development of improved neuroanatomical methods for staining of the nerve cells of the brain and the discovery that the cortex could be divided into areas of different cytoarchitecture that the general principles of the functional organisation of the brain were disclosed.

10

Development of the Brain

The nervous system develops from primitive cells, the neuroblasts. When a neuroblast matures and forms a nerve cell, it loses its ability to divide again. The transition from neuroblast to neuron occurs during foetal life. The total number of nerve cells in the central nervous system is fixed at this stage, since mature neurons generally cannot divide nor can injured cells be replaced.

The growth and maturation of the various parts of the brain do not occur uniformly. Different parts of the central nervous system grow at different rates. In general, the spinal cord and the midbrain develop earliest, during the foetal stage, followed by the medulla, pons, hypothalamus and finally the cerebral hemispheres. The attendant increase in the brain's volume or weight indicates its development only roughly, as we shall see below. As late as the third foetal month, the brain surface is still completely smooth, and not until the fifth or sixth month are the convolutions distinct (Fig. 10.1). Their development proceeds rapidly thereafter but is not complete until well after birth.

Since the number of nerve cells is set early in foetal life, the later rapid growth of the brain is due mainly to maturation. This consists primarily of the outgrowth of dendrites and axons (Fig. 10.2) from the nerve cells and the formation of synaptic contacts. The maturation of the cells includes myelination as well as the appearance of cytoplasmic organelles, particularly Nissl granules and neurofibrils. In addition non-neuronal elements, the glial cells, grow to occupy a considerable portion of the brain.

That the maturation of the spinal cord precedes that of the brain is evident from the fact that, early in development, the motoneurons in the spinal cord already contain Nissl granules and neurofibrils. At this time the general structure of the cortex is clearly laid out, and the cells are grouped into the characteristic six layers, but their relative immaturity is indicated by the scarcity of Nissl substance and neurofibrils. Because the development of cortical cells lags behind that of spinal cord cells at birth, activity in the newborn has been thought to be mainly controlled by the spinal cord and perhaps the lower parts of the brain stem. Within the cortex, the precentral area develops first; again, maturation is not uniform. The motor areas for the arm and shoulder lead, and the sensory areas follow closely after the motor regions. The visual cortex matures before birth, but the visual association areas develop somewhat later, which may imply that a child can see at birth, but not derive meaning from what is seen. The auditory centres develop along with or slightly after the visual centres.

The first year after birth is marked by relatively rapid cortical growth (see Fig. 10.3). It is in particular the fifth cell layer with the large pyramidal cells that develops through the outgrowth of dendrites and nerve fibres which descend to the spinal cord. Between the third and sixth months of life, a rapid outgrowth of dendrites occurs in all parts of the cortex, and the synaptic connections between different systems are established.

As mentioned above, the motor system develops faster than other parts of the brain at first but this

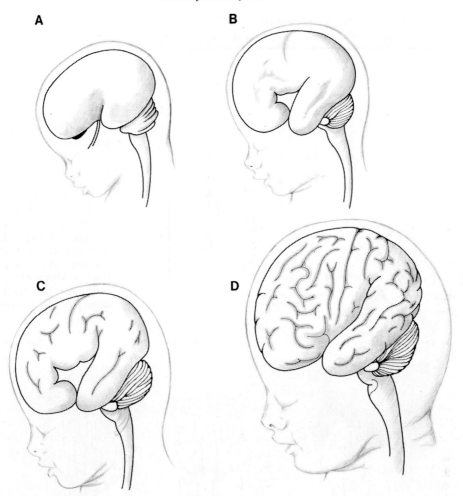

Fig. 10.1 Development of the human brain: (A) 4 month foetus; (B) 6 month foetus; (C) 8 month foetus; (D) newborn infant.

gradually evens out, until by an age of eight years the degree of maturation is relatively equal in all parts of the brain. This does not imply that the brain is now fully mature. During the following years, the myelination of nerve fibres continues; most parts of the motor and sensory systems do not complete this process until puberty. Within other areas, including association areas and the reticular system, myelination continues to some degree until about age 20 or even later. Late myelination also occurs in the frontal lobe. The late progressive functional maturation of the frontal lobe presumably underlies intellectual development, although no direct evidence correlates

myelination with the increase in functional capacity. The increase in number of synaptic contacts between neurons may be more important functionally.

At birth, the brain has reached 25% of its final weight. Its growth during the first weeks of life outstrips that of other organs, and at six months the brain is half its final weight. By age 10 the brain weighs about 95% of its eventual weight. The remaining increase occurs slowly up to 20–30 years of age, when the weight becomes relatively constant, until in old age a gradual reduction sets in (Fig. 10.4).

It is a characteristic feature of the brain that in

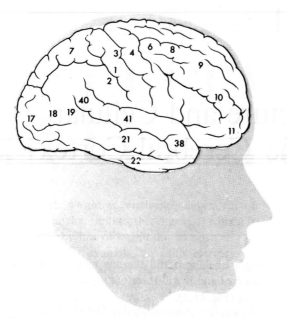

Fig. 11.2 Localisation of some of the principal areas of the cortex according to the chart introduced by Brodmann.

represent the phylogenetically older part of the cortex and are usually referred to as the *rhinencephalon* (see p. 287).

According to their specific input–output characteristics, the different areas of the cerebral cortex can be grouped into three types: motor, sensory and association. It should be realised, however, that this division is not always so distinct as was at first anticipated. Thus the precentral gyrus is by no means a purely motor area nor is the postcentral gyrus purely sensory. It is therefore more appropriate to talk about these areas as being motosensory or sensorimotor. The finding that motor areas receive afferent inputs and that sensory areas have motor functions has prompted a revision of the earlier terminology for cortical areas. For instance, the precentral gyrus which is predominantly a motor area is at present generally termed MsI and the postcentral gyrus which is predominantly sensory is termed SmI. It should be noted, however, that large regions of the cerebral cortex are neither sensory nor motor areas. These are the associational or 'silent' areas which are most likely concerned with the interpretation and analysis of sensory information.

It has been estimated that the total number of cortical nerve cells is in the range of 14 000 million. The great majority of these cells may be divided into two groups, pyramidal cells and stellate or granule cells (Fig. 11.4). The pyramidal cells, which are the most typical of the cerebral cortex, vary in size from small cells to the giant cells of Betz. They have as their name indicates the form of a triangle whose upper end points towards the surface of the cortex. From this part of the cell, a thick *apical* dendrite ascends towards the overlying outer cortical layers. The basal corners of the cell body give off *basal dendrites* which arborise in the vicinity of the cell. The dendrites carry a large number of protrusions, so-called 'spines', which are the sites of axodendritic synapses (Fig. 11.5). The richness of synaptic connections is apparent considering that a single neuron in the motor cortex may be connected to about 600 other cells. In the striate area the interconnections are even more numerous; here a single neuron may connect with 2000–4000 other neurons. The majority of axons of the large pyramidal cells pass out of the cortex to subcortical nuclei and to the spinal cord whereas the axons of the small cells usually remain within the cortex, some passing towards superficial cortical layers. The second main type of cell, the stellate cell, which is often referred to as the granule cell, is small and has a number of dendrites passing in all directions. Its axon is usually short and ramifies in the near vicinity of the cell body. However, some cells have long axons which pass in a vertical direction in the cortex. In addition to pyramidal and stellate cells, there are many other forms of nerve cell with varying structural features.

Neurophysiological studies have provided evidence showing that the cortical neurons are arranged in vertical columns. In the somatosensory cortex, all of the neurons in a particular column are activated by the same kind of peripheral stimulus and all have the same, or nearly the same, peripheral receptor field (see p. 257). Similar functional columns have been demonstrated in the visual and acoustic areas in the cerebral cortex. It may be concluded that a column of cells represents an

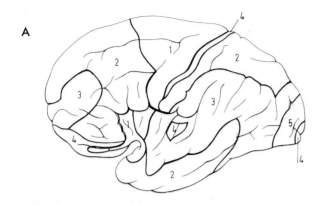

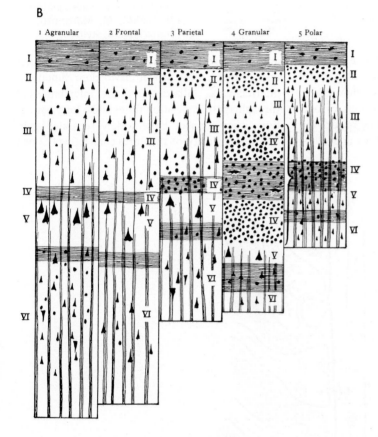

Fig. 11.3 The five major types of cortical cytoarchitecture and their distribution in the cerebral cortex. (From *Gray's Anatomy*, Longman, London, 1973.)

elementary functional unit of the cortex. The cells of a column within a predominantly sensory region all receive similar inputs concerned with the same sense. The activity within such a column may excite or inhibit the neurons of adjacent columns by horizontal short neuronal links represented primarily by the axons of the stellate cells. Similarly the neurons in a predominantly motor column all affect the same group of muscles and adjacent columns interact in a corresponding way (see p. 232).

In addition to the short horizontal links between columns, there are also fibre systems which connect

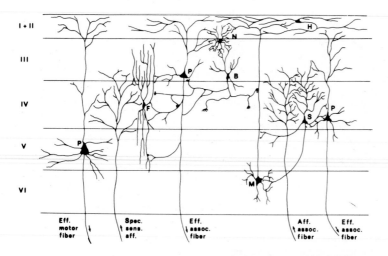

I + II

III

IV

V

VI

Eff. motor fiber   Spec. sens. aff.   Eff. assoc. fiber   Aff. assoc. fiber   Eff. assoc. fiber

Fig. 11.4 Diagrammatic representation of typical features of various types of cortical neurons: P, pyramidal; F, fusiform; N, neurogliaform; B, basket; M, Martinotti; H, horizontal; S, stellate.

different cortical areas. (Fig. 11.6). Some of these, so-called *association fibres*, interconnect cortical regions of the same side of the cortex, while others (*commissural fibres*) interconnect regions of one side of the cortex with corresponding regions on the other side. Both association fibres and com-

missural fibres are arranged in an orderly manner and connect areas which have close functional interrelations. Adjacent gyri are interconnected through short association fibres while long association fibres connect more widely separated gyri. The vast majority of the fibres connecting the two

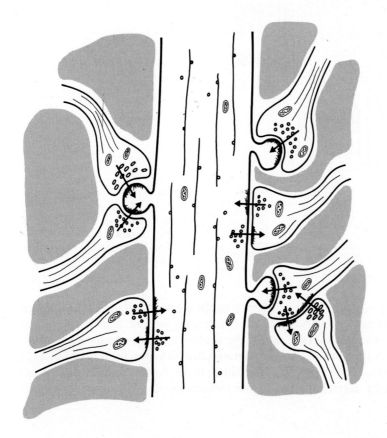

Fig. 11.5 Synaptic arrangement of excitatory and inhibitory endings around the spines of a dendrite of a pyramidal cell. Glial cells (shaded) surround the whole synaptic complex.

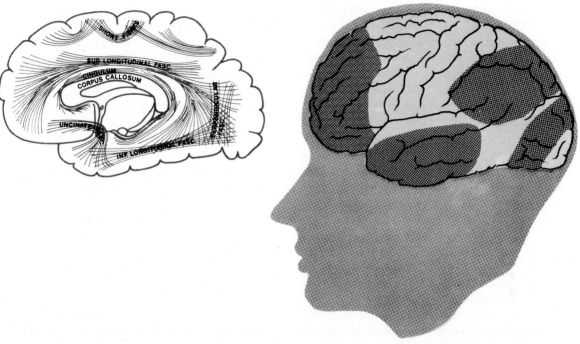

Fig. 11.6   The principal association connections of the cerebral cortex and the corresponding cortical areas.

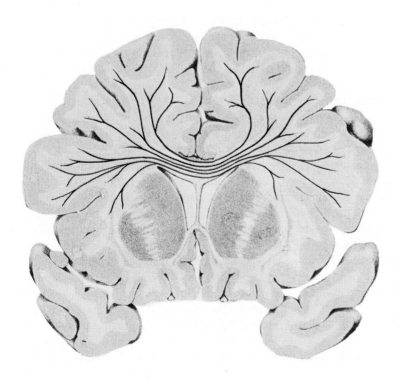

Fig. 11.7   Schematic drawing of frontal section of the brain to illustrate the distribution of the fibres of the corpus callosum.

hemispheres pass in the *corpus callosum* (Fig. 11.7). The wealth of interconnections provided by the corpus callosum is enormous. It has been estimated that there are about 700 000 fibres per square millimetre of a transverse section of the corpus callosum. The connections are highly specific in the sense that fibres from one area pass to the same area on the opposite side. It is thus obvious that through commissural linkages cortical regions on one side receive information about what is going on in the corresponding regions on the other side. It should be noted that some regions, such as the striate area and the hand area of the somatosensory cortex, do not receive commissural fibres. It is probable that these areas receive information through adjacent cortical regions. In view of the intimate linkage between the two hemispheres provided by the finer system of the corpus callosum, it would be expected that profound deficits should result by interruption of these connections. However, it appears that the effects can only be demonstrated by careful testing, as will be discussed later (see p. 320).

The neuroglia

Of the total volume of the brain, more than half is occupied by glial tissue. The neuroglia have long been assumed to serve as a sort of supporting tissue for the nerve cells, since practically all nerve cells in the central nervous system appear to be embedded in glial cells. Anatomically, the cells that constitute glial tissues are of two types (Fig. 11.8): astrocytes and oligodendroglia. The latter are situated mainly in the white substance and are responsible for the formation of myelin around the nerve fibre, in the same way that the cell of Schwann is responsible for myelin formation around peripheral nerves. Astrocytes, which appear within both white and grey matter, comprise two types; both are characterised by so-called end feet contacts with blood vessels and nerve cells in their vicinity. Glial cells, unlike nerve cells, are able to regenerate; after injury to the central nervous system, the glial cells replace the damaged nerve cells.

That little is known about the function of glial cells becomes all the more surprising when we consider what a significant proportion of the brain

they occupy. Their lack of axons indicates that they do not participate directly in signal transmission. In vertebrates and invertebrates, glial cells are electrically passive, i.e. they do not generate action potentials. Instead they may have some metabolic function, possibly serving to transport substances between blood vessels and nerve cells. It has been observed in tissue cultures that glial cells exhibit rhythmic movements, which suggests their participation in some pumping mechanism conveying substances to and from the nerve cells. Another hypothesis, presented originally by Cajal, is that the glia serve to insulate the nerve cells electrically from one another. A later modification of this hypothesis is that they form barriers for the spread of transmitter substances released at the synapses.

Important evidence bearing on the significance of glial cells for the function of nerve cells has been provided by electron microscope studies. It has been found that glial cells and nerve cells are tightly intermingled, separated by a cleft of only 100–200 nm. The extracellular space around the nerve cells is thus considerably less than was earlier believed.

The difficulty in identifying and isolating glial cells has been a major obstacle to the study of their function. During recent years, however, electrophysiological studies of special tissues have clarified several points. Intracellular recordings have disclosed that the glial cells have a negative resting potential determined by the concentration gradient for potassium. Electrical stimulation does not evoke impulse generation; moreover, the glial cells do not seem to be necessary for impulse generation in nerve cells, since the latter still respond after the glial cells have been dissected away. The glial cells lie tightly against the nerve cells, in certain cases completely surrounding them, but there are no conventional synaptic contacts between neurons and glial cells. In contrast glial cells are linked to each other by gap junctions. Ions may pass from one glial cell to another without passing through the extracellular space. The gap junctions thus provide for low-resistance coupling between the glial cells. The extracellular space around the nerve cells would appear insufficient for the passage of ions in impulse activity. Studies of the glial cells of the leech indicate, however,

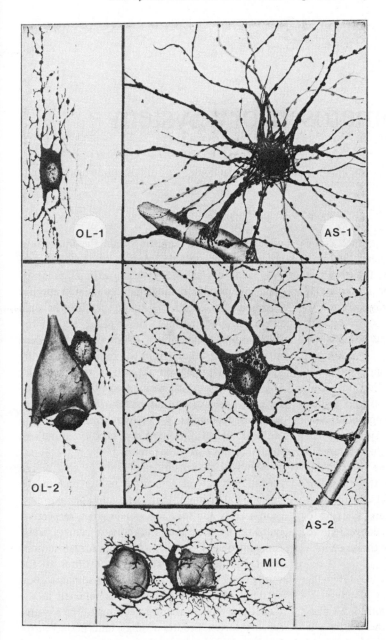

Fig. 11.8 Different types of neuroglia cells: AS-1, fibrous astrocyte with two footplates in contact with a blood vessel; AS-2, protoplasmic astrocyte with one footplate in contact with a blood vessel; MIC, microglia cell whose processes embrace the cell bodies of two neurons; OL-1, 2, oligodendrocytes. (From Penfield, in *Cytology and Cellular Pathology of the Nervous System*, vol. II, ed. W. G. Penfield, Hoeber, New York, 1932.)

that the intercellular system of channels between the glial cells is quite adequate for ion diffusion. During impulse activity in a nerve cell, the extracellular current flows through this intercellular system; little or none passes through the glial cells, yet they are not completely uninfluenced. Repetitive stimulation of the optic nerve of the frog causes slow potential changes in the glial cells, probably due to extracellular accumulation of potassium ions. It thus appears that neuronal activity leads to diffuse depolarisation of glial cells. This potassium-mediated spread of activity is nonspecific and not linked to the presence of synapses. Excitatory and inhibitory neuronal activity has the same effect on the glial cells. The depolarisation of the glial cells might somehow contribute to the generation of slow electrical potentials in the brain (the EEG).

12

The Somatosensory System

Sensory information from body tissues such as the skin, muscles, joints and viscera reaches the brain via two distinct routes represented by the *lemniscal system* and the *extralemniscal* or *anterolateral system*. Together these two pathways form the somatosensory afferent system. In some respects the two divisions resemble the pyramidal and the extrapyramidal motor systems.

The lemniscal system is a large-fibre system for fast transmission of precise information from low-threshold receptors in skin, muscles and joints, while the extralemniscal system is a predominantly slow and less precisely organised system which transmits information mainly from high-threshold receptors. The input from both these two systems is relayed to the cortex through the thalamus. For the understanding of the functional contribution of the lemniscal and the anterolateral systems to somatic sensibility, it is therefore convenient to consider first the organisation of the thalamus.

Thalamus

The thalamus is the final relay station for all sensory input to the brain. Therefore the thalamus is often called the gateway to the cerebral cortex. In addition, the thalamus receives a massive input from the neocortex. This feedback is arranged so that a given group of cells in the thalamus gets signals from the same cortical areas to which they project.

Anatomically, the thalamus consists of a complex of nuclei which are separated by laminae of white matter. The laminae divide the nuclei into three main groups; within each of these are subgroups of nuclei. From the functional point of view, it is usual to distinguish between non-specific and specific nuclei. The non-specific thalamic nuclei are located near the midline and in the internal medullary lamina of the thalamus. These nuclei receive inputs from the reticular activating systems and project to all parts of the neocortex (Fig. 12.1). Electrical stimulation of the non-specific nuclei gives rise to responses which spread over wide cortical areas of the two hemispheres. The 'arousal' effect produced by sensory stimuli is mediated through these nuclei.

The specific sensory nuclei are located in the medial and lateral geniculate bodies and in the ventrobasal group of thalamic nuclei. The two first groups relay auditory and visual signals, respectively, to the acoustic and visual cortical centres, while the ventrobasal complex transmits somatosensory input to the cortex. The afferent fibres to the ventrobasal nuclei are grouped in a somatotopical pattern, and this arrangement is retained in the nuclei as well as in their projections to the somatosensory cortex. Studies of single units in the ventrobasal nuclei have shown that most neurons respond only to one particular type of stimulus and only to stimulation within a restricted field on the contralateral side of the body. The receptive fields from the fingers and toes are small while those on the proximal parts of the limbs are large (Fig. 12.2). The small receptor fields on the fingers provide for the high spatial discrimination in these regions.

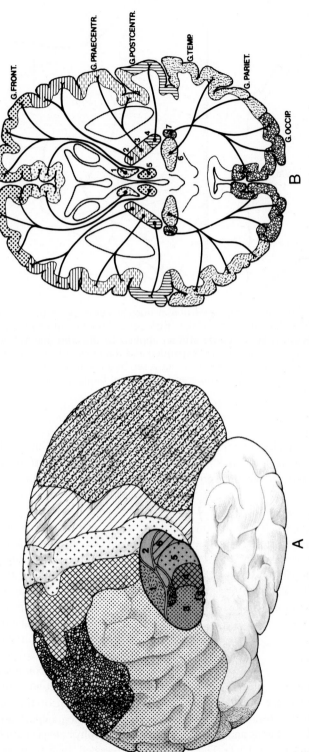

Fig.12.1 The major nuclei of the thalamus and their cortical projections. *Left diagram*: lateral view of left hemisphere. The areas of the cortex interconnected with these nuclei are indicated by coding. 1, dorsomedial nucleus; 2, anterior nuclear group; 3, pulvinar; 4, ventral posteriolateral nucleus; 5, ventral intermediate lateral nucleus; 6, ventral anterior nucleus; 7, lateral dorsal nucleus; 8, geniculate body. *Right diagram*: diagrammatic horizontal section. 1, cingulum; 2, anterior ventral nucleus; 3, lateral ventral nucleus; 4, posterior ventral nucleus; 5, medial nucleus; 6, posterior lateral nucleus and pulvinar; 7, lateral geniculate body.

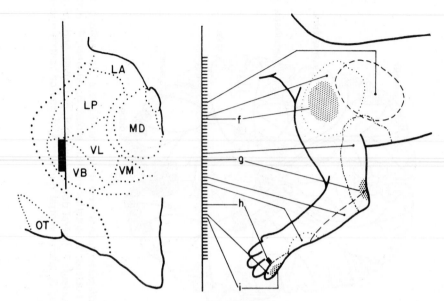

Fig. 12.2   Receptive fields of neurons in the ventrobasal nuclear complex of the thalamus. The diagram to the left shows the microelectrode penetration, the thick part of the line indicating the region in which recordings were made from neurons activated by stimuli applied to the contralateral side of the body. In the diagram to the right, the scale of this region is expanded and the lines indicate the receptive field areas of the neurons observed; f, g, and i represent neurons activated by light touch; h, by rotation of the joint. Note the small size of the peripheral fields as compared to proximal fields. (From Poggio and Mountcastle, *Bull. Johns Hopkins Hosp.*, 106, 1960.)

Stimulation of the ventrobasal nuclei in conscious patients produces sensations of tingling, pricking, or numbness in restricted fields on the opposite side of the body.

Two nuclei located in the ventrobasal part of the thalamus, the anterior and the lateral ventral nuclei (VA and VL), which receive input from the basal ganglia and from the cerebellum, project onto the motor cortex. It is supposed that the main influence of the basal ganglia on motor functions is mediated via this pathway through the thalamus.

The lemniscal system

The lemniscal system is composed of the thick myelinated fibres which enter the spinal cord through the medial portion of the dorsal roots and then ascend in the dorsal white columns and terminate in the dorsal column nuclei (Fig. 12.3). This

is the first relay station in the lemniscal system, the second being the ventrobasal complex of the thalamus. The third final link of this system is the thalámocortical projection to the somaesthetic area of the cerebral cortex.

The salient feature of this system is that it provides for precise information about the quality, site, temporal sequence and duration of a stimulus. The primary afferent fibres are somatotopically arranged in the dorsal columns so that for instance those from the hand are grouped together.

The second link in the ascending lemniscal fibre system is made up of the neurons of the dorsal column nuclei and their axons. The neurons are strictly arranged corresponding to the somatotopical input of dorsal column fibres. There is thus in these nuclei a map of the body surface represented by the topographical arrangement of the neurons. Neurophysiological studies of these neurons have revealed that their receptive fields are

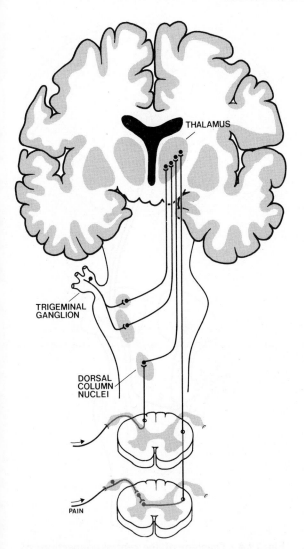

Fig. 12.3 A highly simplified diagram illustrating the course of the ascending sensory tracts in the spinal cord, medulla and midbrain.

The axons of the neurons in the dorsal column nuclei cross the midline and form the medial lemniscal tract that ascends through the brain stem and terminates in the lateral part of the ventrobasal complex of the thalamus (VPL). Recent findings suggest that, contrary to what has been generally assumed, these fibres give off collaterals during their passage through the brain stem. The crossing of the fibres provides the basis for sensory representation of the body in the contralateral side of the cerebral cortex. As in the dorsal column nuclei, the body surface is represented in an orderly topographic manner in the VPL nuclei. All neurons are strictly *modality specific*; that is, a given cell can only be activated by one form of mechanical stimulation involving activation either of superficial skin receptors or deep tissue receptors, such as muscle and joint receptors. The cells are also *place specific* and each neuron responds only to stimulation of a restricted region of the contralateral side of the body. Within a given receptive field the sensitivity is greatest in the centre and decreases towards the periphery of the field. The input of this system conveys information of discriminative tactile sense and kinaesthetic sense for the entire body to the thalamus, except for the head, and from here to the cerebral cortex.

A second component of the lemniscal system is formed by fibres which originate in the main sensory and spinal trigeminal nuclei. These fibres provide the main input to the somatosensory system from the head (see below).

The extralemniscal system

The second major division of the somatic afferent system is the extralemniscal or anterolateral system. It lacks the precise somatotopical organisation of the lemniscal system and serves more general functions. It projects mainly upon the reticular formation and the non-specific thalamocortical system; through these connections it exerts a powerful control of cortical excitability. In addition to these general functions, it conveys information of temperature and pain. The primary afferent fibres of this system are mainly small myelinated and

considerably larger than those of the incoming primary fibres. This shows that there is a high degree of convergence at this level. An implication of this would appear to be a reduced capacity in spatial resolution. It seems, however, that the effect of convergence is counteracted by lateral afferent inhibition (see p. 344) which contributes to spatial discrimination by sharpening of the activity patterns in the nuclei.

unmyelinated axons which upon entering the spinal cord pass to cells in laminae II–III (see p. 154) and probably also to cells in lamina V. It should be noted that many of the secondary cells also receive collaterals from A fibres. The main portion of the ascending system is formed by axons from cells in laminae I, IV and V but there is also a contribution of axons from cells in laminae VII and VIII. Many of the neurons of the extralemniscal system have short axons and form multisynaptic pathways before joining the anterolateral tract. Some of these fibres terminate in the reticular formation; from here the efferent axons of the reticular neurons project upon the non-specific thalamic nuclei. The majority of the cells in these nuclei are activated by various types of strong stimuli that are destructive to the tissue and provoke withdrawal reactions in the awake animal. Their receptor fields are large and usually bilateral. Furthermore, there is no distinct topographical representation of the body surface as in the lemniscal system. It may therefore be concluded that the anterolateral system does not serve tactile discriminative functions. Its main task appears to be to subserve the perception of pain.

The trigeminal system

The sensory input from the head has the same dual characteristics as the general somatosensory system of the other parts of the body. Its primary neurons are located in the Gasserian ganglion. Here the cell bodies are arranged in a topographically orderly fashion. As they enter the brain stem, their axons bifurcate into short ascending and long descending branches. The ascending fibres enter the main sensory nucleus, while the descending fibres, which form the major portion of the descending spinal tract, terminate in the spinal trigeminal nucleus (Fig. 12.4). In addition, this nucleus receives Aδ and C fibres which convey pain and temperature impulses from the face and buccal regions. A salient feature of these fibres is that they do not give off ascending fibres. An important implication of this arrangement is that C fibre pain from these regions of the head is selectively transmitted to the neurons in the spinal trigeminal nucleus.

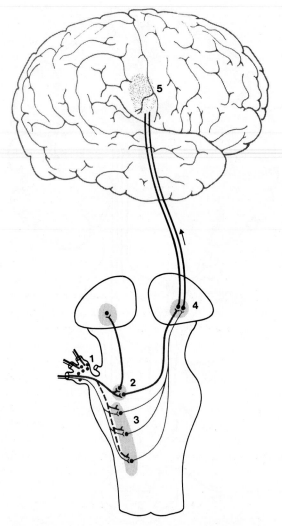

Fig. 12.4   Diagram of the central connections of the trigeminal nerve fibres: 1, trigeminal ganglion; 2, principal sensory nucleus; 3, mesencephalic nucleus; 4, thalamus; 5, somatotopic representation in *gyrus postcentralis*.

The main sensory nucleus is homologous to the dorsal column nuclei, while the nucleus of the spinal tract corresponds to a neuronal complex of the laminae I–V of the dorsal horn. The majority of the axons of the neurons of the main sensory nucleus cross the midline and join the ascending medial lemniscus; some axons which do not cross project to the ipsilateral thalamus. This dual organisation accounts for the bilateral representation of the face at thalamic and cortical levels. Neuroanatomical and clinical data suggest that the main nucleus is concerned mainly in the transmission of tactile sensations from the face region and that the spinal tract nucleus transmits mainly pain and thermal sensation. On the basis of this differentiation, a neurosurgical method, *medullary trigeminal tractotomy*, was introduced by Sjöqvist for the treatment of trigeminal neuralgia. This method involves a transection of the spinal tract at the level of the obex. Following this operation, the patients are usually relieved of their pain while the tactile sensitivity in the face region is on the whole unaffected.

The axons of the neurons in the main nucleus ascend with the medial lemniscus after having crossed the midline and terminate in the VPM nucleus of the thalamus. The fibres of the neurons of the spinal tract join the medial lemniscus after crossing; some of them end in the intralaminar nuclei while others terminate in the reticular formation.

In summary, the somatic afferent system is composed of two major divisions, the lemniscal and the extralemniscal systems. The first of these is largely contralateral; it transmits precise information of the modality, intensity, spatial and temporal characteristics of mechanical stimuli and serves the senses of touch, pressure, vibration and muscle sense. The second division is a fine-fibre system which serves mainly pain and temperature senses. It is bilaterally represented in its cortical projections and is less precisely organised than the lemniscal system. Besides conveying information about thermal and noxious stimuli, it has a powerful influence on the excitability of the cerebral cortex.

Central control of somatosensory input

It is a characteristic feature of all relay stations of the somatosensory system that in addition to the sensory input they also receive fibres from descending supraspinal systems. Studies of the organisation of these systems have encountered considerable experimental difficulties, and knowledge about their functions therefore has lagged greatly behind that of the afferent somaesthetic systems. The recent discovery of the powerful action that some of these systems exert on the input of pain impulses has, however, directed attention to their important role in the control of afferent transmission in somaesthetic pathways.

The afferent input of the lemniscal system is controlled by a massive projection of corticofugal fibres upon the dorsal column nuclei. These fibres arise in the postcentral gyrus and the system is topographically arranged so that, for instance, fibres from the cortical hand area project upon dorsal column neurons receiving afferent input from the hand. This descending system also projects upon the neurons of the ventrobasal complex of the thalamus. Thus there are two control stations in the lemniscal pathways, one at the level of the dorsal column nuclei and another at the thalamic level.

The afferent input through the anterolateral system is under the control of a corticofugal system originating mainly in the postcentral gyrus but also in other cortical areas. The fibres of this system descend in the pyramidal tract and project upon dorsal horn cells (see p. 162). Electrophysiological studies have demonstrated that the predominant effect of the corticofugal system is inhibition. However, recent observations showing that cortical stimulation may have an excitatory effect on some cells in the dorsal column nuclei indicate that the descending system has a dual function.

The somatosensory representation in the cortex

Extensive studies on monkeys have demonstrated that the primary cortical centre for skin and muscle sense, the first somatosensory area (SmI), occupies the postcentral gyrus corresponding to Brodmann's areas 3, 1 and 2. The afferent input to this area comes from the ventral posterior nuclei (VPL and VPM) in the thalamus. The incoming fibres are arranged in a distinct somatotopical pattern such that the body is represented upside down, with the leg in the upper part of the postcentral gyrus and the head in the lower region (Fig. 12.5). The sizes of the areas for different parts of the body vary in relation to the functional significance of the sensory input from each region. The somatotopical map

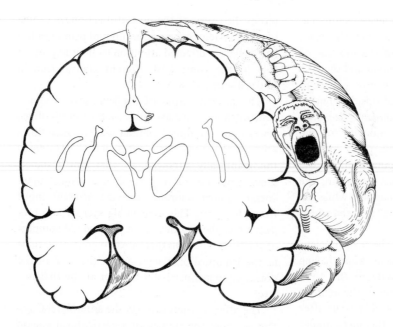

Fig. 12.5   The sensory homunculus showing proportional somatotopic representation in the somaesthetic cortex. (After Penfield and Rasmussen, *The Cerebral Cortex of Man*, 1950.)

therefore differs considerably from one animal species to another. Within the postcentral gyrus there is a cytoarchitectonic differentiation which was first described by Brodmann, who divided this gyrus lengthwise into three areas (3, 1 and 2). Each of these zones receives its afferent input from a specific part of the VPL nucleus in the thalamus. This anatomical arrangement suggests that there might be a corresponding functional differentiation, an idea borne out by the finding that area 2 receives inputs mainly from joint receptors and muscle receptors, while area 3 receives inputs mainly from skin receptors. Area 1 has no such clear distinction. The dermatomes (see p. 157) of the body are represented by zones which run transversely across the three areas.

The first attempts to map out the human cortex were made in the early 1930s by electrical stimulation of the brain in awake patients during brain surgery; since brain tissue is devoid of pain receptors, this does not cause discomfort. It was found that electrical stimulation of the postcentral gyrus evoked sensations which the patients identified as coming from the opposite side of the body. The sensations generally had an unfamiliar quality and the patients had difficulties in describing them. Usually they were perceived as tingling, vibration,

numbness, or a sense of movement. With weak stimulation the sensation was sharply localised, particularly if it was in the face or the hand area. Characteristically, those parts of the body which have a relatively high density of somatic receptors, such as the fingers, the lips and the tongue, were found to occupy larger gyrus areas than other parts of the body (Fig. 12.5). In general the sensations evoked were referred to the contralateral side of the body. However, stimulation of the cortical areas for the face and particularly the oral region produced bilateral sensations; this was also the case for the genital organs, the larynx and the rectum.

Single-cell recordings in monkeys have disclosed that each cell in the somatosensory cortex receives impulses from a given limited skin area, which represents the receptive field of the cell. The size of this field varies; it is usually larger for those parts of the skin that are sparsely innervated. For most cells the receptive field is situated on the opposite side of the body, but some have fields on the same side. Cells activated by the same type of stimulus are organised in vertical columns (Fig. 12.6) and all cells within a given column have receptive fields which lie close together. Columns with cells representing different modalities are clearly distinct

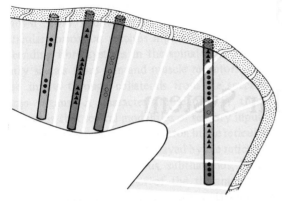

Fig. 12.6   Schematic representation of the columnar organisation of the somatosensory area in the postcentral gyrus of the macaque. The elementary functional unit of the cortex is a vertically oriented column of cells. The neurons encountered in microelectrode penetrations normal to the cortical surface are all of the same modality. When the microelectrode is inserted at an angle to the cortical surface, changes of modality types occur as the electrode passes from one column to another. Neurons activated by cutaneous stimulation are indicated by filled circles, joint receptors by triangles and fascial receptors by open circles. (Adapted from Powell and Mountcastle, *Bull. Johns Hopkins Hosp.*, 105, 1959.)

from one another, as there are relatively few lateral connections between different columns. The lateral connections which do exist serve to convey an inhibitory influence, implying that the cells in one column can inhibit the cells in neighbouring columns.

Lesions of the postcentral gyrus produce sensory defects which primarily affect somaesthetic discriminative capacities. Thus in monkeys, removal of the postcentral gyrus is followed by loss or impairment of tactile discrimination and what appears to be a lack of awareness of movements of the contralateral limbs. Information about the effect of lesions restricted to the postcentral gyrus in man are fragmentary. However, there is reason to believe that the sensory defects are similar to those observed in the monkeys.

In summary, the somaesthetic area of the cerebral cortex contains a topographical overall representation of the body, so that each area corresponds to a given area of the body. There is in addition an organisation in vertical columns with respect to the modality of the sensory input. A similar vertical organisation has also been found in the cortex of other primary sensory areas, such as in the visual cortex (see p. 383).

Other cortical areas receiving somatosensory input

In mapping out the somatosensory area in animals by recording evoked potentials, it was found in early studies that responses to stimulation of sensory nerves could be obtained not only in the postcentral areas but also in what was considered as pure motor areas. It was at first thought that these responses were mediated by association fibres, but later studies disclosed that the motor cortex actually receives a direct sensory input of its own. Several lines of evidence suggest that this input serves an important function in modulating the output from the motor cortex (see p. 257). It also appears that the sensory input to the motor cortex is less related to conscious sensory experience than is the input to the postcentral gyrus. We may thus distinguish a 'motor' somatosensory input and a 'perceptual' somatosensory input to the cortex.

The body surface is also represented in a relatively small area (SmII) of the parietal cortex on the superior bank of the Sylvian fissure. Its somatotopical pattern is similar to that in the first somatosensory area, but less precise. The representation of the body is bilateral, with the contralateral side dominant. Electrical stimulation of this area in human subjects gives rise to sensations resembling those evoked by stimulation of the first somatosensory area. Still another cortical area that receives a somatosensory input is the supplementary motor area (MsII) located on the medial surface of the hemisphere. Knowledge about the functional organisation of the sensory input to this area is still incomplete.

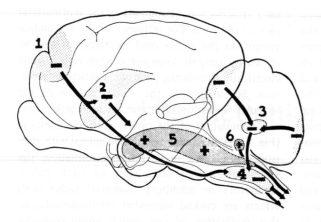

Fig. 13.3   Inhibitory and facilitatory regions of the reticular formation concerned with control of muscle tone and reflex activity: 1, motor cortex; 2, basal ganglia; 3, cerebellum; 4, reticular inhibitory area; 5, reticular facilitatory area; 6, vestibular nuclei. (From Lindsley *et al., J. Neurophysiol.,* 12, 1949.)

for the maintenance of muscle tone. By modulating this tonic activity, the reticular formation exerts its control of muscle tone and reflex activity. The descending system also participates in the control of tone in the respiratory muscles and in the regulation of autonomic motor functions.

The ascending system

The main function of the ascending reticular system is to exert an activating influence on the cortex. If, in a sleeping animal, the reticular formation is stimulated with implanted electrodes, the animal will awaken, and the EEG will show the changes typical of arousal (see p. 238). This suggests that the ascending part of the reticular system plays a significant role in regulating sleep and wakefulness. A great deal of evidence suggests that the state of consciousness is dependent on a tonic input; the ascending reticular system is therefore generally called the *reticular activating system* (RAS). If this input to the cortex is blocked or eliminated by lesions of the reticular formation, loss of consciousness and a sleep-like state result.

As already mentioned, a portion of the ascending reticular fibres pass to the thalamus. Electrical stimulation of this system elicits cortical responses which gradually grow in amplitude with repetitive stimulation, the so-called recruiting responses. Such responses, which are especially conspicuous in the associative areas of the cortex, arise from the summation of dendritic synaptic potentials. There seems to be a functional difference between this thalamocortical system and the brain stem part of the ascending reticular system. Conceivably, the former mediates rapid changes, thus being responsible for cortical functions such as focusing attention, whereas the latter system might be responsible for maintaining wakefulness over long periods.

14

Electrical Activity of the Brain

The electroencephalogram

In 1875 a young English physiologist, Caton, reported in the *British Medical Journal* that he had succeeded in recording weak electrical currents from the brain of rabbits and monkeys. Caton had found that a sudden potential change occurred when the animal turned its head or chewed some food. Even more fascinating was the observation that a potential change was induced when a flame, which was the only source of light available, in the room, was placed in front of the animal's eyes. Caton's report passed unnoticed and remained unknown for many years, and several other authors later claimed priority for the discovery of 'brain currents'. About 15 years after Caton's discovery, a Polish physiologist, Beck, reported in *Centralblatt für Physiologie* that there were waxing and waning potential changes in the cortex and that these rhythmic potentials disappeared when the animal's eyes were stimulated with light; this appears to be the first description of the arousal reaction. Beck's claim to the discovery of the electrical activity of the brain was brought into challenge shortly after the publication of his report by an Austrian physiologist, Fleischel von Marxow, who called attention to a sealed letter that he had deposited in 1883 at the Academy of Sciences in Vienna. This letter was opened and published in the *Centralblatt*. There Fleischel reported that potential variations were induced in the brain by stimulation of sense organs and concluded that: 'Perhaps, it will be even possible to observe, by recording from the scalp, currents evoked by various psychological acts of one's own brain'. During the ensuing discussion between Beck and Fleischel, the editor of the *Centralblatt* received a letter from Caton in which he directed attention to his report in the *British Medical Journal* 15 years earlier, and this ended the fight for priority to the discovery of the brain currents.

Despite the interest which this struggle for priority attracted, 50 years would pass before attempts were made to record the electrical activity of the human brain. The first to do so was a German psychiatrist and neurologist, Berger, who showed that it was possible to record rhythmic electrical fluctuations from the brain (Fig. 14.1) with electrodes placed on the scalp. Berger was also the first to study the changes in the electrical patterns of the brain waves in certain states of altered brain functions and it was he who introduced the term electroencephalogram (EEG).

In ordinary practice, EEG recordings are usually

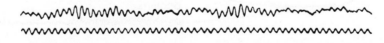

Fig. 14.1   The first published electroencephalographic recording in man made by Berger in 1929, the subject being his son Klaus. *Upper trace*: electroencephalographic recording showing typical alpha rhythm. *Lower trace*: 10 Hz sine wave from an oscillator.

carried out with several pairs of electrodes placed at different sites on the skull. The recording is commonly made between each of a pair or between a given electrode and an inactive 'distant' electrode usually connected to one ear. The recordings are generally analysed by direct inspection; for a more precise study, other methods such as computer frequency analysis have to be used.

As was first demonstrated by Berger, the EEG is composed of four basic rhythms: alpha, beta, theta and delta. The alpha rhythm is most prominent in recordings from the parieto-occipital regions (see Fig. 14.2), has a frequency of 8–12 s^{-1} and has an amplitude of approximately 50 μV. The beta rhythm, which is considerably lower in amplitude (10–15 μV), has a frequency of 15–30 s^{-1} and appears over the frontal parts of the brain. The theta wave frequency is 4–7 s^{-1} while that of the delta waves is 1–4 s^{-1}; the latter have an amplitude of 10–50 μV. In the adult, the delta waves are rarely seen during wakefulness and may then be a sign of pathological activity, but their occurrence is a regular and normal phenomenon in children. Under certain conditions another EEG pattern, the so-called lambda waves, whose frequency is 4–5 s^{-1}, may be recorded from the occipital lobes.

The alpha rhythm is recorded in its purest form from the parieto-occipital region of a subject at rest and with the eyes closed. It varies considerably in amplitude and spatial distribution from one individual to another. However, for a given person the alpha rhythm remains remarkably constant from time to time. When the eyes are opened (Fig. 14.2), the alpha activity is replaced by low-voltage, high-frequency waves representing a desynchronisation of cortical activity. The change in activity, the alpha blocking or *arousal effect*, is obtained with all types of sensory stimuli as well as during mental activity, for instance, focusing of attention.

The electrical activity of the brain appears before birth and may be recorded with electrodes placed on the mother's abdomen from the seventh month. Recordings from foetuses have revealed slow brain waves as early as the third foetal month. In the sixth foetal month, the EEG changes markedly, with the appearance of periodically occurring regular waves, the theta waves. Somewhat later the slower delta waves appear against a background of more rapid activity.

The EEG of a newborn child is varying and therefore not easily characterised. During the first days of life, the EEG of an awake child shows irregular delta activity superimposed upon a background of high-frequency waves. The more sleepy and passive the child, the more pronounced the delta rhythm. The activity also varies with the

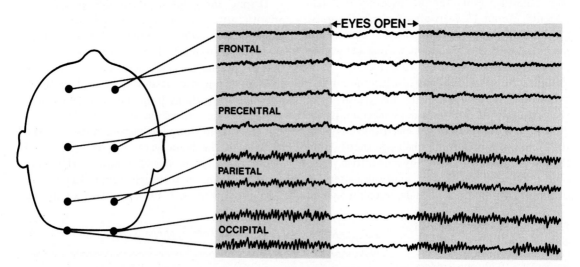

Fig. 14.2   EEG of resting, awake human subject. Simultaneous recordings from different sites on the skull. Note blocking of alpha rhythm during opening of the eyes.

nature of sleep, so that peaceful sleep has alternating periods of discharge and insignificant activity, whereas the activity is continuous when the child sleeps lightly and restlessly. Both the frequency and amplitude of activity increase gradually after birth; and by age one year the typical frequency is $6-9 \text{ s}^{-1}$. Up to six months after birth, symmetrical recordings from both sides of the head show differences, but by the age of one year the activity in the two hemispheres is generally the same. During the second and third years of life, the pattern of the EEG stabilises. Theta activity, still noticeable, now decreases; it is rarely seen after the age of 10 except in the frontal parts of the brain, where it normally remains up to the age of 16–18. The theta activity seems to be related to the child's emotional state, for it tends to occur when the child feels sad or angry. By the age of 10, both delta and theta activity have generally disappeared, and the basic rhythm is $7-9 \text{ s}^{-1}$. The maturing of the EEG continues relatively slowly, the process terminating at age 17–18.

The relation of the EEG to the degree of wakefulness and attention is reflected in the changes typically occurring as a person goes to sleep and during different stages of sleep. By recording these changes in the EEG, it has been possible to divide the depth of sleep into different levels (see sleep on p. 304). During narcosis, changes in the EEG occur which in many respects resemble those during sleep. In the first stage of barbiturate narcosis, before the patient has lost consciousness, rapid waves of high amplitude appear in the frontal lobes. When the patient loses consciousness, large and slow waves appear. At a yet deeper level, these waves gradually diminish, and isopotential recordings show small waves or none at all. Upon reawakening, the EEG gradually returns, together with the rapid activity typical of the initial stage of anaesthesia.

The EEG pattern is also affected by changes in the oxygen or carbon dioxide content of inspired air. A decrease in oxygen slows the rhythm; if the reduction is large, delta waves will occur. During long-lasting and profound lack of oxygen, the EEG waves are markedly reduced in amplitude, and the recording may become completely flat. In hypogly-

caemia, similar effects may occur; when the blood sugar drops below 60 mg %, delta waves appear. The rate of change matters, for the faster the blood sugar falls, the more pronounced are the changes in the EEG. Hyperglycaemia, in contrast, has little effect on the EEG.

Disturbances of brain function are often associated with changes in the EEG pattern, and the EEG has therefore become a valuable tool in the diagnosis of cerebral disorders such as epilepsy and brain tumours. Epileptic seizures are characterised by the appearance of bursts of spike-like potentials, sometimes followed by wave-like components. In cases of tumours or haemorrhage, normal activity may vanish or slow waves occur in the damaged area. If the pathological activity is 'latent', as sometimes occurs, so that the EEG seems to be normal, it may be provoked by hyperventilation or flickering light. Brain tumours are usually electrically inactive, but the pressure they exert on surrounding tissue may produce abnormalities in the EEG; such changes are usually focal and characterised by slow, delta-like waves.

Few electrical phenomena in the nervous system have been the subject of such intense studies as the EEG. Despite this, we do not adequately understand its underlying mechanisms. At first it was thought that the EEG expressed summed impulse activity in cortical cells, but many properties of the EEG, especially the relatively slow rhythms of the alpha waves, did not fit this hypothesis. Studies of cortical activity in the early 1930s disclosed that dendrites differ from cell bodies in several functional respects. These findings suggested that EEG waves might represent synchronous activity of the dendrites. The nature of brain waves as rhythmic, oscillating potential changes indicated that they must come from structures with a uniform geometrical orientation. The apical dendrites from the pyramidal cells appeared to meet this requirement, having a relatively large membrane surface suitable for generating the current flow underlying the EEG. In recent years, data have accumulated that provide strong evidence supporting the idea that the EEG derives from summed postsynaptic potentials in the dendrites.

Even if the EEG reflects the activity of the

cortical dendrites, the source of the rhythm must be sought. Some kind of pacemaker mechanism was at first thought to synchronise the activity of the cortex, and since the sensory inflow to the cortex comes via the thalamus, this part of the brain was looked at as a possible centre for coordinating cortical activity. Since the early 1940s, stimulation of peripheral nerves has been known to arouse rhythmic activity in the cortex. The importance of sensory inflow in maintaining normal EEG activity is also evident from the fact that interruption of afferent pathways by a transection of the brain stem at the level of the oculomotor nucleus produces EEG activity similar to that of deep sleep. This change is not due to loss of the input to the cortex via the specific sensory pathways, but rather depends upon elimination of the input via the ascending reticular system. In an awake person at rest, without distracting stimulation, there is probably a constant influx to the cortex via this system. The input undergoes a rhythmic modulation in the thalamus. When the alpha waves dominate, cortical activity is controlled from the thalamus; the rhythm apparently results from a rhythmical alternation between excitation and inhibition in the cells in the thalamus. The output to the cortical cells is therefore characterised by regular, alternating activity which in the EEG is reflected as rhythmical alpha waves.

The mechanisms for the desynchronisation of the EEG evoked by sensory stimulation have been studied in a similar way by electrical stimulation of the thalamus. Intracellular recordings have shown that high-frequency stimulation produces a summation of excitatory postsynaptic potentials, while at the same time the inhibitory potentials are supressed. The modulating effect of the thalamus is thereby eliminated and its function as a pacemaker blocked. In the cortex this appears as desynchronisation and the elimination of alpha activity, accompanied by behavioural arousal.

Evoked potentials

Caton was the first to report that sensory stimuli induce potential changes in the cortex. Later these so-called *evoked potentials* were used extensively in mapping the sensory areas of the cortex in experimental animals. Early attempts to record evoked potentials from the human scalp were unsuccessful because it was difficult to separate the sensory signals from the background activity in the cortex. The advent of computer techniques have made such recordings possible, and the electrical response of the human brain to sensory stimuli can nowadays easily be tapped with electrodes attached to the scalp. This technique requires that the computer stores each recording during repetitive sensory stimulation and extracts the signals from the background noise. This method has now been widely used in order to obtain clues to the processing of sensory information in the brain and to approach the problems of the central correlates of human perceptual and cognitive processes. The same technique has been applied to record brain potentials accompanying voluntary movements. The motor potentials differ from the somatosensory potentials in being more localised.

It has been suggested that cortical potentials

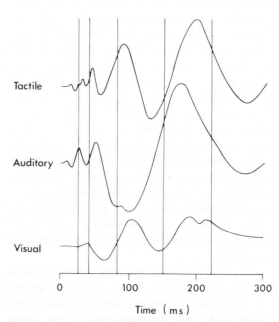

Fig. 14.3 Sensory evoked cortical responses to tactile, auditory and visual stimulation. (From Vaughan, *Average Evoked Potentials*, NASA SP-191, 1968.)

which display a distinct time relation to a given event should be termed 'event-related potentials'. Four categories of event-related potentials have been distinguished: (1) evoked potentials induced by stimulation of sense organs; (2) motor potentials associated with voluntary movements; (3) long-latency potentials related to stimulus evaluation; and (4) steady potential shifts occurring during anticipation or expectancy of a sensory stimulus.

Sensory evoked potentials have been studied extensively using visual, auditory, or somatosensory stimuli or electrical stimulation of peripheral sensory nerves. As illustrated in Fig. 14.3, the waveforms of the responses are different for different sensory modalities. The various components of the responses vary in amplitude and peak delays with the stimulus strength and also with the arousal level of the subject. In general it is possible to distinguish between a primary evoked response which is confined to the specific cortical area and a secondary response which may be more widely distributed. It is supposed that the primary response signals the arrival of the input from the specific thalamo-cortical system while the secondary response is attributed to the modality-nonspecific input. The long-latency responses have similar distributions for auditory and visual stimuli and have their centres overlying the parietotemporal association cortex. These responses appear with discriminatory tasks or in connection with orienting responses. As seen in Fig. 14.4, the regions of maximum amplitude of the somatosensory responses are located

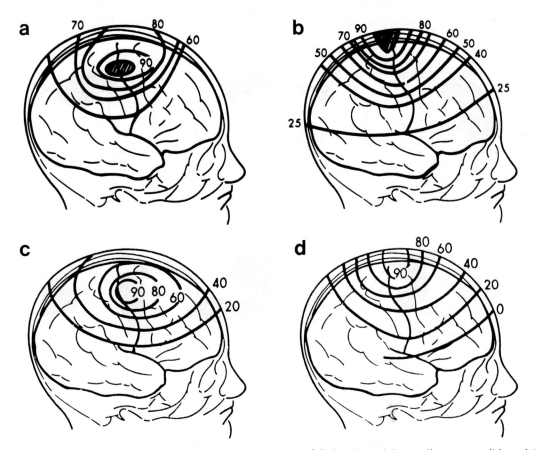

Fig. 14.4   Isopotential maps of evoked cortical responses: (a) shock to right medium nerve; (b) to right peroneal nerve; (c) evoked motor potential associated with hand movement; (d) with foot dorsiflexion. (From Vaughan, *Average Evoked Potentials*, NASA SP-191, 1968.)

Adrian, E. D. and Matthews, R. (1927). The action of light on the eye. The discharge of impulses in the optic nerve and its relation to electric changes in the retina. Part I, *J. Physiol. (Lond.)*, **63**, 378–414

Beck, A. (1890). Die Bestimmung der Localization der Gehirn-und Rückenmarkfunctionen vermittelst der electrischen Erscheinungen, *Cbl. Physiol.*, **4**, 473–476

Beck, A. (1890). Die Ströme der Nervencentren, *Cbl. Physiol.*, **4**, 572–573

Berger, H. (1929). Uber das Elektroenkephalogramm des Menschen, *Arch. Psychiatr.*, **87**, 527–570

Brooks, V. B., Rudomin, P. and Slayman, C. L. (1961). Sensory activation of neurons in the cat's cerebral cortex, *J. Neurophysiol.*, **24**, 286–301

Brooks, V. B., Rudomin, P. and Slayman, C. L. (1961). Peripheral receptive fields of neurons in the cat's cerebral cortex, *J. Neurophysiol.*, **24**, 302–325

Caton, R. (1875). The electric currents of the brain, *Br. Med. J.*, **2**, 278

Caton, R. (1891). Die Ströme des Centralnervensystems, *Cbl. Physiol.*, **4**, 758–786

Chang, H.-T., Ruch, T. C. and Ward, A. A. (1947). Topographical representation of muscles in motor cortex of monkeys, *J. Neurophysiol.*, **10**, 39–56

Ferrier, D. (1876). Experiments on the brain of monkeys, *Phil. Trans.*, **165**, 433

Fleischl Von Marxow, E. (1890). Mittheilung betrieffend die Physiologie der Hirnrinde, *Cbl. Physiol.*, **4**, 538

Foerster, O. (1936). The motor cortex in the light of Hughlings Jackson's doctrines, *Brain*, **59**, 135

Hernandez-Peon, R., Jouvet, M. and Scherrer, H. (1957). Auditory potentials at cochlear nucleus during acoustic habituation, *Acta Neurol. Latinoam.*, **3**, 144–156

Magoun, H. W. (1952). An ascending reticular activating system in the brain stem, *Arch. Neurol. Psychiat.*, **67**, 145–154

Magoun, H. W. and Rhines, R. (1946). An inhibitory mechanism in the bulbar reticular formation, *J. Neurophysiol.*, **9**, 165–171

Moruzzi, G. and Magoun, H. W. (1949). Brain stem reticular formation and activation of the EEG, *Electroencephalogr. Clin. Neurophysiol.*, **1**, 455–473

Mountcastle, V. B. (1957). Modality and topographic properties of single neurons of cat's somatic sensory cortex, *J. Neurophysiol.*, **20**, 408–434

Mountcastle, V. B., Poggio, G. F. and Werner, G. (1963). The relation of thalamic cell response to peripheral stimuli varied over an intensive continuum, *J. Neurophysiol.*, **26**, 807–834

Poggio, G. F. and Mountcastle, V. B. (1960). A study of the functional contributions of the lemniscal and spinothalamic systems to somatic sensibility, *Bull. Johns Hopkins Hosp.*, **106**, 266–316

Purpura, D. P. (1967). Comparative physiology of dendrites, in *The Neurosciences. A Study Program*, eds G. C. Quarton, T. Melnechuk and F. O. Schmitt, Rockefeller University Press, New York, pp. 372–393

Regan, D. (1968). Evoked potentials and sensation, *Percept. Psychophys.*, **4**, 347–350

Rhines, R. and Magoun, H. W. (1946). Brain stem facilitation of cortical motor response, *J. Neurophysiol.*, **9**, 219–229

Scheibel, M. E. and Scheibel, A. B. (1970). Elementary processes in selected thalamic and cortical subsystems – the structural substrates, in *The Neurosciences. Second Study Program*, ed. F. O. Schmitt, Rockefeller University Press, New York, pp. 443–457

Smith, W. K. (1944). The frontal eye fields, in *The Precentral Motor Cortex*, ed. P. C. Bucy, University of Illinois Press, Urbana, pp. 307–342

Vaughan, H. G., Jr, Costa, D. and Ritter, W. (1968). Topography of the human motor potential, *Electroencephalogr. Clin. Neurophysiol.*, **25**, 1–10

Werner, G. and Whitsel, B. L. (1967). The topology of dermatomal projection in the medial lemniscal system, *J. Physiol. (Lond.)*, **192**, 123–144

Whitsel, B. L., Dreyer, D. A. and Roppolo, J. R. (1971). Determinants of body representation in post-central gyrus of macaques, *J. Neurophysiol.*, **34**, 1018–1034

Section VII: Central Control
of Locomotion

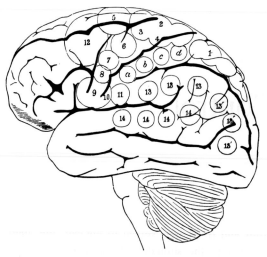

Fig. 15.1   Ferrier's map of the human brain. This map, which is the first of its kind, was worked out on the basis of observations on the cortical functions in the monkey brain. (From Ferrier, *The Functions of the Brain*, London, 1876.)

of the motor cortex is to initiate and modulate activity of spinal patterns.

The patients upon whom the early studies of the motor regions were carried out (Fig. 15.2) were not under general anaesthesia and the effect of electrical stimulation of the motor cortex on voluntary movements could therefore also be studied. It was found that electrical stimulation interfered with the ability of the patients to perform movements. For instance, if asked to move the foot or the hand while the corresponding area of the motor cortex was stimulated, the patient was unable to carry out the movement and would report that he felt as if the leg or the arm was paralysed. This effect occurred even if the electrical stimulation elicited no movement.

Motor areas

The precise localisation of the cortical areas involved in motor control was outlined through the work of Sherrington. He used lightly anaesthetised apes and unipolar stimulation that allowed a finer localisation. Sherrington's work established that the primary motor areas were confined to the

imitations of voluntary movements, and coordinated movements were never obtained. This led to the notion that the patterns of discrete movements are organised at the spinal level and that the role

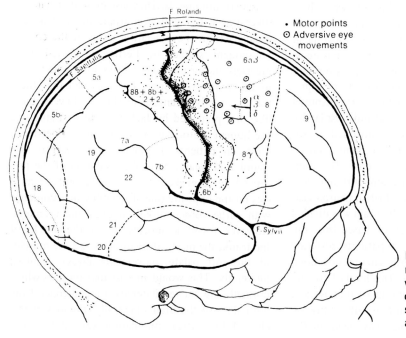

Fig. 15.2   Regions of the right hemisphere in man from which discrete movements can be elicited by electrical stimulation. (From Penfield and Boldrey, *Brain*, 60, 1937.)

region in front of the central sulcus. This area includes a relatively small strip of the cortex, Brodmann's area 4. Here each muscle group is represented by a field, and the different muscle groups are arranged in a strict and regular pattern in the following order, starting from the top of the gyrus: toes, legs, body, arms, face, mouth and tongue. The cortical areas controlling the muscles of the thumb, the face, the tongue and the toe are larger than the areas controlling, for example, the trunk musculature. In other words, cortical representation has a direct relation to the degree of precision of the movements of different muscle groups (see Fig. 15.3); the larger the cortical area, the greater is the precision with which movements may be carried out.

The effect obtained by stimulating a given area varies greatly with the duration and strength of the electrical stimulus. For example, prolonged stimulation of the thumb area first produces movement of the thumb, then gradually gives movement in the forefinger and, if the stimulation continues, movements of the wrist. If the stimulus is increased in strength beyond the threshold for evoking contraction of a given muscle, neighbouring synergistic muscles may also contract.

There is a close connection between the cortical motor and sensory systems as indicated by the finding that movements may be induced by electrical stimulation of the postcentral area (SmI). The effects elicited were at first believed to result from a spread of the stimulating current from the postcentral to the precentral gyrus. Later it was found that the movements could still be obtained after removal of the cortex of the precentral area. This finding suggests that the postcentral gyrus can itself exert motor control functions. Normally, however, its contribution to the control of movement is probably mediated through the precentral area. In its somatotopical representation of the various muscle groups, the postcentral area mirrors the precentral (Fig. 15.4).

Another region that participates in the control of movement is the *second somatosensory area*

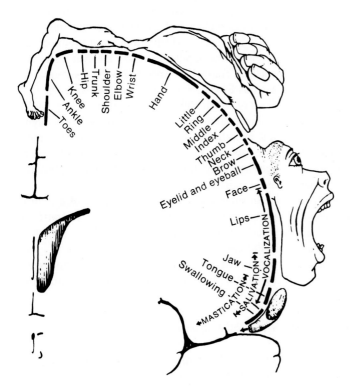

Fig. 15.3 Diagram showing the relative size of various regions of the human primary motor cortex from which movements of different parts of the body can be elicited by electrical stimulation. (From Penfield and Rasmussen, *The Cerebral Cortex of Man*, New York, 1950.)

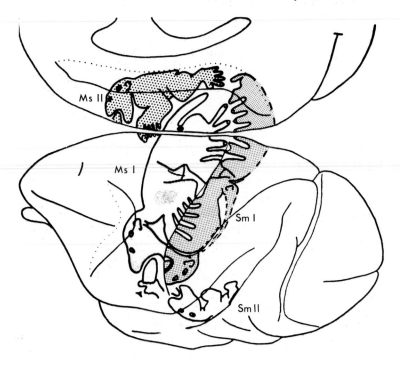

Fig. 15.4   Diagram of left hemisphere of the monkey brain showing the locations of the four main sensorimotor areas. MsI, precentral motor; MsII, supplementary motor; SmI, primary somatic sensory; SmII, secondary somatic sensory. (From Woolsey, *Biological and Biochemical Basis of Behavior*, eds Harlow and Woolsey, University of Wisconsin Press, Madison, 1958.)

(SmII) in the parietal lobe, located close to the Sylvian fissure. This area receives somatosensory signals from both sides of the body. The finding that strong electrical stimulation in this area evokes bilateral movements has been taken as evidence that it may play a part in motor control.

Still another area involved in motor control is the *supplementary motor area* (MsII) situated on the medial surface of the hemisphere in the region of the gyrus cinguli (see Fig. 15.4). The movements elicited by stimulation in this area involve muscle groups on the contralateral side of the body. They are less precise and usually slower than those evoked from the precentral area. The movements generally involve large groups of muscles of the extremities, the trunk, or the head. In man, vocalisation, autonomic effects or inhibition of voluntary movements may also be produced.

Besides the cortical areas that regulate the skeletal muscles, there are also regions which control special groups of muscles, such as the eye muscles and those involved in speech functions. The eye muscles are controlled from an area in the frontal lobe, the so-called frontal eye field (Fig.

15.5). Electrical stimulation in this region gives rise to movements of the eyes and blinking. Nearby is an area in which stimulation produces dilatation of the pupils and makes the eyes water. The cortical control of speech involves several areas such as Broca's area and Wernicke's area, the functions of which will be discussed later (see p. 317).

Visceral motor functions are generally regulated by reflexes, but certain regions in the frontal lobe appear to exert control of visceral motor activity. They display no somatotopic organisation as do those for skeletal muscle, however.

In summary, considerable regions of the cortex participate directly or indirectly in the control of muscle movements, as illustrated in Fig. 15.4. Although the functional organisation of these regions remains far from clear, there is good reason to believe that each motor area has specific functions.

The cellular organisation of the motor cortex

In the early studies of the somatotopic organisation of the primary motor area, coarse electrodes

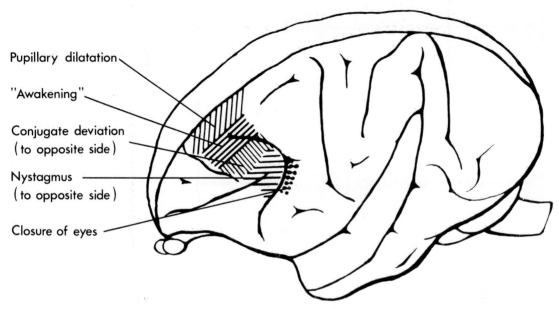

Pupillary dilatation

"Awakening"

Conjugate deviation
(to opposite side)

Nystagmus
(to opposite side)

Closure of eyes

Fig. 15.5   Frontal eye field from which movements of the eyes, eyelids and pupils can be elicited with electrical stimulation. (From Smith, *The Precentral Motor Cortex*, ed. P. C. Bucy, University of Illinois Press, 1944.)

were used to stimulate the cortex; hence large regions were activated, and the resulting effects were rather difficult to interpret. In recent years a technique has been developed for stimulating and recording from single cortical cells. The results obtained have greatly deepened our insight into the organisation of the cortex at the cellular level. These studies have disclosed that the cells in the motor cortex are arranged in columns, and that each column participates in the control of several muscles. This implies that a given muscle is controlled by cells in a group of columns. Moreover, muscles with fine controlled movements are represented in more columns than those with less precise control. This organisation represents the cellular basis for the cortical map of muscles as shown in Fig. 15.3. An important feature of the functional organisation as revealed by the recordings from single cells in the motor cortex (Fig. 15.6) is that all cells of a given column affect movements in the same joint. This suggests that the cellular neurons of the motor cortex do not represent individual muscles as was earlier thought but rather are organised on the basis of the principle of

movements. Furthermore, recordings from single cells in the motor cortex of monkeys trained to perform certain arm and hand movements show that the pyramidal cells (the cells whose axons form the pyramidal tract) may be divided into two main groups: (1) large cells with rapidly conducting axons, which are active only while a movement is in progress, and (2) small cells which are constantly active and whose activity decreases or increases during a movement. It has been suggested that these two types of cells correspond to the large and small motoneurons in the spinal cord (see p. 156). However, the possibility also exists that the small cortical neurons control the gamma-neurons. Simultaneous recordings from both types of cortical cells show that both may be active at the same time, or one type may be silent while the other is firing. This shows that there is a plastic functional relationship between the two types of cell. Consequently, during certain movements, cortical neurons in a column may operate as synergists, as antagonists, or in still other cases completely independently of one another. This in turn seems to reflect the fact that the cells of a column control

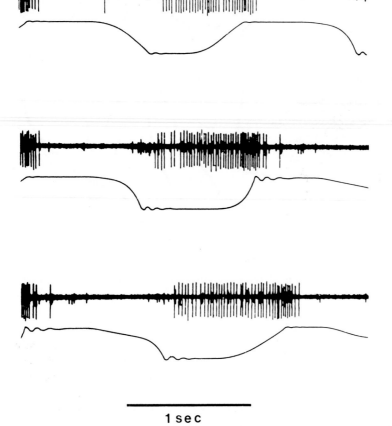

1 sec

Fig. 15.6 Activity of cortical neuron in monkey during flexion—extension movement of the wrist. Recordings from three successive cycles of movement with no opposing load. Lower trace in each recording indicates movement, extension downwards and flexion upwards. (From Evarts, in *Neurophysiological Basis of Normal and Abnormal Motor Activities*, Raven Press, 1967.)

the activity of several muscles. Single-cell recordings have demonstrated that the cellular activity in a column undergoes continuous alteration in the process of executing the movement as a result of an interaction between the cells which participate in the control of the movement in a joint. The plastic organisation of the cells in the motor cortex thus permits, for example, activation of a flexor muscle and inhibition of its antagonist for the performance of a movement; in another situation a flexor muscle and its antagonist may be activated together, for instance to stabilise a joint. It is therefore not surprising that the activity pattern of a pyramidal tract neuron varies greatly with the parameters of movement. An important question arising from this is whether cortical activity is related to the actual movement of a limb or to

the force exerted. Analysis of the activity patterns of single cortical neurons in monkeys during the performance of various voluntary movements strongly suggests that the activity is primarily related to force and the rate of change of force.

Recent studies have demonstrated that there is an 'internal feedback' system within the motor cortex that plays an important role in the control of movement. The function of this feedback system is reminiscent of the recurrent inhibition by the Renshaw cell in the spinal cord (see p. 172). The feedback control is mediated by recurrent collaterals from the pyramidal neurons (Fig. 15.7). These collaterals return to the second and third layers and terminate on stellate cells which in turn feed back on the pyramidal cells. The effect may either be inhibitory or excitatory and results

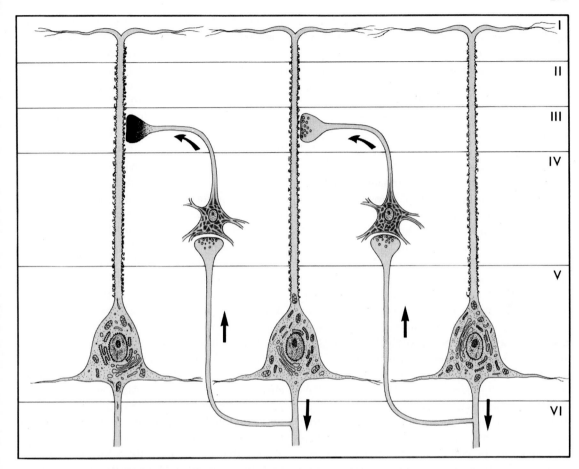

Fig. 15.7   Schematic diagram showing positive and negative feedback from pyramidal cells in the motor cortex. Inhibitory action is indicated by synapse in black.

in alterations of the cortical activity profile. The function of the inhibitory projection may be to restrict the cortical activity to a small number of columns and thereby to provide for a fine and precise motor control.

15.2   The cortical command signal

Muscle movements are of two kinds: voluntary and reflexive. Voluntary movements may be elicited without any obvious external stimulus, whereas reflex movements, by definition, are always provoked and controlled simply by sensory input signals. Since the very earliest studies of the motor

system, an important question has been which part of the motor cortex initiates voluntary activity; in other words, in which part of the cortex does the motor command signal arise?

Studies of the disorders that ensue from injuries of different brain areas in man suggest that there are three sequential phases in the neuronal processes underlying the cortical control of voluntary movement. The first is the act of decision. This may stem from an intellectual process, an emotional sensation, or memories evoked by external stimuli. Next, the decision is transferred to that part of the motor cortex where the movement has been programmed by earlier learning. The third phase comprises the neuronal processes involved in the performance of the movement. A disturbance of the first phase is probably the source of some forms of *apraxia*, particularly characterised by an inability to perform a given movement on command, despite there being neither motor nor sensory deficit, nor a reduced capacity for understanding. Asked to wave his hand, the apractic patient may be unable to do so and yet he is fully capable of waving his hand spontaneously. In other types of apraxia, the patient may not be able to execute the movement spontaneously; presumably the program for this movement in the motor cortex has been destroyed.

The development of the technique for recording brain potentials associated with voluntary movements has offered new possibilities for studies of the cortical processes underlying cortical motor control. It has been demonstrated by averaging EEG activity during repetitive self-paced contractions that the initiation of voluntary movements is associated with 'motor potentials' of complex waveform comprising four components (Fig. 15.8). The first component is a negative wave, 'the readiness potential', which appears 1–2 s before the actual movement starts and builds up gradually. It is maximal at the vertex and bilaterally distributed. The second component is a positive wave, 'the premotor potential', which for finger movements begins 80 ms before the onset of movement. It is followed by the third component, 'the motor

potential', which is a sharp negative wave, whose topographical representation depends on which muscle group is active. It precedes the movement by an interval that varies with the muscles being activated; with movements of facial muscles, for instance, the latency is 30–50 ms, while with movements of the foot or the leg, it is 150–200 ms. The fourth wave is positive and accompanies the movement.

These potentials have been interpreted variously. One theory is that the readiness potential reflects the act of planning and decision and that the following premotor potential represents the actual command signal. Spreading to the motor cortex, the command signal initiates the motor potential, which initiates the activity in the motor cortex.

A pertinent question in relation to the command signal is which cortical region generates this signal. Anatomical studies and clinical observations suggest that areas 5 and 7 of the parietal lobe are essential for integration of somaesthetic and motor functions. Recently, Mountcastle has succeeded in recording the activity of single neurons in these areas in waking monkeys which were trained to perform stereotyped movements in response to sensory stimuli or to fixate or track visually a target. Neurons in area 5 were found to discharge at high frequencies when the animal performed a particular movement. Mountcastle concluded from his observations that these cells generate the com-

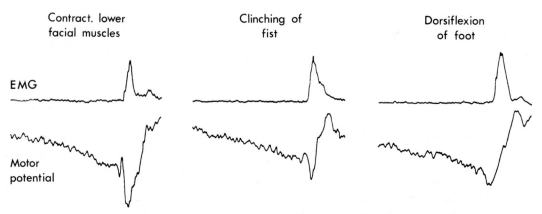

Fig. 15.8   Cortical motor potentials (*lower trace*) associated with voluntary movements. Upper trace in each recording shows movement as indicated by EMG. (From Vaughan, *Average Evoked Potentials*, NASA SP-191, 1968.)

mand signal for the execution of a behavioural motor act. An interesting feature of these cells is that their pattern of discharge is not congruent with the spatial and temporal pattern of the movement commanded. The neurons in area 7 appear likewise to function in generating command signals for the direction of visual attention. There are in the brain probably many sources of commands and whether or not the parietal lobe command centres receive input from higher command centres located elsewhere in the cortex can only be answered by future experiments.

The sensory input to the motor cortex

As we have seen, the motor cortex receives a considerable sensory input of which the somatosensory inflow is pre-eminent. The functional significance of this input has been studied in monkeys whose dorsal roots to one or more extremities were sectioned. When the dorsal roots to the arm of a monkey are cut, the arm appears to become completely paralysed. If the other arm is tied down, the animal will not use the deafferented arm to take offered food. This 'paralysis' is not due to a motor deficit, however, since electrical stimulation of the motor cortex can provoke movement of the deafferented limb. Moreover, specific movements learned earlier in life may sometimes still be performed. In short, the sensory input from the skin, muscles and joint is of clear importance for the control of movement, but the motor cortex does not absolutely require such input in order to produce motions. Just how the previously learned movements are controlled is not known. It may be that the movement becomes programmed into the cortex by learning. Or, since in the course of a movement the somatosensory area continually receives information about the output from the motor cortex, perhaps this information fulfils the same function as the sensory input.

In addition to the input from the skin, muscles and joints, the cortex receives sensory input from the non-specific thalamic system. The latter system is less important for precision in movement; however, it has great significance for the general level of activity in the cortex. The input to the primary motor cortex is distributed to the cells within the first and fourth cell layers (Fig. 15.9), the first layer receiving the input from the non-specific thalamic system, and the fourth the somatosensory input conveyed by the specific system. In addition, the fourth layer receives input from the cerebellum and from other motor areas.

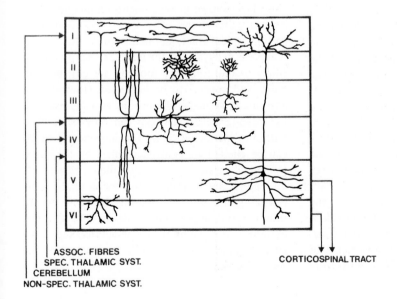

ASSOC. FIBRES
SPEC. THALAMIC SYST.
CEREBELLUM
NON-SPEC. THALAMIC SYST.

CORTICOSPINAL TRACT

Fig. 15.9 Schematic diagram showing distribution of the input from various sources to the different layers of the motor cortex.

The cells of the first and fourth layers can be considered as interneurons which convey the incoming impulses to the cells of the fifth and sixth layers from which the output of the primary motor cortex is passed to the motoneurons via the pyramidal tract. The second and third layers are, with respect to their functional organisation, strongly reminiscent of the substantia gelatinosa in the spinal cord; it is here that the interaction underlying the intracortical feedback of the motor cortex primarily occurs.

The first studies of the sensory input to the motor cortex, which were carried out on the cat, indicated that the cortical cells are activated particularly by cutaneous stimulation but show little response to stimulation of muscle and joint receptors. This observation was surprising since the input from muscles and joints had long since been assumed to be an important component of the integrated activity in the motor cortex. Later studies appear to have resolved this enigma. It has been found that the relative importance of different kinds of sensory input varies significantly by species. In monkeys, for instance, the cells in the motor cortex receive considerable input from joint and muscle receptors but very little from the skin. Unlike the cells in the somatosensory area (where the cells in a given column are activated only by one kind of stimulus), the cells within a given motor column can be activated by more than one kind of stimulus but are usually most sensitive to one modality. All the cells within a column have their receptive fields in the same part of the contralateral part of the body, although some cells, which have large receptive fields, may receive input from both sides of the body. The size of the receptive fields varies; in general those on the trunk are greater than those on the extremities, and of the fields on the extremities those in the distal parts of the limbs are smaller than the proximal ones (Fig. 15.10). Studies on monkeys have shown that the location of the distal fields on the limbs often bears a given relation to the direction of the movement. For instance, a cell which participates in the control of flexor movements of the hand receives its afferent input mainly from the palm, whereas a cell which participates in extension has its receptive fields on the dorsal side of the hand. The sensory input may, in some situations, be extremely powerful, as is illustrated by the *grasping reflex*. This is a grasping movement of the hand elicited by tactile stimulation of the palm. It is most easily demonstrable in newborn children but may also appear in adults after injuries of the frontal brain. The most characteristic feature of this reflex is that a weak tactile stimulus of the palm leads to a forced and sustained grasping movement.

Effects of lesions of the motor cortex

The effect of an injury to the primary motor area depends on the extent of the lesion. If the entire motor cortex in area 4 of the monkey is removed by neurosurgery, a complete paralysis of the contralateral body results. After a time, some movements may return, but the motions are clumsy, slow and strongly dependent upon visual guidance. Spasticity also develops, characterised by hypertonia in the hindlimb extensor muscles and in the forelimb flexor muscles. Since an injury of area 4 affects the pyramidal system as well as the extrapyramidal (see p. 262), it was at first unclear if the spasticity was accounted for by the effect on the former or the latter system. It has since been shown in experiments on monkeys that no spasticity ensues after selective sectioning of the pyramidal tract, and neither does this lead to complete paralysis. If, for instance, the pyramidal fibres to the arms in a monkey are cut, the arm hangs and appears to be paralysed. However, the animal can be made to move the arm, for example by offering a banana which can only be reached with the 'paralysed' arm. The movements which can be elicited are controlled solely by the extrapyramidal system. Typically these movements are clumsy and coarse. After a lesion of the postcentral gyrus in monkeys, all fine and precise movements disappear but no spasticity results. The extremity affected by the lesion is often kept in an awkward position, apparently due to loss of the sense of position.

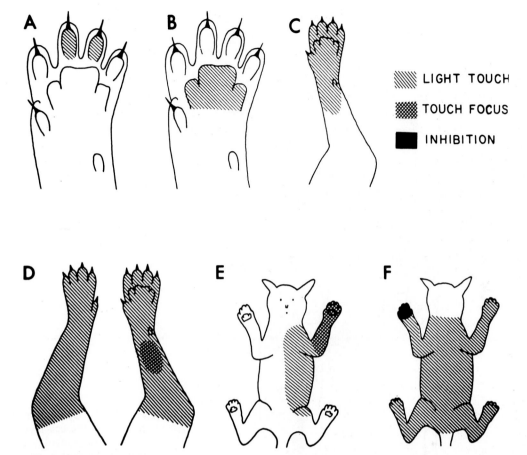

Fig. 15.10   Receptive fields of motosensory cortical neurons in the cat. (From Welt *et al.*, in *Neurophysiological Basis of Normal and Abnormal Motor Activities*, Raven Press, 1967.)

15.3   The pyramidal tract

The output from the primary motor cortex was for a long time thought to come from the giant Betz cells of the fifth cell layer (Fig. 15.11). However, this notion had to be modified when later neuroanatomical studies revealed that there are only around 30 000 Betz cells in the primary cortex of man, while the pyramidal tract contains more than 1 000 000 nerve fibres. This discrepancy was resolved when subsequent studies showed that the small cells within the motor area send fibres to the pyramidal tract, and that a significant supply comes from other cortical areas as well. Thus it has been demonstrated that, in the monkey, 31% of the fibres come from area 4, 29% from area 6 and 40% from areas 3, 2, 1, 5 and 7. This means that 40% of the pyramidal tract fibres come from postcentral areas, i.e. regions earlier regarded as purely sensory. That a considerable portion of the pyramidal fibres derive from small cells is reflected in the pyramidal tract fibre spectrum. Only 2–5% are coarse (10–20 μm in diameter) and rapidly conducting (70 m s^{-1}); these fibres seem to come largely from the Betz cells. The overwhelmingly greater part of the fibres in the pyramidal tract are thus thin and slowly conducting.

From the cortex the pyramidal tract fibres descend and enter into the internal capsule. Here

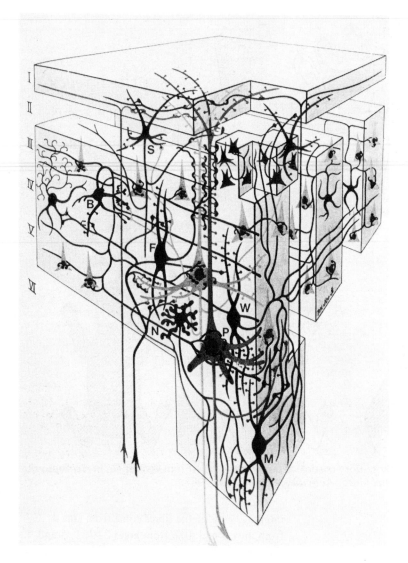

Fig. 15.11 Cytoarchitectural picture of the cell layers and fibre arrangement of the cerebral cortex: P, pyramidal cell; S, stellate cell; B, basket cell; M, Martinotti's cell; F, N and W, fusiform, neuroglia-form and 'wide-field' Golgi cells. (From *Gray's Anatomy*, Longman, 1973.)

they become grouped together in an arrangement strictly corresponding to their place of origin in the cortex (Fig. 15.12). In its further downward course, the pyramidal tract passes through the pons. In this passage the fibres split into several bundles which make their ways between the large masses of the pontine nuclei where some fibres end. When leaving the pons the remaining fibres of the tract are gathered together again and form a distinct bundle. In the further course of the tract in the brain stem, fibres are given off to supply the

motor nuclei of the cranial nerves. Some of these fibres cross to the opposite side while others do not. This implies that the muscles supplied by these nerves are controlled from both sides of the cerebral motor cortex. It is of clinical importance that the part of the facial nucleus innervating the lower part of the face receives only crossed tract fibres. In a unilateral lesion, resulting for instance from a haemorrhagia, only the corresponding muscle on one side of the face will therefore be paralysed. The majority of the remaining fibres

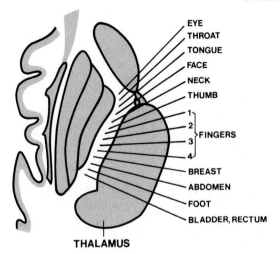

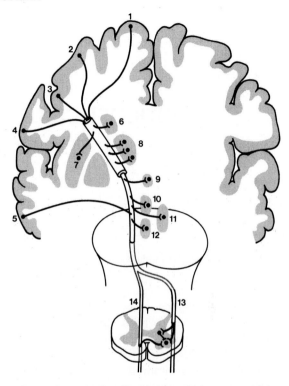

Fig. 15.12 Diagram showing the somatotopical pattern of the corticospinal fibres on their passage through the *capsula interna*.

of the tract cross in the pyramidal decussation and proceed downwards into the spinal cord forming the lateral corticospinal tract (Fig. 15.13). The few fibres that do not cross descend in the ventral funiculus forming the ventral corticospinal tract. This tract rarely descends below the thoracic level of the spinal cord.

Fig. 15.13 Simplified diagram of the pyramidal system and its neuronal connections: 1, frontal cortex; 2, area 6; 3, area 4; 4, area 3; 5, parietal cortex; 6, nucleus caudatus; 7, putamen; 8, thalamus; 9, colliculus superior; 10, nucleus ruber; 11, formatio reticularis; 12, nuclei pontis; 13, lateral corticospinal tract; 14, ventral corticospinal tract.

16

Subcortical Control Systems

16.1 The extrapyramidal system

The discovery of the extrapyramidal system goes back to observations showing that movements could be elicited by brain stimulation in areas which had no obvious relation to the pyramidal tract. Hence, this system was referred to as extrapyramidal. Anatomically it includes large cortical areas, the basal ganglia and their connections. While the pyramidal system controls rapid, finely differentiated movements, the extrapyramidal system primarily participates in the control of involuntary movements and in the maintenance of postural tone. The pyramidal and extrapyramidal systems influence one another in a complex way through their interconnections, and sometimes the pyramidal system may be considered subordinate to the extrapyramidal system.

The basal ganglia, which comprise the nuclei caudatus and lentiformis (*putamen* and *globus pallidus*), represent an important part of the extrapyramidal system. The connections between the basal ganglia and the cortex and the interconnections among the nuclei of the basal ganglia are as yet incompletely known (Fig. 16.1). It has been demonstrated that the basal ganglia receive significant input from the cortex and that nearly the entire cortex sends fibres to the caudate nucleus and the putamen. The largest and most important is the projection from the somatosensory motor cortex, which probably includes collaterals from the pyramidal tract.

Most of the output from the basal ganglia passes to the nucleus ventralis anterior of the thalamus, which in turn projects to the cortex and primarily to the frontal lobe. Other thalamic nuclei which receive input from the basal ganglia project to the sensory motor cortex (Fig. 16.2). Many of the nerve fibres from the basal ganglia descend in the brain stem and make synaptic connections with various nuclei that send fibres to the spinal cord.

Injuries to the basal ganglia produce disorders of muscular tone and involuntary movements. In Parkinson's disease both are present. The increase in muscular tone in this disease affects both extensor and flexor muscles, and is usually referred to as plastic rigidity. It is characterised by a soft plastic resistance to passive movements of a joint. Voluntary movements become slow and weak owing to the rigidity. Involuntary movements appear as regular rhythmical alternating contractions of opposing muscle groups at rest. They are best seen in the fingers and the thumbs which perform 'pill-rolling' movements. This tremor is absent during voluntary movements. Histological studies have shown that this disease is accompanied by degeneration of cells in the substantia nigra and in the globus pallidus and a reduction of the content of dopamine in these nuclei.

Injury to the basal ganglia may also give rise to other types of involuntary movements such as *athetosis*, *chorea* and *ballism*. Athetosis is characterised by slow writhing movements of the hands

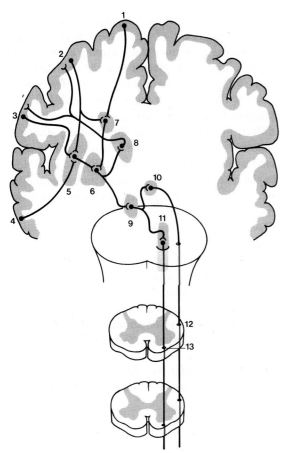

Fig. 16.1 Simplified diagram of the principal connections of the extrapyramidal system: 1, frontal cortex; 2, area 6; 3, area 4; 4, parietal cortex; 5, putamen; 6, pallidus; 7, nucleus caudatus; 8, thalamus; 9, substantia nigra; 10, colliculus superior; 11, formatio reticularis; 12, rubrospinal and tectospinal tracts; 13, reticulospinal tract.

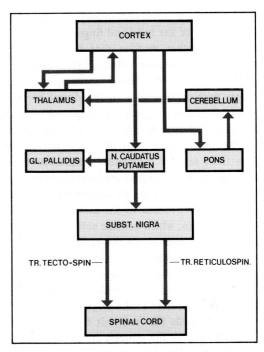

Fig. 16.2 Summarising diagram of the main circuits of the extrapyramidal system.

and feet. Chorea involves rapid, jerking movements, mainly affecting the distal parts of the extremities, but may also appear in the muscles of the face. Ballism takes the form of violent movements of the extremities; it may also involve the trunk muscles as well.

16.2 Organisation of corticospinal motor control in the spinal cord

As the fibres in the lateral corticospinal tract approach their terminal levels in the cord, they veer aside and enter the dorsal horn. Until the early 1950s, it was generally thought that the impulses in the pyramidal tract are transmitted to the motoneurons in the anterior horn via interneurons. This concept was based on findings from the cat, but later work on monkeys suggested that some muscles receive descending impulses over a direct, monosynaptic pathway, without intermediate links. The muscles under such direct cortical control are mainly those of the fingers and forearm: muscles with fine, precise movements. The immediate connection between the nerve fibres from the cortex and the motoneurons allows for a direct and subtle control of the movements in these muscle groups. The cortical areas from which these muscles may be activated are typically delineated more sharply than those of multisynaptically innervated muscles. This direct control over motoneurons seems to have developed relatively late in evolution in connection with the need for meticulous movements of certain muscle groups. The cat, for example, requires less precision in moving its paw than the monkey needs for its fingers. By

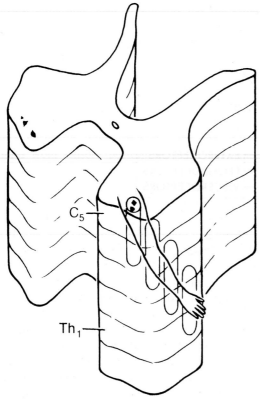

Fig. 16.5 Columnar arrangements of motor ventral horn cells. (From Brodal, *Neurological Anatomy*, Oxford University Press, 1969.)

effect; this control is mediated by the extrapyramidal system.

Neuroanatomical studies have shown that the
fibres from the precentral area terminate upon
cells in laminae VI and VII of the spinal cord,
while those from the somatosensory area terminate
in laminae IV and V. When the pyramidal tract is
stimulated, the cells in laminae IV and V are
inhibited, whereas the cells lying ventrally in
lamina V and those in lamina VI are activated.
This control of sensory input appears to affect

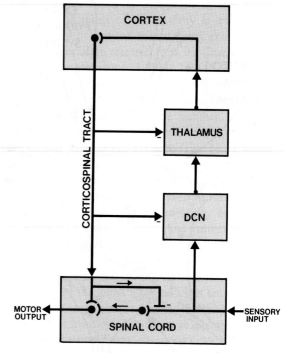

Fig. 16.6 Schematic diagram illustrating cortical
control of sensory input at different levels of the
sensory afferent pathways.

only the part of the somatosensory information
which does not reach perception and only pertains
to motor control. Evidence of this is the fact that
selective damage of the pyramidal tract does not
impair cutaneous sensation. The output of the
motor cortex thus has two different functions: to
activate and control the motoneurons and to
regulate the sensory input to the motor cortex. In
view of the functional importance of the sensory
input in the performance of fine and precise movements, it has been suggested that the motor cortex
exerts its control functions mainly by modulating
the sensory input which in turn governs the output
to the motoneurons.

17

The Cerebellum

It has been known since the early nineteenth century that injuries to the cerebellum cause disturbances in equilibrium and in coordination of movements. These symptoms appeared to be accounted for when it was discovered in neuroanatomical studies that the cerebellum has extensive connections with both motor and sensory systems. The complexity of the input—output relations of the cerebellum as revealed by these studies is perhaps most easily understood if the phylogenetic history of the cerebellum is considered (see Fig. 17.1).

The oldest part of the cerebellum, the *archicerebellum*, is an outgrowth from the vestibular nuclei; this indicates that this part of the cerebellum serves the sense of balance. The next part to appear is the *palaeocerebellum*, which develops in connection with the increase in proprioceptive input from the skeletal muscles. Last to appear is the *neocerebellum*, the development of which is associated with the increased cortical control of movements. The phylogenetic development of the cerebellum is accordingly reflected in the distribution of the incoming fibres. Impulses from the vestibular organ are transmitted to the phylogenetically oldest parts of the cerebellum, the *nodulus* and *flocculus*, which together form the

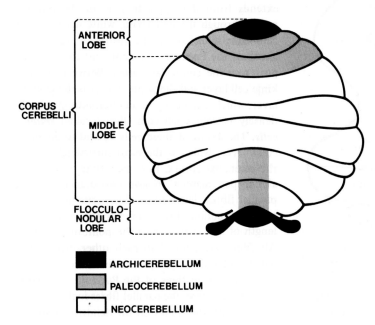

Fig. 17.1 Simplified diagram showing the three main subdivisions of the mammalian cerebellum.

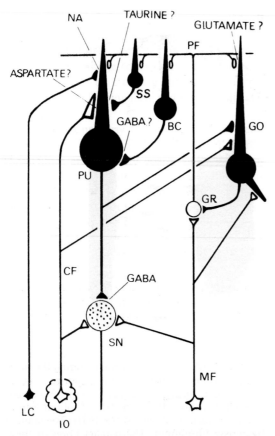

Fig. 17.5 Transmitter substances of the cerebellum: PU, Purkinje cell; BC, basket cell; SS, superficial stellate cell; GO, Golgi cell; GR, granule cell; CF, climbing fibre afferent; MF, mossy fibre afferent; PF, parallel fibre; SN, subcortical nucleus cell; IO, inferior olive; LC, locus coeruleus; NA, noradrenalin. (From Ito, in *Advances in Neurology*, 21, Raven Press, 1978.)

These studies have provided evidence of an elaborate interaction between the different types of neurons in the cerebellar cortex (Fig. 17.7). The climbing fibres from the inferior olive nuclei have a strong excitatory action on the Purkinje cells. A single fibre, however, excites very few Purkinje cells. The mossy fibres have a relatively weak excitatory effect on the Purkinje cells and this is mediated by the granular cells through their parallel fibres. In contrast to the climbing fibres, each mossy fibre may excite a large number of Purkinje cells.

Since the axons of the basket and stellate cells run at right-angles to the parallel fibres, they mainly inhibit Purkinje cells lying on both sides of the excited region (see above). The effect may be demonstrated by local stimulation of the cortex of the cerebellum. The stimulus activates a small bundle of parallel fibres which in turn excite the underlying Purkinje cells, the basket and stellate cells and the Golgi cells. Only those Purkinje cells which are passed by the bundle of active parallel fibres are excited, while those on both sides of this region are strongly inhibited. This inhibition is mediated by the axons of the basket and stellate cells which extend at right-angles to the parallel fibres. The effect of the inhibitory neurons is

regions of the cerebellar cortex and that there was a somatotopical localisation similar to that found in the cerebral cortex (Fig. 17.6). Responses were easily obtained from skin and muscle receptors but could also be evoked by acoustic or visual stimuli. Furthermore, it was found that stimulation of the sensorimotor region of the cerebral cortex produced responses in the cerebellar cortex. These findings confirmed what was already known from neuroanatomical studies but provided little insight into the functional organisation of the cerebellar cortex. Such information did not become available until recordings were made from single neurons.

Fig. 17.6 Cerebellar homunculus showing the distribution of proprioceptive and tactile afferent input from various parts of the body. (From Snider, *Proc. Assoc. Res. Nerv. Ment. Dis.*, 30, 1952.)

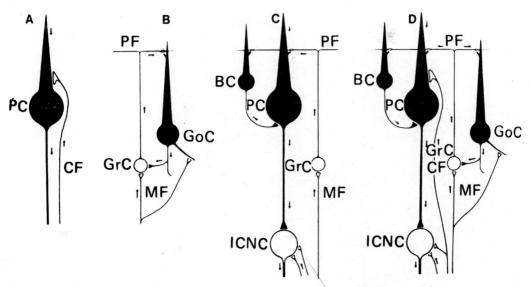

Fig. 17.7 Schematic diagram of the neuronal connections in the cerebellum. Inhibitory cells are shown in black. The component circuits of (A), (B) and (C) are assembled in (D). PC, Purkinje cell; CF, climbing fibre; GrC, granule cell; PF, parallel fibre; GoC, Golgi cell; MF, mossy fibre; BC, basket cell; ICNC, intra-cellular nuclear cell. (From Eccles, *The Understanding of the Brain*, McGraw-Hill, 1973.)

therefore to sharpen the boundaries of the active zone. The effect is closely similar to that of lateral inhibition in the retina. However, the basket and stellate cells also exert a certain inhibitory action on the Purkinje cells in the active zone. The main effect of this inhibition is to cut off the activity of the Purkinje cells.

The studies of the behaviour of the different types of neurons in the cerebellar cortex led to the surprising discovery that the Purkinje cells themselves are inhibitory neurons. This implies that the excitatory input to the cerebellar cortex is transformed into an inhibitory output to the cerebellar nuclei. The functional significance of this inhibition is understood if we consider that the cerebellar nuclei receive a strong excitatory input from the collaterals of the climbing and mossy fibres and that this input is relayed to spinal motor systems and to the cerebral cortex by the efferents of the cerebellar nuclei. This output is in turn modulated by the inhibitory action of the Purkinje cells. The excitatory influx to the cerebellum is thus processed in the cortex and transformed into inhibitory signals which modulate the output from the cere-

bellum (Fig. 17.8). This is the key to the understanding of cerebellar functions.

Coordination of motor functions

The cerebellum does not initiate movements but is essential for the coordination of voluntary movements and for the control of muscular tone, posture and equilibrium. The importance of the cerebellum for various motor functions has been studied by disrupting the connections between the cerebellum and the other parts of the nervous system. Three main syndromes are produced: disturbances of equilibrium, inability to perform rapid alternating movements and tremor during performance of voluntary movements.

Recent studies of the activity of Purkinje cells have provided interesting insight into the mechanism underlying the coordinating functions of the cerebellum. It appears that the command signals sent out from the cerebral cortex reach the Purkinje cells before they arrive at the motoneurons. This has been disclosed by the discovery that some Purkinje cells begin to fire about 25 ms before the

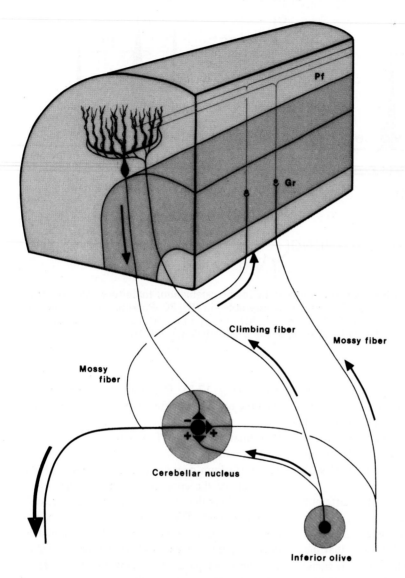

Fig. 17.8 Summary of principal afferent and efferent connections of the cerebellar cortex.

muscle movement. This suggests that the cerebellar cortex exerts its modulatory influence on the output of the descending motor pathways before the command signal has reached the motoneurons. With some exaggeration it may thus be said that the cerebellum is able to correct for cerebral mistakes before they are committed. It is important to note that the coordinating function of the cerebellum during the performance of a given movement is dependent on the continuous input from muscle and skin receptors as well as from sub-

cortical motor centres. By comparing this information with the cortical command signal, the cerebellum controls and adjusts the movement. The principle by which the cerebellum appears to work is that of feed-forward control and corresponds to a surprising extent to procedures widely used in modern technology. In the control of airplanes, missiles or automatically controlled industrial processes, stabilisation and adjustment is based on sampling of data in centres from which the controlling signals are sent out.

It should be noted that the cerebellum is able to exert its coordinating functions without the feedback from muscle and skin receptors. An example of this is the control of rapid movements such as in playing the piano. The movements involved appear to be too fast to allow for correction on the basis of sensory feedback. The performance of this kind of movements is based entirely on programming by previous training.

A basic condition for the coordinating functions of the cerebellum is that they are carried out with great speed. An indication that this actually occurs is the high frequency of the cerebellar EEG waves. The resting rhythm of the cerebellar cortex has a basic frequency of 150–300 Hz, upon which there are superimposed still more rapid waves of 1000–2000 Hz, i.e. the resting activity is more than 10 times faster than that of the cerebral cortex.

The importance of cerebellar mechanisms in the control of movements in humans is illustrated by the deficits which appear after lesions in various parts of the cerebellum. In man, the most noticeable signs of cerebellar dysfunction are disturbances of balance and changes in precision, rate, extent and force of muscle movements. A person with cerebellar damage has a broad-based and uncertain walk, and must think about each step in order not to lose his balance. Such a person walks with his cerebral cortex, without the coordinating function which the cerebellum normally provides. Another symptom is difficulty in carrying out precise movements. Simple movements become extremely difficult, and require correction from the cortex during the whole performance of the movement. The patient initially has difficulty in finding the intended direction of movement, and is not able to carry it out rapidly and precisely. This may be due partly to the disturbance of the normal control of muscle tone via the gamma system. The loss of gamma activity might also be the reason for the general decrease in tone, which is another characteristic symptom of cerebellar injury.

BIBLIOGRAPHY FOR SECTION VII

Suggested Reading and Reviews

Asanuma, H. (1975). Recent developments in the study of the columnar arrangement of neurons within the motor cortex, *Physiol. Rev.*, **55**, 143–156

Chan-Palay, V. (1977). *Cerebellar Dentate Nucleus. Organization, Cytology and Transmitters*, Springer-Verlag, Heidelberg

DeLong, M. R. (1974). Motor functions of the basal ganglia: single-unit activity during movement, in *The Neurosciences. Third Study Program*, eds F. O. Schmitt and F. G. Worden, MIT Press, Cambridge MA, pp. 319–325

Eccles, J. C. (1969). The inhibitory pathways of the central nervous system, *The Sherrington Lectures* IX, C. C. Thomas, Springfield

Eccles, J. C., Ito, M. and Szentagothai, J. (1967). *The Cerebellum as a Neuronal Machine*, Springer-Verlag, Berlin

Evarts, E. V. (1967). Representation of movements and muscles by pyramidal tract neurons of the precentral motor cortex, in *Neurophysiological Basis of Normal and Abnormal Motor Activities*, eds M. D. Yahr and D. P. Purpura, Raven Press, New York, pp. 215–251

Evarts, E. V. (1975). Activity of cerebral neurons in relation to movement, in *The Nervous System*, vol. 1, ed. D. B. Tower, Raven Press, New York, pp. 221–233

Evarts, E. V. (1979). Brain mechanisms of movement, *Scient. Am.*, **241**, 146–156

Granit, R. (ed.) (1966). *Muscle Afferents and Motor Control*, John Wiley & Sons, New York

Granit, R. (1970). *The Basis of Motor Control*, Academic Press, New York

Grillner, S. (1975). Locomotion in vertebrates – central mechanisms and reflex interaction, *Physiol. Rev.*, **55**, 247–304

Iggo, A. (ed.) (1973). *Somatosensory System, Handbook of Sensory Physiology*, vol. 2, Springer-Verlag, Berlin

Ito, M. (1974). The control mechanisms of cerebellar motor systems, in *The Neurosciences. Third Study Program*, eds F. O. Schmitt and F. G. Worden, MIT Press, Cambridge, MA, pp. 293–303

Ito, M. (1978). Recent advances in cerebellar physiology and pathology, in *Advances in Neurology*, vol. 21, eds R. A. P. Kark, R. N. Rosenberg and L. J. Schut, Raven Press, New York, pp. 59–84

Kornhuber, H. H. (1974). Cerebral cortex, cerebellum, and basal ganglia: an introduction to their motor functions, in *The Neurosciences. Third Study Program*, eds F. O. Schmitt and F. G. Worden, MIT Press, Cambridge, MA, pp. 267–280

Llinas, R. (1969). Neuronal operations in cerebellar transactions, in *The Neurosciences. Second Study Program*, ed. F. O. Schmitt, Rockefeller University Press, New York, pp. 409–426

Llinas, R. (1975). The cerebellar cortex, in *The Nervous System*, vol. 1, ed. D. B. Tower, Raven Press, New York, pp. 235–244

Magoun, H. W. (1950). Caudal and cephalic influences of the brain stem reticular formation, *Physiol. Rev.*, **30**, 459–474

McGeer, P. L., Eccles, J. C. and McGeer, E. G. (1978). *Molecular Neurobiology of the Mammalian Brain*, Plenum Press, New York

Mountcastle, V. B. (1961). Some functional properties of the somatic afferent system, in *Sensory Communication*, ed. W. A. Rosenblith, MIT Press, Cambridge, MA, pp. 403–436

Oscarsson, O. (1973). Functional organization of spinocerebellar paths, in *Somatosensory System*,

Handbook of Sensory Physiology, vol. 2 ed. A. Iggo, Springer-Verlag, Berlin, pp. 339–380

Oscarsson, O. (1976). Spatial distribution of climbing and mossy fibre inputs into the cerebellar cortex, in *Afferent and Intrinsic Organization of Laminated Structures in the Brain*, ed. O. Creutzfeldt, Springer-Verlag, Heidelberg

Penfield, W. and Rasmussen, T. (1950). *The Cerebral Cortex in Man*, Macmillan, New York

Porter, R. (1973). Functions of the mammalian cerebral cortex in movement, in *Progress in Neurobiology*, vol. 1/1, eds G. A. Kerkut and J. W. Phillips, Pergamon Press, New York

Sherrington, C. S. (1906). *The Integrative Action of the Nervous System*, Yale University Press, New Haven

Stein, R. B. (1974). Peripheral control of movement, *Physiol. Rev.*, **54**, 215–243

Welt, C., Aschoff, J. C., Kameda, K. and Brooks, V. B. (1967). Intracortical organization of cat's motorsensory neurons, in *Neurophysiological Basis of Normal and Abnormal Motor Activities*, eds M. D. Yahr and D. P. Purpura, Raven Press, New York, pp. 255–289

Wiesendanger, M. (1969). The pyramidal tract. Recent investigations on its morphology and function, *Ergebn. Physiol.*, **61**, 73–136

Original Papers

Asanuma, H. and Rosen, I. (1972). Topographical organization of cortical efferent zones projecting to distal forelimb muscles in the monkey, *Exp. Brain Res.*, **14**, 243–256

Asanuma, H. and Sakata, H. (1967). Functional organization of a cortical efferent system examined with focal depth stimulation in cats, *J. Neurophysiol.*, **30**, 35–54

Asanuma, H. and Ward, J. E. (1971). Patterns of contraction of distal forelimb muscles produced by intracortical stimulation in cats, *Brain Res.*, **27**, 97–109

Axelrad, H. (1976). Identification of pyramidal tract cells and determination of spontaneous unitary activity in immature rat somatomotor neocortex, *Exp. Brain Res.*, **227**, 277–281

Bernhard, C. G. and Bohm, E. (1954). Mono-synaptic corticospinal activation of forelimb motoneurones in monkeys (*Macaca mulatta*), *Acta Physiol. Scand.*, **31**, 104–112

Desmedt, J. E. (1980). Patterns of motor commands during various types of voluntary movement in man, *Trends in Neurosci.*, **3**(11), 265–268

Eccles, J. C. (1973). The cerebellum as a computer: Patterns in space and time, *J. Physiol. (Lond.)*, **229**, 1–32

Eccles, J. C., Fatt, P. and Landgren, S. (1956). Central pathway for direct inhibitory action of impulses in largest afferent nerve fibres to muscle, *J. Neurophysiol.*, **19**, 75–98

Eccles, J. C., Llinas, R. and Sasaki, K. (1966). The inhibitory interneurones within the cerebellar cortex, *Exp. Brain Res.*, **1**, 1–16

Eccles, J. C., Llinas, R. and Sasaki, K. (1966). Parallel fibre stimulation and the responses induced thereby in the Purkinje cells of the cerebellum, *Exp. Brain Res.*, **1**, 17–39

Eccles, J. C., Llinas, R. and Sasaki, K. (1966). The excitatory synaptic action of climbing fibres on the Purkinje cells of the cerebellum, *J. Physiol. (Lond.)*, **182**, 268–296

Eccles, J. C., Sasaki, K. and Strata, P. (1967). The potential fields generated in the cerebellar cortex by a mossy fibre volley, *Exp. Brain Res.*, **3**, 58–80

Eccles, J. C., Sasaki, K. and Strata, P. (1967). A comparison of the inhibitory actions of Golgi cells and of basket cells, *Exp. Brain Res.*, **3**, 81–94

Evarts, E. V. (1966). Pyramidal tract activity associated with a conditioned hand movement in the monkey, *J. Neurophysiol.*, **29**, 1011–1027

Evarts, E. V. (1968). Relation of pyramidal tract activity to force exerted during voluntary movement, *J. Neurophysiol.*, **31**, 14–27

Evarts, E. V. (1974). Precentral and postcentral cortical activity in association with visually triggered movement, *J. Neurophysiol.*, **37**, 373–381

Hamori, J. and Szentagothai, J. (1965). The Purkinje cell baskets: ultrastructure of an inhibitory synapse, *Acta Biol. Acad. Sci. Hung.*, **15**, 465–479

Hamori, J. and Szentagothai, J. (1966). Identification under the electron microscope of climbing fibres and their synaptic contacts, *Exp. Brain Res.*, **1**, 65–81

Hyvärinen, J., Poranen, A., Jokinen, Y., Näätänen, R. and Linnankoski, I. (1973). Observations on unit activity in the primary somesthetic cortex of behaving monkeys, in *The Somatosensory System*, ed. H. H. Kornhuber, Georg Thieme Verlag, Stuttgart

Ito, M. (1970). Neurophysiological aspects of the cerebellar motor control system, *Int. J. Neurol.*, **7**, 162–176

Ito, M. (1972). Neural design of the cerebellar motor control system, *Brain Res.*, **40**, 81–84

Ito, M. and Yoshida, M. (1966). The origin of cerebellar-induced inhibition of Deiters neurones. I. Monosynaptic initiation of the inhibitory postsynaptic potentials, *Exp. Brain Res.*, **2**, 330–349

Lindsley, D. B., Schreiner, L. H. and Magoun, H. W. (1949). An electromyographic study of spasticity, *J. Neurophysiol.*, **12**, 197–216

Llinas, R. and Precht, W. (1969). The inhibitory vestibular efferent system and its relation to the cerebellum in the frog, *Exp. Brain Res.*, **9**, 16–29

Marr, D. (1969). Theory of cerebellar cortex, *J. Physiol. (Lond.)*, **202**, 437–470

Mountcastle, V. B. (1957). Modality and topographic properties of single neurons of cat's somatic sensory cortex, *J. Neurophysiol.*, **20**, 408–434

Oscarsson, O. (1969). Termination and functional organization of the dorsal spino-olivocerebellar path, *J. Physiol. (Lond.)*, **200**, 129–149

Oscarsson, O. and Sjölund, B. (1977). The ventral spino-olivocerebellar system in the cat. I. Identification of five paths and their termination in the cerebellar anterior lobe, *Exp. Brain Res.*, **28**, 469–486

Oscarsson, O. and Sjölund, B. (1977). The ventral spino-olivocerebellar system in the cat. II. Termination zones in the cerebellar posterior lobe, *Exp. Brain Res.*, **28**, 487–503

Penfield, W. and Boldrey, E. (1937). Somatic motor and sensory representation in the cerebral cortex of man as studied by electrical stimulation, *Brain*, **60**, 389–443

Powell, T. P. S. and Mountcastle, V. B. (1959). Some aspects of the functional organization of the cortex of the postcentral gyrus of the monkey: a correlation of findings obtained in a single unit analysis with cytoarchitecture, *Bull. Johns Hopkins Hosp.*, **105**, 133–162

Rosen, I. and Asanuma, H. (1971). Peripheral afferent inputs to the forelimb area of the monkey motor cortex: Input–output relations, *Exp. Brain Res.*, **14**, 257–273

Snider, R. S. and Stowell, A. (1944). Receiving areas of the tactile, auditory and visual systems in the cerebellum, *J. Neurophysiol.*, **7**, 331–357

Section VIII: Neural Control of Visceral Functions and Behaviour

18

The Autonomic Nervous System

Functional anatomy of the autonomic system

The autonomic nervous system contributes through its various actions to the homeostasis of the organism, that is to the maintenance of the optimal internal environment of the body. It fulfils this function by a fine control of smooth muscles, cardiac muscle, exocrine glands and some endocrine glands. Anatomically it is composed of two divisions: the sympathetic and the parasympathetic systems (Fig. 18.1). The sympathetic fibres stem from cells situated in the thoracic and two upper lumbar segments, while the parasympathetic fibres have cells in the brain stem and in the second to

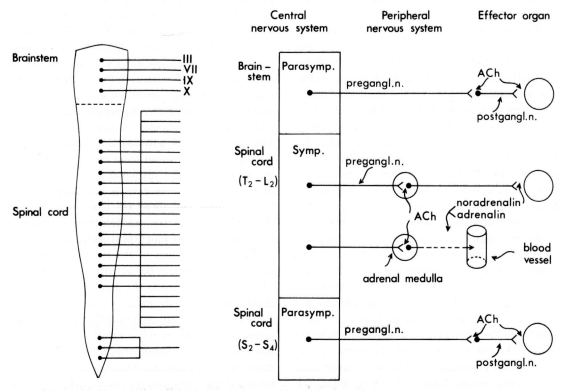

Fig. 18.1   Schematic diagram showing general organisation of the autonomic nervous system.

The parasympathetic effects on different organs thus lack a common denominator like that seen in the functions of the sympathetic system; for example, parasympathetic activity causes a slowing of the heart, increased gastrointestinal activity, contraction of the bladder, and constriction of the pupils.

Transmitter substances

The idea that autonomic effects are mediated by chemical transmitters was first presented in 1904 by Elliot, who based his hypothesis on the observation that the effects of adrenalin resemble those produced by stimulating sympathetic nerves. Two decades passed before Elliot's hypothesis was experimentally proven. In 1921 Loewi showed that the vagal inhibition of the heart is mediated by the release of a chemical transmitter later identified as acetylcholine (ACh). When further studies indicated that the transmitter substances in the autonomic system were adrenalin or acetylcholine, the autonomic fibres were classified as cholinergic and adrenergic. Noradrenalin is the transmitter at the postganglionic sympathetic terminals except those to the sweat glands (see Fig. 18.1). Acetylcholine is the mediator in all autonomic ganglia, all parasympathetic postganglionic terminals and the sympathetic postganglionic terminals to the sweat glands. It remains in an inactive form, stored in small vesicles, until its release during activity of the nerve fibre, whereupon it diffuses from the terminals to the effector organ. The released acetylcholine is rapidly hydrolysed to choline and acetic acid by an enzyme, acetylcholinesterase, whose action may be inhibited by a number of drugs, e.g. physostigmine (eserine) and neostigmine (prostigmin).

Later experiments found a discrepancy between the effects obtained with adrenalin and with stimulation of sympathetic nerves, suggesting that some other substance was the transmitter. In 1946 von Euler showed that extracts from the splenic nerve of the ox contained noradrenalin and he therefore suggested that it was this substance that was released from the sympathetic nerves. Extensive studies have confirmed that noradrenalin serves as a transmitter in most of the postganglionic sympathetic nerve fibres, although some nerve terminals simultaneously release traces of adrenalin as well. Unlike acetylcholine, which is rapidly broken down, adrenalin and noradrenalin are relatively stable and can be found in the blood and urine after stimulation of the sympathetic system. In this system the effect is terminated mainly by 'removal' or by uptake into sympathetic nerve terminals where they may be 're-used' as transmitters or broken down enzymatically by monoamine oxidase (MAO), or by non-neuronal cells where they are metabolised either by MAO or by catechol-*O*-methyl transferase (COMT).

The observation that adrenalin causes contractions in some smooth muscles and relaxation in others has led to the assumption that different types of receptors exist in the effector organs. The adrenergic receptors are classified into two main types: (1) alpha receptors (which can be subdivided into $alpha_1$ and $alpha_2$), mediating either excitation (e.g. in smooth muscle in most tissues) or inhibition (of many neural or metabolic functions); and (2) beta receptors (subdivided into $beta_1$ and $beta_2$), mediating either excitation (of myocardium, neural and metabolic functions) or inhibition (of some smooth muscle). The action of noradrenalin or adrenalin on alpha receptors is often to alter the permeability of the cell membrane in target organs to certain ions, while their effects on beta receptors are in many cases mediated by activation of adenylate cyclase and formation of cyclic AMP as an intracellular second messenger. The situation is complicated by the fact that most organs contain both alpha and beta receptors. Noradrenalin and adrenalin are about equally potent with regard to their action on $alpha_1$, $alpha_2$ and $beta_1$ receptors, but $beta_2$ receptors are relatively selectively activated by adrenalin. Consequently, both are about equally strong as vasoconstrictors in many tissues (skin, viscera), but they differ with regard to effects on the huge vascular bed of skeletal muscle, where adrenalin is a vasodilator while noradrenalin is a vasoconstrictor. Noradrenalin will, when infused into the circulation (e.g. from the adrenal medulla), tend to cause a rise in (both systolic, diastolic and mean) arterial blood pressure, while adrenalin has a mixed effect, enhancing the systolic but depressing the diastolic pressure, and therefore often not altering the mean pressure. A distinction can also be made between two types of cholinergic receptors at the endplate in skeletal muscle and those in smooth muscle. The former receptors are excited with nicotine whereas the latter are excited by muscarine. Hence the former are called nicotinic receptors and the latter muscarinic receptors.

The activity of the autonomic nerves may be mimicked by administration of different drugs. Some of these influence the ganglia, others the cholinergic or adrenergic effectors. Many of these substances have seen wide use in clinical medicine, for treating disorders of the digestive circulatory and respiratory systems. More recently, drugs have been developed which have been classified as alpha or beta receptor blocking agents depending on which type of receptor they act on. Drugs with alpha receptor blocking effect have found limited clinical application, whereas beta receptor blocking drugs are widely used in the treatment of, for instance, angina pectoris, essential hypertension and certain types of cardiac arrhythmias.

Neurophysiology of Behaviour

19.1   The limbic system

The limbic system is a part of the brain consisting of a band of cortical tissue on the medial sides of the hemispheres and, partly, of deeper structures including the amygdala, the hippocampus and the septal nuclei (Fig. 19.1). The limbic areas are phylogenetically among the oldest parts of the brain. In the course of evolutionary development, they have been more or less covered by the cortex of the cerebrum, but the limbic system has relatively few connections with it. The neocortex has therefore been likened to a rider astride the limbic system but unable to steer it. As our instincts and emotional life seem centred in the limbic system, they appear to be outside the control of the cortex. In electrophysiological studies of the limbic system, single stimuli often give very long-lasting responses, which may explain why emotional reactions may long outlast their stimulus.

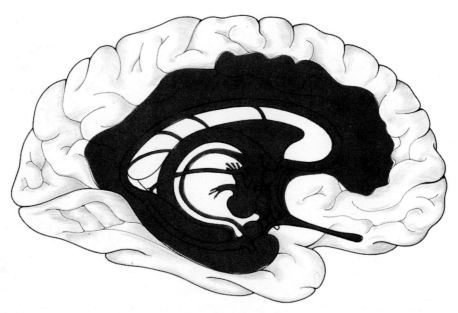

Fig. 19.1   Midline sagittal section of the brain to show the principal regions included under the term 'the limbic system' (shaded areas).

The limbic system was earlier called the rhinencephalon, the olfactory brain (Fig. 19.2), and was thought to deal mainly with smell and eating. It was known that stimulation of one of the nuclei in the amygdala causes chewing, swallowing, licking and other movements of food ingestion, and that injuries to the amygdala produce hyperphagia, characterised by indiscriminate consumption of nearly anything available. It was later found that the limbic system also controls sexual behaviour and emotional reactions; furthermore, electrical stimulation of certain parts of its region affects visceral functions. The limbic system may thus serve as a superior regulatory control system for visceral and vascular functions; or, alternatively, the vegetative effects may only be links in a chain of events started by the emotional reactions elicited from the limbic system.

It has long been known that injuries within certain parts of the limbic system in animals can alter their reactions to external stimuli. Calm and affectionate animals become aggressive and wild; weak or neutral external stimuli produce bursts of anger, during which the animals attack other animals, the experimenters, or nearby objects. Lesions elsewhere in the limbic system may eliminate normal fear or flight reactions, typical of which is the reaction of monkeys to snakes. At the sight of a snake, monkeys normally show signs of great fear and try to flee, but after bilateral lesions in the amygdala this fear vanishes; the monkeys will even try to catch and eat the snake. Wild rats, which are very aggressive and difficult to handle in captivity, become calm and quiet after lesion in the amygdalae, although the aggression returns if parts of the hypothalamus are stimulated. Two counterbalancing systems seem to operate, one producing a calm and peaceful behaviour pattern and the other producing aggression. The mechanism may well differ in man, of course, since the basis for human emotions is probably more complex and subtle; still, anatomically our limbic system is very like that of monkeys, and injuries in the amygdalae of humans after brain operations prompt reactions similar to the effects described above in animals. For example, injuries in the hypothalamic ventromedial nuclei are followed by personality changes involving pronounced aggressiveness.

In animals, bilateral lesions in certain parts of the limbic system markedly increase sexual activity. The animals are attracted not only by the opposite sex but by other species, and they attempt copulation with almost any available object. Further evidence links the hypothalamus with the control of sexual activity. Thus, stimulation within certain parts of the male hypothalamus causes erection, while lesions of other parts abolish sexual activity. The implantation of small amounts of oestrogen within the anterior part of the hypothalamus of the female rat causes the animal to go into heat, an effect not obtained elsewhere in the brain. Clearly cells of this area must be sensitive to oestrogen circulating in the blood.

From many sites in the brain, it is possible to elicit behavioural reactions which are directed to attain a goal. The rewarding effect of brain stimulation was discovered by Olds and Milner in 1954. Quite accidentally they found that some rats appeared to enjoy electrical stimulation of certain

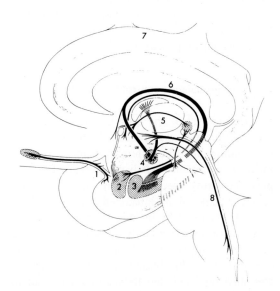

Fig. 19.2 Schematic representation of the principal pathways of the limbic system: 1, olfactory striae; 2, amygdaloid complex; 3, hippocampal formation; 4, mamillary body; 5, thalamus; 6, fornix; 7, longitudinal striae; 8, dorsal longitudinal fasciculus.

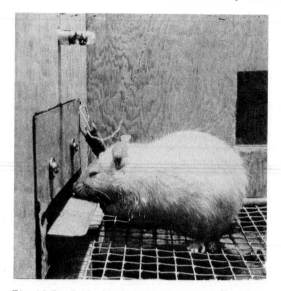

Fig. 19.3 Self-stimulation experiment. Each time the animal presses the pedal, a stimulus is delivered to its brain through implanted electrodes. (From Olds, in *Electrical Stimulation of the Unanesthetized Brain*, Hoeber, New York, 1960.)

regions of the brain (Fig. 19.3). The animals rapidly learned to press a lever to obtain such stimulation. At about the same time Milner and his associates reported that stimulation of certain hypothalamic regions induced 'aversive' responses such as flight or attack reactions. These rats rapidly learned to press a lever to terminate the stimulus that gave the aversive response. These findings suggested that there exist specific brain systems for reward and punishment. The reward system occupies large regions of the brain including the limbic system, the hypothalamus and some regions of the frontal and temporal cortex. Rats with electrodes placed in any of these regions stimulate themselves regularly for long periods of time and may reach a stimulation rate of several thousand shocks per hour. The strength of the drive for stimulation may be so strong that given a choice between food and stimulation the rat may prefer the latter; nor do the rats hesitate to expose themselves to painful electric shocks to reach the lever. The strongest reward effects in terms of stimulation rate are obtained in the posterior and lateral hypothalamus within the regions of the medial forebrain bundle.

This suggests that the reward effects are dependent on structures activated by the fibres of the medial forebrain bundle. A great portion of the fibres in this bundle are adrenergic, indicating that the reward effects are induced by central adrenergic mechanisms. However, the observation that lesions involving large parts of the medial forebrain bundle produce little effect on the reward response indicates that the reward system has a diffuse distribution in the brain. Furthermore, reward responses may be elicited at some sites after injection of drugs that block adrenergic transmission; it would thus appear that the reward system is not purely adrenergic.

The punishment system is more diffusely spread than the reward system and includes parts of the lateral and medial hypothalamus, hippocampus, thalamus, amygdala and the ventricular grey of the midbrain. When stimulated at certain points in these regions, the animal begins to tremble or tries to flee. Often the sites where aversive reactions are elicited are located close to the reward sites. It was at first believed that the aversive reactions were elicited by stimulation of pain pathways. However, this appears not to be so since aversive effects may be obtained from sites with no obvious connections with central pain pathways.

19.2 Hypothalamic control functions

For the survival of the organism, it is a primary prerequisite in all warm-blooded species that the temperature and the internal chemical environment are maintained relatively constant. The complex regulatory mechanisms by which this constancy is achieved are integrated in the hypothalamus. As indicated by its name, the hypothalamus is a portion of the brain lying beneath the thalamus. Its functional significance remained almost unknown until the beginning of this century. It was then observed that lesions or brain tumours in the hypothalamic region were associated with disturbances in various functions controlled by endocrine organs. It was also found that stimulation of the hypothalamus produced various reactions mediated by the autonomic nervous system.

It was, however, not until Horsley and Clarke introduced the stereotactic method for stimulation of precisely localised areas of the brain that a more detailed study of the hypothalamus became possible. These studies have established that the hypothalamus has a vast array of multifaceted functions which embody two main areas: the maintenance of a constant internal environment (*homeostasis*) and the control of behaviour patterns. The hypothalamus exerts its function as controller of homeostatic mechanisms by integration of the functions of the autonomic nervous system. For this reason, the hypothalamus has been designated by Sherrington as the 'head ganglion of the autonomic nervous system'. In broad outline, the anterior part of the hypothalamus activates the parasympathetic system and inhibits the sympathetic system, whilst the posterior hypothalamus activates the sympathetic system. Through its close connections with the limbic system and the forebrain, the hypothalamus plays a key role in the regulation of emotional and instinctual behaviour, including motivated behaviour patterns such as feeding, drinking, copulatory reactions, etc. Extensive studies have provided evidence that the control exerted by the hypothalamus is mediated by the endocrine system. This has led to the development of a new field in neuroscience, termed *neuroendocrinology*.

Anatomically, the hypothalamus is composed of small nerve cells which are arranged in groups or nuclei which in general are not clearly segregated one from another (Fig. 19.4). Except for a few cases, it has not been possible to assign a

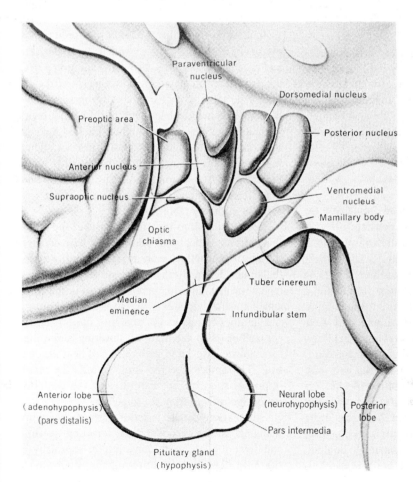

Fig. 19.4   Diagram showing localisation of principal hypothalamic nuclei and the hypophysis of the mammalian brain. (From Noback and Demaret, in *The Human Nervous System*, McGraw-Hill, 1975.)

particular function to a specific nucleus. The hypothalamic connections are numerous and complex. Some of the fibre systems constitute fairly discrete tracts, while others are diffuse. The origin and terminations are established for some of these fibre systems but are unknown for others. In broad outline, the hypothalamus receives its major input from the non-specific reticular system and from the olfactory system and the hippocampus. There are also less well defined pathways connecting the hypothalamus with the limbic system, the frontal cortex, the thalamus and the periaqueductal grey matter. The hypothalamus in turn sends projections to most of these regions. Fibre tracts involved in the regulation of water metabolism pass from hypothalamic nuclei into the posterior lobe of the hypophysis. In addition, there is a direct vascular link 'the hypophysial portal vessel system' between the hypothalamus and the anterior lobe of the hypophysis.

In brief, the hypothalamus exerts its integrating control functions through the autonomic and endocrine systems as well as via efferent somatic systems. Of the many important functions executed by the hypothalamus, only those associated with the regulation of body temperature, food intake and water balance will be considered.

19.3 Temperature regulation

In humans, as in all warm-blooded animals, body temperature remains relatively constant despite changes in the ambient temperature and variations in the heat production of the body. The critical balance between heat production and heat loss is achieved by central regulating mechanisms controlled by the hypothalamus. When body temperature rises, heat loss increases and heat production decreases. Increased heat loss is achieved by dilatation of the blood vessels of the skin, which emit heat through radiation; this can only occur, however, if the temperature of the surroundings is lower than that of the body. For higher ambient temperatures, the body has at its disposal yet another protective mechanism, sweating. Sweating in itself causes no cooling; it is the evaporation of fluid from the skin sur-

face that cools, and this in turn depends upon the humidity of the air. In warm, dry air, evaporation is swift and effects a rapid heat loss, so that even at high temperatures there is little risk of a rise in body temperature. The combination of high temperature and high humidity, on the other hand, may induce hyperthermia and heat prostration, since heat loss through radiation cannot occur and the evaporation of perspiration is slowed. Animals lacking sweat glands (and therefore unable to lose heat through perspiration) resort to polypnea, i.e. rapid, shallow respirations achieving heat loss by exhaled air. A general decrease in muscle tone occurs at high temperatures; it is one reason why we feel comfortably relaxed in warm surroundings. This decrease in tone is yet another heat defence mechanism; it decreases the body's heat production and thus helps slow the rise in body temperature.

In cool surroundings, heat loss is reduced by peripheral vasoconstriction, which cools the skin and decreases the loss through radiation. Heat production is increased by shivering, i.e. irregular muscular activity characterised by phasic muscle contractions which begin in the arm and trunk musculature. Shivering is probably elicited through a direct reflex mechanism as the skin cools. When the body temperature falls substantially, metabolically active hormones such as thyroxine, noradrenalin and adrenalin contribute to a general rise in the metabolism.

Restricted lesions in different parts of the hypothalamus and electrical stimulation have located the centres for temperature regulation in the hypothalamus. These studies suggest that there is a region in the anterior part of the hypothalamus which controls vasodilatation, sweating and panting and another region in the posterior hypothalamus controlling vasoconstriction, shivering and other mechanisms associated with raising of heat production. The anterior region thus controls the reflex responses induced by warmth and the posterior region the reflex responses to cold.

Stimulation of the anterior part of the hypothalamus causes vasodilatation, sweating, panting and lowering of body temperature, especially if the animal is in cold surroundings. Following a lesion in the anterior part of the hypothalamus, an experimental animal is unable to sustain normal body temperature in warm surroundings and may die of hyperthermia at a slight increase in ambient temperature. Similarly, tumours or injuries in the anterior part of the hypothalamus in man may lead to hyperthermia and inability to maintain normal temperature in warm surroundings. Stimulation of the posterior regions causes the opposite effects: vasoconstriction and shivering. Following lesions in this region, the body temperature tends to fall to that of the environment.

The temperature regulating centre of the hypothalamus appears to work as a dual thermostat which prevents major changes in body temperature. When the temperature of the environment increases, the anterior parts of the centre are activated and reflexes mediating heat loss are induced; when environmental temperature decreases, the posterior region is thrown into activity and reflexes mediating heat production and heat conservation are activated.

To fulfil its regulatory functions, the hypothalamus must receive information about the environmental temperature as well as about the internal body temperature. This information is obtained from two sources: (1) cutaneous receptors in the skin, and (2) thermosensitive cells in the hypothalamus. The message arriving from the cold receptors in the skin appears to be distributed to the posterior region of the thermoregulatory centre and that from warmth receptors to the anterior region. The existence of thermosensitive cells in the hypothalamus has been established by warming or cooling the blood of the carotid arteries. In dogs warming the blood causes panting, sweating and vasodilatation while cooling induces shivering, vasoconstriction and piloerection. Microelectrode recordings have provided further evidence of the existence of hypothalamic thermodetectors. It has been shown that there are cells in the hypothalamic thermoregulatory centres which respond to a rise in temperature while others are activated by a fall.

The setting of the central thermostat may be changed by certain toxins known as *pyrogens* which are produced by bacteria or liberated from white blood cells (*endogenous pyrogens*). Under the influence of these toxins, the thermoregulatory centre may behave as if set to maintain the temperature of the body at a higher level than normal. It is not known how this change is induced. It has been suggested that the action of pyrogens is mediated by prostaglandins. This suggestion is based upon the finding that aspirin, which is well known to depress fever, inhibits the synthesis of prostaglandins.

19.4   Regulation of food intake

An adult animal maintains a relatively constant body weight even though its energy expenditure may change considerably from day to day and week to week. This requires that the food intake be regulated to correspond to the energy requirements. If the food intake exceeds the energy expenditure, the surplus is stored in the form of fat; if it is less, some of the reserves must be used. The adjustment of food intake to energy expenditure represents a series of complex regulatory mechanisms in which hunger and satiety are the most important factors.

Hunger may be defined as a diffuse, craving sense of emptiness, usually felt in the abdomen. Hunger is distinct from appetite, the desire for especially palatable food, whose role in food intake bears more on what is eaten than how much. It is hunger that decides the quantitative intake. Since the feeling of hunger is usually related to the abdominal cavity, hunger was at first associated with the stomach, particularly when in the early 1900s so-called hunger contractions were recorded in the stomach. The feeling of emptiness in the stomach is not, however, the decisive factor in regulating food intake. For instance, after vagotomy (transection of the vagus nerve) the motor behaviour of the stomach changes but the food intake is not particularly influenced. Moreover, although hunger contractions disappear after a few morsels of food, the hunger feeling does not necessarily abate. Nor is filling of the stomach correlated with the feeling of satiety. It is well known that hunger can be temporarily eliminated by eating low-caloric food that fills the stomach, but the feeling

intake of water, and (2) release of antidiuretic hormone (ADH) that regulates the output of water through the kidneys. Thirst may not only signal a general lack of water but also an abnormal distribution of water in the body (see Fig. 19.7). Normally the water content of the body is distributed between a sodium-rich extracellular compartment and a potassium-rich intracellular compartment. The latter is larger and comprises two-thirds of the body's total water content. If there is a disturbance in the distribution of water between these two compartments, reactions are elicited which serve to restore the fluid balance. If, for example, there is an increased intake of salt, the concentration of sodium in the extracellular space rises, which in turn leads to a shift of water from the intracellular space to the extracellular. This condition is called *relative dehydration*, while *absolute dehydration* is the condition caused by a deficit in water intake.

In relative dehydration, salt secretion through the kidneys increases and this contributes to the restoration of normal water distribution. The opposite occurs with lack of salt; the sodium concentration in the extracellular space falls, and more water is taken up by cells, creating a condition of cellular overhydration. The decrease of extracellular fluid in turn leads to a decrease of blood

volume, which stimulates the kidneys to release renin, whereby angiotensinogen in the blood is transformed into angiotensin II, a substance extremely active in causing vasoconstriction, thus helping to maintain blood pressure at a normal level. Angiotensin also stimulates the secretion of aldosterone, which increases the reabsorption of sodium by the kidneys.

The hormonal regulation of water reabsorption in the kidneys is mediated by the release of antidiuretic hormone (ADH) from the posterior lobe of the hypophysis. The hormone is carried via the blood to the kidneys, where it reduces water loss and concentrates the urine. Its effect upon the body's fluid balance is the same as drinking water. ADH is produced by nerve cells in the hypothalamus and transported via nerve fibres to the posterior lobe of the hypophysis, the neurohypophysis, where it is stored until released by a neuroregulatory mechanism. If the nervous connection between the hypothalamus and the neurohypophysis is interrupted, the release of ADH ceases, and a disease called *diabetes insipidus* develops. It is characterised by a disturbance of fluid regulation in which enormous amounts of urine are voided, due to the absence of ADH regulation of the reabsorption of water in the kidneys. The water

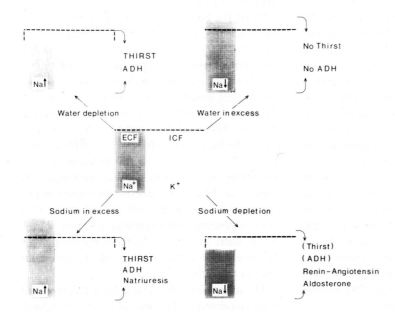

Fig. 19.7　Changes in body fluid distribution following changes in water and sodium intake. Compensatory mechanisms are indicated at the right of each diagram. ECF, extracellular fluid compartment; ICF, intracellular fluid compartment. (From Andersson, *Physiol. Rev.*, 58, 1978.)

losses induce a corresponding increase in the fluid intake.

Thirst and release of ADH can thus be caused by either absolute or relative dehydration. In both cases, the intracellular fluid volume decreases and the sodium concentration increases in the extracellular space. A reasonable conclusion is that one or both of these changes acts to elicit thirst and the release of ADH. Yet thirst is also elicited by an extreme lack of salt, which entails the opposite conditions: an increase in the cellular hydration and a reduction in the extracellular concentration of sodium.

At the end of the nineteenth century, a German physician suggested that centres in the brain regulate water intake. He had observed that a man who had been kicked in the head by a horse suffered from pronounced thirst. Direct experimental evidence that the water balance of the body is regulated by the brain was found in the early 1900s by Mayer. He showed that thirst in dogs, as expressed in drinking, is related to the osmotic pressure of the blood. Mayer concluded that an increase in osmotic pressure activates a thirst centre in the brain and causes drinking. In later experiments on dogs, it was found that the injection of hypertonic salt solutions into the carotid arteries causes ADH secretion by the hypophysis, indicating that certain nerve cells in the brain are specifically sensitive to changes in blood osmolarity and thereby regulate the release of ADH. The sensation of thirst and the ADH secretion thus appear to share a common control mechanism triggered by cellular dehydration of the osmoreceptors.

The location of these osmoreceptors was disclosed early in the 1950s by Andersson, who showed that electrical stimulation of a small area in the hypothalamus of goats causes a copious intake of fluid. The effect is dramatic; the animals immediately begin to drink when the stimulus is turned on and continue almost uninterruptedly as long as it lasts. The fluid intake may be so great that overhydration results, the body weight increasing by as much as 40%. The injection of small amounts of hypertonic salt solutions within the same hypothalamic area produces similar results.

The latter observation suggested that there are cells in the hypothalamus that are activated by an increase in the osmotic pressure of the blood, the balance between intracellular and extracellular fluid volume being the decisive factor. For instance, the intake of salt evokes thirst even though the total volume of fluid in the body remains the same, because the increased concentration of extracellular salt causes the cells to lose water, which moves osmotically into the extracellular space. A salt that is equally distributed intra- and extracellularly can be taken without eliciting thirst, which is further evidence for the existence of osmoreceptive cells.

The idea that fluid balance is regulated through a central neuro-osmoreceptive mechanism was generally accepted until the end of the 1960s. Doubts arose when it was found that hypertonic sugar solutions, which should be as effective as a salt solution, when infused into the third ventricle, failed to elicit thirst or release of ADH. The osmoreceptor theory proved inadequate to meet other observations as well, such as the well known fact that thirst is elicited by severe blood loss. To explain this, it had earlier been assumed that the osmotic regulation is accompanied by a volumetric regulation, mediated by volume or pressure receptors in the heart and large vessels.

It is significant that recent findings show that the role of the kidneys in regulating fluid balance is not limited to the ADH-regulated water reabsorption. Angiotensin when injected into the blood of rats increases drinking. The thirst-producing effect of angiotensin appears to be centrally elicited; an injection of small amounts of angiotensin into the hypothalamus causes intense drinking. These observations may explain why thirst is elicited after severe fluid losses, such as haemorrhage and diarrhoea. The decrease in blood volume causes a release of renin, stimulating angiotensinogen to form angiotensin and thereby producing thirst. That angiotensin elicits thirst and interacts with sodium suggests that the receptors in the hypothalamus are more sensitive to changes in the extracellular sodium concentration than to changes in osmolarity. The role of angiotensin in this process remains unclear. Possibly, it influences

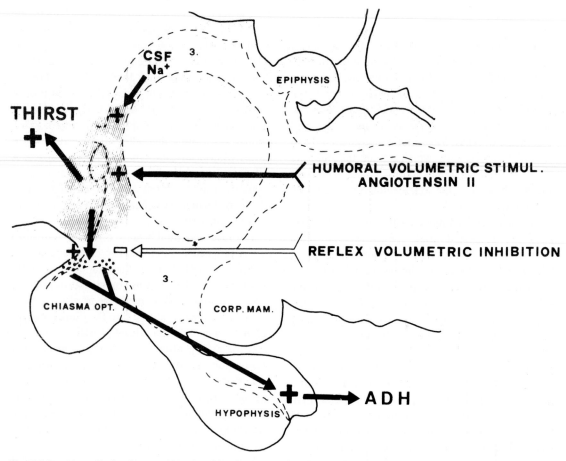

Fig. 19.8   Hypothalamic areas involved in the regulation of water intake. (From Andersson, *Physiol. Rev.*, 58, 1978.)

the permeability of the receptors to sodium and thereby affects the activity of the sodium—potassium pump. As the regulator of the activity of the receptors, angiotensin would thus be the central factor in the complex regulatory mechanisms that elicit thirst and cause the release of ADH (Fig. 19.8).

20

The Physiological Clock

It has long been known to physiologists and biologists that many functions in animals and plants vary in a cyclic way with periods of approximately 24 hours. Such rhythmic activities are now usually referred to as 'circadian' (*circa* = about; *dies* = day). Rhythmic movements of leaves and petals are frequent in the plant kingdom. Linné, the Swedish botanist, referred to them as 'sleep movements' since they were subordinate to the cycles of day and night. Linné actually constructed a 'flower-clock' by planting a number of plants, the petals of which had different times for opening and closing. Early observations provided evidence of corresponding rhythms of certain functions in animals such as the emergence of insects from their pupae or the daily fluctuations in body temperature. In humans the existence of circadian rhythms was demonstrated in studies of glycogen synthesis in the liver, urinary secretion, body temperature and pulse frequency (Fig. 20.1).

The discoveries of these various diurnal rhythms led to the hypothesis that there exists an internal physiological clock which regulates various functions. The idea gained support from the well

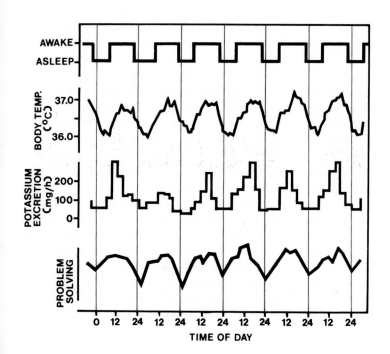

Fig. 20.1   Periodic changes in various body functions in human subject during a day. (Modified from Wever, *Forsk. Framsteg*, 6, 1972.)

known fact that some people are able to estimate with a high degree of precision the actual time of day, with few or no external time clues. They are also able to wake up with great precision at a given time aided only by their internal 'head clock'. Interestingly, the accuracy of this physiological time measurement is greatest under hypnosis.

In early studies on circadian rhythms, the assumption was made that they were modulated by external factors which set the clock and adjust the circadian cycle to a 24 hour periodicity. These external factors were supposed to function as time-keepers or synchronisers of the endogenous rhythm. This hypothesis has since been extensively tested in animals and human subjects kept under conditions which exclude external rhythmical changes as much as possible.

The human subjects of early experiments voluntarily isolated themselves in caves; later studies in specially designed laboratories have followed the circadian rhythms of different functions under more strictly controlled conditions. These studies have shown that the circadian rhythms are still present in the absence of external modulating factors. However, the periods of the physiological rhythms of various functions under these conditions show deviations from the normal 24 hour period. The cycle of sleep and wakefulness in isolation tends to lengthen beyond 24 hours; the subjects awake and go to bed somewhat later every day than normal (Fig. 20.2). The total length of this so-called free-running period is about 25 hours. There are remarkably small differences between different subjects and between subjects of different age. If a subject is kept isolated in this way for 25 normal days, he will experience only 24 days. When emerging from the isolation he has lost one 24 hour day. It is then difficult to convince a subject of the loss since his strong subjective belief is that he has lived a normal 24 hour day. If a subject should stay for instance for a year in isolation, one might ask how much older this person is at the end of the year. His physiological age would no longer correspond with the calendar and he would apparently be younger than the calendar shows!

The demonstration that the sleep–waking period in isolation is longer than normal clearly shows that there exists an internal physiological clock which regulates the activity cycle independently of the 24 hour daily rhythm. Evidence for the existence of an internal clock in humans has also been provided by the finding that several other bodily functions exhibit the same alterations in rhythm when the influence of external factors is excluded. The changes in the circadian rhythm of body temperature during isolation is one example. Normally the maximum is reached late in the afternoon and the minimum in the middle of the night. In subjects kept in isolation, there is a shift in this period in relation to the sleep–waking cycle, and the maximum in body temperature now occurs in the middle of the morning for the subject and the minimum late in the subject's afternoon.

This shows that the rhythm of different functions may be shifted in relation to one another. The conclusion would therefore be that there exists not only one physiological clock but probably several. Normally these clocks are tightly coupled, but their time interrelationships may be altered by elimination of external synchronising factors. Thus there appears to be one physiological clock which controls the sleep–waking rhythm, another which controls the body temperature, etc. The fact that these various clocks are synchronised during normal conditions raises the question of what external factors control their functions. Several lines of evidence suggest that the most important factor in most animal species is the diurnal variations in light and darkness. In humans the influence of variations in light appears to be less dominant but is nevertheless present. The effect of light on the sleep–waking cycle has been studied by varying the lengths of artificial day and night periods in subjects kept in isolation. In one of these experiments, the normal 24 hour period was shifted to 26 hours and 40 minutes. The subject did not notice this change but awoke gradually earlier in relation to the light period until he awoke when the light was turned on and went to bed when the light was turned off. He reported that he felt very well, without knowing of the change. Shortly thereafter the length of the artificial day was reduced to 24 hours. The subject still

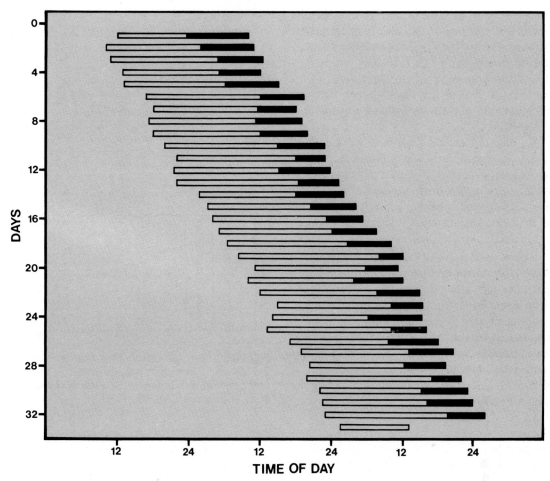

Fig. 20.2 Gradual changes in sleep—wakefulness cycle in human subject kept in isolation. Black bars indicate periods of sleep. (Modified from Wever, *Forsk. Framsteg*, 6, 1972.)

being unaware of the change, reported that he felt very uncomfortable. When the artificial day was later reduced to 22 hours and 40 minutes, the day became too short for him and he returned to the free-running rhythm with a period length of about 25 hours. Studies of this kind suggest that the physiological clock can be made to go faster or slower under the influence of external factors. How much can the rhythm of the physiological clock be altered? The experimental findings on isolated human subjects suggest that the length of the period cannot be extended beyond 27 hours nor reduced to less than 23 hours; once past these limits the clock resets itself to its inherent 25 hour rhythm.

It is common to characterise people, depending on their sleep—waking cycles, as 'morning' or 'evening' people. It has been suggested that the differences in their sleep—waking rhythms reflect variant settings of their physiological clocks; in 'morning' people the period would be shorter than 24 hours and in 'evening' people longer. Since the average duration of the period of the physiological clock is 25 hours, most of us are 'evening' people.

The effect of disturbances of the rhythm of the internal clock is particularly evident after long-distance flights in eastward or westward directions. While individual sleep—waking rhythms are variously affected, most people experience a decrease in intellectual and physical capacities.

Studies of pilots in flight simulators show that the decrease in functional capacities is greatest after eastward flights. These time-zone effects are most obvious during the first 24 hour day, but delayed effects have been demonstrated as late as the fifth day (Fig. 20.3), and they depend upon not only the magnitude of the time shift but also the time of departure.

As indicated above, there is a great deal of evidence suggesting that there is a tight coupling of the various physiological clocks. This has led to the assumption that there is a central clock or a 'master clock' which governs the rhythm of all the other clocks. Despite much research, the identity of this master clock remains unknown.

Recent studies focused interest on the pineal gland as a possible time-keeper. It has been found that removal of the pineal gland in birds leads to disturbances in their activity rhythms. This effect can be eliminated by daily injections of melatonin, a hormone produced by the pineal gland. Normally the melatonin level in the blood rises in the evening, and this has been assumed to indicate that melatonin may act as pacemaker for other physiological oscillators.

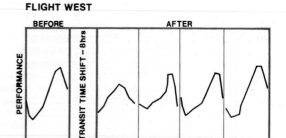

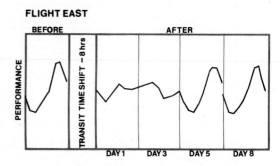

Fig. 20.3 The effects of time displacement on the phase of circadian rhythm of air pilots' performance in a simulator. (Modified from Klein *et al., Aerospace Med.,* 41, 1970.)

21

Sleep and Wakefulness

All living beings show regular rhythmic changes in their general activity. In humans this rhythm is linked to the alternation between day and night, and during each 24 hour cycle an adult sleeps 7–8 hours. This regular alternation between sleep and wakefulness is established during the first year of life. In the newborn child, the alternation has a periodicity of approximately one hour; under the influence of forced habits and other factors, the child gradually begins to sleep more during the night than the day and slowly assumes the adult rhythm (Fig. 21.1). This rhythm would appear to be governed by external factors such as variations in afferent input, and internal factors such as the fatigue that builds up towards the evening. However, even when the influence of these factors is eliminated, a regular rhythm remains (see p. 297).

Sleep has long been considered as a necessary resting period during which the organism restores itself. As we shall see, however, the nervous system as a whole does not rest during sleep, nor does the brain appear to undergo a restitution process

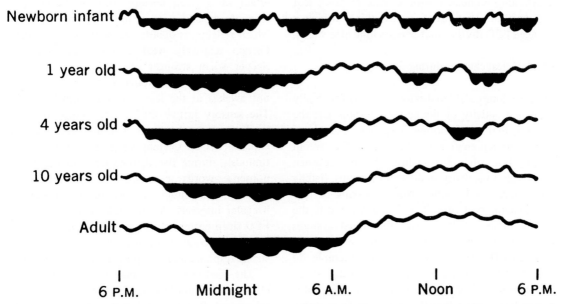

Fig. 21.1   Schematic representation of the change in sleep—wakefulness cycle with age. (From Kleitman, in *Sleep and Wakefulness*, University of Chicago Press, 1963.)

during sleep. On the other hand, long-lasting sleep-lessness has been seen to cause pathological changes in brain cells, psychic disturbances and, in experimental animals, even death. Dogs kept awake up to 500 hours remain in relatively good physical condition but show signs of increased irritability; histological analyses of their brains reveal changes in the cells of the frontal lobe. Human subjects deprived of sleep for several days and nights have a slower EEG pattern than normally. They may solve simple mathematical problems relatively easily, but their lowered intellectual performance is revealed when tasks are more complicated or demand concentration over long periods. A person who has been sleepless for several nights may, therefore, for a short time show the same ability as one who is rested, but he cannot undertake any performance that is long-lasting, requires much attention, or has any high degree of difficulty.

Following prolonged lack of sleep, an increasing inability to think logically, disturbances of perception and personality changes occur. These effects are made use of in brainwashing, which can succeed partly because the victim is isolated, partly because he is prevented from sleeping and partly because he is exposed to monotonous repeated questioning combined with threats creating fear and anguish. Victims of brainwashing display a changed EEG rhythm that persists long afterwards.

Physiological changes during sleep

Sleep was long considered as a condition of generally decreased activity of the nervous system, but the changes that occur during sleep have since been shown to represent no reduction in the overall activity but rather changes in the balance between activity and inactivity in different systems. Falling asleep means a transition from a waking pattern to a sleeping pattern, rather than a decrease in the overall brain activity. Some functional systems may become inactive, while other systems are activated. The cells in the cortex, for example, do not become completely inactive during sleep.

Recordings from single neurons in the motor cortex have shown that the transition from wakefulness to sleep is accompanied by changes in activity, characterised by bursts of impulses at relatively long intervals. It is the whole organism that sleeps and not the individual brain cells.

The shift in brain activity during normal sleep invites the inference that sleep is not a passive process but is actively induced. As evidence of this, sleep can be produced by stimulating parts of the brain. To some extent, sleep also appears to result from an active inhibitory effect. For example, the general decrease in spinal reflex activity during sleep probably derives not only from the decreased sensory inflow but also from an increase in the inhibition from higher levels.

One of the most typical signs of sleep is a decreased reaction to sensory stimuli. It has been assumed that afferent signals fail to reach their central projection areas in the cortex, but neurophysiological studies have provided no clearcut evidence of this. In fact, both a decreased electrical response in the cortex to sensory stimuli and the opposite effect have been observed. For example, single cells in the cortex respond equally well during sleep as during wakefulness.

Since it takes a relatively strong sensory stimulus to awaken a sleeping person, the sensory centres in the cortex have been described as 'asleep'. Yet the effect of a given sensory stimulus during sleep seems to depend more on its 'awakening capacity', which reflects its quality rather than its intensity. Certain relatively weak stimuli may awaken a sleeper when stronger ones will not, as with a mother who sleeps through strong ambient noise but awakes at the least murmur from her child. The sensory inflow during sleep must somehow be analysed in the brain, a notion borne out by experiments on sleeping subjects who listen continuously during the night to a recorded series of nonsense words into which a code word (for instance, the subject's own name) appears at irregular intervals. At the code word, the normal EEG sleep pattern shows a change, and a strongly emotional code word may elicit a particularly strong response and the subject may even awake.

The fact that the brain retains certain discriminative functions during sleep would appear to suggest that learning might also be possible. Intensive studies have been performed to settle this question; it appears that the brain may store information, especially if delivered repeatedly, but only during the stage of falling asleep, while the alpha rhythm is still normal. When the EEG goes into slower activity and the sleep spindles begin to appear, no learning can occur. The ensuing period of sleep contributes to maintaining the knowledge, whereas intellectual activity following the learning period prevents retention.

Usually a sensory stimulus causes a wakening reaction, but with special kinds of stimuli it is possible to produce the opposite effect, i.e. sleepiness and eventually sleep itself. A regularly repeated, monotonous stimulus is needed for this. In animals, stimulation of skin nerves can produce EEG changes similar to those that occur during sleep. In humans, sleep may be induced through monotonous sound stimuli or weak light flashes. Subjects sitting in a dark and silent room fall asleep faster when exposed to regular, weak light flashes than if left in complete darkness. The soporific influence of a monotonous stimulus is, of course, well known and has always been used by mothers rocking their children to sleep. Rhythmical dancing movements also lead to EEG changes similar to those that occur when falling asleep, possibly explaining the trance-like behaviour sometimes seen during ritual dances.

During sleep, a number of vegetative functions alter. Slowing of the heart rate and a decrease in the minute volume of the heart are characteristic, although as we shall see later during certain periods sleep may be accompanied by an increase in the heart rate and in the blood flow to the brain. Body temperature commonly falls during sleep, as is usual during inactivity, but the decline is relatively larger in sleep than in rest. Respiration also decreases, and thereby the gas exchange in the lungs, which induces an increase in carbon dioxide in the blood. At the same time, however, the respiratory centre's sensitivity to carbon dioxide lessens.

The EEG during sleep

As we have seen, sleep is associated with a series of changes both somatic and vegetative, but most are relatively useless as measures of its depth. The finding of changes in the EEG characteristic of different stages of sleep has opened up new possibilities for experimental studies of sleep (Fig. 21.2). The EEG of a subject who is awake and alert shows a random pattern of fast waves of low amplitude. If the eyes are closed, this pattern changes gradually into a pattern dominated by the alpha rhythm. As drowsiness supervenes, the alpha waves become less prominent and large slow waves

Excited

Relaxed

Drowsy

Asleep

Deep sleep

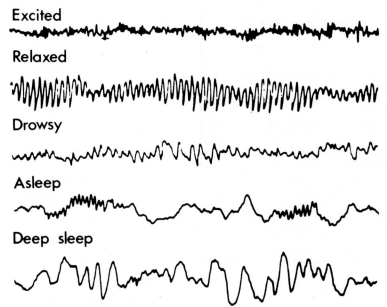

Fig. 21.2   EEG records during excitement, relaxation and various stages of sleep. (From Jasper, in *Epilepsy and Cerebral Localization*, C. C. Thomas, 1941.)

begin to appear. When sleep begins, so-called 'sleep spindles' occur which consist of short bursts of waves which wax and wane in amplitude. As sleep becomes deeper, the spindles become less prominent and may disappear. At this stage the EEG is dominated by large and slow delta waves. The appearance of these waves is associated with an increase in threshold for awakening.

Many attempts have been made to define different stages of the transition from wakefulness to sleep on the basis of the changes in the pattern of the EEG. The most widely used classification is that of Loomis, who distinguished between five stages termed A, B, C, D and E (Fig. 21.3). In stage A, alpha activity is no longer continuous but alpha waves appear in trains of various lengths. In stage B, the alpha waves have disappeared and the EEG is dominated by low-voltage activity. Stage C, or the spindle stage, is characterised by the presence of the sleep spindles. In stage D, the spindles are still present but in addition there are large wave-like potentials (K-complexes). In the last stage, E, the spindles have disappeared and the EEG pattern is dominated by large delta waves. According to another classification, sleep is divided into four stages (see Fig. 21.4).

Two types of sleep

In 1928 two Russian scientists reported that they had observed regular alternations in breathing and motor activity in sleeping infants. The periods of increased motor activity were generally associated with rapid movements of the eyes. These observations remained unnoticed for more than 20 years. In 1953 while studying the motor activity of sleeping children, Aserinsky and Kleitman rediscovered the phenomenon described by the Russian physiologists. By recording the eye movements, they were able to demonstrate that the alternations occurred with great regularity and for discrete periods lasting from a few minutes to half an hour or more. Since the eye movements were jerky and rapid, these periods were referred to as rapid eye movement (REM) periods. Characteristically the REM periods were accompanied by an increased brain activity as indicated by the low-voltage EEG pattern.

Subsequent studies in adults corroborated this puzzling observation; 4–6 such periods per night were seen, each lasting approximately 20 minutes. The outstanding aspect of these observations was that there are two types of sleep, the usual sleep

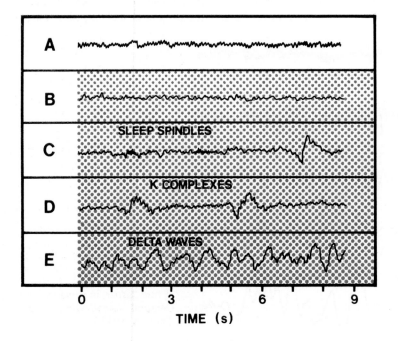

Fig. 21.3 Classification of the stages of sleep on the basis of changes in the EEG according to Loomis *et al.* (1936). In stage A, the subject is awake, relaxed; in B, falling asleep; in C, sleep is light, in D, sleep is moderately deep; and in E, deep. Stage B corresponds to REM sleep.

(ortho-sleep or non-REM sleep), when the EEG is characterised by a slow rhythm, and another with rapid EEG activity called REM sleep. Since the brain seems to be awake although the subject is deep asleep, this type of sleep is often also called paradoxical or para-sleep.

Extensive studies have established that during the night there are regular cyclic variations in the two types of sleep. The usual sequence during a night is that stage 4 is reached fairly rapidly and then persists for a varying time, usually half an hour to one hour (Fig. 21.4). The REM sleep period is heralded by a rapid transition from stage 4 to 3 and 2 and finally to stage 1 during which rapid eye movements appear. After termination of this period, there is a rapid transition to stage 3 or 4 which again is interrupted by a REM period. These cyclic variations of the EEG patterns occur repeatedly throughout the night with intervals of 90–100 min.

If the changes in the EEG are an indication of the depth of sleep, as was generally assumed, the ortho-sleep should be deep and the REM sleep periods with rapid EEG activity should represent light sleep. The evidence is that REM sleep is deeper, however. In animals, for instance, stimulus thresholds during REM sleep are considerably higher than during ortho-sleep; a stronger sound stimulus is necessary to awaken an animal during REM sleep than during ortho-sleep, and a stimulus that merely awakens during REM sleep will cause an animal to leap up and awaken abruptly if applied during slow-wave sleep. In humans the arousal thresholds for sound stimuli are 2–3 times higher during REM periods than they are during stage 1 at the onset of sleep.

Comparative studies have shown that REM sleep does not occur in lower animals such as reptiles and fishes. In the phylogenetic series, it appears first in birds, but the periods are of very short duration (10–20 s) and constitute less than 1% of the total sleep period, whereas in higher mammals REM sleep represents 20–30%. The duration of REM sleep thus seems to increase with the development of the brain. It is not directly related to brain development, however, since REM sleep

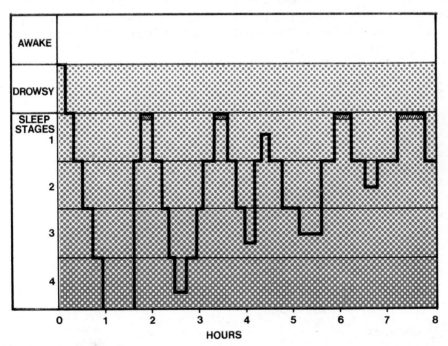

Fig. 21.4 Typical sleep pattern in a young adult subject during a night of sleep. Shaded bars indicate periods of REM sleep.

occupies more than half of the total sleeping period of children. In newborn animals whose brains are incompletely developed at birth (e.g. cat, rabbit and rat), only REM sleep occurs; in species in which the brain is well developed at birth (e.g. sheep and guinea-pigs), the sleeping newborn exhibit both ortho- and REM sleep.

In humans, the relative amount of REM sleep periods decreases gradually with age, until at age 20 they comprise 20–30% of the total sleep time (Fig. 21.5). They are not equally distributed during the night, occurring mostly during the later part of the early morning hours. Both the length and distribution of the REM sleep periods show great individual variations. People who sleep lightly have shorter REM sleep periods than those who sleep heavily. Night workers who sleep during the day have a little over half as much as normal night sleepers. The frequency seems to increase if, before going to bed, the subject has been engaged emotionally, for example watching an exciting film, but such experiences are not necessary for REM sleep. People kept in complete isolation from external stimuli exhibit only slight changes in sleep pattern after the first night and the amount of REM sleep is nearly normal. The most noticeable

change is that the eye movements during the REM sleep become more lively.

During REM sleep periods the blood in the brain and oxygen consumption increase. Blood pressure, heart rate and breathing show wide variations seemingly related to the content of the dreams then occurring (Fig. 21.6). Muscle reflexes and muscle tone are greatly reduced, especially in the neck, although certain muscle groups increase their activity, as for example the eye muscles. The general reduction of muscle tone and reflex activity during REM sleep has been thought to explain the feeling of paralysis sometimes experienced during a nightmare, such as when one dreams that one's life is threatened but, on trying to flee, one is unable to move, or on wanting to call for help, one cannot make a sound.

The discovery of REM sleep raised the question of whether the periods of increased brain activity are connected with dreaming. Subjects awakened during periods of rapid EEG activity usually report that they had been dreaming, and extensive studies have found a regular correlation between the REM sleep periods and dreams. This implies that most people dream several times each night, and that dreams are of longer duration than the

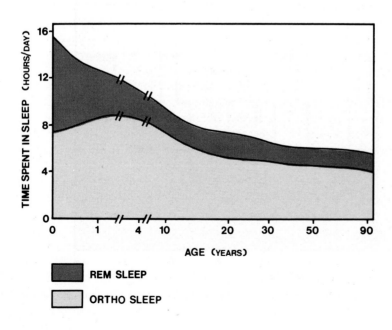

Fig. 21.5   Changes with age in amount of ortho-sleep and REM sleep. (Modified from Roffwarg *et al.*, *Science*, 152, 1966.)

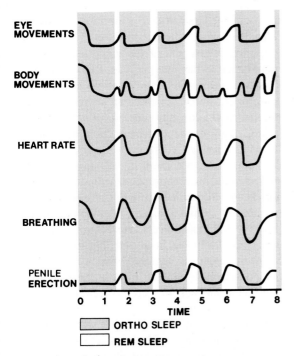

EYE MOVEMENTS

BODY MOVEMENTS

HEART RATE

BREATHING

PENILE ERECTION

0 1 2 3 4 5 6 7 8

TIME

ORTHO SLEEP

REM SLEEP

Fig. 21.6 Patterns of various physiological functions during a typical night of sleep in a young adult male.

flash-like rapid events that they were earlier believed to be. The memory of a dream is very short-lived. A subject awakened immediately after the occurrence of a REM sleep period (as indicated by the change of EEG pattern) can recount his dream clearly, but if awakened 5 minutes after the period his recollection is less clear, and at 10–20 minutes afterwards the dream is vague or has been completely forgotten. Studies of REM sleep and the occurrence of dreams have shown that an adult person dreams for a couple of hours altogether each night but remembers relatively little of it upon awakening. Dreams also occur when the EEG shows activity during ortho-sleep, but they are different in character from the eventful and fanciful dreams of REM sleep; dreams that occur during ortho-sleep seem more realistic.

Because the dreams of REM sleep are associated with rapid eye movements, it has been surmised that the dreamer actually sees dream pictures, the eye movements thus being related to the content of the dream. Indeed, lively dreams coincide with lively eye movements. Moreover, while subjects who have become blind late in life display the usual rapid eye movements during REM sleep, those who have been blind all their lives have normal periods of REM sleep but without the eye movements. It is also suggestive that activity in the visual cortex increases during REM sleep periods.

Since there are two types of sleep, it is natural to assume that a need for both types exists. A person awakened at night will fall back into ortho-sleep regardless of the state from which he was awakened. If awakened repeatedly during REM sleep and thereby deprived of it, he will have a greater frequency of periods of REM sleep during following nights. This indicates an absolute need for a certain amount of REM sleep and dreams, which if not met must be made up during later sleep. The need for both types of sleep makes questionable the long-term efficacy of soporifics, some of which reduce the frequency and duration of the periods of REM sleep.

Dreams are often connected with motor activity related to sexual life; in both humans and animals, periods of REM sleep may coincide with penile erection in males and pelvic movements in females.

In some individuals, periods of greatly increased motor activity occur during sleep, an extreme expression being leaving the bed, walking around and carrying out more or less aimless movements. The phenomenon of *somnambulism*, or sleepwalking, is relatively common in children, but only 1–5% of adults, mainly men, experience it. Laboratory studies of sleepwalkers found that somnambulism occurs during ortho-sleep, not during REM sleep, as might be expected. It usually occurs in the first 3 hours of sleep and at no set time from the REM sleep periods. Since the sleep patterns remain quite normal throughout the night, it is not surprising that a night with one or more periods of somnambulism leads to no increase in para-sleep on following calm nights. The sleepwalking is usually preceded by the sudden appearance of continuous, high-amplitude EEG activity which persists during the event. Sleepwalkers are clearly unaware of their surroundings; their eyes are open, their faces are expressionless, though sometimes frightened in appearance, and their movements are stiff and aimless. Talking while asleep is also common, but rarely is any sense of logic discernible. Typically, sleepwalking terminates with a spontaneous return to bed, and the subject awakens ignorant of what has happened. In cases of long periods of sleepwalking, the EEG becomes desynchronised and assumes the waking pattern.

The control of sleep and wakefulness

In the 1930s a Swiss physiologist, Hess, found that rhythmic electrical stimulation in the diencephalon of cats made the cats fall asleep. The experimental animals began circling, as if to find a place to sleep, then stretched their legs, closed their eyes, curled up and fell into deep sleep from which they could be awakened only by relatively strong stimuli. From this, Hess proposed that a sleep centre in the basal part of the brain actively induces sleep. Hess also showed that stimulation of other regions such as the posterior hypothalamus produced all the signs of normal awakening. These findings suggested that sleep was an active process induced by rhythmic activity in a thalamocortical system which modulated the excitability of the cortical cells. In principle this concept is still generally accepted in a form modified in the light of later findings. Subsequent studies demonstrated that sleep or sleep-like states could be elicited not only from the sleep centres of Hess but also from extensive subcortical parts of the brain as well as by direct stimulation of the cortex. The regions from which sleep may be induced include the cortex, the hippocampus, the thalamus, the entire hypothalamus and the reticular formation. Interestingly, the onset of sleep takes a varying form depending upon the site of stimulation. If stimulated in the thalamus, a cat exhibits the characteristic behaviour of circular movements, stretching, extending the paws, licking, closing the eyes and finally going to sleep; the sleep lasts about 6–8 hours and has phases of both slow and rapid EEG activity. In contrast, stimulation of other areas induces sleep without the preparatory behaviour. The sleep

states obtained also differ. For instance, stimulation of medial parts of the thalamus causes slow orthosleep preceded by general sleepiness, while stimulation of areas in the pons produces REM sleep.

A few years after Hess' discovery, a Belgian neurologist, Bremer, reported an interesting observation that led to many succeeding investigations. In studying the effect of transection of the brain stem in cats at different levels, he found that, if the transection was made at the mesencephalic level, a state resembling permanent sleep was induced, and the animal could not be awakened by any kind of stimulation. This discovery led to the concept that wakefulness requires a maintained sensory input to the brain and that sleep ensues when the input is removed. Accordingly, sleep was considered by Bremer to be a passive process resulting from lack of sensory activation of the brain.

In the animal whose brain stem was transected at the mesencephalic level, the olfactory input and the visual input remain but olfactory and visual stimuli produce only weak and transient changes of the EEG. Thus, there is no arousal effect as in intact animals. This indicates that sensory input *per se* is not sufficient to produce wakefulness but that some other neural mechanism is required. This additional mechanism was found to involve a widespread neuronal system located in the brain stem. That centres in the brain stem have great significance in maintaining wakefulness has long been known from clinical observations. During the First World War a certain form of encephalitis, commonly called sleeping sickness, spread epidemically in Europe. In the early stage of the disease, the patients suffered from insomnia, whereas in the later stages they passed into lethargy or prolonged sleep periods. In autopsies of the brains of these patients, it was found that the disease was associated with widespread death of neurons in certain regions of the brain stem. In 1949 Magoun and Moruzzi found that stimulation of the brain stem produced activation of the EEG. When stimulation was applied via implanted electrodes in sleeping animals, behavioural awakening occurred. These findings strongly supported the idea that sleep was induced by deactivation of the reticular system. The question remained to be answered, however, what it is that turns the reticular activating system off and on. The reduction in sensory input that normally occurs when going to bed at night might account for turning off the system, but awakening in the morning usually occurs without necessarily an increase in sensory input. It is probable that the regulatory mechanism is a dual system composed of a portion that turns on the waking state and another that turns on sleep, very much as Hess originally suggested. Recent observations have provided additional evidence in favour of this idea. There is, for instance, a considerable amount of evidence that the raphe system in the midline of the brain stem controls wakefulness by inhibiting the ascending reticular system (RAS) and thus inducing ortho-sleep. Selective lesions in these regions in experimental animals produce a sleeplessness similar to that seen after transection of the pons. The activity of this sytem appears to be interrupted at more or less regular intervals by increased activity in the cells of the *locus coeruleus*. These neurons have a strong inhibitory influence on descending motor pathways and thereby participate in the reduced muscle tone characteristic of REM sleep. Selective destruction of this nucleus within the

dorsal part of the pons makes REM sleep disappear. The locus coeruleus is therefore considered as the centre for REM sleep.

The cells of the raphe system contain serotonin, and the cells in the locus coeruleus noradrenalin, which has directed interest towards these substances as possible participants in regulating the sleep–waking rhythm. The usual technique for studying their effect is to make local injections into different parts of the brain or into the cerebral ventricles. Another method is to inject precursors of the active substances into the bloodstream, for these easily pass the blood barrier and are then transformed into the active substances. The injection of 5-hydroxytryptamine (5-HT), the precursor of serotonin, has been shown to produce ortho-sleep and suppress REM sleep. Substances that selectively reduce the concentration of serotonin in the brain produce sleeplessness of the type that ensues from a lesion in the raphe system. Another substance considered to be active in causing sleep is ACh; some observations have implicated ACh in REM sleep. Injection of ACh near the locus coeruleus produces REM sleep in cats, while atropine (which inhibits the action of ACh) suppresses REM sleep. Monoamine oxidase inhibitors (which decrease the breakdown of monamines and there-

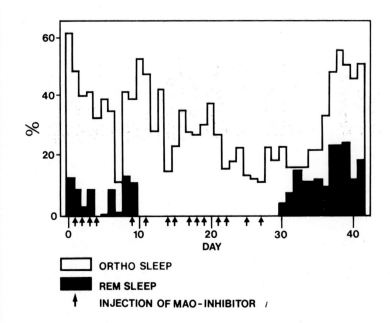

ORTHO SLEEP

REM SLEEP

INJECTION OF MAO-INHIBITOR

Fig. 21.7 Suppression of REM sleep by administration of monoamine oxidase inhibitor (pheniprazinc). Arrows indicate days when the inhibitor was given. (Modified from Jouvet, *Image*, Roche, 1970.)

by increase their concentration in the brain) are strongly inhibitory of REM sleep (Fig. 21.7).

It is an old notion that the fatigue we feel towards evening is due to the accumulation of substances having a sleep-producing effect. This idea gained support at the turn of the century as a result of observations made by the French physiologists, Legendre and Piéron. They found that cerebrospinal fluid from sleep-deprived dogs produced fatigue and sleep when injected into the *cisterna magna* of normal dogs. Piéron concluded that some substance accumulates in the brain during activity and causes sleep when it reaches a sufficient concentration. He proposed the name *hypnotoxin* for the hypothetical endo-genous sleep-inducing humoral factor. Piéron's observations have since been reconfirmed; moreover, intraventricular injections of extracts from brains of sleeping animals have been shown to produce sleep in waking animals. In addition, in cross-circulation experiments in cats, sleep in one animal induces sleep-like changes in the EEG of the recipient animal. The active substance has not yet been identified. Putative candidates are several organic substances that have a strongly soporific effect, one of these being gamma-hydroxybutyric acid. Recent studies further indicate that some polypeptides isolated from the brain have sleep-producing effects.

BIBLIOGRAPHY FOR SECTION VIII

Suggested Reading and Reviews

Akert, K. (1965). The anatomical substrate of sleep, in *Sleep Mechanisms, Progress in Brain Research*, vol. 18, eds K. Akert, C. Bally and J. P. Schadé, Elsevier, Amsterdam, pp. 9–19

Andersson, B. (1978). Regulation of water intake, *Physiol. Rev.*, **58**, 582–603

Bennett, M. R. (1972). *Autonomic Neuromuscular Transmission*, Cambridge University Press, London

Bie, P. (1980). Osmoreceptors, vasopressin, and control of renal water excretion, *Physiol. Rev.*, **60**(4), 961–1048

Bolton, T. B. (1979). Mechanisms of action of transmitters and other substances on smooth muscle, *Physiol. Rev.*, **59**(3), 606–718

Brady, J. V. (1961). Motivational–emotional factors and intracranial self-stimulation, in *Electrical Stimulation of the Brain*, ed. D. E. Sheer, University of Texas Press, pp. 413–430

Bray, G. A. and York, D. A. (1979). Hypothalamic and genetic obesity in experimental animals: an autonomic and endocrine hypothesis, *Physiol. Rev.*, **59**(3), 719–809

Bremer, F. (1954). The neurophysiological problem of sleep, in *Brain Mechanisms and Consciousness*, ed. L. Delafresnaye, Blackwell, Oxford, pp. 137–162

Brobeck, J. R. (1946). Mechanisms of the development of obesity in animals with hypothalamic lesions, *Physiol. Rev.*, **26**, 541–559

Bünning, E. (1973). *The Physiological Clock*, Springer-Verlag, Berlin

Burnstock, G. (1972). Purinergic nerves, *Pharmacol. Rev.*, **24**, 509–581

Burnstock, G. (1979). Past and current evidence for the purinergic nerve hypothesis, in *Physiological and Regulatory Functions of Adenosine and Adenine Nucleotides*, eds H. P. Baer and G. I. Drummond, Raven Press, New York

Butter, C. M. (1969). *Neuropsychology. The Study of Brain and Behaviour*, Brooks/Cole, California

Cannon, W. B. (1934). Hunger and thirst, in *Handbook of General Experimental Psychology*, ed. C. Murchison, Clark University Press, Worcester, MA, pp. 247–263

Deutsch, J. A. (1963). Learning and electrical self-stimulation of the brain, *J. Theor. Biol.*, **4**, 193–214

de Wied, D. (1977). Peptides and behavior, *Life Sci.*, **20**, 195–204

von Euler, U. S. (1961). Neurotransmission in the adrenergic nervous system, *Harvey Lectures* **55**, 43

Evarts, E. V. (1961). Effects of sleep and waking on activity of single units in the unrestrained cat, in *The Nature of Sleep, A Ciba Foundation Symp.*, eds Wolstenholme and O'Connor, Little, Brown & Co., Boston

Fitzsimons, J. T. (1972). Thirst, *Physiol. Rev.*, **52**, 468–561

Fitzsimons, J. T. (1976). The physiological basis of thirst, *Kidney Intern.*, **10**, 3–11

Hardy, J. D. (1961). Physiology of temperature regulation, *Physiol. Rev.*, **41**, 521–606

Hartmann, E. L. (1973). *The Functions of Sleep*, Yale University Press, New Haven

Hess, W. R. (1954). *Diencephalon, Autonomic and Extrapyramidal Functions*, Grune & Stratton, New York

Hess, W. R. (1965). Sleep as a phenomenon of the integral organism, in *Sleep Mechanisms, Progress in Brain Research*, vol. 18, eds K. Akert, C. Bally and J. P. Schadé, Elsevier, Amsterdam, pp. 3–8

Hillarp, N.-Å. (1960). Peripheral autonomic mechanisms, in *Handbook of Physiology*, section

Section IX: Higher Functions of the Brain

22

Speech Functions

The ability to speak depends upon the coordination of a series of motor, sensory and perceptual functions in which large areas of the cortex participate. The first stage in the development of speech is the association of sounds with tactile and visual sensations. These associations, stored in the memory, are later utilised in verbalising the words thus learned. To articulate requires coordinated movement of the muscles of the vocal cords, throat, tongue and lips. When a child learns to read, the spoken words are combined with visual symbols; through this association the child also learns to write. Hence, the ability to express ideas in spoken or written words combines a number of closely related functions involving extensive cortical areas.

Studies of the cortical control of speech were long focused on speech disorders, known as *aphasia*, resulting from injuries of the brain. It was initially thought that two kinds of aphasia exist, motor and sensory. The former includes speech disorders mainly affecting motor functions. Although there is no paralysis of the musculature involved in speech, the formation of words is faulty in motor aphasia, and the patient is unable to express his thoughts in spoken words. Because of this disability, motor aphasia is also called expressive aphasia. The ability to speak is not entirely lost, but speech becomes telegraphic, endings of words are omitted and multisyllabic words avoided. Oddly, the disturbance is less pronounced during singing, particularly at rapid tempos. As speaking and writing are intimately connected, the ability to express ideas in writing is often lost, whereas the comprehension of spoken or written words remains.

Sensory aphasia is characterised by disturbances of perceptual functions involved in speech. The patient does not understand what is said, nor the content of what he reads, although hearing and vision are normal; he is word-deaf and word-blind. It is just as if a healthy person were to hear or read a language he does not know. The motor functions of speech are unaffected but, because the patient does not understand the meaning of what he or she is saying, speech becomes confused. Brief sentences can often be formulated without error, but the disorder is evident in longer ones. Unable to find the right words, the patient gropes for synonyms and seizes on inappropriate words, and speech becomes incoherent. Sensory aphasia has also been called receptive or perceptual aphasia.

Motor aphasia was for some time attributed to damage of Broca's area and sensory aphasia to damage of Wernicke's area (Fig. 22.1), but this has proved not always to be so. Not only the site of the damage but also its extent determines which type of aphasia emerges. Also other factors such as the patient's premorbid personality and intellectual level are important. Moreover, even though an aphasia may be categorised as motor or sensory, it seldom appears in pure form.

The cortical centres for various aspects of speech have been inferred from the locus of lesions giving rise to certain disturbances. Whether this inference is justifiable is uncertain. Any one area involved in

23

The Split Brain

Anatomically the brain can be considered as a symmetrically bilateral organ, whose halves are joined by a system of interconnections. In view of the symmetrical anatomical organisation of both the motor and sensory systems, it would be reasonable to assume that there is a corresponding functional symmetry, but we have seen that this is not the case. One of the hemispheres dominates, usually the left. This dominance shows itself in that several important functions, such as the abilities to speak and read, normally depend on cortical centres in the left hemisphere. For the motor system, this asymmetry is correlated with a preference for the use of one hand, usually the right.

The earliest information of the functional asymmetry of the brain derives from the observation of Broca in 1861 on a patient who, following localised damage in the left hemisphere, had lost the ability to speak. This and later clinical observations led to the notion that was prevailing until the middle of the present century that not only speech but all higher functions of the brain are associated with the activity of the left hemisphere. The right hemisphere was generally considered as subordinate and secondary to the left. Consequently the left hemisphere became known as the 'dominant' or 'major' hemisphere and the right hemisphere as the 'non-dominant' or 'minor' one.

The two halves of the brain are linked together by the *corpus callosum* which contains more than 200 million nerve fibres. The size of the corpus callosum and the orderly distribution of its nerve fibres would suggest that it has an important role

for the functions of the two hemispheres. However, observations in the early 1940s on patients who had undergone complete transection of the corpus callosum (Fig. 23.1) to prevent the spread of epileptic seizures from one hemisphere to the other failed to reveal any consistent neurological or neuropsychological dysfunctions as a result of the operation. Personality, temperament, speech, verbal reasoning and memory functions were all preserved almost unchanged. It was therefore concluded that the corpus callosum contributed next to nothing to higher brain functions.

This was the situation when in the 1950s Sperry and his collaborators set out a series of experiments on cats and later on monkeys in which they transected not only the corpus callosum but also the *chiasma*. In keeping with the findings in the patients with 'split brain', the animals behaved quite normally in most activities. However, when the relevant sensory information (by a special testing procedure) was restricted to one hemisphere at a time, the story was quite different. In brief, Sperry's studies revealed that the corpus callosum is necessary for interhemispheric integration of sensory and motor functions and also for the interhemispheric transfer of learning and memory. These findings, which clearly established an important function of the corpus callosum in subhuman mammals, prompted a reconsideration of its role in man. This became possible in the early 1960s when Vogel and Bogen carried out surgical section of the commissure to treat severe convulsive disorders in a series of patients. This kind of sur-

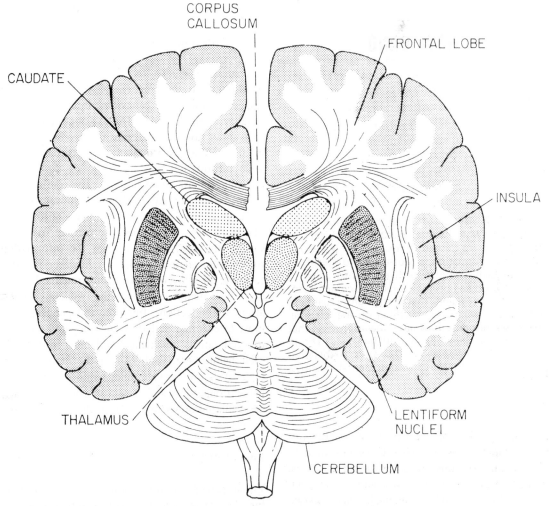

CORPUS
CALLOSUM

FRONTAL LOBE

CAUDATE

INSULA

THALAMUS

LENTIFORM
NUCLEI

CEREBELLUM

Fig. 23.1 Surgical separation of the two hemispheres by midline section of the brain commissures. (From Sperry, *The Neurosciences, Third Study Program*, MIT Press, 1974.)

gery involves a complete section of the corpus callosum, the smaller anterior commissure and the *massa intermedia*. The operation is undertaken as a last resort to control life-threatening epilepsy. Since then, a modified form of transection has been introduced involving section of only the anterior part of the corpus callosum.

Sperry and his collaborators examined these patients from a neuropsychological viewpoint. Over the years since these studies were started, 16 persons with complete transection of the corpus callosum have been examined for sensory, motor and cognition functions.

In testing the response to visual information, Sperry took advantage of the orderly projection of the nerve fibres from each half of the two retinas. As indicated in Fig. 23.2 when the eyes are fixed on a central point on the viewing screen, visual stimuli to the left of this point are projected only to the right hemisphere and stimuli to the right of the fixation point only to the left hemisphere. Normally the eyes make voluntary and involuntary

for instance verbs such as smile, nod, frown, knock were presented visually to the right hemisphere and the subject was instructed to carry out these acts, he was unable to do so. When the same stimuli were presented to the left hemisphere, the actions were promptly performed. It appears that the inability of the right hemisphere to carry out commands when these were presented visually in the form of verbs was due to lack of comprehension. This could be demonstrated by presenting pictures instead of verbs for the different acts; the subject then readily carried out the actions. The right hemisphere would thus appear to possess a fair auditory comprehension while its reading vocabulary is restricted to object-nouns.

Learning and memory

As we have seen in the foregoing, the right hemisphere in the 'split brain' patient can easily learn and remember visual, auditory and tactile information of spatial patterns, relations and transformations. Similarly, linguistic and mathematical functions are readily processed and preserved in the left hemisphere. All evidence thus favours the conclusion that processing and basic memory functions in each hemisphere are not affected significantly by the separation of the two hemispheres. Nevertheless, the commissurotomised patient suffered a general impairment of memory functions. This memory deficit affected mainly short-term memory, whereas there was no conspicuous loss in old memory. This suggests that established engrams remain unaffected whereas establishment of new engrams is impaired in the 'split brain'. The memory impairment appears to be due to the lack of interhemispheric integration. In this context it is also interesting to note that the 'split brain' patient after the commissurotomy suffered a general reduction in what might be called 'mental grasp'. They were simple, sometimes logorrhoic (wordy) in their conversation and lacked perseverance in carrying out mentally demanding tasks.

Summary

It has been realised for more than a hundred years that the two hemispheres of the brain are not functionally equivalent. Until recently, most of our information about hemispheric specialisation derived from clinical observations of various kinds of functional impairments following asymmetric brain damage. In the last 20 years, direct and unprecedented opportunities for studies of the specialisation of the two sides of the adult human brain have been provided in a small group of patients in whom the main interhemispheric commissures have been transected as a treatment for epilepsy. These studies have borne out earlier observations in animal studies that transection of the entire corpus callosum causes little disturbance of ordinary behaviour. A person who has undergone this operation might go through routine psychological and medical tests without revealing any particular symptoms.

In the 'split brain' patients it is possible with special testing techniques to examine and measure various capacities of each hemisphere. The results of these studies indicate that, following surgical disconnection of the two hemispheres, things experienced, learned and remembered by one hemisphere remain unknown to the other. Each hemisphere has its own realm of conscious awareness, thoughts and ideas, its own private experience and memories inaccessible to recall by the other hemisphere. Moreover, these studies have revealed interesting and significant functional differences between the two hemispheres (Fig. 23.11). The minor right hemisphere is mute, agraphic and has a restricted comprehension of language; upon cursory examination it may therefore appear illiterate and agnostic. However, with special tests it can be demonstrated that the right hemisphere has a high order of mental activity and in certain aspects is superior to the left. These aspects in general involve functions requiring apprehension and processing of three-dimensional patterns and relations. It also has a greater capacity for imaginal perception and is in general superior to the left in recognising and remembering tunes of songs. The left hemisphere on the other hand is superior to the right in analysing temporal patterns. Thus it has a greater ability than the right in judging the order of verbal and non-verbal auditory stimuli as well as visual

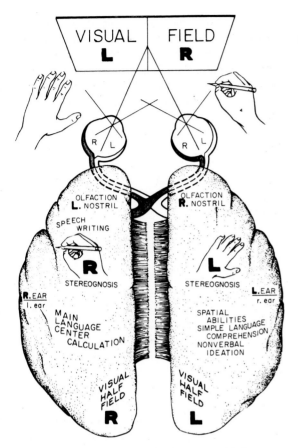

Fig. 23.11 Functional specialisation of the two hemispheres. (From Sperry, *The Neurosciences, Third Study Program*, MIT Press, 1974.)

each other. The left hemisphere has almost the same capacity as the normal brain in remembering verbal material but has difficulties in memorising complex visual and tactile information. The memory capacities of the right hemisphere are almost the opposite; verbal material is poorly memorised while pictorial or tactual sensations of complex nature are readily committed to memory. Furthermore the left hemisphere in its processing of information is applying an abstract, conceptual and analytical mode of thinking, in contrast to the right hemisphere that has a concrete, synthetic mode of information processing and a greater capacity of imaginative thinking.

The right hemisphere is incapable of theoretical thinking and is unable to analyse perceptions in logical forms but perceives the external world in all its aspects of richness and diversity. In the normal brain, the two hemispheres are interconnected and therefore not independent of each other. This means that one hemisphere may complement the capacities of the other. Although direct evidence is sparse, there appears to be strong reason to believe that the interhemispheric interaction also involves mutual inhibition. This would allow for instance the left hemisphere to suppress the right hemisphere in situations where the capacities of the left hemisphere are specifically required, such as for instance in solving mathematical problems. In situations where imaginative thinking is more important, such as in artistic creative work, the right hemisphere might achieve its full capacity by inhibiting the left hemisphere.

About 40 years ago Pavlov suggested that people could be divided into two types — thinkers and artists. At that time there was no direct evidence to support such a classification. Today it appears that there actually is a real basis for this distinction. Thinkers are people who in their general activities are governed by the left hemisphere, while artists are people whose right hemisphere is the more powerful. It has been suggested that the differences between the Western world and the East in culture and ways of thinking would reflect a dominance of the left hemisphere in Western people, while the cultures of the East have resulted from a relatively greater influence of the right hemisphere.

and tactile events. It has been suggested that the greater capacity in analysing acoustic events is the basis for the superiority of the left hemisphere for language.

The language-dominant hemisphere is, to quote Sperry, 'the more aggressive, executive leading hemisphere in the control of the motor system. This is the hemisphere that we mainly see in action and the one with which we regularly communicate'. The right hemisphere in contrast is the 'silent passenger who leaves the driving of behaviour to the left hemisphere'. But 'the minor hemisphere is nevertheless clearly the superior cerebral member for certain types of tasks'.

The memory capacity of the two hemispheres has certain characteristics in which they differ from

The discovery that the two hemispheres function independently and also without knowledge of each other after transection of the corpus callosum raises the question of whether they might come into conflict. Is the split brain patient no longer one person but two? Studies of humans show no signs of this, but in animal experiments such situations have been observed. Another question, perhaps more philosophical than physiological, concerns intellectual functions. Are willpower, emotional life and intelligence equally represented, or are there differences between the hemispheres? Only future research can tell.

BIBLIOGRAPHY FOR SECTION IX

Suggested Reading and Reviews

Buser, P. (1976). Higher functions of the nervous system, *Ann. Rev. Physiol.*, **38**, 217–245

Darwin, C. J. (1974). Ear differences and hemispheric specialization, in *The Neurosciences. Third Study Program*, eds F. O. Schmitt and F. G. Worden, MIT Press, Cambridge, MA, pp. 57–63

Eccles, J. C. (ed.) (1966). *Brain and Conscious Experience*, Springer-Verlag, Berlin

Eccles, J. C. (1973). *The Understanding of the Brain*, McGraw-Hill, New York

Gazzaniga, M. S. (1970). *The Bisected Brain*, Appleton–Century–Crofts, New York

Grossman, S. P. (1967). *A Textbook of Physiological Psychology*, John Wiley & Sons, New York

Grossman, S. P. (1973). *Essentials of Physiological Psychology*, John Wiley & Sons, New York

Hecaen, H. (1979). Aphasias, in *Neuropsychology, Handbook of Behavioral Neurobiology*, vol. 2, ed. M. S. Gazzaniga, Plenum Press, New York, pp. 239–292

Heilman, K. M. (1979). The neuropsychological basis of skilled movement in man, in *Neuropsychology, Handbook of Behavioral Neurobiology*, vol. 2, ed. M. S. Gazzaniga, Plenum Press, New York, pp. 447–461

Hollien, H. (1975). Neural control of the speech mechanism, in *The Nervous System*, vol. 3, ed. D. B. Tower, Raven Press, New York, pp. 483–491

Kimura, D. (1975). Cerebral dominance for speech, in *The Nervous System*, vol. 3, ed. D. B. Tower, Raven Press, New York, pp. 365–371

Liberman, A. M. (1974). The specialization of the language hemisphere, in *The Neurosciences. Third Study Program*, eds F. O. Schmitt and F. G. Worden, MIT Press, Cambridge, MA, pp. 43–56

Milner, B. (1964). Some effects of frontal lobectomy in man, in *Frontal Granular Cortex and Behavior*, eds Warren and Akert, McGraw-Hill, New York

Milner, B. (1974). Hemispheric specialization: scope and limits, in *The Neurosciences. Third Study Program*, eds F. O. Schmitt and F. G. Worden, MIT Press, Cambridge, MA, pp. 75–89

Milner, P. M. (1971). *Physiological Psychology*, Holt, Rinehart & Winston, London

Nottebohm, F. (1979). Origins and mechanisms in the establishment of cerebral dominance, in *Neuropsychology, Handbook of Behavioral Neurobiology*, vol. 2, ed. M. S. Gazzaniga, Plenum Press, New York, pp. 295–344

Penfield, W. (1971). The neurophysiological basis of thought, *Mod. Perspect. Psychiat.*, **1**, 313–349

Sperry, R. W. (1962). Some general aspects of interhemispheric integration, in *Interhemispheric Relations and Cerebral Dominance*, ed. V. B. Mountcastle, Johns Hopkins Press, Baltimore, pp. 43–49

Sperry, R. W. (1970). Perception in the absence of the neocortical commissures, in *Perception and its Disorders, Assoc. Res. Nervous & Mental Dis.*, **48**, 123–138

Sperry, R. W. (1974). Lateral specialization in the surgically separated hemispheres, in *The Neurosciences. Third Study Program*, eds F. O. Schmitt and F. G. Worden, MIT Press, Cambridge, MA, pp. 5–19

Sperry, R. W., Gazzaniga, M. S. and Bogen, J. E. (1969). Interhemispheric relationships: the neocortical commissures; syndromes of hemisphere disconnection, in *Handbook of Clinical Neurology*, vol. 4, eds P. J. Vinken and G. W.

Bruyn, North-Holland, Amsterdam, pp. 273–290

Springer, S. P. (1979). Speech perception and the biology of language, in *Neuropsychology, Handbook of Behavioral Neurobiology*, vol. 2, ed. M. S. Gazzaniga, Plenum Press, New York, pp. 153–177

Wilson, J. P. (1974). Psychoacoustical and neurophysiological aspects of auditory pattern recognition, in *The Neurosciences. Third Study Program*, eds F. O. Schmitt and F. G. Worden, MIT Press, Cambridge, MA, pp. 147–153

Original Papers

Akelaitis, A. J. (1943). Studies on the corpus callosum. VII: Study of language functions (tactile and visual lexia and graphia) unilaterally following section of corpus callosum, *J. Neuropathol. Exp. Neurol.*, **2**, 226–262

Bogen, J. E., Fisher, E. D. and Vogel, P. J. (1965). Cerebral commissurotomy: A second case report, *J. Am. Med. Assoc.*, **194**, 1328–1329

Broadbent, D. E. and Gregory, M. (1964). Accuracy of recognition for speech presented to the right and left ears, *Q. J. Exp. Psychol.*, **16**, 359–360

Broca, P. P. (1861). Perte de parole, ramollissement chronique et destruction du lobe antérieur gauche du cerveau, *Bull. Soc. Antropol., Paris*, **2**, 235

Gazzaniga, M. S. and Hillyard, S. A. (1971). Language and speech capacity of the right hemisphere, *Neuropsychologia*, **87**, 415–422

Gazzaniga, M. S. and Sperry, R. W. (1967). Language after section of the cerebral commissures, *Brain*, **90**, 131–148

Kimura, D. (1961). Some effects of temporal-lobe damage on auditory perception, *Can. J. Psychol.*, **15**, 156–165

Kimura, D. (1961). Cerebral dominance and perception of verbal stimuli, *Can. J. Psychol.*, **15**, 166–171

Kimura, D. (1964). Left–right differences in the perception of melodies, *Q. J. Exp. Psychol.*, **16**, 355–358

Kimura, D. (1967). Functional asymmetry of the brain in dichotic listening, *Cortex*, **3**, 163–178

Levy, J., Trevarthen, D. and Sperry, R. W. (1972). Perception of bilateral chimeric figures following hemisphere deconnection, *Brain*, **95**, 61–78

Mills, J. N. (1964). Circadian rhythms during and after three months in solitude underground, *J. Physiol. (Lond.)*, **174**, 217–231

Milner, B. (1954). Intellectual functions of the temporal lobe, *Psychol. Bull.*, **51**, 42–62

Milner, B. (1971). Interhemispheric differences in the localization of psychological processes in man, *Br. Med. Bull.*, **27**, 272–277

Myers, R. E. (1959). Function of the corpus callosum in interocular transfer, *Brain*, **79**, 358–363

Nebes, R. D. (1973). Perception of spatial relationships by the right and left hemispheres in commissurotomized man, *Neuropsychologia*, **11**, 285–289

Section X: Sensory Systems

24

The Neural Basis of Perception

Sensory organs may be considered as instruments with which we measure the physical and chemical properties of the outer world. Consequently the information received by the brain depends upon the properties of these instruments. Although most of our sense organs have exquisite sensitivity, high resolution and a wide measuring range, they nonetheless do not convey an exact reproduction of the outer world. The information in different sensory channels undergoes processing and may be subjected to inhibition at several levels before finally reaching its end station in the cerebral cortex. It is consequently far from certain that the message received by the cerebral cortex faithfully reproduces the original signals evoked from the sense organs. In addition, the various sensory channels have very different representations in the brain. In lower vertebrates, for example, the olfactory system predominates; in many of these species the perception of the outer world may be totally dominated by olfactory sensations. With increasing development of the cortex and particularly of associative centres, olfactory predominance decreases. In man and higher primates, smell plays a relatively subordinate role; it is visual sensations that dominate. Ours is a world of forms, colours and contours, whereas most animals live in a world of odours.

According to the common classification of sense organs (which goes back to Aristotle), we have five senses: vision, hearing, smell, taste and touch. The incompleteness of this list is obvious; it neglects, for example, the senses of balance, position, temperature and pain. Aristotle's exclusion of pain was deliberate, and it introduced a bias which has persisted for centuries. He maintained that pain like pleasure merely is a 'passion of the soul' and therefore cannot be considered as a sensory modality like the other five.

Coding mechanisms

A primary concern in sensory physiology is to establish the relation between neural activity and perception. As early as 1927, Adrian (Fig. 24.1) and Matthews pointed out the close relation between the discharge in the eel's optic nerve and the intensity of the same light as perceived by the experimenter. Later studies have provided evidence of a similar correlation in other systems.

To establish firmly the neural basis of sensory perception would ideally require simultaneous recordings at different levels of a sensory pathway in human subjects, along with measurements by psychophysical methods of the sensations evoked. Naturally the possibilities for doing this are very limited. However, in a few cases such studies have been performed and, as will be described below, the data obtained have greatly enlarged our insight into the neurophysiological mechanisms involved in the processing of sensory information.

Intensity coding

In psychophysical studies of sensory functions, attention has to a great extent been focused on the

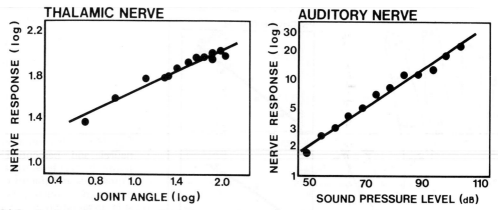

Fig. 24.8 Coding of sensory magnitude in central sensory pathways. Left diagram shows the response of a single thalamic neuron as a function of joint angle; right diagram shows the response of the whole auditory nerve and the stimulus intensity. (Left diagram from Mountcastle, Poggio and Werner, 1963; right diagram from Teas, Eldridge and Davis, 1962.)

is the importance of the focusing of attention on a stimulus. As is illustrated in Fig. 24.9 in the cat, the cortical evoked potential to a regularly repeated tone remains unchanged in amplitude as long as the cat is focusing attention towards the stimulus; if not, or if the cat is exposed to a distracting stimulus, the cortical response is depressed.

Quality coding

The specific sensitivity of receptors is the neurophysiological basis for signalling the particular quality of a stimulus. The activity of a given type of receptor is carried by specific pathways, which serve as private lines to the cortex. This can be demonstrated for cutaneous sensations by stimulating a nerve from the skin and recording the impulse traffic in that nerve in human subjects. In this way it has been shown that activation of thick, rapidly conducting fibres gives rise to the sensation of touch or pressure, while stimulation of thin C fibres evokes pain (see p. 463). For most, but not all, sensory systems, the fibres transmit the input from only one kind of receptor and the afferent message is carried to a given area in the cortex. It should be noted, however, that on their way to the cortex, the fibres give off collaterals at different levels which together with fibres serving other modalities form non-specific pathways. These pathways do not convey information about what kind of receptors are being stimulated, but only signal an unspecified sensory input. The signals are not carried to the primary sensory area in the cortex; they are fed into non-discriminatory parts of the brain. This input sets the overall level of excitability of the cortex and thus plays an important role in determining states of consciousness such as sleep and wakefulness.

Coding of stimulus localisation

The concept of receptive field

The peripheral terminals of an afferent fibre subserving the sense of touch spread over a restricted area of the skin; this is the *receptive field* of the primary afferent neuron. In a given area of the skin, there is a considerable overlap of the receptive fields of the individual afferent fibres. In the spinal cord the terminals of these afferents converge upon interneurons which transmit information exclusively from that restricted area. The receptive field of each of these interneurons is thus composed of the receptive fields of the primary neurons from which it receives afferent input. In Fig. 24.10 the receptive field of the interneuron 'a' consists of the peripheral fields 1 and 2 and that of the interneuron 'b' of the peripheral fields 2, 3 and 4. At

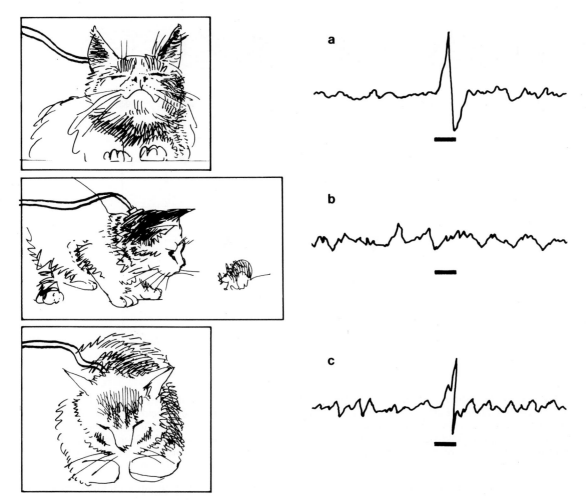

Fig. 24.9 Selective attention: suppression of auditory evoked response by a novel stimulus. The click response recorded from the cochlear nucleus is diminished when the cat is watching the mouse. (From Hernandez-Peón *et al., Science*, **123**, 1956.)

higher levels there is a corresponding increase of the receptive fields of individual neurons as a result of the convergence of the afferents in the ascending pathways. It may be noticed that the neurons of the motor systems also have receptive fields. Thus the pyramidal neurons in the motor cortex have receptive fields corresponding to the sensory input that they receive.

In the multineuronal network of the central afferent system, there is an interaction which involves an inhibition between parallel afferent pathways. This type of inhibition corresponds to

lateral inhibition in the *Limulus* eye. Owing to lateral inhibition, the receptive field of a postsynaptic neuron in the sensory pathway consists of two concentric zones, one central zone from which the neuron is activated and a surrounding zone from which it is inhibited (Fig. 24.11). In the visual system there are receptive fields with the opposite organisation (see p. 375). By definition the receptor field of a central neuron therefore is the area from which it is influenced by peripheral stimulation. Lateral inhibition in sensory systems has important functional significance for information

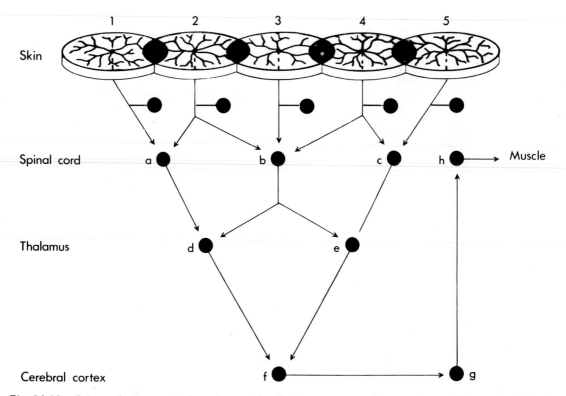

Fig. 24.10 Schematic representation of receptive field arrangement for neurons at different levels in the somatosensory system. Each neuron receives the input from a given peripheral field. Owing to convergence in the afferent pathways, this field tends to increase in size at successively higher levels in the system. The increase in receptor field size is reduced by lateral inhibition (not depicted in the diagram). Note that the neurons in the motor cortex have receptive fields corresponding to the sensory input that they receive.

processing in the central nervous system since it provides for an enhancement of the acuity by increasing the contrasts of the pattern of the message carried to the brain. Direct evidence of this has been achieved in recordings from single cells within the somatosensory area. Typically, a cell in this area is activated by stimulation of a small, relatively well demarcated area in the skin (see Fig. 24.11). If surrounding areas are stimulated, the cell is inhibited. The inhibitory effect is schematically illustrated in Fig. 24.12; incoming impulses from receptive fields in the skin are relayed to spinal cord cells, whose axons carry the impulses to higher centres and also to interneurons that inhibit the activity of cells receiving input from neighbouring receptive fields. A given skin area represents the excitatory field for some cells and the inhibitory field for other cells. Stimulation of a restricted skin area therefore activates one group

of cells while another group is inhibited. Since the cells in the relay nucleus are arranged somatotopically in a representation of the body surface, the result is that a group of cells lying close together is activated, while the surrounding cells are inhibited. This means a sharpening of the profile of activity within the nucleus (Fig. 24.13). This inhibitory mechanism is also present in all relay centres of the sensory afferent pathway. Within the dorsal column nuclei, the inhibition appears to be mainly of presynaptic nature, while in the thalamus and the cortex it is postsynaptic. In addition to these lateral inhibitory mechanisms, there are also inhibitory influences exerted from the sensory cortex on the thalamus and the relay nuclei in the dorsal column. All these inhibitory effects play a significant role in modulating and controlling the sensory input to the cortex. By suppressing the input from one or several sensory sources, they may allow for

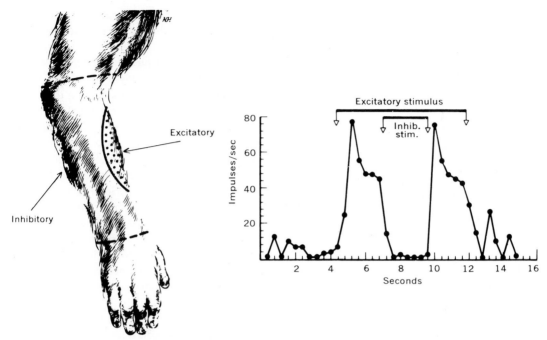

Fig. 24.11   Lateral inhibition in the somatosensory system demonstrated by the interaction of excitatory and inhibitory effects of cutaneous stimulation on the activity of a neuron in the postcentral gyrus of the monkey. The neuron was excited by stimuli within a field on the arm and inhibited by stimulation within surrounding areas. (From Powell and Mountcastle, *Bull. Johns Hopkins Hosp.*, 105, 1959.)

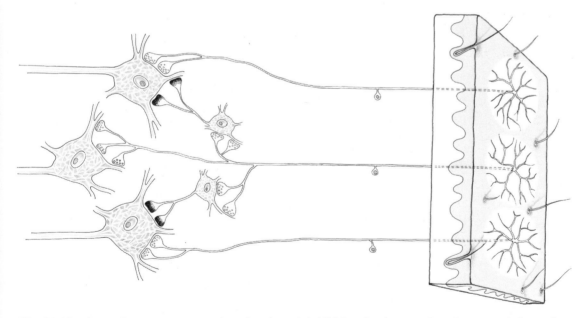

Fig. 24.12   Synaptic arrangement subserving lateral inhibition in the transfer of sensory information from the skin. The primary afferent axon from the central receptive field terminates on secondary spinal neurons, the axon of which conveys the impulses to higher centres. The primary axon also gives off branches with synaptic contacts on neighbouring inhibitory interneurons which have synaptic terminals (black) on adjacent relay neurons.

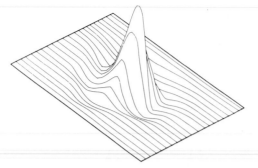

Fig. 24.13 Lateral inhibition in sensory systems illustrated by the activity profile within a nucleus in the lemniscal system. Note the decreased activity surrounding the peak of activity. (From Mountcastle, *Medical Physiology*, C. V. Mosby, St Louis, 1974.)

the selective passage of one particular sensory message. This is most likely the neuronal mechanism underlying, for instance, focusing of attention. Such a process may also be the basis for the suppression of pain.

The psychological mechanism behind localising a given stimulus to the site of stimulation without visual guidance appears to build upon the development in the cortex of a perceptual map of the body. This map is formed early in childhood by combining the sensations evoked by touch with visual observation of the location of the stimulus. This explains why the ability to localise a stimulus on the back is considerably inferior to the ability to localise a stimulus on the front of the body: the cortical map of the back is poorly developed for want of visual input. Furthermore, the skin of the back has a lower density of innervation and so the receptive fields of its neurons are quite large, especially when compared to the tips of the fingers.

25

Vision

Introduction

Sensitivity to light is a widespread functional feature in the animal world. It is present in one-celled animals and in species which do not have a specialised optical apparatus for refraction or any system for image forming. Many species of worms, for example, have light-sensitive cells scattered over the body surface. The next stage in evolutionary development is for light-sensitive cells to be clustered in pits on the body surface. In this way the cells are protected and, at the same time, the grouping contributes to an increased functional precision. As a further step for the protection of these specialised cells, a transparent covering membrane is developed and thus the primitive eye is transformed into a closed cavity. This covering membrane, which makes up the first primitive cornea, also bends the rays of light so that an image is formed. Later a lens develops from the membrane and gives the eye the capacity to vary the bending of the light rays so that it can be adjusted for sharp vision of objects at different distances. From these relatively simple eyes, the step to the eye of lower vertebrates is not long. Furthermore, in the whole vertebrate series, the same principles for the structure of the eye are retained. Thus the human eye does not differ significantly in structure from the eye of the frog; this in turn implies that the basic functional principles are the same for the eyes of most vertebrates (Fig. 25.1).

25.1 The optics of the eye

Light is part of the spectrum of electromagnetic

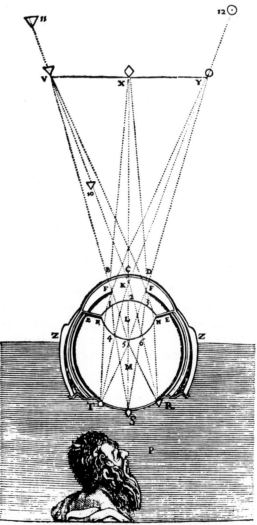

Fig. 25.1 Descartes' illustration of image formation in the eye. (From Descartes, La Dioptrique, in *Discours de la Méthode*, 1637.)

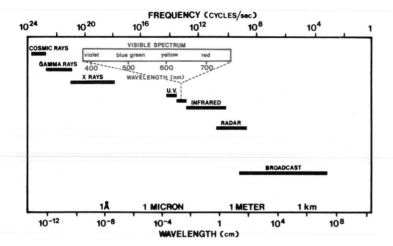

Fig. 25.2 Spectrum of electromagnetic radiation. Only a narrow range (expanded in the diagram) of wavelengths is capable of stimulating the receptors of the eye. (Modified from McKinley, *Lightning Handbook*, Illuminating Engineering Society, New York, 1947.)

radiation which includes X-rays, γ-rays and broadcast bands (Fig. 25.2). The optical system of the eye allows wavelengths of a relatively narrow part of this spectrum to reach the retina; it is relatively transparent for the wavelengths of light between 295 nm and 1200 nm. The cornea absorbs most of the ultraviolet light but is transparent for light of long wavelengths. Absorption of light of longer wavelengths is due in large degree to the lens. The visible part of the spectrum is limited to a range from approximately 370 to 740 nm, blue light having the shortest and red light the longest wavelength.

The eye may be considered as an optical instrument for focusing light from external objects upon the retina (Fig. 25.3). The image is formed by virtue of the refractive power of the cornea and the lens. The bending or change in direction of the light rays is called refraction. During their passage into the eye, the light rays are refracted at three surfaces: the anterior surface of the cornea, the anterior surface of the lens and finally at the posterior surface of the lens.

The refraction of lenses or surfaces is measured in units of dioptres (D), which is the reciprocal of their focal distances in metres. The optical power of refracting surfaces is determined by their radii of curvature and the index of refraction of the light-transmitting media. Focusing of the visual image on the retina is performed by the cornea and the lens. Their optical properties are therefore of major significance for image formation in the eye. As can be seen in Table 25.1 the anterior corneal surface has a refractive power of +48.2 D, the posterior surface of −5.9 D, the anterior lens surface of +5 D and the posterior lens surface of

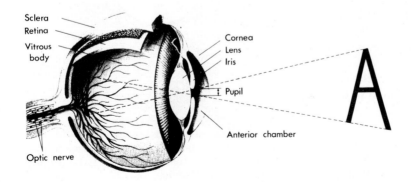

Fig. 25.3 Refraction of light of the optical system of the eye.

Table 25.1 Optical properties of parts of the eye.

	Radius of curvature (mm)	Refractive power (D)
Cornea, ant. surface	7.8	+48.2
Cornea, post. surface	6.8	−5.9
Lens, ant. surface	10.0	+5.0
Lens, post. surface	−6	+8.3

+8.3 D. Simple addition of these values does not provide an accurate measure of the eye's total refractive capacity. One reason for this is that the lens does not have a homogeneous refractive index; it varies from 1.3 to 1.4. Another is that these surfaces are separated by the anterior chamber and the lens, respectively.

Optical defects of the eye

In the normal eye with accommodation (see below) relaxed, a clear image of objects at a distance of more than 6 m is produced on the retina. Such an eye is said to be *emmetropic* (Fig. 25.4). If the image of distant objects is formed in front of the retina, the eye is said to be *myopic*. This may occur if the eye is too long in relation to the focal length of the dioptic apparatus or if the optical refracting system is more powerful than normal. The light rays are then brought to focus in front of the retina and diverge before reaching the retina. The image formed will therefore appear blurred. Myopia may be corrected by placing a negative or diverging lens in front of the eye. If, on the other hand, the axial length of the eye is too short in relation to the focal length of the optical system of the eye, light rays from a distant object reach the retina before they are brought to focus. An eye with this kind of refractive error is said to be *hyperopic*. This refractive error can be corrected by placing a positive lens in front of the eye.

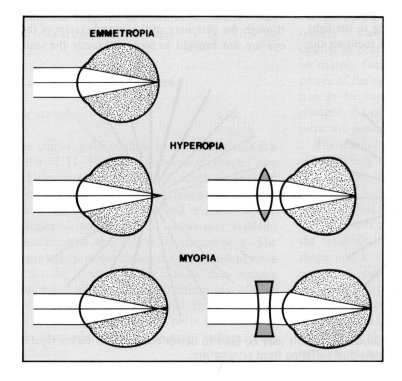

Fig. 25.4 Optical defects of the eye. In the normal (*emmetropic*) eye with relaxed accommodation, parallel rays are brought to focus on the retina. In the far-sighted (*hyperopic*) eye, parallel rays reach the retina before being brought to focus and each point source of light is represented by a diffusion circle. A converging lens placed in front of the eye corrects this defect and allows for a clear image to be formed on the retina. In the near-sighted (*myopic*) eye, parallel rays are focused in front of the retina and diverge again to form diffusion circles on the retina. A concave lens placed in front of the eye causes the light waves to diverge slightly so that they are brought to focus on the retina.

The changes in the form of the lens that underlie accommodation can easily be observed by holding a candle in front of the eye of a subject (Fig. 25.7). Three distinct separate reflections of the light may be seen; one bright erect image that is from the anterior surface of the cornea, a second erect and larger image from the anterior surface of the lens and a third small inverted image from the posterior surface of the lens. The difference in size between the two lens images indicates that the anterior surface of the lens is less curved than the posterior surface. When a subject is asked to focus upon a near object, the corneal image does not change in size, but the two lens images become smaller. It is primarily the larger image that is affected, indicating that the increase in refractive power during accommodation can mainly be attributed to the change in curvature of the anterior surface of the lens (Fig. 25.8). Under normal conditions, accommodation occurs simultaneously in both eyes. The reaction time is approximately one-third of a second and it takes about a half-second for the fully accommodated state to be reached.

As noted above, the elasticity of the lens capsule decreases with increasing age and thereby the lens gradually loses the ability to change its curvature. This means that the near-point, i.e. the shortest distance at which a small object can be brought into focus, recedes. At the age of 8 the near-point is normally 8 cm from the eye, at age 20 it is about 10 cm, and at age 60 about 90 cm. At the age of 8, it is possible, by accommodation, to increase the refractive power of the eye by 12 D, at age 30 by 9 D, and at age 50 by 2 D (Fig. 25.9). The reduction is thus relatively slow in the beginning but increases rapidly after age 30, and at the age of 60 the ability to accommodate is almost entirely lost. At the time when the near-point has moved so far that the subject cannot read fine print, the eye is said to be *presbyopic*. Normally this occurs around the age of 45 when the near-point is about 20–25 cm in front of the eye. The loss in refractive capacity can then be compensated for with spectacles with convex lenses, worn only to view nearby objects.

Vitreous humour

The vitreous humour is a gelatinous transparent substance which fills the eyeball behind the lens. Its structural elements consist of collagenous fibres which form a kind of supporting skeletal network. The chemical constitution of the vitreous humour agrees closely with that of the aqueous humour, yet no steady flow of fluid like that in the anterior chamber takes place in the vitreus. The vitreous humour commonly contains small particles which appear as spots when gliding past in the visual field. In most cases they consist of blood corpuscles or of condensed proteins.

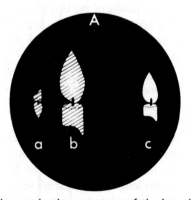 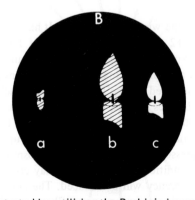

Fig. 25.7   Changes in the curvature of the lens demonstrated by utilising the Purkinje images. (A) Eye at rest and (B) eye accommodated for near objects: a, image reflected from the posterior surface of the lens; b, from the anterior surface of the lens; c, from the anterior surface of the cornea.

A   **B**

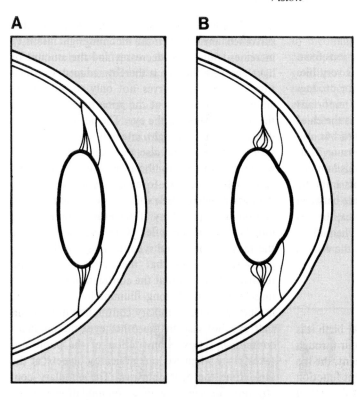

Fig. 25.8 Changes in lens shape during accommodation. At rest (A) the lens is held under tension by the lens ligaments and the lens has a flattened shape. When near objects are viewed, the ciliary muscle contracts and the lens ligaments are relaxed. Owing to the elasticity of the lens capsule, the lens acquires a more convex shape (B). As indicated, it is principally the curvature of the anterior surface of the lens that is changed.

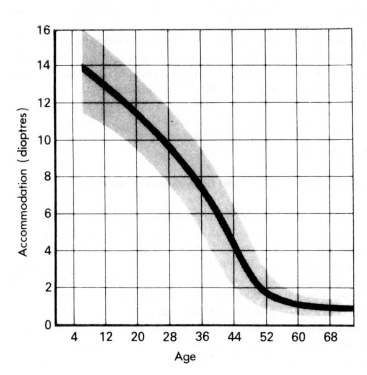

Fig. 25.9 Changes in accommodation with age. (From Gregory, *Eye and Brain. The Psychology of Seeing*, World University Library, London, 1966.)

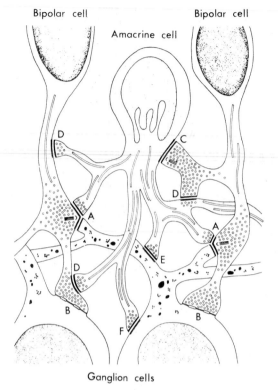

Bipolar cell

Bipolar cell

Amacrine cell

Ganglion cells

Fig. 25.16 Schematic representation of arrangement of bipolar synaptic contacts in the inner plexiform layer of the retina; A, axodendritic synapse involving terminals of amacrine and ganglion cells; B, axosomatic contact with ganglion cell; C, axosomatic contact with amacrine cell. The amacrine cells make contact with axons of bipolar cells (D) and with dendrites (E) and somata (F) of ganglion cells. (From *Gray's Anatomy*, Longman, 1973.)

other bipolar cells and upon ganglion cells. The organisation of the synaptic contact is complex; in some species the activity of the bipolar cells seems to pass first through amacrine cells instead of directly to the ganglion cells. The elaborate synaptic arrangement suggests that a correspondingly complex information processing exists in the inner plexiform layer.

25.4 Spectral sensitivity of the eye

If the visibility to monochromatic light of different wavelengths and equal energy is examined in moderately bright light, it will be found that the sensitivity of the eye is greatest in the region around 550 nm and decreases in a regular way towards shorter and longer wavelengths (Fig. 25.17). The curve obtained is called the *photopic luminosity* curve of the eye. If the same measurements are made in dim light, it will be found that the sensitivity is greatest at 507 nm and decreases towards shorter and longer wavelengths in the same way as in the light-adapted eye. The curve thus obtained is termed the *scotopic luminosity* curve. It is important, however, to note that the dark-adapted eye is colour-blind and that different wavelengths are seen as different intensities of grey as is expressed in the folk saying: 'At night, all cats are grey'. The difference between the photopic and the scotopic luminosity curves indicates that with increasing dark adaptation the sensitivity of the eye is shifted towards shorter wavelengths. This means that in weak light the blue part of the spectrum is seen more clearly than the red. Thus when walking in the fields on a summer evening it is easier to find bluebells than wild strawberries. The change in sensitivity with decreasing illumination was first observed by Purkinje and has been called the *Purkinje shift*.

The scotopic luminosity curve represents the sensitivity of the rods to light of different wavelengths. As the light-absorbent pigment in the rods consists of rhodopsin, it is reasonable to assume that the shape of the scotopic luminosity curve is determined by the photochemical properties of rhodopsin. A comparison shows that the absorption curve for rhodopsin is almost identical to the scotopic luminosity curve of the eye. The rhodopsin curve has its maximum at 503 nm while the scotopic luminosity curve, as mentioned, has its maximum at 507 nm (Fig. 25.18). The difference between the curves is explained by the fact that light is absorbed in passing through the media of the eye.

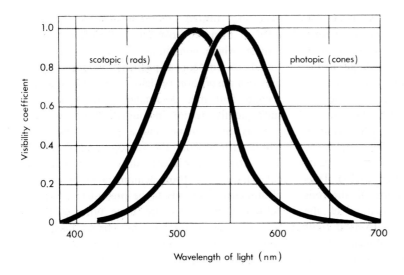

Fig. 25.17 Scotopic and photopic visibility curves. The scotopic curve shows the sensitivity of the eye to various wavelengths in dim light; the photopic curve shows the corresponding sensitivity of the light-adapted eye. The shift in sensitivity with light adaptation is known as the Purkinje shift. In the diagram, both curves are adjusted so that peak sensitivity is taken as a value of 1.0. In absolute values, rod sensitivity is much greater than cone sensitivity.

25.5 The photochemical basis of vision

The retina of the dark-adapted eye has a deep purple colour. Under the influence of light, this colour disappears and the retina becomes greyish. If the retina is returned to darkness, the colour reappears. Early investigators attributed the colour of the retina to the presence of a pigment, visual purple or *rhodopsin*, which was isolated in 1877 by Boll. However, the chemical structure of rhodopsin remained unknown until well into the present century. Interest in the functional role of rhodopsin in vision was revived by the observation that lack of vitamin A results in poor night vision. This led to the assumption that vitamin A is a component of the visual pigment. This notion was supported by the finding that the retina contains vitamin A. Subsequent studies showed that the visual pigment is formed by a chromophore group, *retinene*, identical with vitamin A_1-aldehyde and a protein, *scotopsin*. Other kinds of visual pigments have since been found, each with specific light-absorbing properties. In these pigments the chromophore group is always the same, but the protein part, the *opsin*, differs.

Since vitamin A_1-aldehyde contains a number

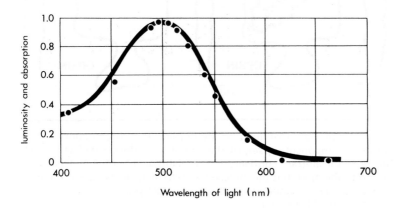

Fig. 25.18 Spectral sensitivity of human rod vision (full curve) and spectral sensitivity of rhodopsin (dots). The two are nearly identical, indicating that vision in dim light is a function of the absorption of light by rhodopsin.

This can be demonstrated by looking into the sky on a dark night after the eyes have been completely dark-adapted. If vision is directed to a faint star (i.e. by using foveal vision), the star seems to disappear.

It has generally been assumed that the time course of dark adaptation is determined by the regeneration of the photopigments. Although this may be true in part, it is now recognised that other factors may contribute. First, in the dark-adapted eye the pupil may expand in diameter from about 2 mm to about 8 mm. This implies that the eye becomes capable of gathering light more efficiently. In addition, dark adaptation involves an increased spatial summation which augments the responsiveness of the retina. Recent studies suggest that there is still another neuronal mechanism for adaptation. This so-called network adaptation is a relatively fast process and precedes visual pigment regeneration. The network adaptation is not associated with synaptic events; some evidence suggests that it may be related to alterations in the extracellular levels of potassium. It thus appears that the increase in sensitivity of the retina is not a simple function of the regeneration of photopigments but rather the summed effect of a number of processes, some neuronal in origin, which permits more efficient utilisation of small quantities of light energy.

If colour vision is tested during dark adaptation, it will be found that the subject is able to identify colours only during the first 5–10 min of dark adaptation, corresponding to the initial phase of the curve in Fig. 25.20. As dark adaptation proceeds, the ability to distinguish colours gradually disappears and the fully dark-adapted eye is colour-blind. Colour discrimination is thus linked to cone vision, while the rods are insensitive to colours and only able to distinguish different intensities of illumination. It should be noted, however, that the rods in contrast to the cones are relatively insensitive to red light; that is why a red object appears black in dim light. As a consequence, partial dark adaptation of the rods may take place in red light.

Light adaptation

When a dark-adapted eye is exposed to bright light, its sensitivity falls rapidly within the first 10–20 s and the change is nearly complete in the following 5 to 10 min (Fig. 25.20B). Light adaptation is accompanied by a series of changes opposite to those occurring during dark adaptation. The decrease in sensitivity is partly due to the reduction of the amount of photosensitive material in the visual cell, but in addition to this several other processes may be involved. At high levels of illumination, there is also a change in retinal organisation leading to a reduced 'gain' of the system.

The electrical signals of the eye

The electroretinogram (ERG)

In 1865 a Swedish physiologist, Holmgren, discovered that a characteristic sequence of potential changes is produced in the eye when the retina is exposed to light. The response, which is called the electroretinogram (ERG) has several features (Fig. 25.21) which may vary separately in magnitude with the intensity of the light stimulus and the state of adaptation of the eye. Generally, the initial component of the ERG is a fast negative deflection, the *a-wave*, which appears shortly after the light stimulus is turned on. This wave, which is

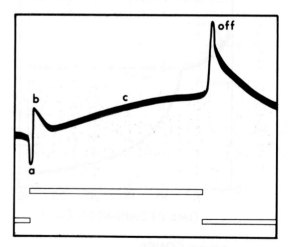

Fig. 25.21 The principal features of the electroretinogram: the negative initial a-wave, the positive b-wave, the slow positive c-wave and finally the 'off' effect or the d-wave. (By courtesy of K. Holmberg.)

believed to arise in the receptor layer, is followed by a slower, positive deflection, the *b-wave*, which most likely originates in the bipolar cells and in the outer synaptic layer. A third, slower deflection, the *c-wave*, is also positive and may outlast the stimulus; it has been attributed to the activity of the pigment epithelium. When a light of long duration is turned off, a fourth feature appears, the *d-wave*, often termed the off-response. This wave is accompanied by an increased discharge of the optic nerve fibres at the cessation of illumination; it may be related to the perception of contrast.

Single-cell recordings

Studies of the ERG have provided relatively little information about signal processing in the retina, mainly because of the uncertainty in relating the various waves to defined retinal structures. A direct study of signal transmission in the retina did not become possible until the advent of the technique for intracellular recording. The first recordings of this kind were made in simple invertebrate eyes. It was found that the receptors responded to illumination with a slow, graded, depolarising potential which increased in amplitude with the intensity of the stimulating light (Fig. 25.22). The photoreceptors thus respond in the same way as other types of receptors. It came as a surprise when later studies showed that in the vertebrate retina photoreceptors

respond to light with hyperpolarising potentials: the inside of the cell becomes more negative than in darkness. Apart from this, the vertebrate photoreceptors behave similarly to the invertebrate visual cells. The hyperpolarisation of the vertebrate photoreceptors occurs because in darkness a constant current, known as the *dark current*, flows through the plasma membrane of the outer segment. This current is borne by sodium ions (Fig. 25.23). When light strikes the receptor, the sodium permeability of the membrane decreases, reducing the influx of sodium ions. As a result, the inside of the cell becomes more negative. There are indications that the sodium current is regulated by calcium ions. As the rhodopsin molecules in the discs of the outer segment absorb light, calcium ions sequestered in the discs are released and close the sodium channels in the plasma membrane. In darkness, the calcium ions are taken up again and the channels for sodium reopen. The dark current also seems to be associated with a constant release of transmitter substance from the receptor terminals. This transmitter release is reduced when light strikes the receptor. The hyperpolarisation of the vertebrate photoreceptors by light would appear to contradict the general rule that associates activity of nerve cells with depolarisation. However, this is actually not so, since light simply reduces the depolarisation associated with the activity in the dark. But as we shall see later, the activity of several

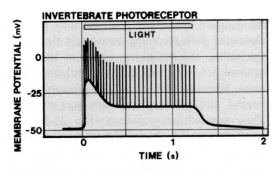
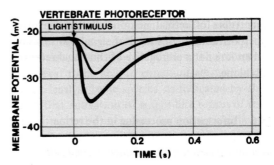

Fig. 25.22   A comparison of receptor potentials of invertebrate and vertebrate photoreceptors. *Left*: Response of photoreceptor of the horseshoe crab. Light depolarises the receptor and gives rise to an impulse discharge that lasts for the duration of stimulation. The response of the invertebrate photoreceptor thus is of the same type as the responses of slowly adapting vertebrate mechanoreceptors. *Right*: Response of a single cone in the turtle retina to brief flashes of light of three intensities. The vertebrate photoreceptor responds to light by a graded hyperpolarisation and does not generate spikes. (Left part from Fuortes and Poggio, *J. Gen. Physiol.*, 46, 1963; right part from Baylor and Fuortes, *J. Physiol.*, 207, 1970.)

response of a horizontal cell to illumination is a sustained hyperpolarisation similar to that of the receptor cells. Studies on goldfish have demonstrated that some horizontal cells respond either with hyperpolarisation or depolarisation depending on the wavelength of light.

The bipolar cells respond to illumination either with sustained hyperpolarisation or depolarisation; like receptor cells and horizontal cells, they do not generate conducted impulses. Explorations with small light spots have demonstrated that the retinal region from which a bipolar cell receives input is roughly circular and consists of a central zone and a surrounding zone which are antagonistic in their effects. For a given cell, stimulation of the central zone may cause either excitation or inhibition; stimulation of the surround always has the opposite effect to that obtained by stimulation of the central zone. As we shall later see, this is also the characteristic functional arrangement of the receptive fields of the ganglion cells. Like the ganglion cells, the bipolar cells are relatively insensitive to diffuse illumination of the whole receptive field. The functional implication of this is that the bipolar cells, like the ganglion cells, signal differences in the levels of illumination, that is contrasts in the retinal image rather than brightness of light. The

interesting conclusion that derives from these observations is that some of the fundamental accomplishment of information processing in the retina is achieved already at the level of the bipolar cells.

The amacrine cells are interesting from the point of view that it is at this level that conducted impulses are first met in the neuronal chain by which signals are transmitted from the receptors to the ganglion cells. The amacrine cells receive their input from bipolar cells and from other amacrine cells but have no direct connections with the receptors. The amacrine cells respond to light with transient depolarising potential changes at onset and offset of illumination. Superimposed upon the slow potential changes there appear short bursts of impulses. The output from the amacrine cells is fed to the ganglion cells which also receive input from the bipolar cells. The ganglion cells represent the final stage in the integrative processes in the retina and their responses reflect the transformation and integration of visual information that occurs in the transmission of signals through the sequential layers of cells in the retina (Fig. 25.25).

The receptive field organisation of the retina

The behaviour of ganglion cells was first studied

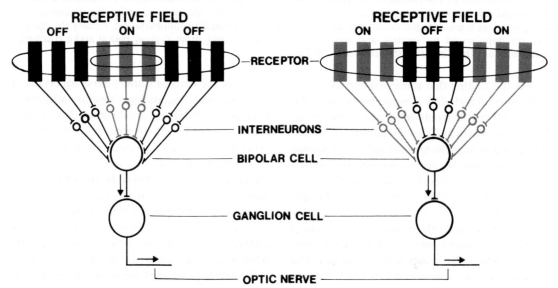

Fig. 25.25 Schematic diagram illustrating synaptic arrangement underlying the organisation of the receptive fields of the retina in 'on' and 'off' regions.

by recording the pattern of action potentials in single fibres in the optic nerve. It was found that some of the fibres responded when light was turned on as well as during illumination. Other fibres responded only when light was turned off, while still others gave both on- and off-responses. The explanation for these differences in behaviour of the ganglion cells was found later by Kuffler (Fig. 25.26) in experiments in which he stimulated the retina with small spots of light while recording the responses of single ganglion cells.

A characteristic feature of the ganglion cells is that they discharge continuously at a low rate even in the absence of illumination. While exploring how this activity was influenced when selective areas of the retina were stimulated, Kuffler observed in the retina of the cat that the cell increased or decreased its rate of firing only when a limited region of the retina was stimulated. The *receptive field* was circular or slightly elongated and the ganglion cell was generally located in the geometrical centre of the field. The size of the receptive field varied with the location of the ganglion cell in the retina. In the foveal region where the resolving power of vision is highest, the fields were smaller than in the periphery of the retina. Depending on its position in the field, a spot of light either excited a cell or suppressed its spontaneous activity. Following suppression of activity by illumination there was always an off-discharge when light was turned off. By systematically mapping out the excitatory and inhibitory regions of the receptive fields of different cells, Kuffler demonstrated that there were two basic receptive field types which he

Fig. 25.26   Stephen W. Kuffler.

termed 'on'-centre and 'off'-centre fields (Fig. 25.27). In the 'on'-centre fields a spot of light excited the cell when shone onto the centre of the field, while it suppressed the activity when shone onto the periphery of the field. In the 'off'-centre field the arrangement was the opposite. If the entire field of a cell was illuminated, the antagonistic action of the centre and the periphery cancelled each other's effects and there was usually only a weak discharge when light was turned on and another similar weak discharge when light was turned off; that is, the cell was relatively insensitive to diffuse light.

The important functional implication emerging from Kuffler's studies was that the ganglion cells do not convey information about the absolute level of illumination but rather measure differences in illumination in different regions of their receptive fields. This implies that they are exquisitely designed to detect contrasts.

To understand the functions of the ganglion cells, it is important to remember that even a very small spot of light may cover the receptive fields of many ganglion cells, some of which are excited and others inhibited. Moreover, the interaction between the on and off regions varies with the state of adaptation as well as with the location of the receptive field in the retina. The central zone enlarges in darkness and shrinks in light; thus with strong background illumination, the receptive fields often consist of only a small central zone with no surrounding zone of opposite functional polarity.

Within the framework of the above described general organisation of the receptive fields, later studies in the cat have disclosed three types of ganglion cells, which differ from each other with

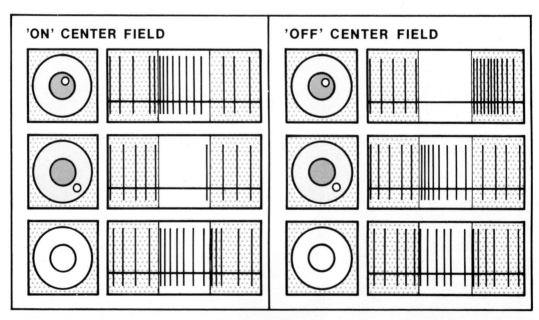

Fig. 25.27 Functional organisation of receptive fields of ganglion cells in the retina. The cells can be grouped into two classes: 'on'-centre and 'off'-centre cells. 'On'-centre cells respond to a spot of light shone onto the central part of their receptive field and are inhibited by illumination of the peripheral region of the field. Note that illumination of the entire receptive field causes only slight increase in activity. The 'off'-centre cell has the opposite organisation, the cell being excited by a spot of light shone onto the peripheral part of the receptive field and inhibited by central illumination. Like the 'on'-centre cell, the 'off'-centre cell is weakly excited by illumination of the entire receptive field. (Modified from Kuffler, *J. Neurophysiol.*, 16, 1953.)

respect to the specific features of their discharge patterns. One type of cell (X-cell) gives a sustained discharge. Another type of cell (Y-cell) discharges only transiently, while the third type (W-cell) can be excited both by light or dark spots.

Central visual pathways

Anatomical organisation

The eye is often compared to a camera. Inherent in this concept is the assumption that the image formed on the retina is transferred to the visual cortex point by point, the cortical image thus being a copy of the retinal image. Early anatomical studies on the projection pathway in the visual system gave support to this idea, since they provided evidence showing that the entire visual system displays a point-to-point localisation, in the sense that each small part of the retina corresponds to a given area within the visual cortex (Fig. 25.28). The structural basis for this correspondence is a topographical arrangement of the fibres in the visual pathways. In the optic nerve, the fibres are arranged in such a way that those coming from the upper quadrants of the retina congregate in the upper half of the optic nerve, and the fibres from the lower quadrants occupy the lower part of the nerve. In the optic chiasma, a regrouping occurs, so that nerve fibres from the right half of each

retina pass to the right hemisphere, and those from the left half join the visual pathway of the left hemisphere (Fig. 25.29). This implies that impulses from the right half of each retina are transmitted to the lateral geniculate body on the right side and thence to the visual centre in the right occipital lobe. Thus the visual centre in the right occipital lobe receives information about objects in the left part of the visual field and the left occipital lobe receives information about objects in the right visual field.

The first synaptic relay of optic impulses in the brain occurs in the lateral geniculate body. Its cells are arranged in six layers and the connections from both eyes retain a strictly topographical organisation. Fibres from corresponding areas of the two retinae end within alternating layers, the uncrossed fibres in layers 2, 3 and 5 and the crossed ones in layers 1, 4 and 6 (Fig. 25.30); there is thus no convergence of the impulses from the two eyes in the lateral geniculate body. It is only when the impulses reach the visual cortex that the input from the two eyes is integrated. Recordings from single cells in the lateral geniculate nucleus have shown that the discharge patterns are largely the same as those of the retinal ganglion cells. Certain differences exist, however. In particular, the peripheral zone of the receptive field seems to have a relatively greater influence on the centre than is the case with the retinal ganglion cells. Functionally, this implies

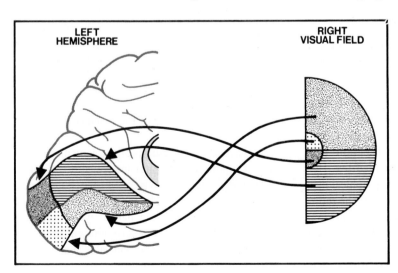

Fig. 25.28 Cortical projection of the retina. Left-hand drawing shows the medial aspect of the cerebral hemisphere with the calcarine fissure spread apart. The projection of different regions of the contralateral half of the visual field as indicated by the coding. Note that the macular region is represented posteriorly and relatively large; the peripheral regions of the retina are represented anteriorly and relatively small.

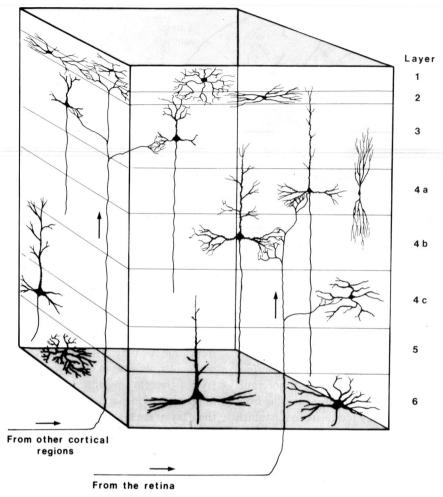

Layer

1

2

3

4 a

4 b

4 c

5

6

From other cortical regions

From the retina

Fig. 25.33 Schematic diagram showing the main features of the organisation of the visual cortex into different layers and their typical types of neurons.

25.7   Cortical processing of visual information

Receptive fields of cortical cells

It was in studies of the response characteristics of cells in area 17 that Hubel and Wiesel (Fig. 25.34) made the important discovery in the late 1950s that the neurons were only activated when the stimulus had a certain shape and position in the receptive field. This observation represents a dramatic breakthrough in the understanding of the analytical mechanisms of processing of visual information at the cortical level. Hubel and Wiesel

found that the cortical cells, like the ganglion cells, did not respond to diffuse illumination. In order to activate the cells they had to use slits of light, dark lines or edges. On the basis of their sensitivity to these stimuli, the neurons could be grouped into four classes forming a series of increasing complexity: (a) circularly symmetrical, (2) simple, (3) complex, and (4) hypercomplex cells. The cells of the first three groups were found in area 17 and the hypercomplex cells in areas 18 and 19. Later studies have shown that cells with properties similar to the hypercomplex cells are also present in area 17 (see below). The circularly symmetrical

Fig. 25.34
Torsten Wiesel
and David Hubel.

and the simple cells are present in the highest proportion in layer 4, while the complex cells are found in layers 2, 3, 5 and 6. Both the circularly symmetrical and the simple cells are monocular; that is, each type can only be influenced from one eye. About half of the complex cells are monocular, the remainder being binocular.

The circularly symmetrical cells behave like the geniculate cells from which they receive input. The simple cells have receptive fields composed of antagonistic on and off regions, but each field is in general elongated rather than being circular as are

those of the ganglion cells, the geniculate cells and the circularly symmetrical cells. The configuration of a simple cell's receptive field may vary but usually consists of a long and narrow region flanked by two antagonistic areas (Fig. 25.35), or it may consist of one excitatory and one inhibitory longitudinal region facing each other. Depending on the arrangement of the antagonistic areas, the simple cells tend to respond maximally to a line, a slit or an edge. The simple cells have therefore often been called *feature detectors* and have been divided into categories called line detectors, slit detectors or

Fig. 25.35 Receptive field organisation of simple cortical cells in cat's visual cortex. In this and following figures, 'on' areas are indicated by plus signs and 'off' areas by minus signs. The receptor fields are organised to provide information about lines and borders. In the diagram, the left cell is most effectively activated by a slit of light in the centre (slit detector), the middle cell by a dark bar in the centre (line detector) and the right cell by an edge with dark on the left (edge detector). (Modified from Hubel and Wiesel, *J. Physiol. (Lond.)*, **160**, 1962.)

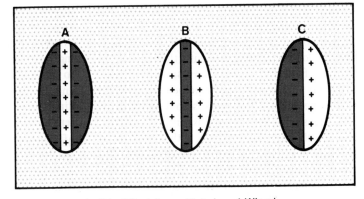

Table 25.2 Characteristics of cells in the visual system.

Type of cell	Shape of receptive field	On and off areas	Specific sensitivity to	Responsiveness to diffuse light	Orientation sensitivity	Position sensitivity	Movement sensitivity	Binocular sensitivity
ganglion	circular ellipsoid	+	small spots	(+)	−	+	−	−
geniculate	circular ellipsoid	+	small spots	(+)	−	+	−	−
cortical simple	rectangular	+	bar or edge	−	+	+	(+)	(+)
complex	rectangular	−	bar or edge	−	+	−	(+)	+
hypercomplex	rectangular	−	corner or angle	−	+	+	(+)	+

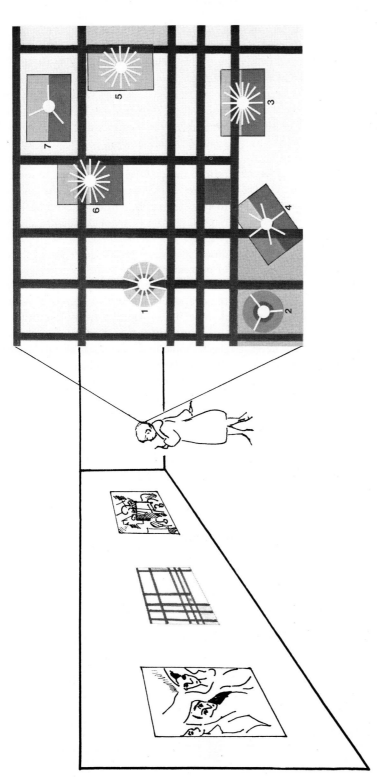

Fig. 25.41   When a person looks at the painting of Mondrian in the museum the ganglion cells (1) in the retina with 'on' centres signal the boundaries between different fields, while those 'seeing' a field without contrasts respond only weakly (2). Among the cortical cells, the simple cells (3) are strongly excited when the boundaries or lines of the picture coincide with the axis orientation of their receptive fields, while other orientations are less effective (4); complex cells (5) signal boundaries and lines but the position of the stimulus within their receptive fields is less important; hypercomplex (6) cells are maximally excited by an angle or a corner in the picture. Cortical cells seeing fields without contrast are, like the ganglion cells, only weakly excited, as illustrated by the simple cell (7) in the right upper field. (Based on a postcard courtesy of the Museum of Modern Art, Stockholm.)

from the visual cortex to other cortical regions comes from the neurons in layers 2 and 3; cells in layer 5 project to the superior colliculus and cells in layer 6 to the lateral geniculate nucleus. The cells in layer 4 are predominantly simple cells whereas layers 2 and 3 contain almost exclusively complex cells. It is most likely that the receptive field differences between cells in the different layers are related to the specific projection patterns of their dendritic connections. For instance, cells in layer 5 which are characterised by large receptive fields have large dendritic fields. There is also evidence to suggest that the pattern of branching of the basal dendrites is an important factor in relation to the geniculate input.

Binocular interaction

As we have seen, most of the neurons in the fourth layer are monocular; that is, they receive afferents from only the left or only the right eye but never from both. The convergence of information coming from both eyes occurs in the cell layers above and below layer 4. Here half of the complex cells receive input from both eyes. In general, the influence of the two eyes is not equal and the activity of individual cells is dominated by the input from one eye. There are all nuances of influence from complete ocular dominance from one eye to nearly

equal influence from the two eyes (Fig. 25.42). The majority of the binocular cells in area 17 have their receptive fields in corresponding parts of the two retinae.

As indicated earlier, visual information passes from area 17 to area 18. Here the binocular cells have receptive fields which are not located at exactly corresponding points in both eyes. For optimal activation, they require a disparity of the retinal images and have therefore been termed *disparity detectors*. Other cells respond optimally to objects at different distances and thus play an important role in binocular depth discrimination (Fig. 25.43). Some binocular neurons are in addition specialised for the detection of the direction of movement of the object. For instance, some of these cells respond to objects moving away from the eye and other cells to objects moving towards the eye. These neurons therefore provide information about changes of objects in three-dimensional space. Some neurons appear also to be sensitive to the velocity of a moving object.

In summary, the message sent from the retina to the visual cortex is not the simple point-to-point transmission as previously surmised. In the retina as well as in the cortex, the image undergoes an elaborate analysis. The ganglion cells, particularly those in the foveal region that have small centres, appear to provide for the resolution of the fine

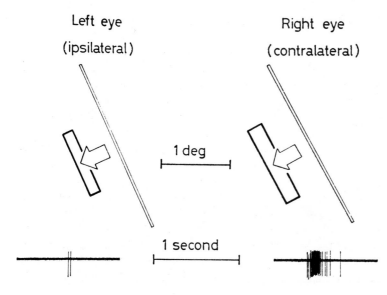

Fig. 25.42   Eye dominance in the visual cortex. Recordings from a binocular neuron in the visual cortex. The cell is clearly more strongly activated by a stimulus to the contralateral eye than by the same stimulus to the ipsilateral eye. (From Blakemore and Pettigrew, *Nature*, 225, 1970.)

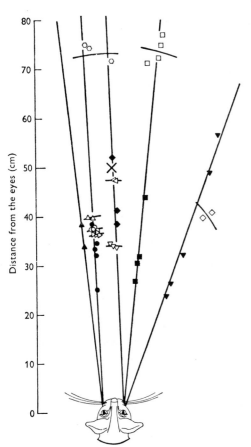

Fig. 25.43 The representation of three-dimensional visual space in the visual cortex. Distribution of points in space for optimal stimulation of binocular units in the cat's striate cortex. For each neuron there is a three-dimensional locus in space at which the stimulus must lie for the cell to be most effectively driven. The cells are arranged in two types of columns called *constant depth columns* and *constant direction columns*. The cells in a depth column view a thin sheet of visual space a few degrees wide and those in a direction column view a cylinder of visual space directed towards the contralateral eye. The filled symbols represent spatial positions for optimal activation of units in direction columns (different symbols for different columns), and the open symbols represent corresponding positions for units in depth columns. (From Blakemore, *J. Physiol.*, 209, 1970.)

details of the retinal image and at the same time, by virtue of the antagonistic action between the centre and surround of their receptive fields, provide information about contrast. The transforma-

tion from circular to rectangular receptive fields which occurs as signals pass from the retina to the cortex enables the orientation of the retinal image's pattern to be analysed. At this stage in the processing of the signals, the movement of the image is also incorporated into the message. The more sophisticated analyses carried out by the complex and hypercomplex cells bring out still other features of the image.

According to this model, the cortical processing of the features of the retinal image occurs in successive stages from simple cells to complex cells and thence on to hypercomplex cells. It would appear that for the final perceptual process the components of information have to be combined again by some still higher-order neurons that are able to synthesise all the details into a whole picture. Some observations suggest that such so-called 'pontifical cells' may actually exist in areas 18 and 19. Particularly suggestive is the finding that some cells in the inferotemporal cortex of the monkey respond best to a picture of a monkey's hand: optimal activation was obtained when the hand was pointing downwards, i.e. the very view the monkey might habitually have of its own hand. Such cells may represent the synthesis of features analysed at lower levels in the hierarchical cascade; in addition, these cells would have the capacity of storing visual information.

Functional architecture of the visual cortex

It is a basic principle of the functional organisation of the brain that cells with common functional properties are grouped together. In the cortex this grouping occurs in columns orientated at right-angles to the cortical surface. This organisation was first demonstrated in the somatosensory cortex, where the neurons subserving a given modality such as touch or pressure form columns which are separated from those cells subserving other modalities. It has since been shown that a similar organisation exists in other sensory areas of the cortex. By making a large number of penetrations with microelectrodes into the visual cortex, Hubel and Wiesel have demonstrated that cells with similarly oriented receptive fields are stacked in discrete columns (Fig. 25.44) lying perpendicular to the cortical surface. This discovery was followed some years later by the demonstration that a similar arrangement also exists for the binocular cells which are dominated by the afferent input from one eye. Hence, there are two independent systems of vertical subdivisions; one of these subserves receptive field orientation and the other ocular dominance. These columns have been termed *orientation* and *ocular dominance* columns respectively. Later neuroanatomical studies have provided evidence that the columns are not shaped like pillars but rather form parallel slabs.

The orientation columns are slender and intersect the ocular dominance columns. All the simple, complex and hypercomplex cells within a column have the same receptive field axis orientation. If the visual cortex is penetrated with a microelectrode at right-angles to the cortical surface and parallel to the length axis of a column, all the cells encountered will show the same axis orientation of their receptive fields. If the electrode is passed in a direction parallel to the cortical surface and at right-angles to the columns, there occurs a regular shift in the axis orientation of the receptive fields.

At intervals of 25–50 μm there is a shift in axis orientation of about 10°, and over a distance of 1 mm in parallel with the cortical surface there is roughly a 180° rotation.

To permit visualisation of the anatomical arrangement of the ocular dominance columns, Hubel and Wiesel used autoradiographic techniques. The method is based on the observation that, after injection of radioactive amino acids, label is taken up by the ganglion cells and transported to the geniculate body and from there to the visual cortex. Fig. 25.45 shows a section through the right striate cortex of a monkey where the right eye had been injected with radioactive amino acids. The light patches correspond to the injected eye and the dark patches to the other eye. By three-dimensional reconstructions, Hubel and Wiesel were able to show that the labelled patches correspond to parallel bands representing the ocular dominance columns which form a pattern closely like that of a fingerprint (Fig. 25.46). When exploring the arrangement of the ocular dominance columns with an electrode passing in parallel with the cortical surface, it can be shown that there is an alternation of eye dominance at intervals of about 400 μm. It

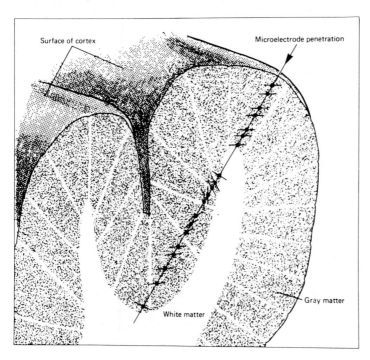

Fig. 25.44 Orientation columns of the visual cortex. Diagrammatic representation of typical results obtained in microelectrode recordings from the visual cortex. Each dot on the track represents a single cell and the line drawn through the dot represents that cell's orientation preference. Note that in each column all cells have the same orientation preference. As the electrode penetrates from one column to another there is an abrupt change in orientation preference. (From Blakemore, in *Handbook of Psychobiology*, Academic Press, 1975.)

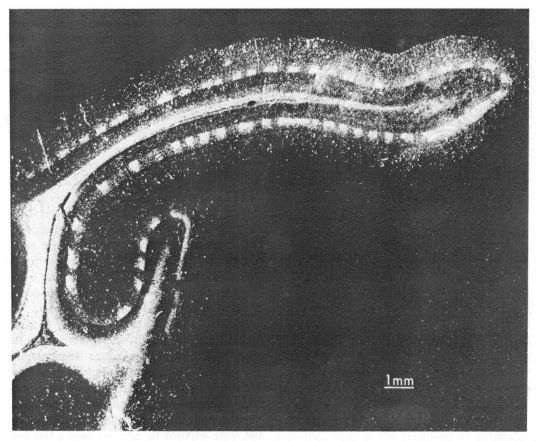

Fig. 25.45 Ocular dominance columns of the monkey's visual cortex visualised by an autoradiographic technique. Radioactively labelled amino acid was injected into the right eye. The amino acid is transported via the lateral geniculate body to the cells in the visual cortex. Labelled areas represent columns of cells which respond more actively to the right eye than to the left; the dark areas separating the bright patches represent columns of cells dominated by the left eye. (From Hubel, *The Harvey Lectures,* Academic Press, 1978.)

would thus appear that for the system of ocular dominance columns as well as for that of orientation columns all variables are represented in a region occupying about 1 mm^2 of the cortex. In this region there is a rotation in axis orientation of $180°$ and a shift from left eye to right eye. A set of orientation columns representing a full rotation of $180°$ together with an intersecting pair of ocular dominance columns form a *hypercolumn* that has a width of about 1 mm. Such a hypercolumn may be regarded as an elementary unit of the visual cortex (Fig. 25.47). Each hypercolumn has within it a complete set of simple, standard complex and special complex cells, which by their activity encode a complete feature description of the input image. This information is sent to other brain areas for further image processing, leading to the final perceptual process underlying the awareness of the image being seen.

25.8 Plasticity of the visual system

Soon after the discovery of the specialisation of the neurons in the visual cortex, the question was raised whether the connections that underlie the

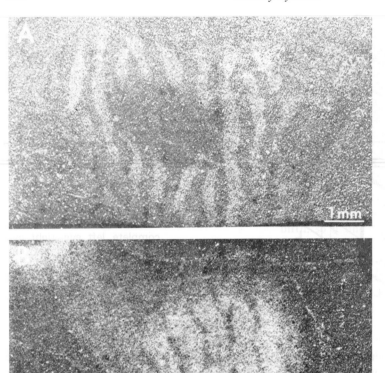

Fig. 25.48 The effect of monocular deprivation on development of ocular dominance columns. Tangential sections of the visual cortex through IV in (A) normal monkey and in (B) a monkey whose right eye was closed at 2 weeks of age. Note the difference in size of the two groups of columns as indicated by the dark and bright stripes. Those representing the normal (left) eye (bright stripes) are greatly increased in width, while those corresponding to the closed eye are reduced to half the normal width or at irregular intervals completely obliterated. (From Hubel, Wiesel and LeVay, *Cold Spring Harbour Symp. Quant. Biol.*, 40, 1975.)

may last even longer (up to 4–6 years of age). Deprivation of visual experience or exposure to monotonous patterns during this time may lead to changes in the normal maturational processes in the visual cortex and thereby to persistent deficiencies in visual capabilities.

Subcortical vision

It has long been known that destruction of the visual cortex in man leads to complete blindness. It has therefore generally been assumed that the visual cortex is absolutely essential for vision. Recent observations in monkeys suggest, however, that subcortical centres may contribute to visual perception. Thus it has been found that following complete ablation of the striate cortex the animals are still able to follow with their eyes objects appearing in or moving across their visual field. These findings have raised the question whether a similar persistence of visual perception may also occur after lesions of the visual cortex in man. Some early reports which appeared to indicate this have generally been dismissed since the lesions were thought to be incomplete. Recent studies on patients with lesions of the primary visual cortex have revealed that, although they deny seeing anything at all, they may nevertheless be aware of a light stimulus presented in the visual field. For instance, if a line is flashed they can tell the orientation of the line although they cannot 'see' it. This phenomenon has been called 'blind-sight'.

It is most likely that the persistence of crude visual perception following ablation of the visual cortex is subserved by subcortical systems. It is well established that some of the optic nerve fibres do not pass to the lateral geniculate body but terminate in the superior colliculus (Fig. 25.49). Thus there are two main visual pathways: the retinogeniculate striate pathway that projects to the striate cortex and the retinotectal pathway to the superior colliculus (from here it projects to secondary visual cortical areas). The first system is primarily responsible for detailed analysis of the visual message while the second system is mainly involved in reflex control of ocular movements. Studies of the response properties of single neurons in the superior colliculus have provided evidence to support the idea that the retinotectal system subserves the detection of visual stimuli and particularly the dynamic properties and spatial relationship of stimuli. It appears most likely therefore that the residual vision in patients with complete ablation of the visual cortex is mediated by this system.

Temporal discrimination

When a series of light flashes are presented to the eye, a sensation of flicker is evoked. However, as the frequency of the light stimuli is increased, a point is reached at which the flashes appear to fuse and are seen as steady light. This is known as the *critical fusion frequency* (CFF). Measurement of the critical fusion frequency has been widely used in studies of the temporal discrimination capacity of the visual system. In general the critical fusion frequency increases with the intensity of the stimulating light, with the size of the stimulus and with light adaptation. With strong illumination and a large stimulating field, fusion may not occur until a value of 120 Hz. The frequency at which flickering disappears also varies with the wavelength of the stimulating light. As seen in Fig. 25.50 for red light (670 nm), which stimulates mainly the cones, the fusion frequency increases almost linearly with the logarithm of the stimulating light. For blue light (450 nm), there is a discontinuity in the curve corresponding to the transition from predominantly rod to predominantly cone vision. This suggests that rods are able to discriminate flickering light only at low intensities of illumination.

25.9 Colour vision

Few problems in sensory physiology have been the subject of such extensive interest and aroused so much passionate debate as the question of how colours are perceived. Of all the theories advanced to explain the perception of colours, that presented in 1807 by the English physiologist and physicist, Thomas Young, has stood up best to the experimental research of later times. Young, who was also the first to demonstrate the principles of light

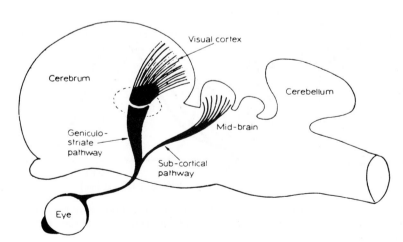

Fig. 25.49 Schematic diagram showing central visual pathways. Following damage of the visual cortex or lesions of the pathways to the visual cortex, the subcortical pathways remain and may mediate a visual sense called 'blindsight'. When presented with visual stimuli, such patients deny seeing anything, but asked to guess where in the visual field the stimulus might be they are often able to locate it accurately. (From Humphrey, *New Scient.*, 53, 1972.)

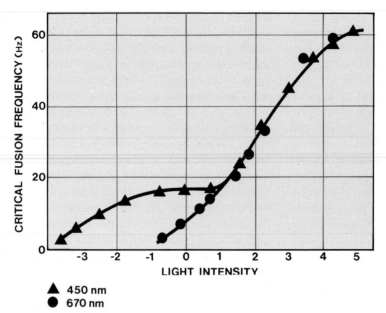

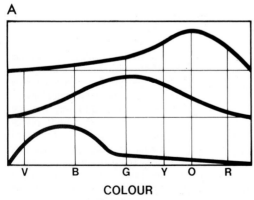

Fig. 25.50 The critical fusion frequency CFF of the central region of the retina as represented by data obtained with two wavelengths of light. Note that the curves are composed of a low-intensity section corresponding to rod function and a high-intensity section associated with cone function. (After Hecht and Shlaer, *J. Gen. Physiol.*, 19, 1936.)

interference, was interested in a number of problems relating to vision. Thus he was the first to describe the mechanisms for accommodation and it was he who discerned that a refractive defect is responsible for astigmatism. Young was also the first to develop a method for deciphering Egyptian hieroglyphs. His colour theory was built upon the assumption that there are three principal colours: red, yellow and blue. He demonstrated that any other colour in the visible spectrum can be produced by mixing monochromatic light of the primary colours in appropriate proportions. Young assumed

that the eye has separate mechanisms to perceive the 'principal colours' and that the sensation of other colours comes from activating these mechanisms to varying degrees. Young's idea went unnoticed for many years, until in 1850 Helmholtz brought it forward again. Helmholtz concluded from psychophysical studies that perception of the three primary colours as suggested by Young was mediated by three photopigments with broad absorption curves each with a maximum in three different spectral regions (Fig. 25.51). This so-called *trichromatic theory* implicated the existence of

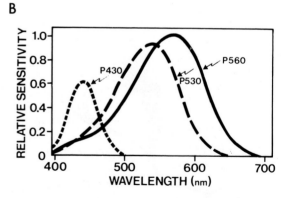

Fig. 25.51 A comparison of the spectral sensitivities of cone photopigments as proposed by Helmholtz (A) and the corresponding curves obtained by recent physiological measurements (B). (From Ratliff, *Neurosci. Res. Prog. Bull.*, 15, 1977.)

three types of colour-sensitive cones, specifically sensitive to blue, green or red light. Sensations of other spectral hues were assumed to be evoked by activation of the three types of cone in different proportions.

A little later Hering developed another theory, which became known as the *'opponent colour theory'*. According to this, the retina contains three photochemical substances, each capable of existing in two states, thus allowing six basic qualities of visual sensation to arise. White light is assumed to break down what he called the white—black substance, thereby producing the sensation of white. Breakdown or build-up of the two other substances, red—green and yellow—blue, would similarly yield red and green or yellow and blue, respectively. Complementary colours are considered antagonistic; they neutralise one another. That an antagonistic interaction between primary colour discrimination mechanisms exists is supported by a considerable amount of psychophysical evidence. Hering's ideas were met with scepticism in his own time and it is not until recently that his theory has received renewed interest in connection with neurophysiological findings of an antagonistic interaction between pairs of cone systems. These studies show that the response of the ganglion cells is the result of excitatory and inhibitory interactions between different parts of the spectrum and also depend on the spatial and temporal pattern of illumination. The interactions between the three primary processes of the Young—Helmholtz system yield the colour opponent pairs of red—green and yellow—blue of Hering's system. It would thus appear that both these theories are valid and complementary to each other.

Photochemistry of colour vision

There is little doubt that colour vision is mediated by the cones. In poor light, when the cones are inactive and only the rods are functioning, the eye does not see colours. Colours can only be perceived when the light is of intensity sufficient to excite the cones. The rods contain just one pigment (rhodopsin) and therefore they cannot possibly mediate information about different colours.

The trichromatic theory predicts that there are three types of cone, each containing a photopigment with specific spectral absorption characteristics. Experimental evidence for the existence of three kinds of cone was obtained in the late 1930s in recording from single ganglion cells. Some cells were found to respond only within a narrow range of the spectrum, while others had broad sensitivity curves. Among the former, three types could be distinguished which were maximally sensitive to the blue, green or red parts of the spectrum. These findings strongly supported the Young—Helmholtz theory but provided no direct proof of the existence of three types of cone or cone pigments. This was not obtained until 1970 when microspectroscopic measurements of the absorption characteristics of single cones in human retinae demonstrated that there were three types of cone, one with its absorption maximum at 445 nm, another at 535 nm and still another at 570 nm. These findings provided (Fig. 25.52) the final confirmation of the Young—Helmholtz theory. That the pigments responsible for the absorption characteristics of the cones subserve the perception of colour is borne out by the finding that the 535 nm pigment and the 570 nm pigment are absent from the eyes of subjects with green blindness and red blindness, respectively.

The absorption curves for the three kinds of cone overlap considerably, especially the 535 nm and the 570 nm curves. This indicates that light of

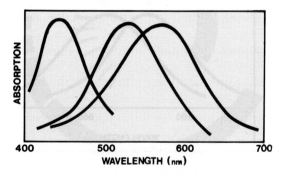

Fig. 25.52 Spectral sensitivity curves of individual cones of human retina. Maximum absorption has been adjusted to the same level in all three curves. (After Marks *et al., Science*, 143, 1964.)

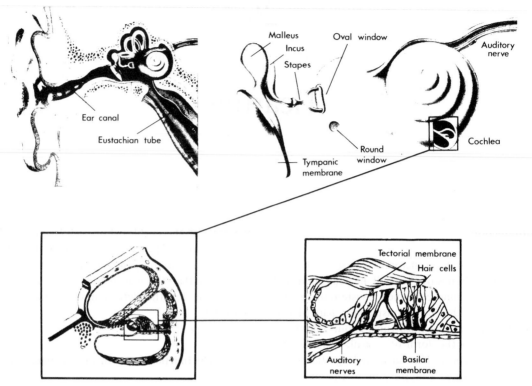

Fig. 26.1 Drawing illustrating some of the main structural features of the external, middle and inner ear.

stimuli, do not spread through the helicotrema from one channel to the other. The scala vestibuli arises in the middle ear at the oval window, in which the footplate of the stapes is inserted. The scala tympani also begins in the middle ear, but at the round window. Vibrations of the footplate of the stapes produce pressure changes in the fluid of the scala vestibuli and the extreme fineness of Reissner's membrane permits the vibrations to be transmitted rapidly and without distortion to the fluid in the scala media. From a mechanical point of view, the scala vestibuli and scala media thus function as a unit, and the basilar membrane is in effect directly exposed to the pressure changes in the scala vestibuli. Since the fluid in the three channels is incompressible, no displacement of the basilar membrane would be possible if the channel system were completely enclosed in bone. But because the scala tympani in the middle ear ends with a distensible membrane, pressure changes can

give rise to movement of the fluid and hence of the basilar membrane. When the footplate of the stapes moves inwards, the pressure increases momentarily in the scala vestibuli and scala media and displaces the basilar membrane. The pressure increase is thereby transmitted to the scala tympani and finally to the round window, the membrane of which is displaced outwards in direct relation to the inward displacement of the footplate. As shown by von Békésy, the motions of the basilar membrane are propagated from the base of the cochlea towards the apex like a travelling wave, the base being displaced in phase with the footplate, whereas the apical parts move after a certain delay.

The perilymph of the scala vestibuli and scala tympani has the same composition as the fluid in the semicircular canals (see below). The fluid in the scala media is endolymph and resembles intracellular fluid in composition. It has a high potassium content but a relatively low protein content, whereas the perilymph is high in both sodium and protein.

The organ of Corti

The sensory cells of the organ of Corti lie in rows, one row of inner hair cells separated by a tunnel from three rows of outer hair cells (Fig. 26.2). It has been estimated that there are about 3500 inner hair cells and 15 000–20 000 outer hair cells in each ear. Thus, the total number of sensory cells in the ear is far fewer than the number of receptors in the eye (about 150 million). The sensory cells carry hairs (stereocilia) on the surface of their free outer ends. The hairs are 3–5 μm long and reach the overlying tectorial membrane with their tips.

Each outer hair cell has some 120 sensory hairs arranged in three rows (Fig. 26.3), resembling a W open towards the *modiolus*; each inner hair cell has about 50–60 hairs arranged in two slightly curved rows. Whether or not the tips of the hairs are attached to the overlying tectorial membrane is contested.

Functionally, one of the key structures in the organ of Corti is the basilar membrane. Although Helmholtz's concept of radially arranged strings functioning as resonators is no longer accepted, it is obvious that the mechanical properties of the basilar membrane are crucial for the transmission

of sound stimuli to the sensory cells. Recent electron microscope studies have partially confirmed Helmholtz's hypothesis in showing that the basilar membrane consists of thin filaments embedded in an amorphous, structureless material. The basilar membrane changes in structure from the base of the cochlea towards its apex, in such a way that the stiffness of the membrane decreases towards the apex.

Cochlear nerves

The sensory cells in the organ of Corti have no axons of their own. At the base of each cell are terminals of the auditory nerve fibres which carry the signals to the brain. The afferent auditory fibres come from the ganglion cells in the *modiolus* and number 25 000–30 000; that is, about as many as the receptor cells. Anatomically, the afferent fibres can be divided into radial and spiral types (Fig. 26.4). The former pass in a radial direction into the organ of Corti to make contact with both the inner and the outer hair cells; those to the outer cells cross the tunnel of Corti on their way. The spiral fibres run lengthwise along the scala media and the basilar membrane close to the base of the hair cells, innervating both outer and inner hair cells. All the fibres lose their myelin sheath before leaving the basilar membrane to form syn-

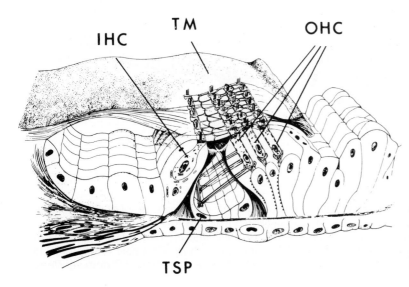

Fig. 26.2 The organ of Corti in mammal. IHC, inner hair cells; TM, tectorial membrane; OHC, outer hair cells; TSP, tunnel spiral fibres. (From Wersäll *et al.*, *Cold Spring Harbour Symp. Quant. Biol.*, 30, 1965.)

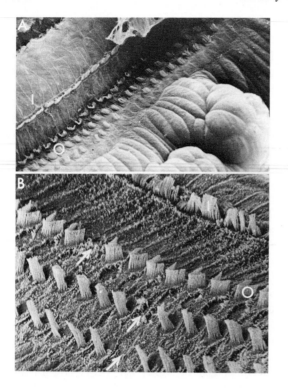

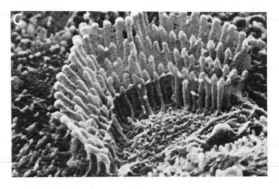

Fig. 26.3 Scanning electron micrograph of the organ of Corti (A) showing three rows of outer hair cells (O) and a single row of inner hair cells (I). (B) The arrangement of the hairs at higher magnification; arrows mark cells missing sensory hairs. (C) Typical arrangement of hairs on an outer hair cell. (From Lundqvist *et al., Monatsschr. Ohrenheilkd., Wien*, 105, 1971.)

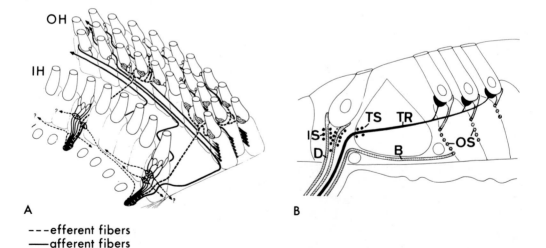

---efferent fibers
——afferent fibers

Fig. 26.4 Schematic diagram illustrating the innervation of the organ of Corti. (A) Stereodiagram of afferent and efferent innervation of outer (OH) and inner (IH) hair cells. (B) Vertical section of the organ of Corti showing synaptic organisation of the afferent (shaded) and efferent (black) fibres: D, radial dendrites to inner hair cells; IS, inner spiral fibres; TS, tunnel spiral fibres; TR, upper tunnel radial fibres; B, basilar fibres; OS, outer spiral fibres. (From Spoendlin, in *Frequency Analysis and Periodicity Detection in Hearing*, Sitjhoff, Leiden, 1969.)

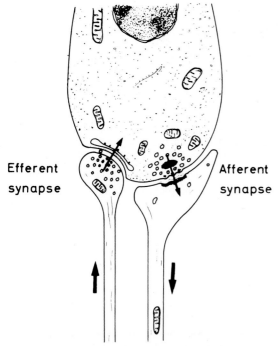

Efferent synapse   Afferent synapse

Fig. 26.5 Schematic diagram showing main features of the afferent and efferent synapses of an outer hair cell. (From Flock, *Cold Spring Harbour Symp. Quant. Biol.*, 30, 1965.)

aptic contacts with the sensory cells. Transmission of activity from sensory cells to afferent nerve fibres takes place by release of chemical transmitters, as indicated by the accumulation of vesicles and mitochondria within the receptor cell in the region of synaptic contact (Fig. 26.5). The terminals of the efferent fibres are filled with vesicles, while corresponding regions of the receptor cell are devoid of vesicles (Fig. 26.5).

Histological studies of the innervation of the cochlea show an uneven distribution of auditory nerves, with inner hair cells receiving more than 95% of the fibres and only about 5% going to the more numerous outer hair cells (Fig. 26.6). Consequently, each nerve fibre to the outer hair cells sends branches to an average of 10 hair cells, whereas the opposite relationship holds for inner hair cells: each cell transmits its activity to at least 20 afferent auditory fibres. The functional significance of this convergence from outer hair cells is that it permits spatial summation. In contrast, each nerve fibre to the inner hair cells reaches only a few receptor cells which are grouped together. The functional consequence of this is a sharp tonotopic discrimination since each fibre is responsible for a limited section of the basilar membrane

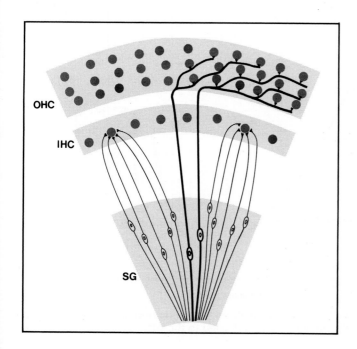

OHC

IHC

SG

Fig. 26.6 Schematic representation of the typical innervation pattern of inner (IHC) and outer (OHC) hair cells. SG, spiral ganglion.

and is excited only when that portion vibrates. The anatomical arrangement indicates that inner hair cells are mainly responsible for tone discrimination. Outer hair cells, on the other hand, can be assumed to have a considerably lower threshold by virtue of spatial summation of activity of cells distributed over relatively large areas of the basilar membrane. It is interesting to note how the functional arrangement of sensory cells in the organ of Corti resembles that of the retina. The inner hair cells, like the cones of the retina, are responsible for high resolution at relatively high stimulus levels, while the outer hair cells, like the rods, are involved in events at low stimulus levels and have low discrimination capacity.

The functional capacity of the inner ear

Intensity range

The range of intensities over which the ear can perceive sounds is tremendous. For frequencies from 1000 to 4000 Hz, which is the most sensitive region of the ear, the range from the minimum intensity that can be detected to the maximum

intensity that nearly causes damage to the organ of Corti represents a 10^{12}-fold increase in sound intensity. To define different sound pressure levels in this extreme range, a logarithmic scale for sound intensity has been adopted. The unit used is the decibel (dB) which is a tenth of a bel, which in turn is the logarithm of the ratio of the energy of a given sound to that of a standard sound. Thus it is important to note that the decibel is not an absolute unit but is always related to some reference level, and this level must be known in order to interpret data expressed on a decibel scale. The standard sound is the pressure of a just audible 1000 Hz tone; this is about 0.0002 dyn cm^{-2} or 10^{-6} W cm^{-2} (Fig. 26.7).

Thresholds

The sensitivity of the human ear to tones of different frequencies is greatest in the range 1000–4000 Hz (Fig. 26.8). Above and below this range it falls off rather steeply, and frequencies lower than 20 Hz or over 20 000 Hz cannot be perceived as sound. The range of frequencies to which the ear can respond is determined mainly by the mechanical

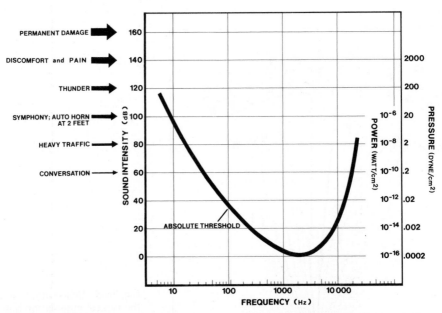

Fig. 26.7 Human audibility curve. Sound intensities in decibels on left-hand ordinate and in pressure and power on right-hand ordinate. Intensities of common sounds indicated to the left.

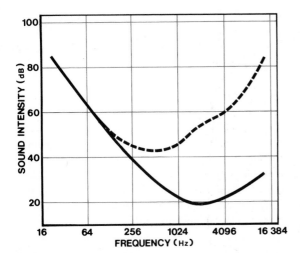

Fig. 26.8 Hearing ability for young adult (full curve) and aged individual (broken curve).

properties of the sound-transmitting system, and particularly by the characteristics of the tympanic membrane, the small bones of the middle ear, the coupling between these bones and the fluids of the inner ear and finally by the properties of the basilar membrane. Hearing declines gradually with age and particularly in the high-frequency range (Fig. 26.9). This alteration is called *presbycusis*. The high-frequency loss with increasing age causes only little difficulties in the understanding of speech since the frequencies which are most important (100–5000 Hz) for speech discrimination are relatively unaffected.

Pitch is the perceptual correlate of the frequency of a tone. The ear can detect pitch differences as small as 2–3 Hz for tones in the frequency range from 60 to 1000 Hz at sound pressure levels above

30 dB. For tones about 1000 Hz, there is an approximately constant ratio between the smallest frequency increment that can be perceived and the frequency of the reference tone.

Most sound sources produce sounds composed of a fundamental frequency plus various amounts of harmonics or overtones which are integral multiples of the fundamental frequency. In general it is the fundamental frequency that determines the pitch of a sound. However, the overtones may also be distinguished with their own characteristic pitches; they give the sounds of the human voice and those of musical instruments their *timbre* or *quality*.

Loudness

Loudness is the perceptual correlate of the intensity of a sound. At threshold all frequencies are by definition equally loud. When tones of different frequencies are increased in intensity above threshold, they are no longer perceived as being of equal loudness although the increase in terms of change in sound pressure is equal. To make sounds above hearing threshold appear equally loud, different frequencies have to be raised differently in intensity. Measurements of how much different frequencies have to be raised to obtain equality in loudness may be carried out by the following procedure. A subject first listens to a tone of 1000 Hz of a given intensity. After this the subject is presented with a second tone of another frequency but of equal physical intensity. The subject is then asked to adjust a potentiometer so that the loudness of the tone is perceived as being of the same loudness as

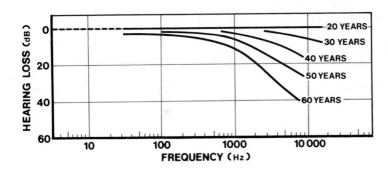

Fig. 26.9 Progressive loss of hearing ability with age.

the 1000 Hz reference tone. The loudness of a tone as compared to that of a 1000 Hz tone is expressed in *phons*. The phon is thus an expression of the perceived loudness. By plotting the phon values for different frequencies and sound pressure levels a family of isophonic contours or equal-loudness curves are obtained as illustrated in Fig. 26.10. For each of these curves, all frequencies are perceived as equally loud. As seen the curves tend to flatten out with increase in intensity level. This implies that for high-intensity sounds, different frequencies of the same intensity appear equally loud. It can also be seen that the rate of increase in loudness with increased sound intensity is much greater in the low-frequency range than in the 1000–4000 Hz range and the same is to some extent also true for high-frequency tones.

The loudness of a tone may also be expressed in *sones*. Measurement of loudness according to the sone scale is made by asking the subject to estimate how much louder a given test sound is in relation to a 40 dB reference tone at 1000 Hz. The perceptual intensity measured in this way involves discriminatory judgments of higher complexity than estimation of equality. If the sone values are plotted in a double logarithmic diagram versus phon values, a straight line is obtained for loudness levels above 40 phon, indicating that the sensation of loudness

is a power function of sound pressure. Below 40 phon the curve decreases more rapidly; that is, loudness increases relatively more with increase in sound pressure.

Audiometry

The acuteness of hearing of an individual is conveniently tested with an audiometer by which various tones are presented to the subject through earphones. The curve obtained is called an *audiogram* and plots the subject's auditory threshold for different frequencies relative to normal. Audiometry is an important clinical tool in measuring hearing ability. There are several types of audiometers and testing techniques. In the pure-tone audiometer, the output of the earphones represents the standard reference threshold value when the attenuation control is set at zero. The 'normal' (international) standard threshold level has been obtained for each frequency by measurements on a large number of young people. The standard procedure in testing hearing with a pure-tone audiometer is to increase the setting of the attenuation control so that the patient can just hear the tone of a given frequency. The reading of the attenuator control then gives the sound pressure over normal standard that is required to be per-

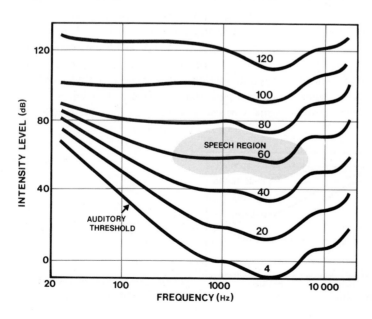

Fig. 26.10 Equal-loudness curves. Each curve represents the intensity level in decibels for different frequencies of sounds which are perceived as being of equal loudness. The number above each curve indicates loudness level in phons. The average auditory threshold is 4 phon. The shaded area represents the range of intensities and frequencies involved in ordinary speech.

ceived by the patient. In the standard audiogram, the normal hearing threshold is represented by the straight '0 dB' line and the hearing loss for the frequencies tested is given in decibels as compared with the normal level (Fig. 26.11).

In another method for audiometry, developed by von Békésy, continuous tones at levels slightly above threshold are used and the frequency spectrum is swept slowly from 100 to 10 000 Hz. The patient is instructed to press a button as long as he hears the tone and to release it when he can no longer perceive the tone. As long as the button is depressed the intensity of the tone is gradually decreased; when the button is no longer depressed the tone begins to increase in intensity. In the recording the intensity changes are traced as upwards and downwards deflections. The midpoint between the reversals of these deflections is taken as an index of the hearing threshold at different frequencies.

Sound localisation

It is a common experience that the source of a sound in general can be localised with a relatively high degree of accuracy. However, it is also well known that under certain circumstances it is extremely difficult to locate the origin of a sound.

Early work on the localisation of sound established that hearing with two ears, or binaural hearing, is a primary requisite. Two binaural cues appear to be essential: difference in time and difference in intensity. A sound originating on one side of the head will reach the ear on the side of the sound source before it reaches the other ear, and there will consequently be a time difference in stimulation of the two ears which gives a cue to localisation of the source of the sound. For continuous tones, the time delay will introduce a phase difference that serves as cue. There is a considerable amount of experimental evidence showing that the time difference is the most important cue for localisation of sounds below 1400 Hz. Above this frequency, the auditory system is less sensitive to temporal differences and must therefore rely on other cues for sound localisation.

The second cue, binaural intensity difference, is present at all frequencies but is the most important cue for localisation of sounds at frequencies above 4000 Hz. The intensity difference arises because the head casts a sound shadow for the ear away from the sound source; intensity is therefore reduced on this side. When a sound is originating in

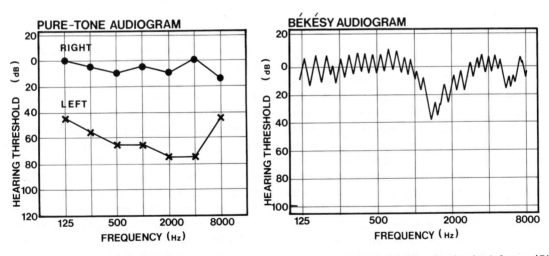

Fig. 26.11   Audiometry. (A) Pure-tone audiogram in patient with impaired hearing in the left ear. (B) Von Békésy audiogram of patient with impairment of hearing in the region of 1000 to 2000 Hz. (From Andersson, *Acta Otolaryngol.*, 62, 1966.)

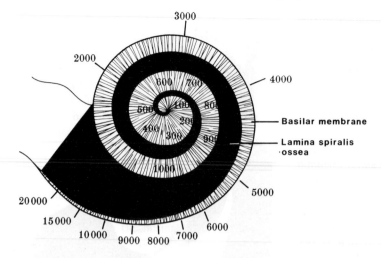

Fig. 26.13 Schematic representation of human cochlear duct showing location of maximal displacement for tones of different frequencies. The 20 000 Hz tone has maximum effect at the base, the 100 Hz near the apex. (From Rohen, in *Funktionelle Anatomie des Nervensystems*. F. K. Schattauer Verlag, 1971.)

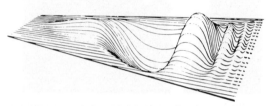

Fig. 26.14 The travelling wave. Schematic diagram illustrating the displacement of the basilar membrane induced by a sound of 400 Hz. (From Tonndorf, in *Neural Mechanisms of Auditory and Vestibular Systems*, Thomas, Springfield, 1960.)

agreed today that the mechanisms of frequency discrimination of the cochlea are far more complex than envisaged by Helmholtz, but his theory of tonotopic localisation in the organ of Corti is nevertheless correct in principle.

An intriguing problem is how the displacements of the basilar membrane induce activity of the hair cells. The cilia are, as mentioned earlier, in close contact with the tectorial membrane which extends out over the hair cells. The tectorial membrane is attached by connective tissue to the central spiral laminar bone and may therefore move relative to the hair cells. When the basilar membrane is set in motion under the influence of the travelling wave, the tectorial membrane slides over the hair cells and the cilia are bent. It has been thought that all the cilia in a bundle of sensory hairs are anchored at their tips in the overlying tectorial membrane. Recent observations suggest, however, that only the longest cilia are attached to the tectorial membrane. It would therefore appear that only the longest cilia are bent when the basilar membrane vibrates. This view has been seriously challenged by recent electron microscope findings showing that the stereocilia are interconnected by a network of fine fibrils which, with certain fixation procedures, appear as bridges by which the stereocilia are attached to each other (Fig. 26.15). This suggests that all the hairs in a bundle actually move in unison.

Clearly the mechanical properties of the cilia must be of fundamental importance for the transducer functions of the hair cells. It has generally been assumed that the stereocilia are flexible. Recent observations by Flock suggest that the stereocilia are rather stiff. When the distal end of a sensory hair bundle in the frog inner ear is displaced by a microprobe, the stereocilia pivot as stiff rods and tend to break at a sharp angle if subjected to excessive bending (Fig. 26.16). This raises the question of what structural components of the stereocilia are responsible for their stiffness. Since removal of the membrane with detergents does not affect the stiffness of the stereocilia significantly, it would appear that their mechanical properties are determined by some intracellular structural components. Early electron microscope observations suggested the presence of thin filaments inside the stereocilia. Later studies with improved techniques have disclosed that the fila-

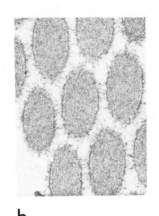
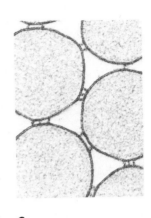

a b c

Fig. 26.15   Arrangement of sensory hairs. (a) Scanning electron micrograph showing arrangement of sensory hair on outer hair cell in human. (b) and (c) Electron micrographs of cross-sections of stereocilia showing that the cilia (of vestibular hair cells) are joined together by fine fibrils. After special fixation procedures, bridges appear between the cilia. (From Flock, in *Psychophysics and Physiology of Hearing*, Academic Press, 1977.)

ments travel in parallel throughout the length of the cilium (Fig. 26.17). At the base of the cilium they gather together into a densely packed bundle. By using a special technique, Flock and Cheung have demonstrated that the filaments inside the stereocilia are composed of actin. The presence of actin would appear to account for the stiffness of the cilia since it is known that actin filaments in other structures exhibit considerable stiffness. The discovery of actin filaments has important bearings on the processes of mechano-electrical transduction in the hair cells. For instance, it is probable that actin can interact with other proteins and thereby influence the stiffness of the sensory hairs. This would imply that the actin filaments by their action might modulate the sharpness of tuning of the hair cells and the auditory nerve responses.

The motion pattern of the basilar membrane is a characteristic of the stimulation frequency. As the intensity is increased, not only will the amplitude of the excursions of the basilar membrane be greater but a greater length of the membrane will be set in motion. It has therefore long been a matter of extensive debate whether the membrane displacements provide for a sufficiently discrete activation to account for the ability to discriminate between different tones. In other sensory systems, discrimination between two stimuli is improved by

lateral inhibition at the receptor level or in relay nuclei in the central nervous system. Lateral inhibition at the receptor level seems unlikely in the inner ear since no synaptic connections have been found which could mediate this kind of interaction. The idea that inhibitory mechanisms in the relay stations of the auditory pathway participate in discrimination gains support from model experiments performed by von Békésy. As we saw earlier (p. 344) the activity profile of the response to a tactile stimulus to the skin is sharpened by a central process corresponding to lateral inhibition. Since the hair cells in the inner ear are mechanoreceptors like the somatosensory receptors in the skin, von Békésy postulated that the auditory and the tactile systems might be similar in their functional organisation. For his experiments, von Békésy constructed a small box with five vibrators, which was placed lightly against the skin of the forearm so that all vibrators touched the skin evenly. He found that if one vibrator oscillated, its frequency could easily be recognised, but if all of them vibrated simultaneously and with equal strength the only vibrations perceived were those of the middle one. Some process of lateral inhibition was evidently at work. Facilitation was present too, however, because the strength of the stimulation perceived from the middle vibrator was dependent on

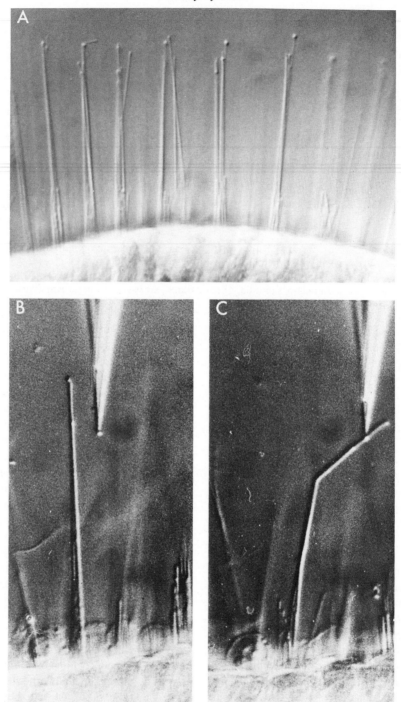

Fig. 26.16   (A) Photomicrograph of cilia in frog inner ear illustrating their rigid structure. (B) and (C) Stiffness of stereocilia demonstrated by displacement of a sensory hair bundle with a microprobe. When exposed to excessive bending, the cilia break at a sharp angle. (From Flock, in *Psychophysics and Physiology of Hearing*, Academic Press, 1977.)

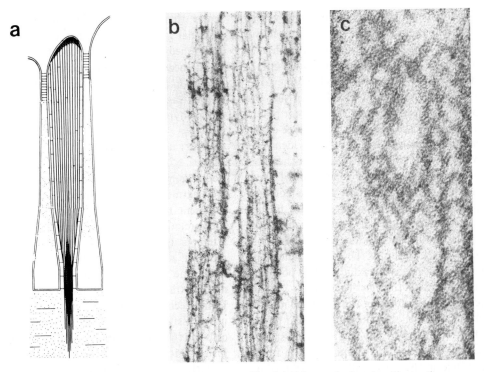

Fig. 26.17   Demonstration of actin filaments in stereocilia. (a) Schematic drawing illustrating arrangement of filaments. (b) Cross-links between filaments. (c) Typical 'arrowhead' decoration indicating that the filaments are composed of actin. (From Flock, in *Psychophysics and Physiology of Hearing*, Academic Press, 1977.)

the amplitudes of the vibrations produced by adjacent vibrators. This was shown by turning off the flanking vibrators, which made the middle stimulus seem weaker. The most probable explanation of these effects is that they are due to inhibitory and facilitatory processes in the relay stations of the spinal cord and thalamus. It would appear probable that similar mechanisms contribute to the discrimination of tone frequencies.

In his studies of the motions of the basilar membrane, von Békésy used isolated cochleas. With the methods then available, high sound intensities were required in order to produce measurable excursions of the basilar membrane; consequently, relatively large regions were set into vibration. Recent studies indicate that with a weaker tone the travelling wave narrows and the membrane becomes much more selective. The results obtained with the use of the Mössbauer effect are pertinent here. This technique permits measurements of the vibration amplitude of the basilar membrane in animals at extremely low intensities of sound. The results show that even though the selectivity of the basilar membrane is much greater than was earlier believed, it still does not approach the degree of resolution observed in recordings of the impulse response of single auditory nerve fibres.

26.3   Electrical activity of the cochlea

The cochlear microphonic response

In 1930 Wever and Bray found when recording from the round window of the cat by means of gross electrodes that the potential changes obtained closely followed the characteristics of the sound stimulus. The cochlea appeared to function like a microphone and the electrical potential changes were therefore called *cochlear microphonics*. At

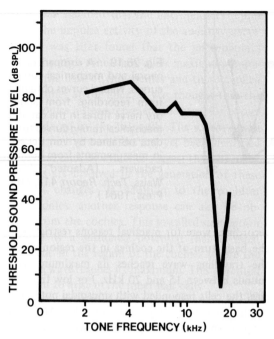

Fig. 26.21 Frequency characteristic of inner hair cell in the mammalian cochlea. Iso-amplitude curve for the DC receptor potential. Note that the inner hair cell receptor potential has the same frequency characteristics as the afferent fibres innervating them (cf. Fig. 26.19). (From Sellick, *Trends in Neurosci.*, 2, 1979.)

For frequencies above 2 kHz, the phase-locking disappears and the frequency of the nerve discharge is determined entirely by the magnitude of the sustained receptor potential.

Of particular interest is the fact that the curves for the intracellular sustained receptor potentials closely resemble the threshold tuning curves for single fibres in the auditory nerve (Fig. 26.19). This suggests that the frequency characteristics of the nerve fibres can be accounted for by the transducer functions of the receptors. This raises the question of how the frequency sharpening is brought about by the receptors. One possibility would be that there is a direct electrical interaction between receptors. However, measurements of resistance changes of the receptors during stimulation provide no support for this. It would thus appear that the tuning of the hair cells occurs at the level of transformation of the vibrations of the basilar membrane.

In short, the sequence of events in the inner ear may be summarised as follows. The sound stimulus gives rise to a wave that travels along the basilar membrane towards the apex of the cochlea, reaching its peak in a restricted region of the basilar membrane characteristic for each tonal frequency. Excitation of the sensory cells occurs when their cilia are bent against the tectorial membrane as a result of the displacement of the basilar membrane. At threshold, a given tone always stimulates a particular group of cells. As the intensity of a tone increases and the travelling wave widens, a greater number of cells are activated. The inner hair cells are highly frequency selective and their response characteristics are faithfully reproduced in the impulse message carried to the brain by the auditory nerve fibres.

26.4 Central auditory pathways

The afferent fibres from the cochlea enter the brain stem and pass to three groups of cochlear nuclei (Fig. 26.22). The distribution of the fibres shows an orderly arrangement so that each fibre divides to send branches to each group of cells in such a way that there is a tonotopical localisation within each group. Thus the cochlea is completely represented in the three separate regions within the cochlear nuclei. The cochlear neurons behave very much like the auditory nerve fibres. Thus at low intensities each neuron is excited only by one frequency. As the intensity is increased, the response range widens towards low frequencies. The response region or the 'tuning curve' is different for different neurons; some have narrow, some broad 'tuning curves'. The 'tuning curve' for a neuron tends to be restricted if a second tone is delivered. This so-called afferent inhibition, which appears to be analogous to lateral inhibition, is often 'single-sided' in the sense that only tones of frequencies lower than the best frequency suppress the spread of the 'tuning curve'.

In studies of response patterns at different levels of the auditory system, pure tones or clicking

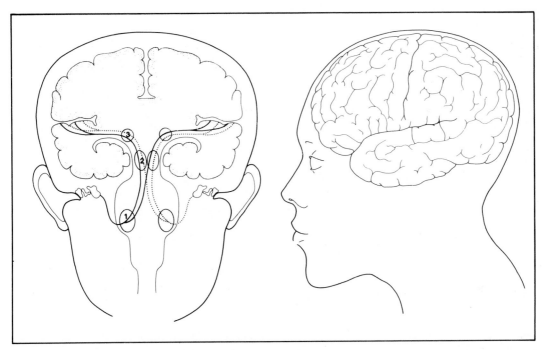

Fig. 26.22 Schematic representation of central auditory pathways: 1, cochlear nucleus; 2, inferior colliculus; 3, medial geniculate body. Drawing to the right indicates auditory cortex in the left hemisphere.

sounds have generally been used for stimulation. These are not, of course, the kind of sound stimuli to which we normally are exposed. To see how the auditory system functions when exposed to more natural sound stimuli, animal experiments have been done in which the frequencies of the sound stimuli have been varied, but the intensity kept constant. A cell in the cochlear nucleus tested with pure tones at different frequencies will then respond over a certain frequency range within which the impulse response is greatest for a given frequency and decreases on either side. If the sound stimulus sweeps rapidly over the same frequency range, the response curve sharpens. Furthermore, many of the cells in the cochlear nucleus do not discriminate specific frequencies at all if presented with pure tones or tones that change slowly in frequency, yet they show a high degree of specificity for rapidly varying frequencies of tone. This effect is probably due to the influence of inhibitory and facilitatory mechanisms at synaptic relays in the auditory pathways. The auditory message that finally reaches

the cortex thus appears to be modulated in the relay stations. Some of the efferent fibres of the cochlear neurons pass to the superior olivary complex and to the inferior colliculus. In each of these relay stations there is a tonotopic organisation. At each of these levels there is a crossing of fibres from one side to the other. This implies that each side of the cortex receives signals from both ears. Other fibres which do not synapse in the superior olivary complex or the inferior colliculus pass into the lateral lemniscus and from here via the medial geniculate body to the auditory cortex. There are observations indicating that the 'tuning curves' of the neurons become gradually narrower for each relay station, from the cochlear nuclei, the superior olivary complex, the inferior colliculus, the medial geniculate and finally to the auditory cortex.

In man, the auditory cortex occupies a region on the superior bank of the temporal gyrus corresponding to Brodmann's areas 41 and 42. In the monkey it has been shown that different tone frequencies are represented in a topographically

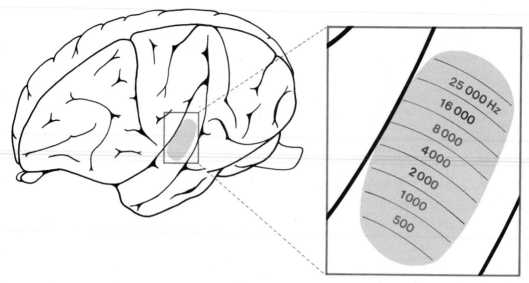

Fig. 26.23   Tonal localisation in the primary auditory area of the left hemisphere in the monkey.

organised pattern corresponding to that of the organ of Corti (Fig. 26.23). It should be emphasised that both organs of Corti are bilaterally represented and overlap each other in the cortex. Cells in the auditory cortex are arranged in columns like the cells in the visual and somatosensory centres to the cerebral cortex, and the cells of each column respond to approximately the same frequencies. The primary auditory region of the temporal lobe is surrounded by a secondary area in which the spatial representation of the cochlea has not yet been defined. There are areas still farther away where responses to sound stimuli can be recorded although the cells of these regions have no tonotopic arrangement and also respond to stimuli other than sound.

27

Vestibular Functions

The functional anatomy of the vestibular organ

In addition to the cochlea, the inner ear contains the vestibular apparatus which is the primary organ of equilibrium. It comprises a system of semicircular canals and sacs that contain mechanoreceptors specialised to signal the position of the head as well as accelerations of the body in space (Fig. 27.1). This system exerts its functions mainly by adjusting the activity of postural muscles and by controlling eye movements during head movements. The sensory input from the vestibular system is normally little noticed from a perceptual point of view and it is only with dysfunction of the system that we become aware of it. Disturbances of the vestibular mechanisms may be accompanied by subjective symptoms of vertigo, dizziness, ataxia and nausea.

The vestibular apparatus is made up of fluid-filled ducts and sacs enclosed in the temporal bone. There are three semicircular canals on each side of the head which are oriented at right-angles to one another in nearly orthogonal planes (Fig. 27.2). When the head is tilted forwards at an angle of 30° the lateral (horizontal) duct is in the horizontal plane. The anterior duct on one side is parallel to the posterior duct on the opposite side and is at right-angles to the posterior duct. Thus, the anterior canal on one side and the posterior canal on the opposite side are maximally stimulated by rotations around a common axis. The arrangement of the canals in parallel pairs provides for detection of rotation about any axis in three-dimensional space.

Each canal has an enlarged portion, the *ampulla*, which contains the sensory cells, and each canal begins and ends in a common sac, the *utricle*, which communicates with another sac, the *saccule*, by way of the utriculosaccular duct. The sensory cells of each of these two sacs are grouped together in a ridge or *macula*, the long axis of which is oriented in the horizontal plane in the utricle and the vertical plane in the saccule. While the semicircular canals signal motion and the rate of motion of the head (angular acceleration), the receptors in the utricle and saccule provide information about the position of the head relative to the direction of the force of gravity and to linear acceleration or deceleration.

The sensory cells of the semicircular canals are grouped together on the crista of the ampulla. On their outer surface, they carry cilia which are embedded in a gelatinous material that forms a wedge, the *cupula* (see Fig. 27.3). The free end of the cupula reaches the opposite side of the wall of the ampulla. Early observations by Steinhausen and Dohlman appeared to demonstrate that the entire cupula was displaced like a swinging door during acceleration. More recent observations suggest that this may occur only with strong (and unphysiological) stimulation. With weak stimulation the cupula rather moves as a diaphragm having its greatest displacement near the centre of the crista and slightly above it, while the tip of the cupula remains stationary and in contact with the ampullar wall.

The receptor cells are of two types, flask-shaped

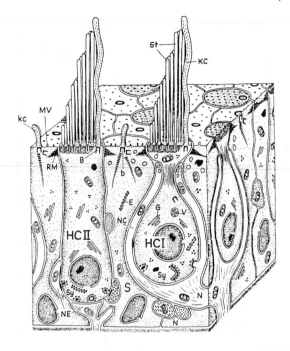

Fig. 27.4   Stereodiagram showing the two types of vestibular sensory cells and their innervation. The flasked-shaped type I cell is enclosed in a nerve calyx (NC). The type II sensory cell makes synaptic contact at its base with afferent and efferent nerve endings. St, stereocilia; KC, kinocilium; kc, modified kinocilium; N, nerve fibre; NC, nerve calyx; NE, nerve endings; Sy, synaptic structures; S, supporting cell; G. Golgi membrane; RM, reticular membrane; E, endoplasmic reticulum; MV, microvilli. (From Spoendlin, in *The Vestibular System and its Diseases*, University of Pennsylvania Press, 1966.)

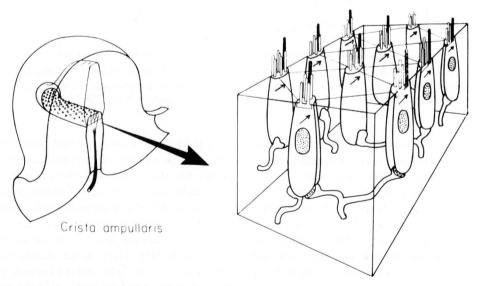

Fig. 27.5   Schematic diagram illustrating the morphological polarisation of the sensory hairs of the crista ampullaris. Note that the kinocilia have the same position in all cells. (From Flock and Wersäll, *J. Cell. Biol.*, 15, 1962.)

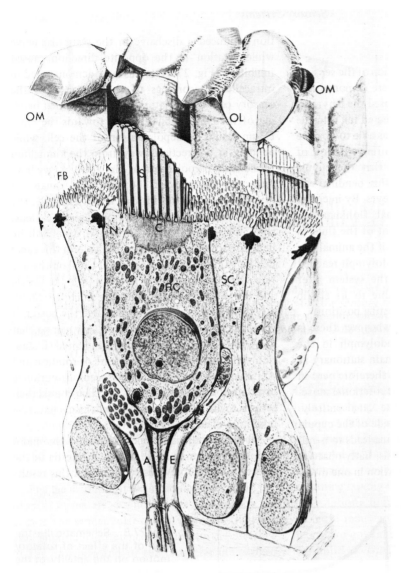

Fig. 27.6 Stereodiagram of saccular receptors in the frog: OM, otolithic membrane; FB, filamentous base; SC, supporting cell; RC, receptor cell; K, kinocilium; S, stereocilia; C, cuticle; A, afferent nerve fibre; E, efferent nerve fibre; OL, otolith. (From Hillman, in *Frog Neurobiology. A Handbook*, Springer-Verlag, 1976.)

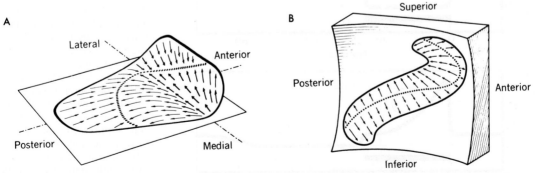

Fig. 27.7 The polarization pattern of the sensory cells in utricular (A) and saccular (B) macula. Arrows indicate the direction of displacement of sensory hair for excitation. (From Spoendlin, in *The Role of the Vestibular Organs in the Exploration of Space*, NASA SP-77, 1965.)

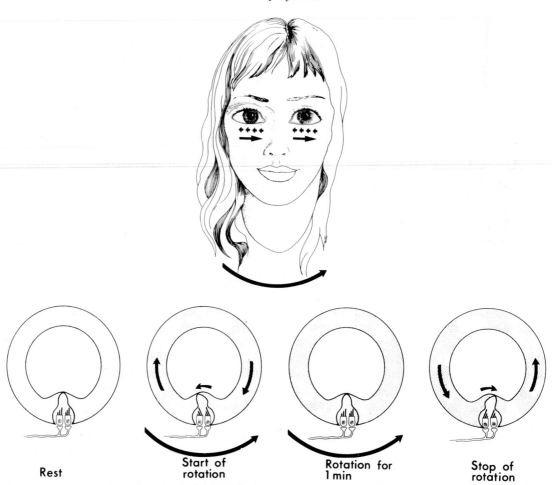

Fig. 27.10   Nystagmus. Jerky movements of the eyes are induced at the start and end of a period of rotation. At the start of rotation, the endolymph is displaced in a direction opposite to that of rotation. The fluid pushes the cupula, bending the sensory hairs. When rotation starts, the eyes move slowly in the same direction as the endolymph, that is opposite to the direction of rotation. When the eyes reach the limit for their movement, they swing back rapidly in the direction of rotation and fix upon a new point and then again move slowly in the direction of rotation. These alternate movements of the eyes are a reflex elicited from the semicircular canals, the slow movement being initiated from the labyrinths and the quick component from centres in the brain. If rotation continues at constant speed, the cupula swings back to its resting position and the eye movements cease. When rotation is stopped, the endolymph is displaced in the direction of the previous rotation and the cupula is displaced in a direction opposite to that during the start of rotation. The eye movements commence again but in the opposite direction, that is the quick phase is opposite to the direction of the preceding rotation; these movements are called post-rotational nystagmus.

When the eyes reach their extreme lateral position and the image can no longer be retained, they return rapidly to their starting position, and a new fixation point is sought. By these movements, the visual field is kept as stationary as possible, so that information about the body's orientation continues to be available. In contrast, post-rotatory nystagmus has no similar purpose; it is the price paid for the useful nystagmus at the beginning of rotation.

The eye movements so far discussed are produced when the body is rotated around its vertical axis and are evoked by excitation of the receptors in the horizontal semicircular canals. The vertical semicircular canals are activated correspondingly by rotation around their respective axis, and the eye movements produced are either vertical or rotatory. Vertical nystagmus is produced when rotation is carried out with the head flexed towards one or other shoulder at an angle of 90°. The vertical canals are then brought into action by rotation of the body around its long axis. *Rotatory nystagmus*, that is movements of the eyes in the frontal plane, is induced by rotation when the head is bent forwards 120° or backwards 60°.

Unlike the horizontal canals, activation of the sensory cells of the vertical canals is induced when the cupula is bent away from the ampulla. This difference relates to the orientation of the kinocilia which on the sensory cells in the horizontal semicircular canals face the utriculus. In the vertical semicircular canals, the ciliary arrangement is the opposite; the kinocilia face away from the utriculus.

The otolith organs

A cat held aloft and suddenly lowered will stretch its leg and spread its toes as if preparing to land. This reaction is not voluntary. It is a reflex mediated by the otolith organs in the inner ear. The impulses from the receptors are conveyed to the vestibular nuclei in medulla oblongata. From here, descending pathways in the spinal cord mediate motor reactions, mainly those of the postural musculature, and participate in righting reflexes (see p. 177). A considerable amount of the outflow from the vestibular nuclei reaches the gamma-neurons and thereby exerts an important influence on the tone of skeletal muscles.

The vestibular nuclei are also connected with autonomic centres. Through these connections, nausea and motion sickness may be produced by vestibular stimuli. In addition, the cerebellum is involved, as shown by the finding that motion sickness cannot be produced in dogs from which the cerebellum has been removed. It is not yet known precisely which type of motion is responsible for motion sickness, but there are indications that it is due mainly to linear accelerations.

28

Taste

What we ordinarily refer to as taste is not in fact a pure taste sensation but includes aspects of smell, touch and temperature; furthermore, the accompanying sights and sounds and the recollections of other flavours also influence our perception of how something tastes. Strictly speaking, taste includes only those sensations mediated by the gustatory nerve fibres. These sensations have four basic qualities: sweet, sour, salty and bitter. Experientially, the perceptions distributed by the gustatory nerves are relatively poor; the finer qualities are mediated by the olfactory nerves, as witnessed by the flatness of taste during an ordinary cold.

Taste receptors

The organs of taste, or the taste buds, are made up of two types of cells, the sustentacular cells and the receptor cells (Fig. 28.1). Most taste buds are on the tongue, but some are embedded in the epithelium of the mucous membrane of the soft palate, in the lining of the throat and on the epiglottis. A single tongue papilla may have 100–150 taste buds, and an adult has approximately 2000 altogether. Electron microscope studies have shown that the free surface of the receptor cells bears microvilli, 1–2 μm long and 0.1–0.2 μm wide. The basal part of the taste bud is surrounded by a network of fine branches from the facial and the glossopharyngeal nerves. The chorda tympani branch of the facial nerve innervates the taste buds in the anterior two-thirds of the tongue, while the

taste buds in the posterior one-third of the tongue are innervated by branches from the glossopharyngeal nerve. The nerve fibres form a reticulum at the base of the taste bud; from here the terminals penetrate the basement membrane of the taste bud and pass towards the receptor cells. The terminal branches are of two types: thick fibres (0.5–1 μm in diameter) which terminate synaptically near the receptor cell and have numerous mitochondria and vesicles, and thin fibres (0.1–0.2 μm in diameter) which nestle in folds of the receptor cell membrane and therefore appear to penetrate the cell. The latter terminations contain only a few vesicles and mitochondria. A single gustatory nerve fibre will innervate several sensory cells in a taste bud, and a cell may receive branches from several such fibres. After transection of the gustatory nerve, the receptor cells in the taste bud degenerate and disappear. When the nerve later regenerates and reaches the periphery, the taste buds reappear. There is a constant turnover of the sensory cells. Each sensory cell has a life cycle of only a few days (in the rat 3–5 days, in the rabbit 10–15 days) and is then replaced by a cell that arises from division of the surrounding supporting cells.

There are four distinct submodalities of taste: sweet, salt, bitter and sour. Application of taste stimuli to various regions of the tongue reveals that there is a topographical distribution of the responses to these four basic qualities (Fig. 28.2). The tip of the tongue is sensitive to all four qualities but mostly to sweet and salt. Sensitivity to sour stimuli is greatest on the lateral edges of the

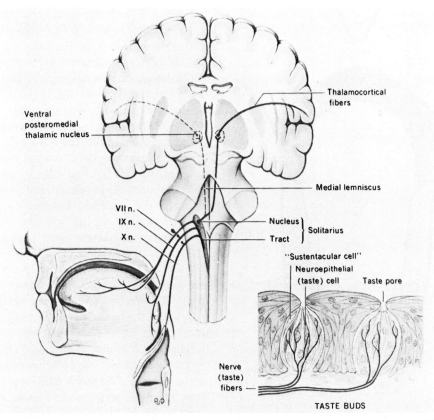

Fig. 28.1   Peripheral and central pathways for taste. (From Noback, in *The Human Nervous System*, McGraw-Hill, 1975.)

tongue, while the base of the tongue is sensitive to bitter stimuli. The differential distribution of the four taste qualities on the tongue would appear to suggest that there exist four distinct types of sensory cells, each specialised to respond to a certain type of taste stimulus. This idea is contradicted by microelectrode recordings showing that most taste cells respond to more than one of the four basic taste qualities. It has therefore been assumed that the receptor sites corresponding to each of the four basic taste stimuli are randomly distributed on the membranes of the sensory cells. Intracellular recordings have demonstrated that taste stimuli in general produce a depolarising receptor potential (Fig. 28.3); some cells, however, are depolarised by stimuli in low concentrations and hyperpolarised by stronger stimuli. The responses are generally, but not always, sustained.

Very little is known about the transduction processes. There is reason to believe that the receptor membrane has sites with specific affinity for certain taste substances. What happens after the molecules of the taste substances are absorbed is still a mystery, although the events very likely are the same as those in other receptors: the membrane permeability changes and the receptor cell is depolarised. The activity of the receptor cell is transmitted to the taste fibres by release of some transmitter substance.

Sensations of taste

If we drink a very lightly flavoured solution and then gradually increase the concentration of the flavour, the taste will change and at a certain concentration it is noticeably different than at first

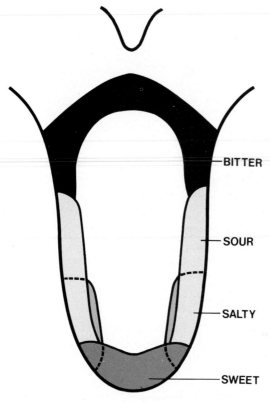

Fig. 28.2   Regional differences in taste sensitivity of the tongue.

perceived. This demonstrates that the unspecific (or detection) threshold is distinct from the specific (recognition) threshold. The latter varies from one individual to another as well as for the same person on different occasions. For one thing, it changes with the temperature; the lowest threshold for recognition generally occurring between 30 and 40°C. Furthermore, taste is influenced by the preceding stimulation that the tongue has undergone. For example, distilled water tastes sweet to someone who has just held a slightly acidic solution in his mouth. Some substances suppress, others enhance one another. Calcium cyclamate, for instance, strengthens the sweetness of sugar, while monosodium glutamate selectively increases the thresholds for sweet and sour. Gymnema acid reduces the sensitivity to sweetness without affecting saltiness or sourness. The leaf of the African plant, *Bumelia dulcificata*, sours sweet and bitter tastes, and the 'miracle fruit', *Synsepalum dulcificum*, makes what is sour taste sweet. If this fruit is chewed, a strong sour lemon solution tastes agreeably sweet, while salty, bitter and sweet tastes are unaffected. The active substance is a glycoprotein, which has been called miraculin, with a molecular weight of 44 000. This substance is not sweet

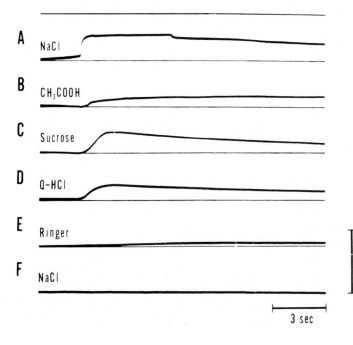

Fig. 28.3   Intracellular recordings of frog taste cell to application of different taste solutions. F shows control after the electrode was withdrawn to extracellular space. (From Sato, *J. Cell. Physiol.*, 80, 1972.)

itself but, after it has been applied to the tongue, acids taste sweet or sour; this effect lasts for about three hours.

Chemical determinants of taste quality

It is generally recognised that the active agent inducing the taste of sourness is the hydrogen ion. In general, a strongly dissociated acid is considerably more sour than an equimolar solution of a more weakly dissociated acid, but no simple quantitative relationship exists between the intensity of the sourness and the hydrogen ion concentration. Certain weakly dissociated organic acids have a more sour taste than would be expected from their pH value. Moreover, for any aliphatic organic acid, sourness depends not only on the hydrogen ion concentration but also on the length of the carbon chain. There are also acids that do not have a sour taste; amino acids, for example, are sweet and picric acid bitter. All this shows that even if the hydrogen ion is mainly responsible for producing the sour taste, its effect may be modified or entirely overridden by other molecular properties.

Many crystalline water-soluble salts yield a salty taste, but only sodium chloride gives a pure taste of salt. Other salts have mixed flavours that are more or less distinct; ammonium chloride, for instance, has a salty–sour taste, and magnesium chloride is bitter–salty. The taste of a salt is determined by both the anion and the cation. In a series of sodium salts, for example, the quality shifts with the anion, a weak solution of sodium chloride tasting distinctly salty, while the same concentration of sodium acetate does not. With respect to the degree of saltiness, the cations may be grouped in the following order: NH_4, K, Ca, Na, Li and Mg; the anions similarly arranged are: SO_4, Cl, Br, I, HCO_3 and NO_3.

Sweetness is evoked mainly by organic compounds with the exception of certain inorganic salts of lead and beryllium. No relationship between the physicochemical structure of the molecules and their sweet taste has been discovered. It is at least clear that the stereochemical configuration of the molecule in a homologous series somehow bears on the sweet taste. Likewise the stereoisomeric form matters; for example, the dextro form of asparagin is sweet but the laevo form is insipid. Recently, two proteins, *monellin* and *thaumatin*, which are intensely sweet have been isolated. Monellin is 2000–3000 times and thaumatin 1000–1500 times as sweet as sucrose by weight.

Bitterness is often linked with sweetness and many sweet substances have a bitter aftertaste, a mixed sensation that is particularly pronounced if the stimulus moves from the tip to the base of the tongue. Even more than with sweetness, it is difficult to relate the physical properties of a substance to its ability to produce a bitter taste. Typical of the bitter substance are alkaloids and complex nitrogen compounds, such as quinine, caffeine, strychnine and nicotine.

Neural activity of taste nerves

Recordings from single gustatory nerves have shown a certain receptor specificity, in that some nerve fibres are more sensitive to certain substances than to others. Some fibres in contrast have no pronounced specificity; all taste substances excite them to some degree. The specificities observed differ strikingly by species. The dog, for instance, has many sweet fibres; the cat, almost none. The dog has receptors that respond to both sugar and salt, and the monkey has fibres specifically excited by quinine. In some animals (e.g. cat, dog, monkey and frog), some fibres have been found which are specifically sensitive to pure water.

For a given taste substance, the frequency of the impulse discharge in a gustatory nerve fibre increases with the logarithm of concentration. In recent studies it has been demonstrated that there is a good correlation between the frequency of the impulse discharge of the gustatory nerves in humans and the intensity of the taste sensation (see p. 341).

The biological value of taste

There is accumulating evidence to show that taste plays a critical role in nutrition in many species. For instance, it has been demonstrated with the preference technique that rats which suffer from dietary deficiencies when offered different food-stuffs or liquids selectively choose those which contain the substances lacking. Thus, adrenal-ectomised animals show a marked appetite for salt and animals in which the parathyroid glands have been removed display an increased appetite for solutions containing calcium. Of particular interest is the finding that animals on a deficient diet are able to detect the lacking elements in lower concentrations in foodstuff or solutions than are normal animals. Although taste may be the most important cue by which the selection is made, olfaction may also be involved in the selection of certain substances which are vital for the organism.

29

Olfaction

Introduction

The ability to react to chemical stimuli is a common functional feature of living tissue. The effect that is elicited by the stimulus varies with the functional characteristics of the cells involved, as well as with the nature of the stimulating agent. Some systems show a broad sensitivity whereas others are highly specific and react only to certain stimuli. In the specialised chemoreceptor organs, such as the chemoreceptors of the carotid bodies or the olfactory sense organ, the cells are able to transduce the stimulus into a coded message that provides the central nervous system with information about the strength and nature of the stimulating agent. Though the cells of different tissues show widely different sensitivities and reaction patterns, they seem to have a great deal in common as regards basic mechanisms of their responses.

29.1 Functional anatomy of the olfactory system

The olfactory organ

The olfactory sensory cells in most vertebrates are uniformly distributed over restricted regions of the nasal mucosa. These regions are easily distinguished because of their yellow-brownish colour. The area covered by the olfactory epithelium varies greatly from one species to another. In man it occupies only a few square centimetres, while in animals with high olfactory acuity it is disposed over extensive areas of nasal mucosa within an elaborate system of folds of the turbinal processes. Although the extent of the olfactory area thus may vary greatly in different species, the structure of the sensory cells and other constituents of the epithelium is essentially the same in all vertebrates.

Receptors

The olfactory sensory cell is a bipolar neuron with an ovoid-shaped cell body (Fig. 29.1). A thin dendrite (1 μm in diameter) extends from the cell body towards the outer limiting membrane where it terminates in a rounded enlargement, the *olfactory vesicle*. The length of the dendrite varies from 10 to 100 μm depending on the thickness of the epithelium. The terminal vesicle, or knob, is approximately 1–2 μm and gives rise to a number of cilia. A cilium has two main parts, an initial thick section of approximately 0.2 μm in diameter and a final section of approximately 0.1 μm. The transition from the thick initial segment to the thin distal one occurs abruptly over a distance of a few micrometres. The length of the two sections varies greatly in different species. In the frog, the initial section is 20–30 μm long and the distal section may be as long as 200 μm. In mammals, the initial section is 1–2 μm while the distal section is about 50–80 μm in length.

The cilia protrude laterally in all directions from the olfactory vesicle (Fig. 29.2). In mammals, each

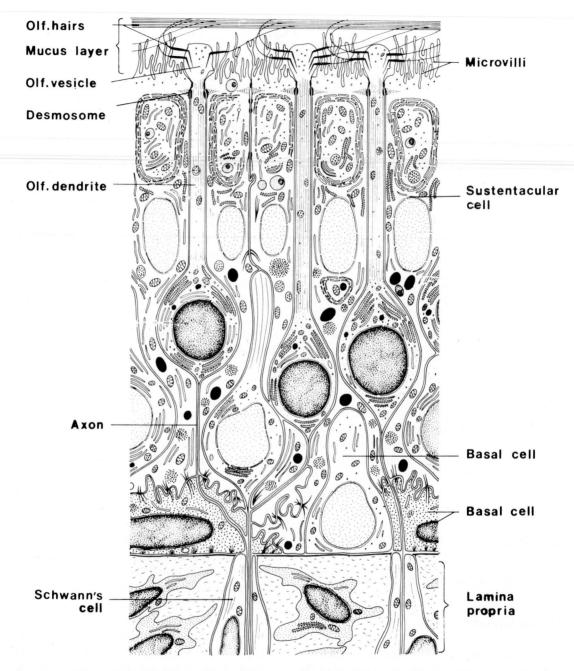

Olf.hairs
Mucus layer
Olf.vesicle
Desmosome
Microvilli
Olf.dendrite
Sustentacular cell
Axon
Basal cell
Basal cell
Schwann's cell
Lamina propria

Fig. 29.1   Schematic diagram of the ultrastructure of the olfactory mucosa. (From Seifert, *Norm. Pathol. Anat.*, 21, 1970.)

vesicle gives rise to 8–20 and sometimes as many as 30 cilia. Their initial parts pass through the dense

matrix of microvilli from the sustentacular cells. The thin sections extend through the mucus to-

A

B

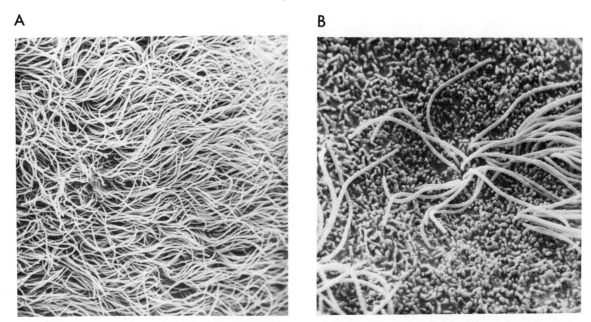

Fig. 29.2   Scanning electron micrographs of olfactory hairs in fish. (From Ottoson, unpublished.)

wards the free surface of the epithelium. In the superficial layer of the mucus, the cilia lie in parallel, apparently along lines of mucus flow.

The initial sections of the cilia have the characteristic internal structures generally found in cilia, there being nine pairs (doublets) of tubules in a ring surrounding a central pair. Each tubule is approximately 20 nm in diameter and resembles microtubules found in other neurons and cells of the body. In the transitional region where the initial section narrows, the doublets end. In mammals the distal cilia of many species, including man, contain only two tubules, which appear to be continuous with the central pair of the initial section.

The distal portions of the cilia form a densely interwoven net in the outer layer of the mucus. Odorant molecules impinging upon the mucosa are most likely trapped in this meshwork. The functional implication of this arrangement would be that there is little chance for the odorous material to pass into the deeper layers of the mucus.

Very close to the outer border of the epithelium, the bipolar cell dendrite is surrounded by a *junctional complex*, by which it is fused to the neighbouring sustentacular cells (Fig. 29.3). These junctional structures have the characteristics of tight junctions and form complete belts around the apices of the dendrites and of the sustentacular cells. Tracer studies have shown that protein molecules injected intravascularly do not pass beyond the junctions, which suggests that they seal off the underlying extracellular spaces from the mucus layer. It would also appear unlikely that olfactory substances dissolved in the mucus would diffuse beyond these barriers to any significant extent. The functional implication of this would be that the action of odorants on the sensory cells is limited to the structures within the mucus layer; the dendrite and the cell body would accordingly not act as receptors. It may be noted that in the respiratory epithelium there are no tight junctions between cells and tracer molecules readily penetrate the intercellular spaces, in contrast to the case of the olfactory epithelium.

The dendrite is enwrapped throughout its course by folds of the plasma membrane of the sustentacular cells, and is in this way isolated from dendrites of neighbouring cells. The axon arises from the

Fig. 29.3   Electron micrograph of freeze—etching replica of olfactory epithelium showing tight junctions surrounding the neck of an olfactory vesicle. (From Ottoson, unpublished.)

lower pole of the cell body. After a short distance, several axons become grouped together in small bundles which penetrate the basement membrane, where they are ensheathed by Schwann cells to form the *fila olfactoria*. These gather into larger bundles during their course and then penetrate the cribriform plate to enter the olfactory bulb.

Supporting cells

The sustentacular cells have a number of fold-like processes which surround the sensory cells and isolate neighbouring dendrites from each other. On the outer surface of the sustentacular cells there are numerous finger-like protrusions, microvilli, which closely resemble the microvilli of cells of the intestinal mucosa. The sustentacular cells contain an extensive system of smooth endoplasmic reticulum in the apical part of the cell body and contribute by their secretion to the production of the deeper viscous layer of the mucus. The basal cells are relatively small and situated in a single row on the basement membrane between the basal

feet of the sustentacular cells. They enclose the axons of the bipolar cells during their passage within the epithelium and are in this respect similar to Schwann cells. The basal cells exhibit a pronounced polymorphism which has been supposed to indicate that they function as replacement cells which provide for the renewal of dying bipolar and sustentacular cells. Recent studies suggest that the receptor cells continue to be renewed even in adult life.

Mucus secretion

A characteristic feature of the olfactory mucosa in mammals, by which it differs from the respiratory epithelium, is the presence of numerous glands, the Bowman's glands. Their secretion issues onto the surface of the epithelium through narrow ducts passing between the sensory and the sustentacular cells out to the outer limiting membrane. The secretory cells are large and their cytoplasm contains yellow pigment granules and secretory granules of varying appearance.

The secretion of the Bowman's gland contributes to the mucus of the olfactory epithelium and may therefore play an important functional role in the olfactory process. There is evidence that in the frog the secretory product of the Bowman's glands forms the outer watery layer of the mucus. It is within this layer that the distal portions of the cilia are floating and it is at this place that the first contact between the odorous molecules and the receptor cells takes place. Before the odorous particles reach the cilia, they must therefore dissolve in the mucus.

Olfactory pigment

The typical colour of the olfactory mucosa can be attributed to the presence of pigments within the cells of the sensory epithelium. The functional role of the pigment has been the subject of much speculation. It has been suggested that it has a function similar to that of the photopigment in the visual cells of the eye. This idea gains support from the finding that the pigment consists partly of carotenoids. It has been proposed that the pigment constitutes receptor sites in the membrane of the receptor cells. The odorous molecules when absorbed on the cell membrane would form weak complexes with the pigment, and as a result of this the cell membrane would be depolarised. It has further been supposed that there are different pigment types and that this would account for the specific sensitivity properties of the receptors and thereby serve the discrimination of odours. However, the presence of the pigment in the receptor cells themselves has not yet been clearly demonstrated. Most of the pigment is present in the form of granules in the cells of the Bowman's glands and in the supporting cells. The role of the pigment in olfactory receptor processes thus still remains an enigma.

The olfactory brain

The parts of the brain which are involved in the transmission of olfactory signals are usually designated as the olfactory brain (Fig. 29.4). Its main parts are the olfactory bulb, the olfactory tract and parts of the basal areas of the forebrain including the prepyriform and para-amygdaloid complex and parts of the striatum. The morphology of the olfactory bulb and centres have remained relatively unchanged in the course of the evolution of the rest of the forebrain and the functional organisation of the olfactory brain is therefore essentially the same in all vertebrates.

The olfactory bulb

The olfactory bulb is the first relay station in the olfactory system (Fig. 29.5). The cells, axons and dendrites are arranged in distinct layers very much like the retina or the cerebellar cortex. The fibres coming from the sensory epithelium reach the bulb aggregated into small fasciculi which split up into fine strands. These form a plexus of densely interwoven fibres on the surface of the bulb. From this layer the fibres turn inwards and enter into spherical regions of neuropile, termed *glomeruli*, which are formed by the exceedingly thin terminals of the incoming fibres and the ramifications of the dendrites of secondary cells (Fig. 29.6). Each glomerulus is encased in a capsule of periglomerular cells. The olfactory axons do not branch before they enter the glomeruli. The synaptic contact between the terminals of the incoming fibres and the dendrites of the secondary cells is thus entirely restricted to the glomeruli.

There is a certain degree of topographical organisation of the incoming fibres so that the upper areas of the epithelium project predominantly to the glomeruli on the upper surface of the bulb. Here the topographical relation is rather precise, whereas the projection of the lower areas of the epithelium is diffuse. Before the incoming fibres enter the glomeruli, there is a re-sorting. It is not known whether this re-sorting involves fibres from a given area or from a given set of receptors.

The secondary bulbar neurons are of two types, *mitral cells* and *tufted cells*. The mitral cells have large triangular cell bodies and are arranged in a distinct layer. In higher vertebrates, each mitral cell has only one main apical dendrite that follows a straight outward course. The dendrite does not branch until it has entered a glomerulus. The mitral

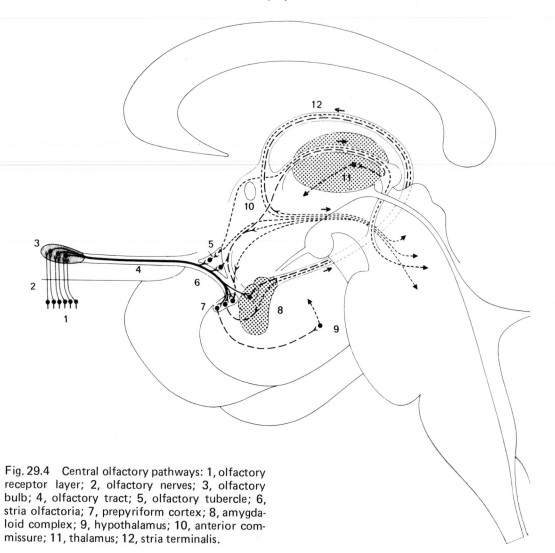

Fig. 29.4   Central olfactory pathways: 1, olfactory receptor layer; 2, olfactory nerves; 3, olfactory bulb; 4, olfactory tract; 5, olfactory tubercle; 6, stria olfactoria; 7, prepyriform cortex; 8, amygdaloid complex; 9, hypothalamus; 10, anterior commissure; 11, thalamus; 12, stria terminalis.

cell also gives off accessory dendrites which connect nearby mitral cells and tufted cells. The tufted cells are somewhat smaller than the mitral cells. Like the latter, they have one main dendrite that terminates in a glomerulus. The axons of the mitral cells and the tufted cells pass into the deeper layers of the bulb. Here they gain myelin sheaths and become grouped together into bundles.

Counts of the number of afferent fibres have demonstrated that there is a very high degree of convergence towards the glomeruli. It has been estimated that each glomerulus in the rabbit re-

ceives about 25 000 afferent fibres. The impulses of these fibres are transmitted through the synaptic connections in a glomerulus to 24 mitral cells and 60 tufted cells. Within the glomerulus, the olfactory nerve terminals make synaptic contacts onto the dendritic branches of the mitral, tufted and periglomerular cells. The connections may be serial, involving a sequence of synapses from one dendrite to the next, or reciprocal. The ultrastructural characteristics of these various synaptic connections suggest that the mitral and tufted cell dendrites are excitatory to the periglomerular dendrites

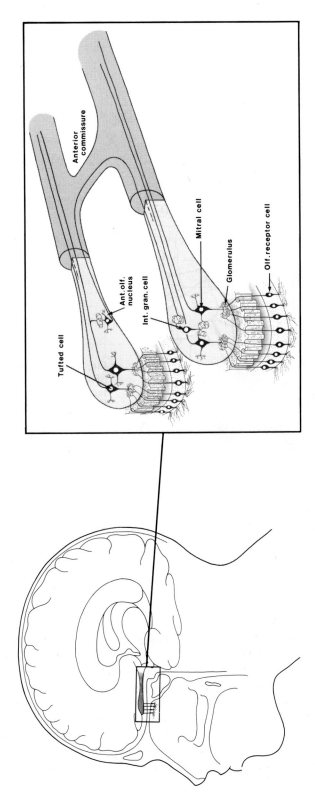

Fig. 29.5 Diagram illustrating the location of the olfactory bulbs at the inferior surface of the brain and their connections via the anterior commissure.

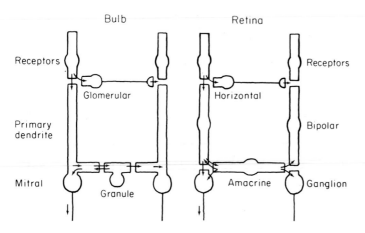

Fig. 29.8 Schematic diagram illustrating the organisation of synaptic connections within the olfactory bulb and the retina in 'vertical' and 'horizontal' systems. (From Shepherd, *The Synaptic Organization of the Brain*, Oxford University Press, 1974.)

retina, there are vertical pathways for 'straight-through' signalling and horizontal pathways for integration of the activity in the vertical pathways. The horizontal integration in the bulb takes place at two levels, the glomerular layer and the external plexiform layer. At the first level, the periglomerular cells appear to be analogous to the horizontal cells of the retina, and, at the second level, the granule cells are analogous to the amacrine cells.

To understand the integrative action of the bulbar neurons it is important to know that the bulb receives a heavy input from the telencephalon. The origin and functional organisation of these central pathways is not yet fully understood. Neuroanatomical studies suggest that the fibres coming to the bulb project mainly upon the granule cells. Since the granule cells are exclusively inhibitory to the mitral cells, the telencephalic input would mainly have an inhibitory action on the activity of the bulb. This is also indicated by observations showing that electrical stimulation of basal and telencephalic structures may have a depressive effect on the activity of the bulb; similar actions may occur through periglomerular cells.

The olfactory cortex

The output of the bulb is carried by the axons of the mitral cells and the tufted cells which are grouped together into the lateral olfactory tract. Before leaving the bulb, these fibres give off collaterals that terminate in the external plexiform layer and in the granular cell layer. The fibres of the olfactory tract end in the pyriform cortex and in the periamygdaloid area and to a lesser extent in the olfactory tubercle and the anterior olfactory nucleus (Fig. 29.9). It is a characteristic feature of all these regions that they give off fibres which feed back to the bulb.

The pyriform cortex is usually considered to represent the primary olfactory cortex. It should be noted that, in contrast to all other sensory systems, the afferent signals reach this cortical area without having passed through the relay stations of the thalamic nuclei. For a long time it was believed therefore that there was no olfactory input to the thalamus. However, recent observations have clearly demonstrated that olfactory tract fibres project upon the mediodorsal and the ventral posterior medial (VPM) nuclei of the thalamus. From here the olfactory input is transmitted to the prefrontal cortex and to the second somaesthetic area (SmII). It has also been demonstrated that the lateral regions of the hypothalamus receive a heavy olfactory input. Recordings from neurons in these regions have provided evidence that odours of biological significance have a powerful excitatory effect. It would appear that the olfactory projection to the hypothalamus has an important role in eliciting behavioural reactions involved in reproduction, feeding, orientation and social organisation. Hence, the olfactory system possesses two distinct

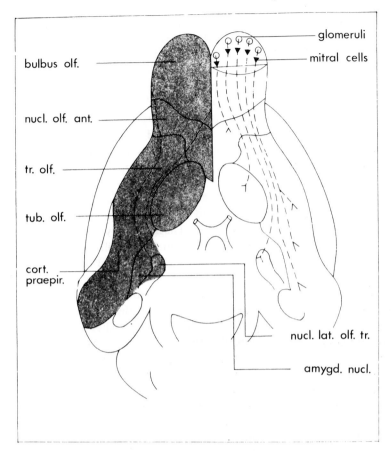

bulbus olf.

glomeruli

mitral cells

nucl. olf. ant.

tr. olf.

tub. olf.

cort. praepir.

nucl. lat. olf. tr.

amygd. nucl.

Fig. 29.9 Basal aspect of the rabbit's brain illustrating structures related to the olfactory system. (From Holley, in *La Recherche en Neurobiologie*, ed. du Seuil, La Recherche, 1977.)

routes, a cortical and a subcortical route. It has been suggested that the cortical system is responsible for fine discriminative functions and that the subcortical system mediates the influence of olfactory stimuli on the hypothalamus and the limbic system.

It should be noted that the significance of the sense of smell in vertebrates is closely related to the phylogenetic development of the brain. In lower vertebrates the cerebral cortex is largely olfactory in function and odorous stimuli have a dominant influence on the life of these species. Evidence of the functional importance of the olfactory system in these species is that odour stimulation has the same awakening action as high-frequency stimulation of the reticular activating system, as is illustrated in Fig. 29.10. With the increasing differentiation of the brain during evolution, the relative size of the olfactory system gradually diminished and in parallel the predomin-

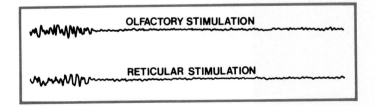

OLFACTORY STIMULATION

RETICULAR STIMULATION

Fig. 29.10 Arousal effect of olfactory stimulation in rabbit: odours produce activation of the EEG closely resembling that obtained by high-frequency electrical stimulation of the reticular activating system. (From Arduini and Arduini, *J. Pharm. Exp. Ther.*, 110, 1954.)

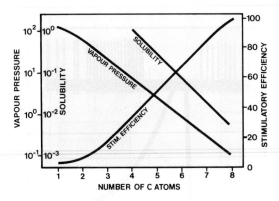

Fig. 29.17   Relation between olfactory stimulating effectiveness of primary aliphatic alcohols to vapour pressure and water solubility. (From Ottoson, *Acta Physiol. Scand.*, 43, 1958.)

Olfactory thresholds

Measurements of threshold sensitivities for different odorants have demonstrated that the human nose is more sensitive to certain substances than the best available physicochemical analysing methods by a factor of between 10 and 100. The extreme sensitivity of the human nose may be illustrated by the fact that 0.01 mg ethylmercaptan can be detected when dispersed in 230 m^3 of air. At this dilution there is only one molecule of mercaptan per 50 000 million molecules of air. A single sniff of 20 cm^3 would then contain 1×10^{10} molecules of mercaptan, part of which would be dispersed onto the sensory epithelium. It has been estimated that only about eight molecules would reach a single receptor. Similar studies on insect receptors suggest that 1–2 molecules of substances to which the insect is most sensitive would be sufficient to excite a single olfactory receptor.

Olfactory adaptation

It is a common experience that an odour, which at first is felt strongly, rapidly weakens and soon becomes almost imperceptible. It has generally been believed that this gradual diminution of the subjective intensity of an odour is due to a rapid adaptation of the olfactory receptors. Early observations by Adrian showed, however, that there is little reduction of the activity induced in the olfactory bulb during repetitive olfactory stimulation. This observation suggested that the olfactory receptors are able to respond to prolonged stimulation. Later studies of the EOG have provided evidence which clearly shows that, contrary to what has been generally believed, the olfactory receptors are slowly adapting and that this is a common property of the olfactory receptors in different species. Additional evidence of this has recently been obtained in recordings of the impulse discharge of single units in the mucosa. When exposed to constant odour stimulation, an olfactory receptor responds with a prolonged discharge that continues throughout the duration of stimulation.

These observations raise the question of what is the origin of the decline in perceptual intensity for a constant odour stimulus. There is at present no clear answer to this question. It has been demonstrated in neuroanatomical and electrophysiological studies that the olfactory bulb receives a heavy input of centrifugal fibres from higher levels in the olfactory system. This centrifugal system appears to exert a powerful control of the transmission of signal from the bulb to higher olfactory centres (see above). The effect may be inhibitory or facilitatory depending on the biological significance of the stimulus. It is likely that the reduction in perceptual intensity may be accounted for by a predominant inhibitory action of the centrifugal control system

Discrimination of odours

It is generally assumed that the ability to discriminate different odours is accounted for by a differential sensitivity of the receptor elements in the olfactory mucosa. It is supposed that the receptor sheet is composed of a limited number of types of receptors, each of which is highly specific to a distinct 'primary' odour, in analogy with primary colours. In the search for these postulated 'primary' odours, Amoore studied more than 600 odorous substances according to similarities in quality, and found that they could be included in seven categories. His assumption was that each category represented a primary odour. By studying various

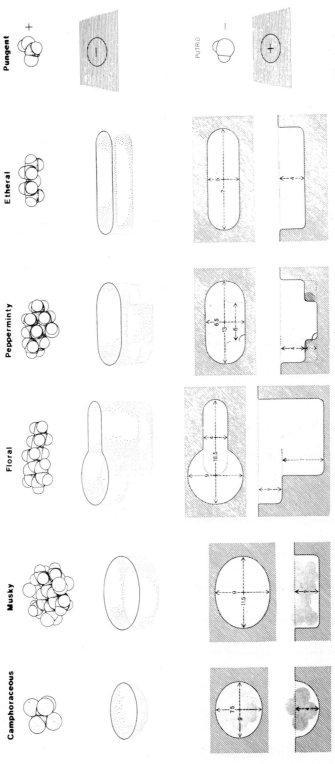

Fig. 29.18 The stereochemical theory of odour. According to this theory there are seven primary odours, and to match these odours there are receptor sites each of a distinct shape and size. Each site will accept a molecule of the appropriate configuration. (From Amoore *et al.*, *Scient. Am.*, 210, 1964.)

characteristics of the molecules, he found that substances of a given category had similar molecular configurations and therefore suggested that the receptor membrane contains corresponding complementary receptor sites (Fig. 29.18). Thus there would be seven distinct receptor sites corresponding to seven primary odours, which could be grouped as follows: camphoraceous, pungent, etheral, floral, pepperminty, musky and putrid. Later studies suggest that, if primary odours exist, there must be more than seven.

According to another theory, the *vibration theory*, proposed by Wright, the odour of a substance is related to its characteristic frequency of intramolecular vibration. There would thus be a close resemblance between olfactory receptors and visual receptors in terms of the mechanisms of excitation.

The idea that different receptors respond selectively to different odours has received support only to some extent from studies on single receptors (Fig. 29.19). Microelectrode recordings in the frog olfactory mucosa have demonstrated that most receptors are excited by a relatively great number

of different odorants. Some receptors have a relatively sharp response profile, while other receptors exhibit a broad spectrum sensitivity. In insects, two types of receptors have been found: 'odour specialists' and 'odour generalists'. The first type has high sensitivity to a few closely related compounds, typically having biological importance for the animal, such as sexual attractants or food odours. The second type is sensitive to a broad range of compounds. An individual receptor of this type appears not to be able to signal the precise quality of the stimulus. Such information is encoded in the pattern of discharge of a multitude of receptors. This mode of encoding has been termed 'cross-fibre pattern coding'.

Several lines of evidence suggest that central mechanisms may play an important role in the discrimination of different odours. Early observations by Adrian have demonstrated that there are large differences in the spatial patterning of excitation in the bulb. For instance, compounds with a fruity smell activated mainly the anterior part of the bulb, and compounds with an oily smell the posterior part. Adrian suggested on the basis of

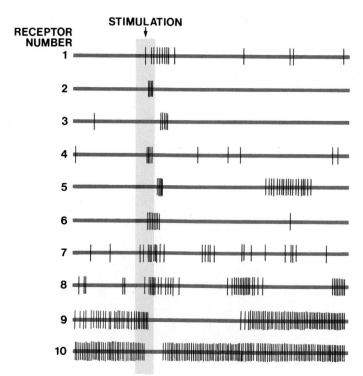

Fig. 29.19   Recordings illustrating differential sensitivity of 10 olfactory receptors to stimulation with anisol. (From Duchamp *et al., Chemical Senses & Flavour,* 1, 1974.)

these observations that spatial patterning of the responses could contribute to the encoding of odour quality. Adrian's observations have recently been confirmed and extended in studies of the responses evoked in the sensory epithelium and in the bulb. By using punctate stimulation of the olfactory mucosa, evidence has been obtained indicating a spatial patterning of receptors with different sensitivity properties in the epithelium. Hence there appear to be restricted receptive fields for different odours in the sensory epithelium. These fields project in a topographical arrangement upon the bulb; this could be the basis for the spatial patterning observed by Adrian. Whether or not this patterning plays a role in the discrimination of odours remains to be settled. As indicated earlier, inhibition is a dominant feature of the activity changes induced in the bulb. The inhibitory effect appears to be analogous to the lateral inhibition in other sensory systems and can be assumed to sharpen the response profiles for different substances.

30

Tactile Sensations, Position Sense and Temperature

Neural basis of tactile sensations

Until the discovery by Blix in 1884 that cutaneous sensibility is point-like, it was generally thought that touch or tactile sensation was a single unitary sense. Thus pressure, cold, warm, tickling, etc., were considered as subqualities of one sense, that of touch or 'skin feeling'. Blix's finding of distinct spots of sensitivity to different kinds of stimulation, together with subsequent histological studies, established that the sense of touch, instead of being a unitary sense, can be divided into separate senses such as touch–pressure, vibration–flutter, warm and cold.

The punctate distribution of sensitivity was thought to reflect a corresponding distribution of specialised receptors or nerve terminals of different types. This conclusion led to a host of studies aimed at correlating the different cutaneous modalities with specific types of receptors. The search procedure was to localise sensory points on the skin, mark them with dye, and remove the skin for histological sectioning; the end organs thus identified were then correlated with the sensation evoked. From this research, it was concluded that cold is mediated by Krause's corpuscles, heat by Ruffini's corpuscles, and touch by Meissner's corpuscles and by nerve endings around the hair roots. Each end organ was assumed to be specifically sensitive to one type of stimulus, its nerve fibre conveying only

information about this stimulus to the brain. In short, the cutaneous sensory cell and its nerve fibre were presumed to function as links in a system which transmitted information of a specific stimulus from a point in the skin to a given end station in the brain.

This so-called '*labelled-line*' theory has been criticised mainly on the grounds that there are more anatomically distinct types of receptors in the skin than there are sensory qualities. It has been suggested as an alternative explanation that the quality of the sensation evoked is determined by the overall pattern of the afferent impulse message rather than by activation of specific groups of receptors. According to this so-called '*common carrier*' theory, the nature of the sensation evoked by a stimulus depends on the temporal patterning of the afferent impulses and the contribution of different components of the population of receptors. The afferent message would be handled by the brain in a synthetic manner like for instance the fusing of colours. There is at present a considerable amount of evidence to show that the message carried by the primary afferent fibres is that of 'labelled-line'. However, in the central nervous system both 'labelled-line' and 'common carrier' principles appear to be employed in the processing of sensory information. Recent observations suggest that this may occur at both subcortical and neocortical levels and that 'labelled-line' information may be used differently from 'common carrier' information.

Nerve endings and afferent fibres

In the skin the branches of the afferent nerve fibres form two nerve nets, one lying relatively deeply and the other more superficially in the skin. The fibres of the superficial layer form a network so intricate that it is impossible to follow any fibre over a long distance. From this network, thin branches extend towards and into the epidermis.

Their terminals are naked, lacking a myelin sheath, and have bud-like swellings. There is a constant turnover since the nerve terminals are continually degenerating and replaced by new endings; this implies that the sensory innervation of skin and mucous membranes is constantly shifting. In the skin, in addition to the naked free nerve endings, there are also many types of encapsulated end organs, such as Pacinian corpuscles, Meissner's corpuscles and Merkel's discs (Fig. 30.1). Hairy skin is well supplied with branchings from myelinated fibres, which form spirals around the hair

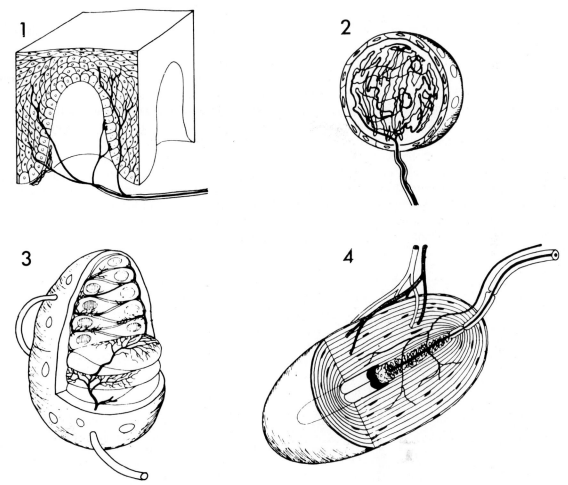

Fig. 30.1 Sensory endings in the skin: 1, free nerve endings; 2, terminal bulb of Krause; 3, Meissner's corpuscle; 4, Pacinian corpuscle. (From Rohen, *Funktionelle Anatomie des Nervensystems*, Schattauer Verlag, 1971.)

roots; there are also many intermediate types in addition to these clearly identifiable end organs. It is noteworthy that there are no encapsulated endings in hairy skin. In contrast, glabrous skin such as that of the finger tips and the lips is richly supplied with encapsulated end organs of different structure in addition to unmyelinated terminals.

The diameter of the afferent fibres from the receptors in the skin vary from the myelinated nerve fibres 15 μm in thickness to fibres only a few micrometres thick. The proportion of thick to thin fibres differs in various skin regions. In the fascial area and the skin of the hands, which have fine discriminative abilities, there is a higher proportion of myelinated fibres than in the skin of the trunk. In general, however, most of the afferent input from the skin comes through thin fibres, which constitute over 75% of all afferent fibres. The conduction velocity of the thickest myelinated fibres is around 90 m s^{-1} while that of the unmyelinated fibres is about 1 m s^{-1} or slower. Since threshold is related to fibre diameter, a relatively light tactile stimulus excites mainly the rapidly conducting thick fibres, while stronger stimulation elicits activity also in the thin fibres. After entering the spinal cord, the fibres conveying information of touch and pressure ascend in the fasciculus cuneatus and gracilis in the dorsal columns to the dorsal column nuclei. Some fibres

also pass up in the dorsolateral fasciculus (Fig. 30.2). In the monkey and probably in man, touch–pressure information is also carried by fibres in the spinothalamic tract.

Adaptation of receptors

Electrophysiological studies have provided evidence that some receptors yield only a few impulses at the onset and cessation of a stimulus. Others are able to respond constantly during maintained stimulation; such a response typically has a relatively high initial frequency followed by slower but enduring activity. Rapidly adapting receptors therefore convey little or no information of the duration of the stimulus; rather they code the dynamic aspects of the stimulus and particularly its velocity or acceleration. The Pacinian corpuscles are typically acceleration detectors; they respond to sinusoidal stimulation with one or a few impulses for each cycle of the stimulus, the discharge frequency being related to the frequency of the stimulus. For a square-wave stimulus they respond only with one impulse at the onset of stimulation and another at cessation. Pacinian corpuscles are abundant in tendons, in joint capsules, in the fasciae of muscles, in the periosteum and in the subcutaneous layers of both hairy and hairless skin. Strange to say, the mesenterium is supplied with a high density of Pacinian corpuscles. .

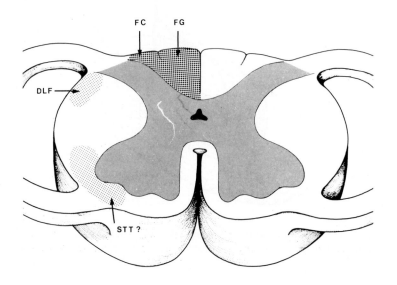

Fig. 30.2   Spinal pathways for touch and pressure sensations. The main pathways are the fasciculus cuneatus (FC) and the fasciculus gracilis (FG). Some fibres pass up in the dorsolateral funiculus (DLF) and probably also in the spinothalamic tract (STT).

Other types of receptors such as the Meissner's corpuscles and the hair-follicle receptors take an intermediate position between rapidly and slowly adapting receptors. They generally respond to a constant stimulus with discharges that cease 100–500 ms after onset of stimulation. Like the Pacinian corpuscles they provide information mainly about velocity and acceleration but may in addition also code the intensity of a stimulus, particularly its dynamic phase.

In hairless skin, there are different types of slowly adapting receptors such as Merkel's discs, Ruffini's endings and tactile discs. They respond to a constant stimulus with discharges that last throughout even prolonged constant stimuli, the frequency of the discharge being directly related to the intensity of the stimulus. They therefore signal both duration and intensity of the stimulus. These receptors are often referred to as tonic or static receptors, whereas rapidly adapting receptors are called phasic or dynamic receptors.

Receptive field and sensitivity

The adequate stimulus for receptors conveying tactile sensations is a deformation of the skin. A given afferent fibre can be activated only from a limited area which corresponds to the distribution of its arborisations and terminals. Within this receptive field, the stimulus threshold is lowest at the centre, increasing towards the periphery. The size of the receptive field varies from one part of the skin to another. Some are only 1–2 mm^2, while others are 100–200 mm^2. Generally, tactile discrimination is finer where the fields are small. A considerable overlap between neighbouring fields is usual; the touch points that Blix observed may have been areas more densely innervated and with more overlapping terminals than elsewhere in the receptive fields.

The sensitivity of the skin to mechanical stimulation varies from one skin area to another. For instance, on the fingertips the threshold for tactile sensation is an indentation of the skin of 6–7 μm, while for the skin on the palm of the hand it is of the order of magnitude of 20 μm (Fig. 30.3). Psychophysical measurements of the increase in

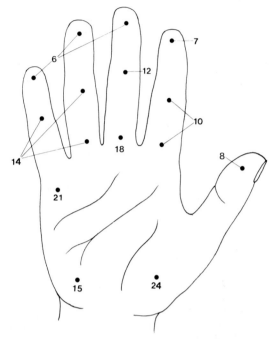

Fig. 30.3 Differences in thresholds for tactile sensation in the skin of the palmar surface of the hand. Thresholds expressed in micrometres of indentation. (From Lindblom and Lundström, in *Sensory Functions of the Skin in Primates*, Pergamon Press, Oxford, 1976.)

sensation intensity with increasing stimulus intensity have provided evidence that the relationship between the strength of the stimulus and the subjective intensity of sensation is best fitted by a power function. For a given subject, this function is remarkably constant, but it varies greatly from one individual to another.

Spatial discrimination

The two-point threshold, that is the distance between two tactile stimuli at which the two can just be discerned to be separate, varies in close correlation with the variations in threshold. It is most precise at the tip of the tongue, the fingertips and on the lips. Here two simultaneously applied point stimuli can be detected as separate if the distance between them is 1–3 mm; for the skin on the back the corresponding distance is of the order of 50–100 mm (Fig. 30.4).

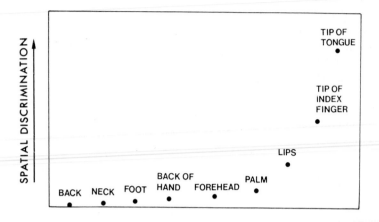

Fig. 30.4   Spatial discrimination in different skin areas.

A gentle touch may sometimes produce the sensation of tickling rather than touch. Tickling is most effectively produced by a light tactile stimulus moved over the skin; typically, it may give rise to strong motor reactions and autonomic reflexes even though the stimulus as such is very weak. Still other kinds of sensation may be induced when the skin is exposed to oscillatory stimulation. With frequencies over 60 Hz, the sensation is perceived as vibration, while with frequencies in the range 10–40 Hz, a sensation of flutter is experienced. Observations in psychophysical studies suggest that these two kinds of sensation are mediated by two different types of receptors. The most obvious candidate receptor for vibration is the Pacinian corpuscle, but the primary afferents of muscle

spindles may also contribute. The sensation of flutter probably results from activation of Meissner's corpuscles and hair-follicle receptors. The spinal pathway conveying vibratory sensation is the dorsal column (Fig. 30.5), while the sensation of flutter is transmitted by several pathways, including the dorsal columns, the anterolateral quadrants and the spinocervical tract.

Muscle sense

According to the ancient classification of sensations introduced by Aristotle, there are five senses: vision, hearing, olfaction, taste and cutaneous sensation. However, some people are often considered to possess a mysterious 'sixth sense' which

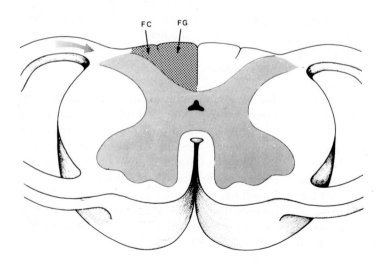

Fig. 30.5   Spinal pathways for the sensation of vibration. FC, fasciculus cuneatus; FG, fasciculus gracilis.

enables them to foresee coming events. It is not clear when the idea of the 'sixth sense' was born, but Sir Charles Bell was most likely one of the first to introduce it. In 1883 he suggested the term 'sixth sense' to designate the sense of positions and movements of the limbs. Later several synonymous terms such as *kinaesthesia*, proprioception or position sense have been used for different aspects of the deep sensibility responsible for cortical awareness of movements of the limbs and of body position in space.

In the tissue around the joints, there is a rich sensory innervation that would appear to be able to provide the brain with information of all aspects of body position and movement. However, as we shall see later, the necessity for any afferent information at all has been questioned. Instead, it has been suggested that kinaesthetic sensations arise within the central nervous system.

There are at least four possible sources of afferent input that might contribute to the muscle sense: cutaneous receptors, muscle receptors, tendon organs and joint receptors.

The skin is richly supplied with rapidly and slowly adapting receptors which project to the cortex. It is well established that cutaneous receptors are of significant importance for cortical motor control. However, relatively few studies have been carried out on their possible contribution to kinaesthetic sensibility. It has been found in experiments in which the skin overlying joints has been locally anaesthetised that there is a severe deficit in the appreciation of position and movement. However, the importance of cutaneous receptors appears to be different for different joints. In distal joints, such as the joints of the fingers and the toes, the contribution seems to be important, while in proximal joints, such as the knee joint, the kinaesthetic role of cutaneous input is less.

Until the early 1960s it was generally agreed that muscle receptors do not contribute to kinaesthetic perception. This notion was mainly based on the failure to demonstrate cortical projections of the muscle afferents. It was therefore concluded that their input did not have access to consciousness. Furthermore, it was demonstrated that stimulation of muscle receptors failed to evoke arousal and

desynchronisation of the EEG. Moreover, it was reported that awake patients undergoing operations did not experience sensations of movement when exposed muscles were pulled. Muscle receptors were for these reasons discarded as possible candidates for subserving kinaesthetic sensibility. As we shall see, this notion had to be revised when later studies disclosed that muscle receptors actually have a key role in kinaesthesia.

Tendon organs lie at the junction between muscles and tendons and would therefore appear to be strategically positioned for providing the brain with information of position and movement of limbs. However, owing to their presumed low sensitivity, they have generally been thought to contribute insignificantly to perception of movement. On the other hand they are well suited for detection of the force of contraction of a muscle and have, therefore, been thought to signal the tension applied to them. This view has been re-evaluated in the light of more recent findings showing that the tendon organs respond not only to high muscle tension but are sensitive to stretching over physiological ranges of movement. It has been claimed on the basis of neurophysiological recordings that the input from the tendon organs does not reach cortical levels and that their message consequently is not perceived. However, other studies suggest a perceptual role for the tendon organs.

There are three types of receptor endings in most joints: Ruffini endings located in the joint capsule, Golgi endings of the spray type and Pacinian corpuscles. In addition, there are free nerve endings which are supposed to be pain receptors. Recordings from joint nerves early in the 1950s provided evidence that one type of ending, presumably the Ruffini endings, was excited over only a small range of joint excursions. Within this range, the frequency of the discharge was proportional to the rate of angular displacement, movements towards the position of maximal excitation causing an increase in firing and movements away from this position a decrease. For a maintained position within its responsive range, each unit gave a tonic discharge that remained constant for hours. Another type of receptor, presumably the Golgi-type spray endings, exhibited little sensitivity to the velocity of movement but responded to tensions applied to the ligament of the joint. Still another type of ending, presumably Pacinian corpuscles, responded only at the onset and during actual movements of a joint. These findings led to the conclusion that the afferent input from the various types of joint receptors provided the brain with all information required for judging movement and position of a joint. This idea was supported by data demonstrating that the joint receptors projected to the cortex; it was therefore concluded that the afferent input from the joints had access to consciousness. Furthermore, a total loss of passive kinaesthetic sensation was reported to occur when the joint afferents were anaesthetised. Until about 1969 the prevailing idea was therefore that joint receptors provided the sole basis for kinaesthetic sensibility. Cutaneous receptors were thought to make some contribution, whereas muscle receptors were considered not to contribute at all. As already mentioned, this view had to be re-evaluated completely under the impact of some ·unexpected neurophysiological and psychological observations in the late 1960s. What first cast doubt on the hypothesis that joint receptors solely are responsible for kinaesthetic sensations was the observation that the majority of the slowly adapting joint receptors are only capable of signalling steady joint angles at positions of extreme flexion or extension; only a small proportion of the receptors respond at intermediate positions. This finding raised the question of what kind of receptors provided the brain with kinaesthetic information in the intermediate range of joint excursions. One possibility appeared to be that the information came from muscle spindles, as was also confirmed in subsequent studies. At about the same time, observations were reported which provided unequivocal evidence that the muscle spindles do in fact project to the cortex. This important finding removed the argument that the input from the muscle spindles lacked access to consciousness. However, if the discharge from muscle spindles contributes to kinaesthetic sensations, how is the brain able to distinguish the input evoked by muscle stretch from that induced by fusimotor activity? There is

no answer to this question yet. Perhaps the fusimotor induced signals are identified and subtracted from the mixed input by some mechanism of central processing of afferent signals.

That muscle afferents play an important role in kinaesthesia is evidenced by the recent demonstration that vibration of muscles may induce kinaesthetic illusions (Fig. 30.6). For instance, if a muscle is vibrated at a rate of 100 Hz, an illusion is evoked that the joint at which the muscle acts is moving in the direction as if the muscle was stretched. When vibration is applied to the antagonist, illusory movements in the opposite direction are perceived. The effect of such illusions on voluntary movements may easily be demonstrated by asking a blindfolded subject to touch the tip of his nose with his finger while vibration is applied to the triceps muscle. The subject misjudges the distance and the motion towards the nose overshoots to one side or the other. Kinaesthetic afferent inputs are also of importance for postural control. If, for instance, vibratory stimulation is applied to the Achilles tendon of a subject standing on that foot only, he sways and tends to fall backwards.

It is well established that the primary afferents of the muscle spindles are extremely sensitive to vibration. This suggests that the illusion of movement is evoked by.excitation of the primaries (see p. 167). The secondaries of the spindle and the tendon organs may also be excited by vibrations, but their sensitivity is considerably lower than that of the primaries. If they contribute to the illusions produced by vibration, it would most likely be that of illusory false position rather than movement. That kinaesthesia and static position sense are signalled by different kinds of receptors is suggested by the observation that illusions of movements and of position can be produced independently.

It has been known for a long time, through clinical studies, that the main pathways for muscle sense is the dorsal column—medial lemniscal system (Fig. 30.7). Experimental studies in the cat suggest that the dorsal column pathways for position sense include the *fasciculus cuneatus* (but not the *fasciculus gracilis*) and the spinomedullothalamic (SMT) pathway. In man and monkeys, the ventral quadrants are also engaged. Whether or not the

Fig. 30.6   Position illusions induced by vibratory stimulation. The subject being blindfolded was asked to align her forearms during vibration of the biceps muscle. The misalignment indicates the illusion in position sense produced by the vibration.

spinothalamic tract contributes to position sense is not yet settled.

As mentioned above, it is an old notion that kinaesthetic sensations may arise within the central nervous system on the basis of centrifugal command signals for voluntary contractions. This idea appears to derive from observations on patients with phantom limbs. Typically these patients perceive that the phantom limb moves in response to motor commands. On the other hand, there is no sensation of movement in response to a command signal to a completely paralysed muscle. The current concept is therefore that cortical command signals do not give rise to the sensation of movement. However, there is strong evidence suggesting that they contribute to the sensation of muscular force accompanying voluntary command signals. It is not clear how this sensation arises. One possibility is that it is produced by corticofugal activity acting on afferent relay stations.

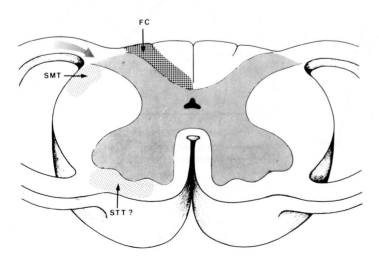

Fig. 30.7   Spinal pathways for position sense. FC, fasciculus cuneatus; SMT, spinomedullothalamic tract; STT, spinothalamic tract. The main spinal pathway is the fasciculus cuneatus. The evidence for the contribution of the spinothalamic tract is less certain.

31

Pain

Historical aspects on the concept of pain

From the earliest dawn of civilisation until the present day, the concept of pain has undergone a continuous process of change. In many primitive civilisations, pain was attributed to the intrusion of objects or spirits into the body. It is interesting to note that this idea still remains among the aborigines in Australia, New Guinea and in some islands of Melanesia. The objects causing pain were thought to be harmful things like an arrow, sword or a spear. For the ancient Persians and Egyptians, pain was considered to be caused by magic influences of spirits of the dead or by demons and devils. In the Hebraic civilisation, pain was thought to be a consequence of sin; the idea of pain as punishment for committed sins derives from this time. The ancient Greeks were greatly interested in the nature of sensations and particularly in pain. For Plato, the knowledge of sensation and pain was of fundamental importance in his search of truth. Plato viewed the heart as the centre of all sensations and considered pain to arise from violent intrusion of elements into the body and, like pleasure, to be an 'affection' of the whole body. To Aristotle, the subject of the nature of sensations was of prime interest, and he considered the sense organs as the sources of all levels of knowledge. However, he did not include pain in the five categories of senses, vision, hearing, smell, taste and touch, because he considered pain to be a 'quale of the soul' and opposite to pleasure. Aristotle's view was strongly criticised by Galen, who maintained that the brain is the centre of all sensations and that each sense is subserved by a specific set of nerves. Sensory stimulation was thought to be mediated to the brain by a psychic pneuma which filled the tubular nerves. This idea remained fundamentally unchanged until the discovery of the electrical phenomena associated with impulse conduction. For a long time it was generally accepted that pain was a consequence of excessive stimulation and could be mediated by all peripheral sensory nerves. It was not until the early twentieth century with the development of methods for recording of nerve impulses that it was proved that the sensation of pain was carried to the brain by specific afferent nerves. Following the important discoveries by Adrian and Gasser in the 1920s, research on pain was to a great extent focused on the peripheral mechanisms of pain. In the last two decades, interest has shifted towards central pain processes and particularly the neurophysiological basis for pain control.

Recent advances in pain research

Pain research has in the last decade witnessed a progress which is almost unprecedented in the history of neuroscience. The explosive development in this field began in 1965. In that year Melzack and Wall put forward the concept of the gate control system which modulates the input of pain impulses to the brain. According to this theory, activity in large afferents would inhibit the transmission of activity in nociceptive small fibres at the spinal level. Wall and Sweet tested this hypothesis on themselves and later also on some patients. The success of this treatment provided the impetus for further applications of electrical stimulation for the relief of pain and initiated development of apparatus and techniques for the treatment of various pain syndromes. Four years after the introduction of the gate control theory, an important discovery was reported by Reynolds. In studying the effect of focal stimulation of different brain regions in rats with implanted electrodes, he found that stimulation of the midbrain central grey resulted in complete analgesia. Even more surprising was the finding that the electrical stimulation did not affect the level of consciousness of the animals nor their reactions to sound or visual stimulation. The analgesic effect was powerful enough to permit abdominal surgery to be carried out without the use of chemical anaesthetics.

Only a few years after Reynolds' discovery it was found that opiates exert their action in the central nervous system by binding to specific opiate receptors. Of particular interest was the demonstration that there is a dense representation of opiate receptors in the regions where electrical stimulation has an antinociceptive effect. The discovery of the opiate receptors led to an intense search for the natural ligand to these receptors. In 1975 these efforts were crowned with success by the isolation of a number of hitherto unknown endogenous opioid peptides, the enkephalins and the endorphins. This discovery was rapidly followed by the demonstration that these peptides exert an inhibitory modulation of the transmission of pain impulses. A further dimension was added to the role of these neuropeptides in pain control by the finding that stimulation which leads to pain relief in patients is correlated with the release of endogenous opioids. Under the impetus of these discoveries in the last decades, not only has pain research experienced a unique progress but moreover the advances achieved have paved the way to the development of a number of new therapeutic approaches in the treatment of pain.

Perceptual aspects of pain

Although pain is easily identified and recognised as a perceptual experience, there exists no adequate definition of pain. As pointed out by Brain in 1962, 'Our vocabulary for the description of pain is relatively poor and we tend to fall back on terms which describe the way in which it might have been produced even though in the particular instance it has not been so produced. Thus we speak of pricking pain, burning pain, bursting pain and so on'.

Pain is generally associated with anxiety and fear, and these emotional variables affect the intensity and quality of the pain perceived. Pain, more than any other sensation, is influenced by anticipation, attention, suggestions, cognitive processes and previous experiences. When anxiety towards pain is reduced, the subjective intensity of pain is also reduced. An example of the powerful effect of psychological mechanisms is given by the observations of Beecher in a study of soldiers wounded during the battle at Anzio in the Second World War. He found that about 50% of seriously wounded men denied having pain or experienced so little pain that they did not want any analgesic. This observation corroborates the well known fact that strong emotional reactions may completely block the perception of pain. Hence, the gates through which the pain impulses have to pass in order to reach consciousness may be closed from the inside by central control mechanisms or – as we shall see later – from the outside by afferent input.

In spite of the complexity of pain as a perceptual experience, it is possible to distinguish two major components, which are often referred to as the sensory—discriminative and the motivated—affective components, respectively. Terms such as physiological and psychological pain are also used to define the two components but are less appropriate since there is implicit in these terms a distinction between 'real' pain versus 'imagined' pain.

For most sensory modalities, the subjective experience of a maintained stimulus gradually weakens and may fade completely. Pain is unique in the sense that its intensity varies only slightly when painful stimulation is prolonged. Central inhibitory processes may sometimes reduce the pain perceived, but more often the opposite happens: a long-lasting influx of pain impulses augments the excitability in the central nervous system, so that the pain increases in intensity with time. This may be seen in phantom pain and trigeminal neuralgia. The excitability of the pain system may in these cases increase to the point that the gentlest touch elicits an intense, unbearable lightning attack of pain. Neurophysiologically, such attacks are similar to epileptic seizures in the motor system. An increase in the intensity of pain may likewise occur with a more short-lived stimulus. Hold a finger in ice water and pain will be perceived in this finger after 5–10 min; soon, the pain intensifies and it will spread to the other fingers, even though they are out of the water. The interesting point is that this may occur even if the other fingers have been anaesthetised before the experiment. Evidently the spreading represents irradiation within the central nervous system, most likely in the spinal cord.

Long-lasting chronic pain may have profound and destructive effects on the personality of the sufferer. An individual who has long suffered from pain often becomes dysphoric and depressed, forgoes social contacts, feels isolated and often becomes addicted to drugs. Severe pain may, within a short time, destroy a human being, transforming a well balanced person into one for whom suicide appears the only rescue. Only a decade ago there was little hope of obtaining permanent relief from pain in these difficult cases. Today the situation is different. Experimental studies in animals have led to the development of new techniques and methods, and the insights they offer into the mechanisms involved have provided us with new and powerful tools in combating pain.

Measurements of pain

Progress in pain research has been greatly hampered by difficulties encountered in quantification of subjective pain experience and in measuring pain experience in relation to the parameters of the pain-producing stimulus. An important issue is whether or not the pain felt in an experimental situation corresponds to the pain produced by pathological processes. Several lines of evidence suggest that experimental pain is different from clinical pain. One such piece of evidence is that morphine is extremely effective in alleviating clinical pain but relatively ineffective in experimental pain.

One of the major difficulties encountered in experimental pain studies is that the pain endings are not specific in the sense that they are particularly sensitive to a given type of stimulation. Any kind of stimulation if strong enough can provoke pain. Since most sensory nerve endings have lower thresholds than the pain endings, a variety of receptors may be activated together with the pain receptors. Experimentally provoked pain is therefore generally not a pure pain sensation but may involve other sensations such as touch, pressure, heat, etc. It is probable that the activity of these other endings contributes to the sensation evoked by adding some particular quality to the pain experience. In this context, it should be noted that visceral organs lack a corresponding representation of touch and temperature receptors; with few exceptions, pain is therefore the only sensation that can be evoked from internal organs.

Of the many techniques used in experimental studies of pain in humans, electrical, mechanical and thermal stimuli appear to give the most reproducible results. To produce cutaneous pain without concurrent activation of mechanoreceptors, Hardy, Wolff and Goodell used a focused light source directed at a black spot on the forehead (Fig. 31.1). The same technique has since been widely adopted in animal studies: light is focused on a rat's tail and the flickering of the tail is supposed to indicate pain. More recently, lasers have been used to deliver controlled temperature pulses. To study deep pain, various methods have been used. The most popular is the tourniquet technique by which ischaemic pain is induced. Another method is to apply calibrated pressure to the Achilles tendon, or to inject hypertonic saline into muscles. Measurements of deep pain are of particular interest since they have been assumed to be

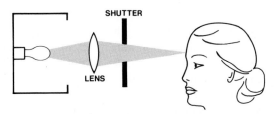

Fig. 31.1   Method for measurement of pain sensibility with radiant heat. The light of a **1000 W** lamp is focused by a lens on the forehead of the subject. The intensity of the light is controlled by means of a rheostat, the duration with a shutter.

more significant for clinical pain than corresponding measurements of superficial pain.

In measurements of pain in humans, verbal reports of the perceived sensation are generally used to obtain measures of the subjective experience. However, verbal reports are not always reliable; the experimental subject may for instance be motivated to deny that pain is experienced. For this reason various physiological reactions are often used, such as evoked brain potentials or changes in heart rate, blood pressure, respiration, skin resistance, etc. These reactions are, however, often influenced by anticipation and emotional reactions and may therefore not necessarily indicate that the subject is experiencing pain.

In experimental studies of pain, it is usually the threshold for eliciting pain or the tolerance level that is measured. Threshold refers to the stimulus strength at which the subject perceives the stimulation as painful; tolerance is the stimulus strength at which the subject is not willing to accept stronger stimulation. Threshold is usually assumed to represent the sensory discriminative component of pain, whereas tolerance is associated with psychological factors such as attitude and motivation. It is of interest in this context to note that, following prefrontal lobotomy, the threshold remains unchanged while pain tolerance is markedly increased. Similar effects may be obtained with pain-relieving drugs.

It is well known that some individuals appear to bear severe pain with equanimity while others react with emotional turmoil to moderately strong stimuli. This raises the question of to what extent the reaction to pain is related to age, sex, personality and cultural background. Most studies suggest that there is no difference in pain threshold between men and women but that pain tolerance in general is higher in men. With age, pain tolerance increases for both sexes. Differences in tolerance have been reported for different cultural and ethnic groups. These differences appear to be related to attitudes towards pain experience. Recent studies suggest that the experience of pain under certain conditions is related to the content of endorphin in the cerebrospinal fluid.

For most sensory modalities, it has been demonstrated that the intensity of a given sensation is a power function of the stimulus strength. This appears to hold also for pain, except that the curve is more steep (see Fig. 24.2). In other words, the intensity of pain increases more rapidly with the strength of a stimulus than do other sensations. From the level of threshold, the sensation of pain rises steeply to the limits of what the subject is able to tolerate. The steep rise of the pain curve also explains why it is difficult to distinguish between different intensities of pain.

31.1   The functional anatomy of pain

Pain receptors

In the late 1800s, when work on the peripheral mechanisms of cutaneous sensation led to the notion that different sensory modalities are mediated by specific receptors, the undifferentiated, naked nerve endings ubiquitous in the skin and mucous membrane were assumed to be the receptors mediating pain. This assumption rested on the finding that free nerve endings are the only type found in the cornea, where the only sensation evoked by stimulation is pain. Similar nerve endings are present in almost all tissues, but the density of innervation differs greatly from one organ to another. Highly sensitive organs like the cornea or tooth pulp are in general densely innervated, whereas the relative insensitivity of muscle and visceral organs has been attributed to the scarcity of free nerve endings there. But even if, as is now widely accepted, the pain receptors are represented by free nerve endings, it is important to note that not all naked nerve endings are pain receptors; some in the skin and in mucous membrane are the endings of fibres that mediate touch and temperature. The receptors mediating the sensations of pain have no specific structural features which make it possible to identify them.

As we have seen, the sensation of pain may be evoked by any kind of stimulation if strong enough. This does not imply that the pain endings are equally sensitive to all kinds of stimuli. Besides the so-called polymodal receptors which respond to all kinds of nociceptive stimuli, there also appear to be specialised pain endings which are particularly sensitive to strong mechanical stimulation. Still another subgroup of pain endings is receptors which are particularly sensitive to pain-producing chemical substances. The sensitivity of the pain endings may change under certain pathological conditions and the endings then become hyperexcitable. This may occur during inflammation of an organ and may lead to a considerable increase in its pain sensitivity. For example, the gastric mucosa which normally is relatively insensitive to most kinds of stimulation may, under inflammatory states, become extremely sensitive to chemical or mechanical stimulation.

Pain-producing substances

Most of the stimuli that provoke pain also cause tissue damage. It has therefore been assumed that the pain is evoked by some substance released from damaged cells. But while pain provoked by mechanical stimulation usually entails a certain amount of tissue damage, this is not true for all kinds of pain. Furthermore, there is no direct relation between the intensity of pain and the extent of tissue damage, after surgical operations or accidents, for instance.

The pain-producing effects of various substances have been studied by techniques such as subcutaneous, intra-arterial, intravenous or intraperitoneal injection into animals and human subjects. The method that has provided the most reliable information was developed by Keele and Amstrong. They produced small blisters on the skin, then removed the epidermis to expose the pain endings, and applied various solutions to study their pain-producing effects (Fig. 31.2). In this way it was demonstrated that acetylcholine produces pain only in concentrations far higher than normally occur in tissue. Adrenalin and noradrenalin provoke no pain; histamine causes itching. Serotonin elicits pain in low concentrations; this is of interest since serotonin comes from disintegrating blood platelets and may conceivably participate in pain arising from blood vessels.

Keele and Amstrong also found that the exudate from blisters had a strong pain-producing effect if kept in a glass syringe for some minutes, whereas fresh it was ineffective; obviously the contact with the glass led to the formation of some pain-producing substance. Further studies identified this substance as *bradykinin*. Proteolytic enzymes

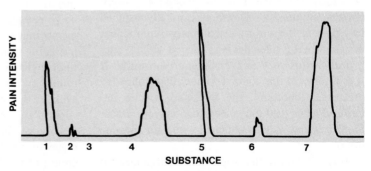

Fig. 31.2   Pain responses to application of different substances to exposed blister base of the skin of the forearm. The intensity of pain was assessed using a visual analogue scale consisting of a pointer moving along a scale and attached to a lever which made records on a moving smoked drum. 1, ACh 10^{-4} g ml^{-1}; 2, ACh 5×10^{-5} g ml^{-1}; 3, fresh plasma; 4, plasma exposed to glass for 4 min; 5, ACh 10^{-3} g ml^{-1}; 6, 5-HT 10^{-6} g ml^{-1}; 7, bradykinin 10^{-5} g ml^{-1}. (From Keele and Amstrong, *Substances Producing Pain and Itch*, Edward Arnold, London, 1964.)

from the alpha-globulins of the plasma form a series of plasmakinins, all of them pain-producing to some degree, and bradykinin is one of them. These agents provoke oedema by increasing capillary permeability. They are also formed during inflammation and probably contribute to the heightened pain sensitivity of inflamed tissue. Bradykinin is the most powerful of the plasmakinins; even in extremely low concentrations it may provoke pain if injected intra-arterially or applied intraperitoneally. It is therefore thought to participate in the pain of peritonitis and pancreatitis, and may also have a share in the pain of angina pectoris and intermittent claudication. Bradykinin is broken down relatively rapidly, and its pain-producing ability soon weakens, suggesting that it only participates in acute pain.

For other types of pain, other agents may intervene. Potassium is one of those proposed. The threshold for eliciting pain with potassium is about 10–20 mM. In view of the fact that the intracellular concentration of potassium is 10 times higher, it is conceivable that the concentration of potassium in damaged tissues may considerably surpass the pain threshold. Changes in the pH of tissue may also be a factor that contributes to pain. It has been found that pain may be provoked at a pH below 6; during inflammation the pH of the tissue may be considerably lower than this value.

There is a great deal of evidence suggesting that pain in inflammatory tissues is due to the release of chemical pain mediators. A number of candidates for this effect have been proposed, such as bradykinin, substance P, acetylcholine, 5-hydroxytryptamine and histamine. Recent observations indicate that prostaglandins synthesised at the site of inflammation sensitise the pain endings by enhancing the pain-inducing effect of bradykinin. Aspirin and aspirin-like drugs appear to exert their pain-relieving effect by inhibiting the synthesis of prostaglandins.

Pain nerves

As already mentioned, any kind of stimulation can provoke pain if the stimulus is sufficiently strong. For this reason, it was once assumed that all afferent nerve fibres could mediate the sensation of pain if they were excessively stimulated. An example of the evidence for this is the finding that a gradually increasing heat stimulus elicits first a sensation of warmth, then heat, and finally pain (Fig. 31.3). The overstimulation theory was originally proposed at the end of the seventeenth century by Erasmus Darwin and still appears in the literature even though it has been discredited experimentally. It has been demonstrated, for instance, that excessive stimulation of nerve fibres mediating touch does

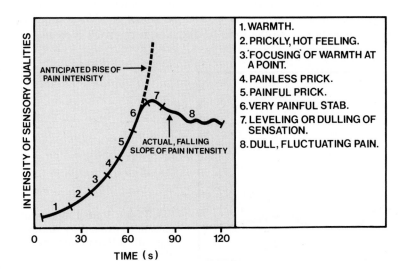

1. WARMTH.
2. PRICKLY, HOT FEELING.
3. FOCUSING OF WARMTH AT A POINT.
4. PAINLESS PRICK.
5. PAINFUL PRICK.
6. VERY PAINFUL STAB.
7. LEVELING OR DULLING OF SENSATION.
8. DULL, FLUCTUATING PAIN.

Fig. 31.3 Verbal reports of sensations produced by increasing radiant heat stimulation. (Adapted from Melzack, in *The Puzzle of Pain*, Penguin Books, 1973.)

not provoke pain reflexes in animals. Furthermore, pain may be selectively eliminated by transecting certain spinal tracts, without blocking other sensory modalities. It is also known from studies in the early 1930s that there is a differential loss of sensations of the skin following blocking of the nerves of the dorsal roots by procaine: first, a loss of sensitivity to cold and warmth, and then loss of sensation of pricking pain and deep pain followed by loss of joint sense, pressure sense and finally touch. Recordings of impulse activity have demonstrated that the nerves are blocked by procaine in the inverse order of their diameters. This experimental evidence strongly supports the notion of specificity of sensory end organs and that pain and other sensory modalities are mediated by specific groups of peripheral nerve fibres.

Early in the studies of the afferent input of pain, it was discovered that there were two types of pain nerves: rapidly conducting delta fibres and thin, slowly conducting C fibres. The quality of the sensation provoked by stimulating each of these two groups proved to be quite specific. This distinction is best illustrated by studies which have been performed in conjunction with surgical operations. Under local anaesthesia, a nerve was dissected from the skin of the leg, stimulated electrically and the resulting impulse volley recorded while the patient described the sensation experienced during the stimulation. A single stimulus activating only rapidly conducting A fibres provoked a sensation of light touch, a tap, or throb, while repeated stimulation gave rise to a sensation

of tingling, scraping, vibration or flutter (Fig. 31.4). In no case was activation of the rapidly conducting A fibre associated with unpleasant or painful sensations. With stronger stimulation, activating also somewhat smaller fibres (the gamma group), the sensation changed and became burning and somewhat unpleasant in quality. With still stronger stimulation, recruiting the delta fibres, single stimuli elicited a distinct, sharp and mildly unpleasant sensation. With repetitive stimulation, a stinging, sticking sensation was evoked that was definitely painful. Finally, at a strength sufficient to activate the C fibres, the sensation changed dramatically: single stimuli evoked pain that was described as severe; with repetitive stimuli, the pain experience became intolerable and the patient refused to continue. These observations show that pain is mediated by two fibre groups, each of which confers a sensation specific in quality. The pain mediated by the delta fibres is distinct, sharp, well localised and definable in terms of time, space and intensity; C fibre pain is diffuse, unpleasant and may be unbearable (Table 31.1). Delta fibre pain is the acute pain experienced when we are exposed to sharp external stimuli; it is less affected by morphine and analgesic substances than the C fibre pain. In clinical medicine, it is the C fibre pain that usually brings patients to seek aid.

The discovery that pain impulses are mediated by two fibre groups with different conduction velocities explains the phenomenon of double pain. Pain evoked by a brief and sharp stimulus to the foot, for instance, is perceived as coming in

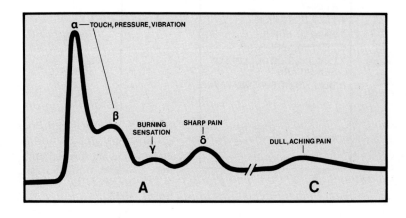

Fig. 31.4 Verbal reports of sensations evoked by stimulation of different groups of afferent fibres.

Table 31.1 Perceptual and physiological characteristics of pain.

General	*Temporal*	*Spatial*	*Evaluative*	*Receptive field*	*Threshold*	*Reflex response*
δ *fibre pain*						
sharp, pricking, distinct	flickering, flashing, stabbing, shooting	localised	discomforting, annoying, intense	small	low	flexor reflexes
C *fibre pain*						
sore, dull, aching, heavy	long-lasting, pounding, throbbing, pulsing, beating	diffuse	annoying, miserable, intense, unbearable	large	high	tonic reflexes

two waves (Fig. 31.5). The first is distinct and brief; a relatively painless interval ensues and then a second wave of pain arises which is long-lasting, diffuse and aching. Obviously, the impulses mediated by the rapidly conducting delta fibres reach the brain considerably earlier than the impulses in the slowly conducting C fibres. Double pain is only perceived from peripheral parts of the body, such as the foot or the hand, because the conduction distance has to be long enough for the difference in conduction velocity to separate the impulse volleys of the two fibre groups. For this reason, double pain cannot be perceived from the facial region.

The pain fibres from skin, mucous membrane, muscle, ligament and fascia join the other somatic nerve fibres in their course towards the spinal cord and the brain. Except for the ones that run in the cranial nerves, all pain fibres, like those of other sensory modalities, have their cell bodies in the dorsal root ganglia. The pain fibres from visceral organs are mainly C fibres which pass together with sympathetic and parasympathetic fibres to the spinal cord (Fig. 31.6). Those innervating the thoracic and abdominal viscera join the sympathetic nerve trunks, whereas the pain fibres of the oesophagus, pharynx and pelvic structures run with the parasympathetic nerves.

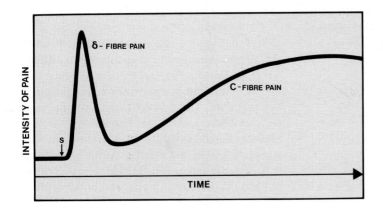

Fig. 31.5 Double pain. Two groups of nerve fibres convey the sensation of pain: Aδ fibres and C fibres. Activation of the first group gives the 'first', sharp, well localised pain, and activation of C fibres the 'second', slow, long-lasting, diffuse, aching or burning pain.

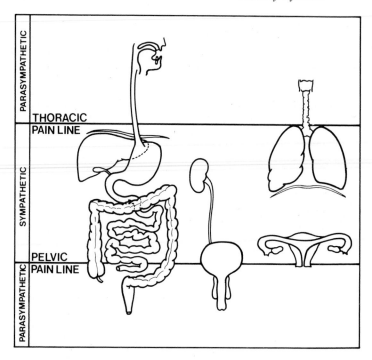

Fig. 31.6 Schematic diagram of pain innervation of visceral organs. (After Ruch and Patton, in *Physiology and Biophysics*, W. B. Saunders, 1965.)

Pain arising from visceral organs is generally diffuse and difficult to localise, probably due to the absence of fibres conveying the sensation of touch. The ability to localise the site of a stimulus depends on a number of factors, the most important being the development of a perceptual image of the body in the cortex. This image develops on the basis of afferent input to the cortex via different sensory channels, mainly those of vision and touch. But visceral organs provide no such information, so there is little or no possibility of localising the source of visceral pain. Often, pain arising from visceral organs is referred to superficial regions of the body (see referred pain in on p. 477).

31.2   Synaptic transmission of pain impulses in the spinal cord

Functional organisation of the dorsal horn

Before the afferent nerves enter the spinal cord, a grouping occurs; all the thin fibres congregate in the lateral part of the dorsal root and the thick fibres run in the medial part (see Fig 31.7). Upon entering the spinal cord, the thick fibres travel in the medial direction and form the large ascending pathways of the dorsal columns, which convey impulses from receptors in muscles and joints as well as from touch and pressure receptors in the skin. The thin fibres, which convey pain, heat and cold, take a different course. After entering the dorsal horn, they divide into ascending and descending short branches, which after only one or two segments pass into the substantia gelatinosa.

Until recently, the dorsal horns of the spinal cord were regarded merely as relay stations, where the afferent impulses were distributed to different tracts or synaptically transmitted to spinal cord systems mediating somatomotor or autonomic reflex functions. This notion was seriously challenged by the finding that the transmission of pain impulses is modulated by the afferent input from receptors in skin and muscles. At the present time it is generally recognised that the dorsal horns are not just the first synaptic relay station encountered

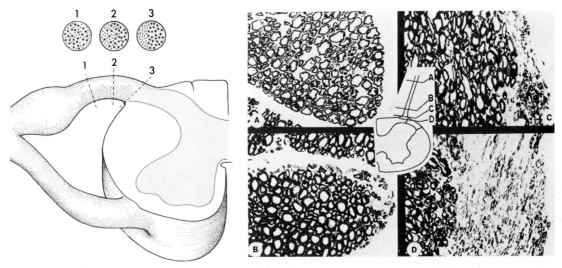

Fig. 31.7 Segregation of coarse and thin afferent fibres at their entrance into the spinal cord. *Left:* Schematic diagram showing distribution of large and small fibres in the dorsal root at different distances from the spinal cord. *Right*: Cross-sections through dorsal root of cat at (A) 5 mm, (B) 1 mm and (C) just before the root entry. (D) Entry zone in the Lissauer tract. (From Kerr, *Pain*, 1, 1975.)

by the pain impulses as they pass to higher centres but rather a most important part of the afferent pain system. As we shall see later, this is corroborated by recent findings showing that the control of the afferent influx of pain impulses mainly takes place in the dorsal horns.

Recent neuroanatomical and neurophysiological studies have demonstrated that the terminals of the pain fibres interact in the substantia gelatinosa with terminals from thick fibres and with endings of fibres from supraspinal centres (see Fig. 31.8). Part of the interaction between these different nerve terminals is mediated by interneurons in the substantia gelatinosa and appear to take place in special structures or conglomerates of synaptic structures (glomeruli, see Fig. 31.9) which are particularly numerous in lamina III. The large central nerve terminal in such a glomerulus (as seen in Fig. 31.9) is most likely the ending of a thick myelinated nerve fibre surrounded by terminals of pain fibres and fibres coming from the brain stem. This intricate structure suggests that the glomerulus has a complex function. Although little is known about the interactions between the terminals in the glomerulus, there are strong indications that it is within these structures that the

large afferents exert their powerful influence on the transmission of pain impulses.

The neurons of lamina IV are medium-sized and send their axons into the contralateral spinothalamic tract. Their dendrites are mainly distributed into the substantia gelatinosa. The afferent input to these neurons comes mainly from the large afferent fibres. In addition to the segmental input, the neurons of lamina IV also receive terminals from descending fibres in the corticospinal tract. Information about the nociceptive input to the neurons of laminae V and VI is still fragmentary. There is experimental evidence indicating that in addition to cutaneous input the neurons of lamina V also receive nociceptive fibres from muscle and visceral organs. This convergence would appear to explain the phenomenon of referred pain. If, for instance, lamina V neurons which have somatic input from the left arm receive nociceptive impulses from the heart, it is not surprising that cardiac pain is experienced as coming from the arm. The neurons of the lamina V also have an input from the corticospinal tract. Their axons pass together with the axons of the lamina IV neurons into the contralateral spinothalamic tract.

The pattern of synaptic transmission described

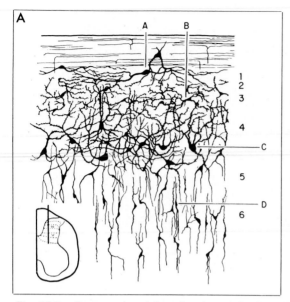 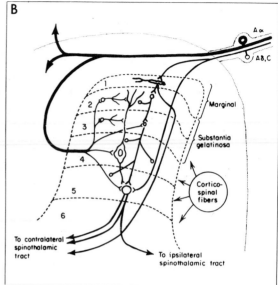

Fig. 31.8 Structural and functional organisation of the dorsal horn. (A) Sagittal section stained by the Golgi–Cox method: A, marginal cell; B, gelatinosa neuron; C, lamina IV cell; D, lamina V cell. (B) Diagrammatic representation of synaptic connections of large and small afferent fibres. ((A) From Scheibel and Scheibel, *Brain Res.*, 9, 1968; (B) from Heavner, *Pain*, 1, 1975.)

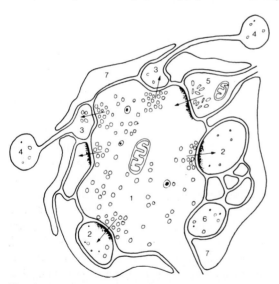

Fig. 31.9 Synaptic organisation of a glomerulus of lamina III in the spinal cord. The large central ending (1) from a primary afferent is presynaptic to dendrites of lamina IV neurons (2), spine heads (3) of gelatinosa neuron dendrites (4), and other dendrites of unknown source (6). It is postsynaptic to boutons with flattened vesicles (5) and surrounded by glial lamellae (7). (From Kerr, *Pain*, 1, 1975.)

above holds for all pain fibres entering via the dorsal roots of the spinal cord. The pain fibres from the trigeminal region have a somewhat different synaptic organisation. After entering the brain stem, the sensory fibres divide into two tracts (see p. 230). The small fibres run caudally and enter into synaptic contact with cells in the medulla; the large fibres in contrast make contact with cells within well defined nuclei soon after the fibres enter the brain stem. The anatomical division between the nociceptive fibres and the other sensory afferent fibres of the facial region may be responsible for some of the specific features of pain arising from this area.

It is generally assumed that the afferent input to the spinal cord enters via the dorsal roots, while the outflow takes place via ventral roots. Many observations indicate, however, that the ventral roots may contain afferent fibres as well. For instance, it has been reported that electrical stimulation of the ventral roots during neurosurgery on the spinal cord may provoke pain. Recent neuroanatomical studies provide conclusive evidence that afferent fibres actually reach the spinal cord via the ventral roots. There is also evidence

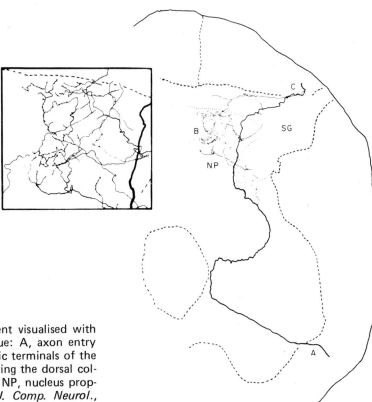

Fig. 31.10 Ventral root afferent visualised with horseradish peroxidase technique: A, axon entry into the spinal cord; B, synaptic terminals of the axon; C, portion of axon entering the dorsal column; SG, substantia gelatinosa; NP, nucleus proprius. (From Light and Metz, *J. Comp. Neurol.*, 179, 1978.)

that these fibres pass into the dorsal horn and make synaptic contact with the cells in the substantia gelatinosa (Fig. 31.10). Most of the fibres are unmyelinated and have their cell bodies in the dorsal root ganglia. Although it would appear probable, there is no rigorous evidence that they are pain afferents.

Ascending pathways

The pain impulses entering the spinal cord are conveyed, after synaptic relay in the dorsal horn, to the thalamus through ascending pathways in the anterolateral part of the spinal cord (Fig. 31.11). The cells that give rise to the ascending axons are located in laminae I, IV and V. Their fibres generally cross to the contralateral side of the spinal cord to form the spinothalamic tract, although some join the ipsilateral spinothalamic tract. The fibres forming the spinothalamic tract cross shortly after

their origin. The crossing is completed within the limit of the segment above the entrance of the dorsal root fibres. The fibres ascending in the spinothalamic tract are arranged in a segmental lamination so that those coming from a given segment are added superficially to those coming from more caudal segments. This somatotopical arrangement is retained during their course through the medulla and pons.

Since most of the ascending pain fibres are grouped together in the spinothalamic tract, it would be reasonable to assume that selective transection of this pathway could interrupt the flow of pain impulses to the brain from levels below the transection. This operation (*chordotomy*) is in fact performed in severe cases of chronic pain. The drawback is that although the pain may disappear immediately after the operation, it usually returns within some months and may worsen. Such surgery is therefore performed only in cases of the most

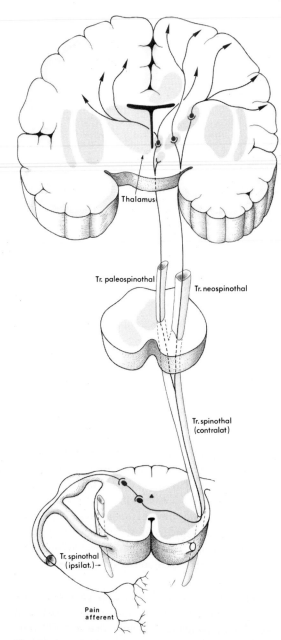

Fig. 31.11 Schematic diagram illustrating the course of the main ascending pain pathway (the lateral spinothalamic tract.)

demonstrated unequivocally, but it seems obvious that the fraction of pain fibres that never cross to the contralateral side must be significant; they would of course be unaffected by a unilateral chordotomy. Another possible route for pain is an ascending pathway that appears to run in the lateral column close to the dorsal horn (Fig. 31.12). These pathways may have what are called 'silent synapses' that are normally used relatively little but may be opened up by facilitatory processes when there is an excessive input or when the ordinary pathways are blocked. The profuse system of intersegmental connections within the grey matter of the spinal cord along with intersegmental contacts mediated by the fibres of Lissauer's tract might also offset the effects of chordotomy. Via these connections pain impulses could pass the level of transection and finally reach higher centres.

Many of the fibres that form the spinothalamic tract derive from cells whose afferent input is not only from pain receptors but also from touch, temperature and proprioceptive receptors; the tract cannot therefore be considered as a specific pain pathway. This has been borne out by studies of the sensations evoked in human subjects by stimulation of the spinothalamic tract; such stimulation may provoke pain as well as sensations of heat, cold and touch.

The fibres of the spinothalamic tract are myelinated, about 5 μm in diameter and conduct at a velocity of about 30 m s^{-1}. The ascending pain fibres when passing through the medulla give off numerous collaterals to the respiratory and cardiac centres; through these connections, painful stimuli may evoke respiratory and circulatory reflexes. En route to the thalamus, they also send branches to the reticular formation and to nuclei in the periaqueductal grey matter (Fig. 31.13). Before reaching the thalamus, the spinothalamic tract divides into a lateral tract, *tractus neospinothalamicus* and a medial tract, *tractus palaeospinothalamicus* (Fig. 31.13). The designation 'neospinothalamicus' indicates that this tract has appeared relatively late in the phylogenetic development of the nervous system; it is present only in higher vertebrates whereas the palaeospinothalamic tract occurs throughout the vertebrate series. The palaeo-

severe pain and when the patient has only a short time to live. The recurrence of pain after transection of the tract suggests that other pain pathways to the brain exist. None have yet been

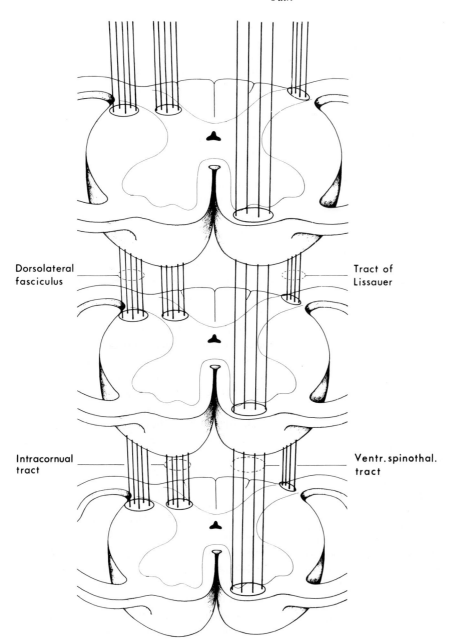

Dorsolateral
fasciculus

Tract of
Lissauer

Intracornual
tract

Ventr. spinothal.
tract

Fig. 31.12 Alternative spinal pathways for pain.

spinothalamic system is characterised anatomically by a wide bilateral distribution within the brain, unlike the neospinothalamic tract, which is strictly contralateral. As we shall see, the two systems are quite different in the quality of the pain sensation that each of them mediates.

The neospinothalamic fibres travel to the ventroposterior lateral (VPL) nuclei in the thalamus (Fig. 31.13). From here, the impulses are conveyed to the somatosensory cortex. The quality of the pain mediated by this system is identical to delta pain. Electrical stimulation of the VPL nuclei in

The pain from somatic tissue is generally diffuse, although it may be localised more easily in relatively superficial layers. In deep-lying tissue, pain is often referred to a place more or less distant from the source of pain. For instance, from neck muscles pain may be perceived as headache radiating in the back of the head. Another characteristic feature of deep somatic pain is the absence of the nociceptive reflexes typical of pain arising in more superficial tissue. Rather, deep somatic pain is accompanied by autonomic reflexes such as perspiration, nausea, vomiting and lowered blood pressure.

The most common form of deep somatic pain is no doubt the pain arising from muscles. It may be provoked in two ways: sustained muscular contraction and/or insufficient blood supply. It is easy to demonstrate the first mechanism by wearing glasses which give double vision. The external muscles of the eye are then forced into sustained contraction to avoid double vision. This soon gives rise to an aching, diffuse pain having all the qualities of frontal headache. Such pain probably comes from pain endings in the connective tissue and the tendons of the eye muscles. In addition, the contraction of the muscle causes compression of the vessels and thereby gives rise to reduced blood flow; this may further increase the intensity of pain. The second source of muscle pain may be demonstrated by arresting the blood supply to a working muscle. Aching arises within 30 s, and a minute later the pain is unbearable. The pain is diffuse but one can easily demonstrate by palpation that it is strictly localised to the muscle that has been working. If the blood flow is released, the pain disappears within a few seconds, and only a slight ache remains. Ischaemic muscle pain has been attributed to the accumulation of metabolic products, such as lactic acid, or other substances, particularly bradykinin and 5-hydroxytryptamine. It has been found that bradykinin as well as 5-HT and potassium may be released in many pathological conditions. Intra-arterial or intramuscular injection of these substances produces an intense discharge in the pain fibres. Certain pain fibres seem to respond only to one substance or another while others are excited by all three. This suggests that pain endings in muscle fall into functionally distinct subgroups.

Visceral pain

It is an old observation that visceral organs are relatively insensitive to many of the stimuli that provoke intense pain in skin and mucous membrane. Perhaps the first direct evidence of this was obtained by Harvey, the discoverer of the circulation of the blood, in his study of the heart of Earl Montgomery. Injured in the chest during a battle, Montgomery survived the injury and his wounds healed but the heart was left exposed. Harvey seized this opportunity to study directly the pumping action of the heart and found that he could touch and even pinch the heart without it being noticed by the the Earl. So remarkable did Harvey find this, that he brought the Earl to His Majesty, King Charles I: 'I carried the young man to the King and His Most Excellent Majesty as well as myself acknowledged that the heart was without the sense of touch'.

The first systematic study of the pain sensitivity of visceral organs was carried out much later in connection with abdominal operations performed under local anaesthesia. It proved possible to cut, burn, or pinch the viscera without eliciting any pain, whereas pulling on the intestines was intensely painful. In contrast to the viscera, the inner abdominal wall was sensitive to any kind of stimulation. It was therefore concluded that visceral organs themselves are devoid of the sense of pain; however, later studies have shown that this is not so.

The pain fibres from visceral organs in the abdomen travel to the spinal cord with autonomic nerve fibres, whereas those from the inner walls of the abdominal and thoracic cavities accompany somatic nerves. Pain impulses from viscera or from the walls of the abdominal and thoracic cavities may thus reach the brain by various routes. The quality of the pain perceived may likewise vary, and three components of pain arising from visceral organs may be distinguished: (1) visceral pain, (2) parietal pain and (3) somatic pain elicited by reflex reactions.

Visceral pain is generally diffuse, difficult to localise and of variable intensity, ranging from weak to severe. It is often called splanchnic pain, because most visceral afferent fibres travel in the splanchnic nerve. Electrical stimulation of the splanchnic nerve during abdominal operations provokes intense diffusely radiating pain in the abdomen.

Pain arising from visceral organs is often felt as coming from regions at a considerable distance from the actual source. Such pain is said to be *referred*. It should be noted, however, that referred pain is not a phenomenon associated exclusively with visceral pain. Perhaps the most common pain syndrome in which referred pain is a prominent component is that of angina pectoris. The pain in attacks of angina pectoris frequently radiates to the left shoulder, thence down the left arm to the elbow or wrist (Fig. 31.15).

Systematic studies of the cutaneous areas to which pain arising in a visceral organ is referred have been made by balloon distension of various portions of the intestinal tract (Fig. 31.16). A rubber bag attached to the end of a tube was passed through the mouth to various levels in the intestinal tract and the position of the bag was identified by fluoroscopy. In this way it was demonstrated that distension of the duodenum was felt in the upper epigastrium, and that of the

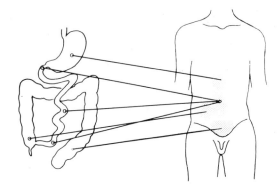

Fig. 31.16   Distribution of pain arising from different regions of the gastrointestinal tract.

jejunum and ileum near the umbilicus. Studies of the effect of distension of the large bowel are difficult with this technique and data therefore incomplete. The few observations made show that distension of the caecum caused pain in an area below and to the right of the umbilicus and that distension of the hepatic flexure and proximal portion of the transverse colon produced pain perceived as coming from regions extending from the umbilicus downwards and to the right. Distensions of the splenic flexure and the descending colon were referred to the left side of the lower abdomen, while pain evoked by distension of the rectosigmoid was perceived as coming from the suprapubic region. Because of its size, the stomach does not lend itself to studies with this technique. However, studies of the pain provoked by distending a balloon filled with hot water show that pain arising in the stomach is referred to the subxiphoid region of the abdominal wall.

Pain provoked by distension of the urinary bladder is referred to the suprapubic region, while pain induced by rapid filling of the ureter with saline is perceived as coming from broad regions in the lower half of the abdomen and flank on the stimulated side (Fig. 31.17). Electrical stimulation or traction of the upper and medial portion of the ureter caused pain in the inguinal region of the same side, while electrical stimulation of the uppermost portion of the ureter and the renal pelvis was perceived as coming from a localised area around the tip of the twelfth rib on the same side.

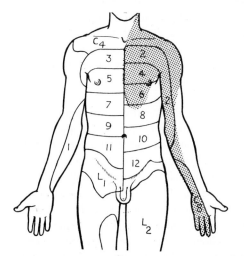

Fig. 31.15   Distribution of referred pain from the heart.

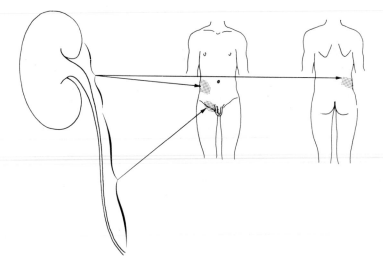

Fig. 31.17   Distribution of pain from different regions of the right urinary tract.

The physiological mechanisms underlying the phenomenon of referred pain have long since been a matter of dispute. The most likely explanation appears to be that the afferents from a diseased visceral organ and the cutaneous pain afferents end upon the same neuron at some level of the central pathway. Such a convergence would explain the dermatomal reference of visceral pain provided that the system is topographically organised. The most likely site for the convergence would appear to be the spinal cord. This idea is strongly supported by recent findings showing that there is a convergence of pain fibres from viscera, skin and muscle on the same neuron in lamina V (see Fig. 31.18). Since superficial pain is considerably more common than visceral pain, the influx that reaches the brain is interpreted as coming from superficial structures. The distribution of referred pain is therefore related closely to the distribution of those cutaneous somatic fibres with which the viscera pain fibres share common central pathways.

Referred pain should be distinguished from projected pain. The latter type represents a psychological process in which pain is referred to some distant part of the body which is actually not exposed to nociceptive stimulation or which may not even exist. The most typical example of projected pain is that seen after amputation. It is a common phenomenon that patients after limb amputation retain a sense of the presence of the limb for a varying time after the operation. In a number of these patients, pain is experienced in the phantom limb. The most common pain is that of a burning sensation. Pain attacks may be triggered off by any kind of stimulation such as by touching the stump or exposure to cold. Emotional stimuli or visceral sensations may also generate attacks of severe pain which is referred to the removed limb.

The cause of phantom limb pain has long since been an intriguing question. Some of the evidence suggests that it is of central origin and due to hyperexcitability somewhere in the neuronal pathways from the limb to the brain. An alternative explanation is that phantom limb pain is of peripheral origin and arises as a result of the formation of a neuroma in the amputation stump (see p. 475).

Parietal pain is mediated by somatic pain fibres innervating the inner surface of the thoracic and abdominal cavities. Such pain may arise when an inflammatory process spreads from the viscera to the abdominal or thoracic wall. For instance, during appendicitis the pain changes in quality if the inflammatory process spreads to adjacent parts of the abdominal wall. From being diffuse and unlocalised, the pain becomes more distinct and localised as the somatic pain fibres of the abdominal wall become involved. The pain mediated by these

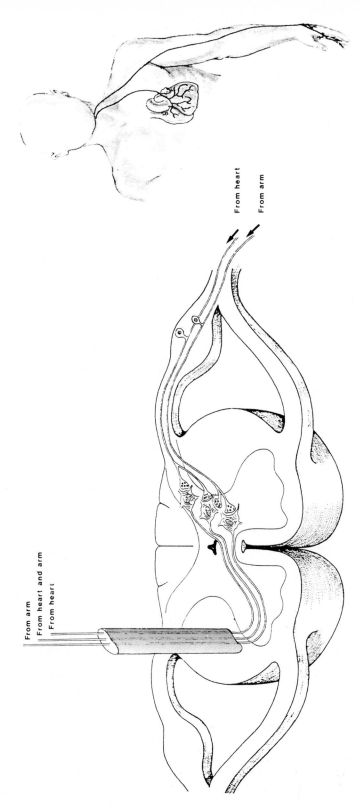

From arm

From heart and arm

From heart

From heart

From arm

Fig. 31.18   Schematic diagram illustrating probable neuronal mechanisms underlying referred pain from the heart.

fibres can be demonstrated by electrical stimulation of the inner surface of the abdominal wall; the pain is perceived as coming from localised regions on the exterior of the abdominal wall. The situation is somewhat different in the diaphragm. Irritation of the margins of the diaphragm causes pain which is perceived as coming from the abdomen (Fig. 31.19). This may lead to diagnostic errors; for instance inflammation of the marginal regions of the diaphragm in pleuritis may provoke pain which is felt as coming from the abdomen in the region of the appendix and lead to unneeded appendectomies. Stimulation of the central parts of the diaphragm, on the other hand, gives rise to pain felt in the neck or the shoulder region within the dermatomes of the third and fourth cervical nerves.

Pain arising from the viscera is often accompanied by increased tone of the abdominal wall muscles; this reflex response is due to the transmission of the visceral pain impulses to the motoneurons in the anterior horns (Fig. 31.20). The resulting muscular pain may be intense and is characteristically long-lasting.

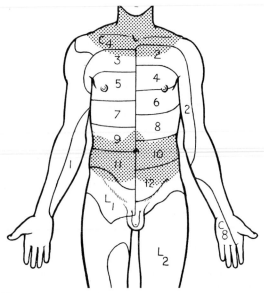

Fig. 31.19 Referred pain arising from the diaphragm. Pain from the central region of the diaphragm is referred to the neck and shoulders, pain from the margins to various parts of the abdominal wall. (After Capps and Coleman, *An Experimental and Clinical Study of Pain in the Pleura, Pericardium and Peritoneum*, Macmillan, New York, 1932.)

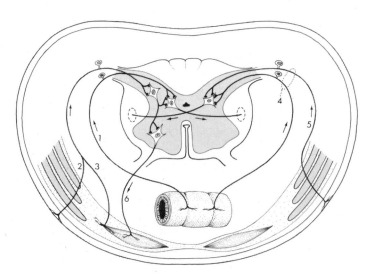

Fig. 31.20 Neuronal connections probably implicated in referred visceral pain and visceromotor reflexes: 1, visceral pain afferent; 2 and 3, cutaneous and deep pain afferents; 4 and 5, visceral and cutaneous pain afferent converging on to the same spinal neuron; 6, efferent nerves to abdominal muscles.

31.4 Physiological mechanisms of pain modulation

Neurophysiological studies in the early 1950s showed that stimulation of widespread regions in the brain caused inhibition of nociceptive reflexes. The important functional implication of these observations was overlooked for nearly 20 years. It was not until Reynolds in 1969 reported that brain stem stimulation produced analgesia in rats that attention was directed to the existence of powerful central mechanisms for the modulation of pain. Reynold's discovery was preceded by the introduction of the gate control theory which emphasised the pain modulation effect of peripheral stimuli. The picture that emerged from the work that was triggered off by these two important events showed that there were two basic physiological mechanisms by which pain could be controlled, one peripheral, induced by afferent input, and one central descending system, the main centre of which was located in the brain stem. Subsequent studies disclosed that these two mechanisms acted upon the substantia gelatinosa neurons in the dorsal horns. Hence, the spinal gate through which the pain impulses have to pass in order to reach higher centres may be closed either from the outside by afferent input or from the inside through the control exerted by the descending system. As we shall see, the two modes for control are generally brought into action jointly.

Pain modulation through peripheral input

Although it is a well known phenomenon that cutaneous stimulation, for instance massage, heat or cold, may have a profound pain-relieving effect, the underlying neuronal mechanisms of the inhibitory action of these stimuli remained largely unknown until Melzack and Wall introduced the gate control theory. Their concept of a spinal gating mechanism was based on observations suggesting that afferent input in large-diameter fibres excited neurons in the substantia gelatinosa (SG) and thereby closed the entrance gate to the spinal cord, whereas afferent input in small fibres inhibited the SG neurons and opened the gate (Fig. 31.21). Melzack and Wall proposed that the inhibitory effect was primarily due to presynaptic inhibition and that the SG neurons acted directly upon the presynaptic terminals. Later studies have shown, however, that the modulating effect is also exerted postsynaptically on the neurons responsible

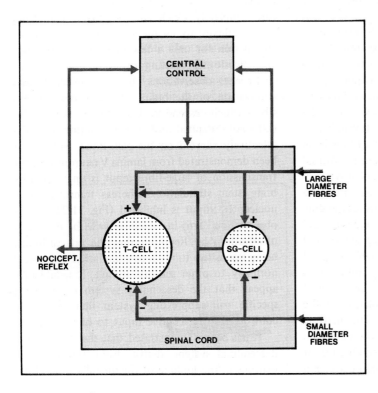

Fig. 31.21 Schematic diagram illustrating the gate control theory. Small- and large-diameter fibres give off collaterals to substantia gelatinosa cells which control the activity of the T-cell implicated in the transmission of pain impulses to higher centres and in nociceptive reflex functions. Activity in the large-fibre system is supposed to inhibit transmission and close the gate by direct action on the substantia gelatinosa cells and indirectly by activating a supraspinal control system which projects back to the spinal gate control system. (After Melzack and Wall, *Science*, 150, 1965.)

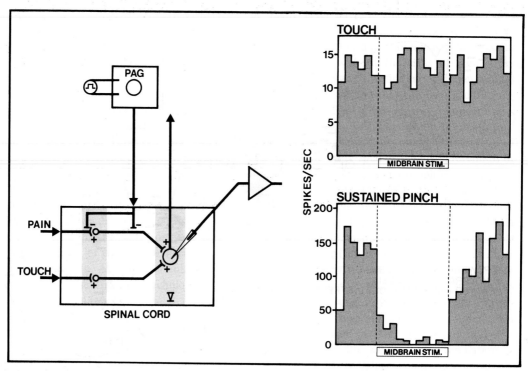

Fig. 31.24   Selective inhibition of nociceptive input by midbrain stimulation. Recordings from neuron in lamina V receiving the input from both nociceptive and non-nociceptive afferent fibres. Upper diagram to the right shows that midbrain stimulation has no effect on the non-nociceptive input but blocks transmission of pain impulses. (Adapted from Oliveras *et al., Exp. Brain Res.*, 20, 1974.)

In addition, they receive a dense input from cells in the reticular formation which in turn receive collaterals from the ascending pain pathways. This suggests that NRM neurons are activated by noxious input. Thus the descending NRM fibres would form part of a negative feedback system by which input from nociceptors is controlled; that is, pain itself appears to be an important factor in activating the pain control system. Direct evidence for this is that NRM neurons are strongly activated by noxious peripheral stimulation. The PAG neurons also receive a large input from nociceptors.

Recent findings suggest that all fibres in the DLF tract do not come from neurons in the NRM. These other fibres appear to originate from non-serotonergic cells in the ventromedial reticular formation of the medulla. Thus the descending pain inhibitory pathways appear to include two

systems, one serotonergic originating in the NRM and one non-serotonergic in the reticular system.

The discovery of the powerful action of the brain stem pain control system makes it pertinent to ask under what circumstances it may be activated and used as a physiological mechanism for the control of pain. There is strong reason to believe that this system can be activated from higher centres as well as by peripheral afferent input. It is conceivable for instance that the absence of pain occurring in states of psychic shock (see p. 459) or associated with strong emotional reactions or auto-suggestion may be accounted for by the action of this system (Fig. 31.25). There is also evidence that sustained pain input exerts a strong activating effect. Whether or not afferent input in large fibres has a similar effect is disputed.

Reynolds concluded the report in which he described the discovery of the brain stem pain con-

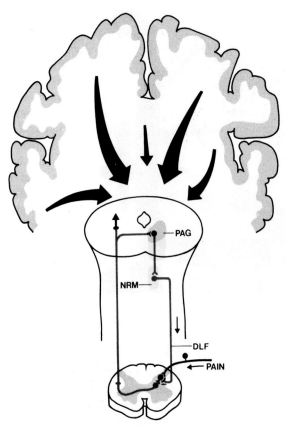

Fig. 31.25 Schematic representation of the cortical and subcortical control of the brain stem pain suppressing system. PAG, periaqueductal grey; NRM, nucleus raphe magnus; DLF, dorsolateral funiculus.

trol centre by suggesting that by identifying the brain stem which upon stimulation induces analgesia 'a safe and reliable electroanesthesia may eventually be developed in man'. Stimulation of the brain stem pain control centre in humans to afford relief of pain involves difficulties which at first appeared insurmountable. The target area is located deep in the brain and close to structures from which aversive or motor effects can be induced. The technical difficulties have now been solved and electrical stimulation of the brain stem centre has been employed with success in patients suffering from chronic, excruciating pain. Other sites where stimulation has proved to be effective include the caudate nucleus, the septum and the

internal capsule. The electrode is implanted permanently (Fig. 31.26) and the patient can turn on the stimulus when in pain. Generally the duration of analgesia exceeds the period of stimulation by up to several hours. The results obtained suggest that the effect of electrical stimulation of the pain control centres in the brain stem in humans is often more effective than in experimental animals.

31.5 Neurohumoral mechanisms for pain inhibition

Enkephalin, the morphine of the brain

In studies of brain stem control over the influx of pain impulses, it was discovered in 1975 that local injection of morphine into some regions of the brain in rats had a powerful analgesic effect whereas injection in other regions had no such effect (Fig. 31.27).

The selective effect proved to be due to the fact that the cells in the regions where an analgesic effect was obtained bear specific receptors, so-called opiate receptors, to which morphine and morphine-like substances bind. Subsequent studies demonstrated that opiate receptors are widely distributed throughout the central nervous system (Fig. 31.28) with high densities in particular regions such as those belonging to the palaeospinothalamic pain pathways. This is of particular interest as it has long been known that it is mainly C fibre pain that is alleviated by morphine and opiates. Opiate receptors have also been found in the hypothalamus and in the limbic system, that is, within regions of the brain generally held to be responsible for motivation and emotions. It may be that the euphoric effect of morphine can be accounted for by the abundant supply of opiate receptors in these regions. Within the spinal cord, opiate receptors occur in the substantia gelatinosa as well as in pain-transmitting regions within the nucleus of the trigeminal nerve. Outside the central nervous system, opiate receptors have been found in a number of peripheral tissues and in particular high density in the gastrointestinal tract.

The discovery of opiate receptors raised the

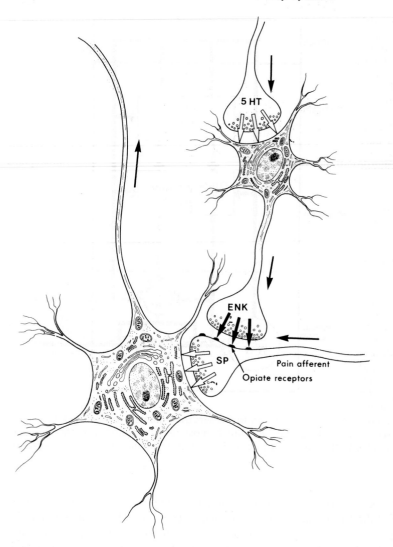

Fig. 31.33   Model for the pain-suppression system at the spinal level. Descending fibres from serotonin- (5-HT-) containing neurons in the midbrain make synaptic contacts with enkephalin neurons in the substantia gelatinosa. Enkephalin released from the terminals of these neurons binds to opiate receptors of the endings of pain afferents (which contain substance P) and inhibit their excitatory action on the pain-transmitting neurons in laminae IV and V.

kinds of pain such as headache, ischaemic pain and psychogenic pain untouched. Recently a modification of the conventional method of transcutaneous nerve stimulation has been introduced in which experiences from Chinese needle acupuncture are utilised. Instead of high-frequency stimulation, brief trains of electrical pulses given at slow repetition rates are used (Fig. 31.35). This so-called acupuncture-like TNS has been found to give relief from pain in many cases where conventional TNS is ineffective. The induction time for analgesia with acupuncture-like TNS is 20–30 min

while that for conventional TNS is only 2–10 min. Furthermore, the analgesia from acupuncture-like TNS is blocked by naloxone while the analgesia obtained with conventional TNS is unaffected. This suggests different mechanisms of action of the two methods and that the analgesia of acupuncture-like TNS is mediated by release of endorphins.

Transcutaneous nerve stimulation activates only a limited number of afferent fibres. In severe and widespread pain, transcutaneous stimulation may therefore not activate a sufficient number of thick fibres to alleviate pain. An alternative method used

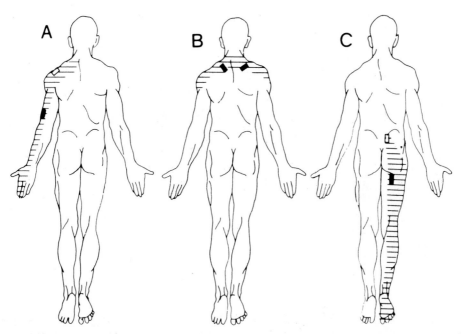

Fig. 31.34   Examples of placement of the electrodes for acupuncture-like transcutaneous nerve stimulation. The black electrode in (A) and (C) is the cathode; in (B) the placement of the cathode is less important and it may be placed either on the right or the left side of the neck. (From Eriksson and Sjölund, 1979.)

in such cases is to stimulate the dorsal surface of the spinal cord by means of implanted electrodes (Fig. 31.36). Thin cables connect the electrodes with a radio receiver that is implanted permanently, usually under the clavicle. The stimulus is delivered transcutaneously to the receiver by a battery-powered radio transmitter, the antenna of which is placed on the skin over the implanted receiver.

During stimulation, the patient experiences a buzzing or tingling sensation radiating through the body below the level of the site of the electrodes. Good pain relief occurs only in areas where the buzzing sensation is evoked. In many patients pain relief persists for several hours after discontinuation of stimulation. There is no impairment of other sensations during stimulation; touch, position

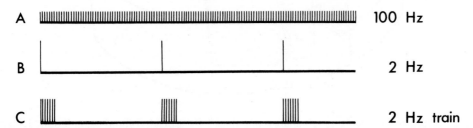

Fig. 31.35   Different methods of transcutaneous nerve stimulation (TNS). (A) High-frequency stimulation involving continuous barrage of brief pulses at 100 Hz. (B) Single brief pulses at 2 Hz. This type of stimulation is generally used in electroacupuncture. (C) Acupuncture-like TNS. Short trains (100 Hz internal frequency, duration 70 ms) of brief pulses at slow (2 Hz) repetition rate. Pulse amplitudes indicate differences in stimulus intensity from induction of analgesia with the three types of stimulation. (From Eriksson *et al., Pain*, 6, 1979.)

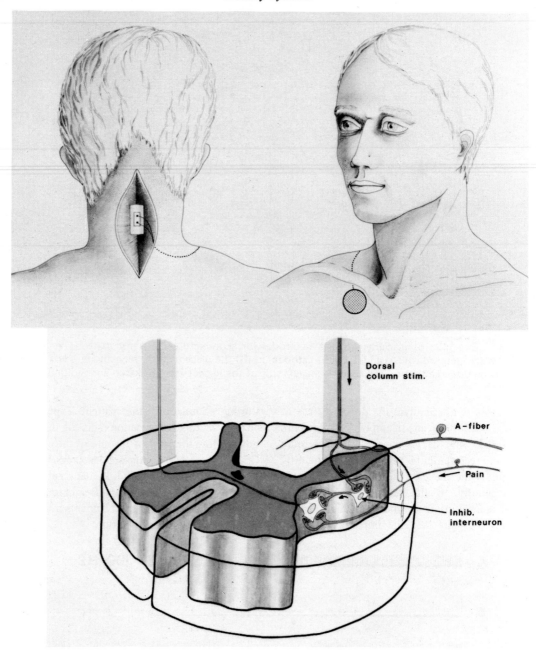

Fig. 31.36 Neuronal mechanisms of analgesia induced by dorsal column stimulation. Electrodes are implanted within the layers of the dura over the dorsal columns of the cord. From the electrodes, a wire is passed subcutaneously to a receiver implanted beneath the skin below the clavicle. To stimulate the dorsal columns, the patient places the antenna of the transmitter over the implanted receiver. When the stimulation is applied, the sensation experienced is normally described as a 'buzzing' or 'vibration' in the body below the electrode level. The pain relief obtained is proposed to be due to antidromic activation of the dorsal column fibres which, through their collaterals, activate substantia gelatinosa neurons controlling the transmission of pain impulses.

sense and vibratory sensations remain intact. Surprisingly, motor control remains unaffected; the patient can walk without difficulty during dorsal column stimulation. Bladder and bowel control also remain unaltered. Dorsal column stimulation (DCS) activates the coarse fibres of the ascending pathways in the dorsal funiculus of the spinal cord. The activity is conveyed antidromically by collaterals which pass into the dorsal horn and inhibit the transmission of afferent pain impulses by activating inhibitory cells in the substantia gelatinosa (Fig. 31.36). The mechanism for inhibition is probably analogous to that in conventional transcutaneous stimulation.

With the tide of enthusiasm provoked by the successful results of TNS, it was forgotten that 'electrotherapy' for the relief of pain was introduced nearly 2000 years ago. The earliest written reference to electrical stimulation in the treatment of pain is by a Roman physician, Scribonius Largus (CE 46) who recommended that: 'For any type of gout, a live black *Torpedo* should, when pain begins, be placed under the feet. The patient should stay like this until his whole foot and leg, up to the knee, is numb'. Electric fish were used to produce local analgesia until well into the nineteenth century and are still used for this purpose in many non-Western cultures. With the technical advancement in the middle of the eighteenth century, electric fish were replaced by various types of electric machines (Fig. 31.37). One of these was an electroanaesthetic apparatus that was guaranteed to make possible extraction of teeth without pain by the application of one electrode to the aching tooth while another was held in the hand by the patient. This apparatus became widely used throughout America and was also introduced to France. To study this new technique, a committee was appointed that reported variable results. One of the members of the committee therefore concluded that: ' . . . there must be something in American teeth which is not in French teeth'. It is interesting to note that in 1975 it was reported by two Czechoslovakian neurophysiologists that they had found in experiments on cats that anodal current blocked activity of nociceptive fibres from the tooth pulp.

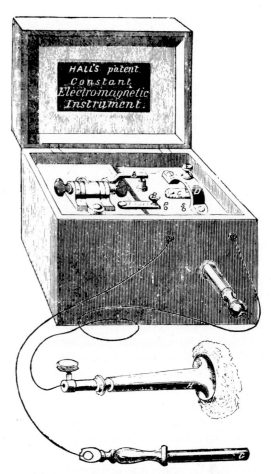

Fig. 31.37 'Magneto-electric machine' with pad and manual electrode recommended for electroanaesthesia. (From Garratt, in *Electrophysiology and Electrotherapeutics*, Tricknor and Fields, 1860.)

Owing to indiscriminate use, the technique for producing anaesthesia by electricity declined in popularity for a time but was rediscovered at the turn of the century. New machines for stimulation were developed and electrotherapy again became widely used. Electrical analgesia was also introduced in surgery in place of general anaesthesia, and there are several reports from this time of the successful use of electroanaesthesia in limb amputation. With the advent of chemical anaesthetics and improved methods for surgical anaesthesia, electrotherapy again declined in popularity until it was

rediscovered and reintroduced in the early 1970s
under the impact of the gate control theory.

31.7   Acupuncture and pain

History of acupuncture

Acupuncture can be traced as far back as the
Stone Age, when sharp-edged tools were used in
China to relieve pain. It is said that the analgesic
effect of acupuncture needling goes back to observations of soldiers who were wounded by arrows
in battle. Trying to pull out the arrows by twiddling
them gently, they found that they were relieved of
the pain from the wound.

The first detailed account in the medical literature of acupuncture is found in *Nei Ching*, or the
Chinese Canon of Medicine, which is also one of
the oldest medical textbooks in existence. Tradi-
tion traces the ideas presented in this book back to
the Yellow Emperor, Huang Ti, who lived around
2800 years BC. The actual writing of the book is
thought to have been carried out during the time
of the Ching Dynasty, i.e. about 250 BC. The *Nei
Ching* links the anatomy and physiology of legend-
ary times with that of Chinese history and carries
it right through centuries to Chinese medicine of
today. In the anatomical–physiological system
presented in *Nei Ching*, man is a microcosm composed of elements from both Heaven and Earth.
Health and long life depend on living according
to the laws of Nature. Vital energy or life force,
ch'i, is continuously circulating through all the
organs of the body and this *ch'i* is under the
influence of two opposing forces, Yang and Yin.
Yang is considered to come from Heaven and
represents maleness, strength, heat and light, while
Yin comes from Earth and represents femaleness,
weakness, passivity, shadow and cold. When Yang
and Yin are in perfect balance, *ch'i* is able to cir-
culate freely and throughout the body in a system
of channels, the *ching-lo* or meridians (Fig. 31.38).
All diseases and pains derive from an imbalance
between Yang and Yin and are due to either loss
of Yang or Yin or impaired flux of one of them in
the channel system. By inserting needles into the

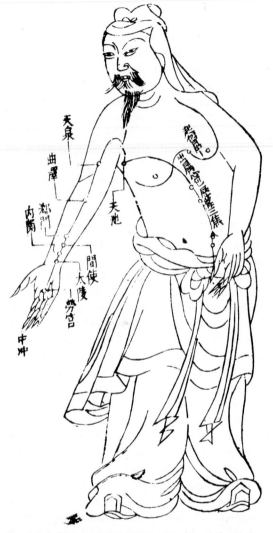

Fig. 31.38   Acupuncture chart from the Ming
dynasty showing meridians and acupuncture points
for treatment of diseases of various organs. (From
Lyons and Petrucelli, *Medicine. An Illustrated
History*, H. N. Abrams, New York, 1978.)

channels, the balance between Yang and Yin can
be restored and the normal circulation in the *ching-
lo* system re-established. The ancient system of
acupuncture includes 14 channels and 365 acupuncture points, each site being related to a diseased organ or pain syndrome. In the *Nei Ching*,
pain is said to arise from intrusion into the *ching-
lo* system of external objects and particularly

from heat and wind resulting in obstruction of the channels. The origin of pain can therefore be detected by the procedure of feeling different types of pulses (Fig. 31.39), which is still an important part of clinical examination by Chinese physicians. One of these pulses is the 'inch pulse'. In the description of pain due to excess of Yang, in *Nei Ching* it is said that: 'When the inch pulse within the hand is short and without volume headache results. When the inch pulse within the hand is too much prolonged extreme pains in the feet and shin bones result. When the inch pulse within the hand roots and strikes upwards the result is a shoulder and back ache'. Relief of pain may be achieved by restoring the circulation and drawing off the minute particles, heat or wind from the channel system.

Although acupuncture treatment has its roots in ancient China, it is interesting to note that similar methods were employed therapeutically in many places in the world without any obvious connections with China or any knowledge of Chinese acupuncture. For instance, the Lapps in Northern Scandinavia have for centuries used — and are still using — pressure stimulation of the

ho-ku point (Fig. 31.40) to get relief from toothache, and some Eskimos practice 'acupuncture' with sharp stones. The cauterisation which was widely practiced in mediaeval Europe may also be considered as a form of acupuncture.

Acupuncture was introduced in the Western world in 1671 by a Jesuit priest who compiled the first European report on acupuncture. Later, many treatises on acupuncture were published in Western languages. However, acupuncture remained largely unknown until the early 1930s, when a translation in French of Chinese methods of acupuncture was published. In 1958 the first operations under acupuncture analgesia were reported from China, and after this acupuncture achieved world fame and became increasingly employed in China and throughout the world.

Acupuncture techniques

Acupuncture stimulation may be performed in four ways: (1) manual acupuncture, (2) electro-acupuncture, (3) injection acupuncture and (4) finger pressure.

The manual method is the traditional one, and

Fig. 31.39 Feeling the pulse, a predominant feature of clinical examination in ancient Chinese medicine. (From Lyons and Petrucelli, *Medicine. An Illustrated History*, H. N. Abrams, New York, 1978.)

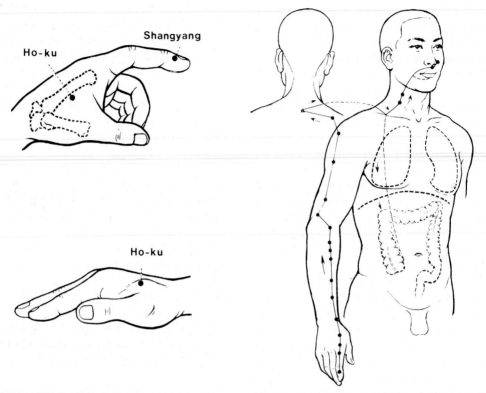

Fig. 31.40 The *ho-ku* point. Acupuncture at this point is proposed for treatment of headache, toothache, tonsillitis, pain of the upper extremities, common cold, etc. The channel mediating the effect of stimulating the *ho-ku* point is 'The Large Intestine Channel of Hand—Yangming' which starts at the tip of the index finger and runs up the arm to the lungs and then to the large intestine, as indicated by the drawing to the right. (From *An Outline of Chinese Acupuncture*, Foreign Languages Press, Peking, 1975.)

is still much employed. Thin flexible needles are inserted into the skin to a depth of 1–4 cm and manipulated by rotation and/or up and down movements of the needle. The most common method today is electroacupuncture, where the needles are connected to an electrical stimulator which delivers biphasic pulses at a frequency of 1–50 Hz. Stimulation frequencies of 2–4 Hz are most commonly used in China. Recent reports from China suggest that the optimal analgesic effect is obtained when the rate is varied. The strength of the stimulus is increased gradually until local muscle contractions appear or to a limit of what the patient can tolerate. Acupuncture by injection uses a few millilitres of a solution (distilled water, saline solution or herb extracts). This

probably stimulates deep pressure receptors. Acupuncture by finger pressure is particularly effective in inducing pain relief when applied to the *ho-ku* point between the first and second metacarpal bones or on the Achilles tendon. Regardless of the method used the analgesic effect takes 20–30 min to develop, but may then persist for several hours with continuous stimulation. When the stimulation stops the analgesia gradually fades, disappearing after 2–3 h. Although the analgesic effect is general, it is most pronounced in the segments where the stimulation is applied. Only the perception of pain alters; touch, vibration and temperature senses remain unaffected. Since acupuncture stimulation does not produce relaxation of muscles, it is inappropriate for surgical procedures that require muscle relaxation such as abdominal surgery. Acupuncture has been found to be particularly effective for operations in the ear, nose and throat, in the chest and in brain surgery. It is less effective in nervous and tense patients or in children.

In the first operations in China under acupuncture analgesia, a large number of needles (40 or more) were used. Later this number was reduced and today a few needles are considered sufficient. Originally the points selected for needling were carefully chosen along the traditonal meridians. The tendency today is to combine 'far points', which are chosen according to the traditional meridian system, with 'near points', which are chosen according to the segmental distribution of spinal and cranial nerves. Stimulation of acupuncture points of the ear is considered to have a generalised analgesic and sedative effect on the whole body since every part of the body is assumed to be represented on the auricula. In the first years after the introduction of acupuncture analgesia in surgery, about 60% of all surgical procedures in China were carried out under acupuncture analgesia. The use of acupuncture in surgery has since been reduced and recent reports give average figures of 15–20%.

Physiological mechanisms of acupuncture analgesia

The physiological mechanisms underlying the powerful analgesic action of acupuncture has been an intriguing problem ever since acupuncture was introduced clinically in China. Systematic and elegant studies by Chang Hsiang-Tung at the Shanghai Academy of Sciences have greatly elucidated the action of the sensory input induced by acupuncture stimulation at different levels in the central nervous system. Furthermore, recent work of Chinese physiologists has added to the understanding of the peripheral mechanisms mediating the analgesic effect. The contribution from the West lies mainly in the discovery that an endogenous pain-suppressing system is involved in acupuncture analgesia.

There is at present unequivocal evidence showing that acupuncture analgesia is dependent on the input to the central nervous system from peripheral afferent fibres. Thus it has been demon-

Fig. 31.41 Chang Hsiang-Tung, Professor at the Shanghai Institute of Physiology under the Chinese Academy of Sciences, has made outstanding contributions to the understanding of the neurophysiological mechanisms of acupuncture analgesia.

strated that the analgesic effect resulting from acupuncture stimulation disappears following injection of procaine deep at the needling points. Several lines of evidence suggest that acupuncture analgesia is mediated by deep, large and medium-sized nerves from the muscles, tendons and periosteum. Cutaneous afferent nerves on the other hand do not appear to contribute significantly to the analgesic effect. The deep fibres activated by acupuncture appear mainly to belong to group II and group III afferents. Attempts to identify the receptors involved have given no clearcut answer. There is indirect evidence that muscle spindles play a key role, but other types of receptors may also be involved.

As indicated above, the maximal analgesic effect is not obtained until after about 20–30 min of acupuncture stimulation. The long induction time and the persistence of analgesia for several hours after termination of stimulation has led to the assumption that some humoral agent is involved in producing acupuncture analgesia. It has, for instance, been thought that some substance might be released at the point of stimulation or in the central nervous system. The first possibility has been ruled out by the observation that the analgesic effect of acupuncture remains after circulatory occlusion. For instance, after vascular occlusion by applying a tourniquet to the upper arm, acupuncture stimulation of the forearm still produces an analgesic effect. The alternative possibility, i.e. that some humoral factor is released in the central nervous system, is supported by a considerable amount of experimental evidence. Before discussing this evidence, let us first consider what is known about the spinal mechanisms of acupuncture analgesia.

As proposed by the gate control theory, there is a gating mechanism at the entrance to the central nervous system. Increased activity in large afferent fibres is supposed to close the gate for transmission of pain impulses whereas increased activity of small fibres tends to open the gate. It would appear reasonable to assume that acupuncture stimulation by activation of large and medium-sized afferent fibres would produce inhibition of pain according to the principle proposed by the gate control theory. Although the interaction of the two inputs in the dorsal horn may play an important role in acupuncture analgesia, it is evident that the effect of acupuncture stimulation cannot be explained entirely on the basis of a spinal gate control.

Chang has demonstrated that the viscerosomatic reflex discharge evoked by stimulation of the splanchnic nerve can be inhibited by acupuncture stimulation and that this effect is abolished by high-level transection of the spinal cord. This suggests that in order to produce analgesia the afferent impulses induced by acupuncture stimulation must activate supraspinal structures which then send back their inhibitory impulses to the spinal cord. Studies on the effect of lesions of different parts of the spinal cord suggest that the ascending pathway of this feedback circuit is located in the anterolateral funiculus. It appears that the

impulses arising from the acupuncture point after entering the spinal cord are transmitted to the bulbar reticular formation where they terminate in the magnocellular nucleus and probably also in the raphe nuclei. The impulses of these neurons pass downwards to the spinal cord and inhibit the transmission of the pain impulses in the dorsal horn. In addition, the neurons of the bulbar reticular formation project upon the centromedian nucleus of the thalamus; this pathway is believed to be mainly of inhibitory nature. There is a considerable amount of experimental evidence suggesting that the centromedian nucleus has a key position in the pain suppressing system. This nucleus is a centre for polymodal sensory input from the whole body. In addition, it is intimately related to the pain receiving intralaminar thalamic nuclei. These connections would appear to explain the generalised analgesic effect obtained by acupuncture stimulation. The nucleus caudatus also appears to be involved in the pain suppressing system, as suggested by the observation that electrical stimulation of the head of the caudate nucleus suppresses the activity induced by nociceptive input to thalamic neurons. It would thus appear that the analgesic effect is due to an interaction of afferent input induced by acupuncture and the pain impulses at several levels of the central nervous system: spinal, midbrain and thalamic.

As pointed out above, the long induction time of acupuncture analgesia and its persistence after cessation of stimulation suggest that some humoral factor may be involved. This notion received strong support from early observations in China showing that injection of cerebroventricular fluid from acupunctured animals into the ventricles of normal animals produced a significant rise in pain threshold in the latter. The nature of this humoral factor remains unknown but there are reasons to believe that endogenous opiate-like substances (endorphins) may be involved. This conclusion is based on the finding that acupuncture analgesia is partially reversed by naloxone. It is therefore probable that acupuncture analgesia involves activation of an endogenous antinociceptive mechanism which incorporates the brain stem pain control system. Since the descending pathway of this system is serotonergic, it would appear likely that serotonin is involved in the process of acupuncture analgesia. Recent observations by Han Ji-Sheng provide evidence of a close relation between the brain level of serotonin (5-HT) and the analgesic effect of acupuncture stimulation (Fig. 31.42). The serotonin-containing neurons of the dorsal raphe nucleus project upon the parafascicular nucleus of the thalamus. This suggests that the serotonergic system may inhibit pain not only through a descending spinal pathway but also via an ascending system acting upon thalamic nuclei. Both of these systems appear to be involved in acupuncture analgesia.

It is well known that acupuncture is more effective in Chinese than in Western people. This suggests that, besides the neurophysiological mechanisms described above, psychological factors may also be involved in acupuncture analgesia. It appears that in Chinese people the confidence in the method together with cultural and social factors contribute to the effect of acupuncture. Anxiety is a major psychical factor in pain experiences and the effect of all methods of pain relief are therefore to a great extent a matter of reduction of anxiety. The close patient–doctor relationship in China and the confidence in acupuncture appear to account for the greater success of acupuncture treatment in Chinese as compared to that in Occidentals.

31.8 Hypnosis and pain

In 1829 a French surgeon, Cloquet, presented to the French Academy of Medicine the report of a remarkable operation on an old woman suffering from cancer of the right breast. Prior to the operation the patient was mesmerised (hypnotised). The patient had not received any drugs, yet talked quietly with the surgeon and showed no signs of experiencing pain during the operation, which involved incision of the breast to the armpit and the removal of the tumour and the glands in the armpit. This report was met with scepticism and Cloquet was accused of being an imposter. However, in the following years several reports of painless surgery under hypnosis appeared and in 1850 Esdaile reported that he had performed over 300 major operations in India utilising only hypnosis

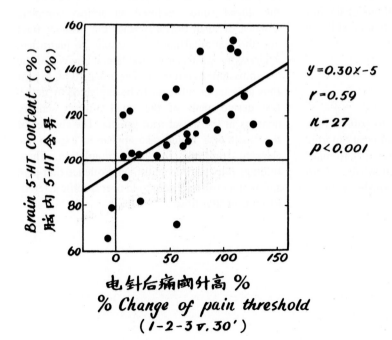

$y = 0.30x - 5$

$r = 0.59$

$n = 27$

$p < 0.001$

Fig. 31.42 Relation between brain serotonin (5-HT) level and the change in pain threshold induced by acupuncture. (By courtesy of Professor Han Ji-Sheng.)

to obtain analgesia. Following the introduction of ether and chloroform as anaesthetics, interest in hypnotism for surgery declined but revived again in the 1930s when several reports appeared about successful use of 'hypnotic analgesia'. These reports also reawakened interest in studies of the psychological mechanisms underlying the pain-reducing effect obtained in hypnosis. It appeared that in most cases it is the anxiety, fear and worry of pain that is reduced. Whether or not pain as sensation is reduced remains a matter of debate. It seems that although pain may have access to some lower level it may not reach the level of awareness under hypnosis. This may be illustrated by the following experiment reported by Hilgard. Circulating ice water was used as pain stimulus and the subject was asked to hold his hand in the water and indicate the intensity of pain by pressing a button with the other hand and at the same time report the pain verbally using a scale from 1 to 10. Under hypnosis the surprising finding was that the subject reported no pain and was totally unaware of the hand in the ice water, yet the hand pressing the button indicated that pain was felt, just as in the normal non-hypnotic state. This finding has been thought to indicate that there are different levels of cognitive functions and that although pain may reach one level of consciousness it may still not have access to the level of awareness.

Congenital insensitivity to pain

Congenital universal insensitivity to pain is rare; until 1965 only about 45 cases had been reported and only in two cases has detailed neuroanatomical examination been carried out. Knowledge about the underlying causes of this abnormality is therefore incomplete.

Patients with congenital insensitivity to pain have no knowledge of pain or aches. The presence or absence of pain is therefore difficult to discuss with the patients. Sometimes these patients may report an upsetting experience as painful, probably because they assume it would be painful to a normal person. Patients with congenital insensitivity to pain may have behavioural responses to pain; this may indicate rather that they try to adapt an appropriate behaviour in order to avoid being regarded as not reacting normally. In most of these patients the corneal reflex is absent, but both itch and tickle are present.

The problem of the possible neural deficit underlying congenital insensitivity to pain has been elucidated in a study of a 12-year-old boy who was totally insensitive to superficial and deep painful stimuli. He also had a greatly elevated threshold for temperature sensation but touch, position and vibratory sensations were normal Although skin biopsies showed normal sweat glands, heating did not evoke sweating. The boy died in a febrile illness during which the body temperature increased to 43°C in 24 hours. At autopsy it was found that there were no small cells in the dorsal root ganglia. Cross-sections of the dorsal roots disclosed an almost complete absence of small fibres. Neither the Lissauer tract nor the spinothalamic tract could be identified, whereas the posterior ventral lateral nucleus of the thalamus appeared normal. The insensitivity to pain thus appears in this case to be explained by defective development of the small primary sensory neurons in the dorsal root ganglia. The absence of the small cells would also appear to explain the elevated threshold for heat stimulation. These findings thus provide additional evidence that pain and temperature are conveyed over specific afferent systems of thin fibres.

32

Sensory Deprivation

Sensory input has been recognised as important for many higher brain functions, but only relatively recently has there been systematic investigations of the effects of reduced sensory input. Various procedures have been used for this purpose. Most often, a human subject is confined in a dark and soundproof room for varying periods of time. It has been found that such reductions in sensory input lead to changes in perceptual and cognitive functions, bizarre hallucinations and delusions. Some of these changes may appear after only a relatively brief period of isolation.

When isolated from the outer world, the subjects usually spend the first few days resting and thinking about their work, personal problems, etc. As time passes, organised thinking becomes gradually more difficult, and the thoughts begin to drift randomly. Continued isolation brings blank periods during which the subjects are unable to think of anything and have difficulty distinguishing whether they are asleep or awake. In this dream-like state, they find coherent thinking impossible; their thoughts, no longer anchored in reality, drift away in capricious fantasies. Many subjects report that during these periods they find it difficult to talk, they feel confused, and are emotionally very labile. Visual hallucinations begin to appear at this point, rather simple ones at first, but more elaborate with prolonged isolation. They are colourful and resemble drug-induced hallucinations. Often they are so frequent and vivid as to prevent sleeping. They usually appear at random, and the subjects have no control over them.

In general no conspicuous somatic changes accompany isolation. Blood pressure, body temperature and other somatic body functions remain normal. The EEG characteristically shifts towards lower frequencies, and this change persists for some time after the individual has returned to a normal environment.

Sensory isolation imposes considerable stress on the subjects, leading to various emotional reactions. The subjects often report that they feel anxious and anguished in the early phase of isolation, as well as being irritated at not being able to think coherently. They become restless and often request to be relieved from isolation; frequently, their panicky reactions necessitate ending the experiment. If the subjects can endure the emotional stress of this first period, a second phase follows during which they adapt to the isolation and feel peaceful and calm. If isolation continues, a third phase ensues in which anguish returns and coherent thought vanishes; violent emotional reactions often follow.

With regard to perception, most isolated subjects develop deficiencies in motor coordination and tactile discrimination, and certain cognitive functions such as problem-solving and reasoning deteriorate. Some reports indicate a reduction in learning ability during isolation. Often the perception of body image changes; for instance, the body feels smaller than normal, the arms seem dissociated from the body, and the subject has a sense of floating in the air. Interestingly, these perceptual changes may occur after only eight hours of isolation. Sensory deprivation for two to three days produces a temporary deficit in colour perception and depth perception. In most cases the decrement in performance is greatest after a two-day period of deprivation; with longer deprivation the subject adjusts to the confinement and improves his performance in perceptual tasks. During isolation many subjects develop symptoms of paranoia. After termination of isolation, there is usually a period during which the subjects report feeling tired, drowsy, confused and disorientated.

What are the neurophysiological mechanisms underlying the various perceptual changes induced by sensory deprivation? The reticular activating system (RAS) provides pathways for diffuse sensory input to the entire cortex. This system plays an important role in alerting, attention and control of sleep—wakefulness. It has been suggested that reduction or elimination of the input via the RAS leads to a general reduction in overall cortical activity and thereby upsets the normal balance. The emotional reactions induced by sensory deprivation may be accounted for by hypothalamic mechanisms.

All studies of sensory deprivation show that there are great individual differences. One of the main determinants appears to be the individual's ability to maintain the integrity of his ego. A firm apprehension of personal identity seems important for maintaining coherent thinking and emotional stability. Such individuals may be relatively unconcerned about the reduction of sensory input from the outer world and may even be able to utilise the isolation constructively for creative work; the value of a restricted input from the environment for intellectual work is well known. For individuals with an immature ego, isolation from the outside world may be intolerable. A person of this type suffers emotional reactions ranging from boredom and restlessness to anxiety and anguish. Moreover, they tend to lose track of time, which makes the situation even worse. Asked after their confinement what was hardest to endure, these individuals answer that it was the feeling of social isolation, loneliness and having no one to talk to.

Studies on experimental animals have provided evidence that deprivation early in life creates permanent deficiencies. Animals reared in isolation show adaptational difficulties and are deficient in social relatedness, exploration and general activity. Corresponding situations may not occur in humans, but there are strong reasons to believe that the sensory input during early life has an important role in the development of higher brain functions in man.

BIBLIOGRAPHY FOR SECTION X

Sensory systems in general

Suggested Reading and Reviews

Adrian, E. D. (1947). *The Physical Background of Perception*, Clarendon Press, Oxford

Adrian, E. D. (1949). *Sensory Integration, First Sherrington Lecture*, Liverpool University Press

Gazzaniga, M. S. and Blakemore, C. (1975). *Handbook of Psychobiology*, Academic Press, New York

Granit, R. (1955). *Receptors and Sensory Perception*, Yale University Press, New Haven

Heinbecker, P., Bishop, G. H. and O'Leary, J. (1934). Analysis of sensation in terms of the nerve impulse, *Arch. Neurol. Psychiatr.*, **31**, 34–53

Hensel, H. (1966). *Allgemeine Sinnesphysiologie Hautsinne, Geschmack, Geruch*, Springer-Verlag, Berlin

Lowenstein, O. (1966). *The Senses*, Penguin Book, Baltimore

Loewenstein, W. R. (ed.) (1971). *Principles of Receptor Physiology, Handbook of Sensory Physiology*, vol. 1, Springer-Verlag, Heidelberg

MacKay, D. M. (1969). Evoked brain potentials as indicators of sensory information processing, *Neurosci. Res. Prog. Bull.*, 7, 181–276

Milner, P. M. (1973). *Physiological Psychology*, Holt, Rinehart & Winston, London

Mountcastle, V. B. (1967). The problem of sensing and the neural coding of sensory events, in *The Neurosciences. A Study Program*. eds G. C. Quarton, T. Melnechuk and F. O. Schmitt, Rockefeller University Press, New York, pp. 393–498

Mountcastle, V. B. and Powell, T. P. S. (1959). Neural mechanisms subserving cutaneous sensibility, with special reference to the role of afferent inhibition in sensory perception and discrimination, *Bull. Johns Hopkins Hosp.*, **105**, 201–232

Penfield, W and Perot, P. (1963). The brain's record of auditory and visual experience, *Brain*, **86**, 596–696

Rosenblith, W. A. (1961). Sensory communication, *Contributions to the Symposium on Principles of Sensory Communication*, MIT Press, Cambridge, MA, and John Wiley & Sons, New York

Stevens, S. S. (1957). On the psychophysical law, *Psychol. Rev.*, **64**, 153–181

Stevens, S. S. (1971). Sensory power functions and neural events, in *Principles of Receptor Physiology, Handbook of Sensory Physiology*, vol. 1, ed. W. R. Loewenstein, Springer-Verlag, Heidelberg

Thompson, R. F. (1967). *Foundations of Physiological Psychology*, Harper & Row, New York

Uttal, W. R. (1969). Emerging principles of sensory coding, *Perspect. Biol. Med.*, **12**, 344–368

Uttal, W. R. (1973). *The Psychobiology of Sensory Coding*, Harper & Row, New York

Werner, G and Mountcastle, V. B. (1968). Quantitative relation between mechanical stimuli to the skin and the neural responses evoked by them, in *The Skin Senses*, ed. D. R. Kenshalo, C. C. Thomas, Springfield

Vision

Suggested Reading and Reviews

Adler, F. H. (1965). *Physiology of the Eye*, C. V. Mosby, St Louis

Bach-y-Rita, P. and Collins, C. C. (eds) (1972). *The Control of Eye Movements*, Academic Press, London

the visual system and the study of receptive fields, *Invest. Ophthalmol.*, **12**, 794–813

LeVay, S., Hubel, D. H. and Wiesel, T. N. (1975). The pattern of ocular dominance columns in macaque visual cortex revealed by reduced silver stain, *J. Comp. Neurol.*, **159**, 559–576

Marks, W. B., Dobelle, W. H. and MacNichol, E. F. (1964). Visual pigments of single primate cones, *Science*, **143**, 1181–1183

Michael, C. R. (1978). Color vision mechanisms in monkey striate cortex: Simple cells with dual opponent-color receptive fields, *J. Neurophysiol.*, **41**, 1233–1249

Michael, C. R. (1978). Color-sensitive complex cells in monkey striate cortex, *J. Neurophysiol.*, **41**, 1250–1266

Nilsson, S. E. G. (1965). The ultrastructure of the receptor outer segments in the retina of the leopard frog (*Rana pipiens*), *J. Ultrastruct. Res.*, **12**, 207–231

Tomita, T., Kaneko, A., Murakami, M. and Pautler, E. (1967). Spectral response curves of single cones in carp, *Vision Res.*, **7**, 519–531

Trevarthen, C. B. (1970). Experimental evidence for a brainstem contribution to visual perception in man, *Brain Behav. Evol.*, **3**, 338–352

Wald, G. and Brown, P. K. (1958). Human rhodopsin, *Science*, **127**, 222–226

Werblin, F. S. and Dowling, J. E. (1969). Organization of the retina of the mudpuppy *Necturus maculatus*. II. Intracellular recording, *J. Neurophysiol.*, **32**, 339–355

Westheimer, G. (1981). Visual hyperacuity, in *Progress in Sensory Physiology*, vol. 1, ed. D. Ottoson, Springer-Verlag, Heidelberg, pp. 1–30

Wiesel, T. N. and Hubel, D. H. (1963). Single-cell responses in striate cortex of kittens deprived of vision in one eye, *J. Neurophysiol.*, **26**, 1003–1017

Wiesel, T. N. and Hubel, D. H. (1974). Ordered arrangement of orientation columns in monkeys lacking visual experience, *J. Comp. Neurol.*, **158**, 307–318

Young, R. W. (1967). The renewal of photoreceptor cell outer segments, *J. Cell Biol.*, **33**, 61–72

Zeki, S. M. (1973). Color coding in rhesus monkey prestriate cortex, *Brain Res.*, **53**, 422–427

Zeki, S. (1980). The representation of colours in the cerebral cortex, *Nature*, **284**, 412–418

Hearing

Suggested Reading and Reviews

Ades, H. W. and Engström, H. (1974). Anatomy of the inner ear, in *Auditory System, Handbook of Sensory Physiology*, vol. V/1, eds W. D. Keidel and W. D. Neff, Springer-Verlag, Heidelberg, pp. 125–158

von Békésy, G. (1960). *Experiments in Hearing*, McGraw-Hill, New York

Brodal, A. (1974). Anatomy of the vestibular nuclei and their connections, in *Vestibular System, Handbook of Sensory Physiology*, vol. VI/1, ed. H. H. Kornhuber, Springer-Verlag, Heidelberg, pp. 239–352

Dallos, P. (1973). *The Auditory Periphery*, Academic Press, New York

Dallos, P. (1975). Cochlear potentials, in *The Nervous System*, vol. 3, ed. D. B. Tower, Raven Press, New York, pp. 69–80

Dohlman, G. F. (1974). Histochemistry and metabolism of the inner ear, *Vestibular System, Handbook of Sensory Physiology*, vol. VI/1, ed. H. H. Kornhuber, Springer-Verlag, Heidelberg, pp. 185–212

Enger, P. S. (1968). Hearing in fish, in *Hearing Mechanisms in Vertebrates, Ciba Foundation Symp.*, eds de Reuck and Knight, J. & A. Churchill, London

Evans, E. F. (1975). Cochlear nerve and cochlear nucleus, in *Auditory System, Handbook of Sensory Physiology*, vol. V/2, eds W. D. Keidel and W. D. Neff, Springer-Verlag, Heidelberg, pp. 1–108

Fex, J. (1974). Neural excitatory processes of the inner ear, in *Auditory System, Handbook of Sensory Physiology*, vol. V/1, eds W. D. Keidel and W. D. Neff, Springer-Verlag, Heidelberg, pp. 585–646

Flock. Å. (1967). Ultrastructure and function in the lateral line organs, in *Lateral Line Detectors*, ed. P. Cahn, Indiana University Press, London, pp. 163–197

Flock, Å. (1977). Physiological properties of sensory hairs in the ear, in *Psychophysics and Physiology of Hearing*, eds E. F. Evans and J. P. Wilson, Academic Press, London, pp. 1–11

Griffin, D. R. (1958). *Listening in the Dark*, Yale University Press, Boston

Harrison, J. M. and Howe, M. E. (1974). Anatomy of the afferent auditory nervous system of mammals, in *Auditory System, Handbook of Sensory Physiology*, vol. V/1, eds W. D. Keidel and W. D. Neff, Springer-Verlag, Heidelberg, pp. 283–336

von Helmholtz, H. L. F. (1870). *Die Lehre von den Tonempfindungen als physiologische Grundlage für die Theorie der Musik*

Hillman, D. E. (1976). Vestibular and lateral line system. Morphology of peripheral and central vestibular systems, in *Frog Neurobiology. A Handbook*, eds R. Llinás and W. Precht, Springer-Verlag, Heidelberg, pp. 452–480

Iurato, S. (1967). *Submicroscopic Structure of the Inner Ear*, Pergamon Press, Oxford

Iurato, S. (1974). Efferent innervation of the cochlea, in *Auditory System, Handbook of Sensory Physiology*, vol. V/1, eds W. D. Keidel and W. D. Neff, Springer-Verlag, Heidelberg, pp. 261–282

Lowenstein, O. (1950). Labyrinth and equilibrium, *Symp. Soc. Exp. Biol.*, **4**, 60–82

Møller, A. R. (ed.) (1973). *Basic Mechanisms in Hearing*, Academic Press, New York

Smith, C. A. (1975). The inner ear: Its embryological development and microstructure, in *The Nervous System*, vol. 3, ed. D. B. Tower, Raven Press, New York, pp. 1–18

Smith, C. A. (1981). Recent advances in structural correlates in auditory receptors, in *Progress in Sensory Physiology*, vol. 2, ed. D. Ottoson, Springer-Verlag, Heidelberg

Spoendlin, H. (1966). *The Organization of the Cochlear Receptor*, Karger, Basel and New York

Spoendlin, H. (1966). Ultrastructure of the vestibular sense organ, in *The Vestibular System and its Diseases*, ed. R. J. Wolfson, University of Pennsylvania Press, pp. 39–68

Spoendlin, H. (1969). Structural basis of peripheral frequency analysis, in *Frequency Analysis and Periodicity Detection in Hearing*, eds R. Plomp and F. G. Smoorenburg, Sijthoff, Leiden, pp. 2–36

Tunturi, A. R. (1960). Anatomy and physiology of the auditory cortex, in *Neural Mechanisms of the Auditory and Vestibular Systems*, eds Rasmussen and Windle, C. C. Thomas, Springfield

Wersäll, J. and Bagger-Sjöbäck, D. (1970). Morphology of the vestibular sense organ, in *Vestibular System, Handbook of Sensory Physiology*, vol. VI/1, ed. H. H. Kornhuber, Springer-Verlag, Heidelberg, pp. 123–170

Wever, E. G. (1949). *Theory of Hearing*, John Wiley & Sons, New York

Wilson, V. J. and Jones, G. M. (1979). *Mammalian Vestibular Physiology*, Plenum Press, New York

Original Papers

Anderson, H. and Barr, B. (1966). Conductive recruitment, *Acta Otolaryngol.*, **62**, 171–183

von Békésy, G. (1947). The variation of phase along the basilar membrane with sinusoidal vibrations, *J. Acoust. Soc. Am.*, **19**, 452–460

von Békésy, G. (1947). A new audiometer, *Acta Otolaryngol.*, **35**, 411–422

von Békésy, G. (1959). Similarities between hearing and skin sensations, *Psychol. Rev.*, **66**, 1–122

von Békésy, G. (1960). Neural inhibitory units of the eye and skin. Quantitative description of contrast phenomena, *J. Opt. Soc. Am.*, **50**, 1060–1070

Dallos, P. J. (1973). Cochlear potentials and cochlear mechanics, in *Basic Mechanisms in Hearing*, ed. A. R. Møller, Academic Press, New York, pp. 335–376

Desmedt, J. E. (1962). Auditory-evoked potentials from cochlea to cortex as influenced by activation of the efferent olivo-cochlear bundle, *J. Acoust. Soc. Am.*, **34**, 1478–1496

Adrian, E. D. (1954). The basis of sensation: some recent studies of olfaction, *Br. Med. J.*, **1**, 287–290

Allison, A. C. (1953). The morphology of the olfactory system in the vertebrates, *Biol. Rev.*, **28**, 195–244

Boeckh, J. (1980). Ways of nervous coding of chemosensory quality at the input level, in *Olfaction and Taste*, vol. VII, ed. H. Van der Starre, IRL, London, pp. 113–122

Cagan, R. H. (1977). Recognition of gustatory and olfactory stimulus molecules at receptor sites, in *Food Intake and Chemical Senses*, eds Y. Katsuki, M. Sato, S. F. Takagi and Y. Oomura, Japan Scientific Societies Press, pp. 131–138

Dravnieks, A. (1964). Physicochemical basis of olfaction, *Ann. N. Y. Acad. Sci.*, **116**, 429–439

Døving, K. B. (1970). Experiments in olfaction, in *Taste and Smell in Vertebrates*, eds G. E. W. Wolstenholme and J. Knight, J. & A. Churchill, London, pp. 197–225

Gesteland, R. C. (1971). Neural coding in olfactory receptor cells, in *Olfaction, Handbook of Sensory Physiology*, vol. 4/1, ed. L. M. Beidler, Springer-Verlag, New York, pp. 132–150

Getchell, T. V. and Getchell, M. L. (1974). Signal-detecting mechanisms in the olfactory epithelium. Molecular discrimination, *Ann. N. Y. Acad. Sci.* (*Odors: Evaluation, utilization and control*), **237**, 62–75

Holley, A. (1977). La perception des odeurs, in *La Recherche en Neurobiologie*, Editions du Seuil, Paris, pp. 91–124

Holley, A. and Døving, K. B. (1977). Receptor sensitivity, acceptor distribution, convergence and neural coding, in *Proc. Sixth Int. Symp. on Olfaction and Taste*, eds. J. Le Magnen and P. MacLeod, IRL, London, pp. 113–123

Holley, A. and MacLeod, P. (1977). Transduction et codage des informations olfactives chez les vertébrés, *J. Physiol. Paris*, **73**, 725–828

Graziadei, P. P. C. (1971). The olfactory mucosa of vertebrates, in *Olfaction, Handbook of Sensory Physiology*, vol. 4/1, ed. L. M. Beidler, Springer-Verlag, New York

Graziadei, P. P. C. and Graziadei, G. A. M. (1978). Continuous nerve cell renewal in the olfactory system, in *Development of Sensory Systems, Handbook of Sensory Physiology*, vol. IX, ed. M. Jacobson, Springer-Verlag, Heidelberg, pp. 55–83

Kaissling, E. E. (1977). Structure of odour molecules and multiple activities of receptor cells, in *Proc. Sixth Int. Symp. on Olfaction and Taste*, eds. J. Le Magnen and P. MacLeod, IRL, London, pp. 9–16

Kleerekoper, H. (1969). *Olfaction in Fishes*, Indiana University Press

Köster, E. P. (1974). Quality discrimination in olfaction, in *Transduction Mechanisms in Chemoreception*, eds T. M. Poynder, L. H. Bannister, H. Bostock and G. H. Dodd, IRL, London, pp. 307–318

Le Magnen, J. (1961). *Odeurs et parfums. Que sais-je?* Presses Universitaires de France, Paris, p. 344

Le Magnen, J. (1971). Olfaction and nutrition, in *Chemical Senses: Olfaction, Handbook of Sensory Physiology*, vol. IV, ed. L. M. Beidler, Springer-Verlag, Heidelberg, pp. 465–482

Ottoson, D. (1963). Generation and transmission of signals in the olfactory system, in *Olfaction and Taste*, ed. Y. Zotterman, Pergamon Press, New York, pp. 35–44

Ottoson, D. (1971). The electro-olfactogram. A review of studies on the receptor potential of the olfactory system, in *Chemical Senses: Olfaction, Handbook of Sensory Physiology*, vol. IV, ed. L. M. Beidler, Springer-Verlag, Heidelberg, pp. 95–131

Ottoson, D. and Shepherd, G. M. (1967). Experiments and concepts in olfactory physiology, *Prog. Brain Res.*, **23**, 83–138

Plattig, K. H. and Kobal, G. (1977). Olfactory and gustatory responses in human electroencephalogram (EEG), in *Food Intake and Chemical Senses*, eds Y. Katsuki, M. Sato, S. F. Takagi and Y. Oomura, Japan Scientific Societies Press. pp. 51–70

Schneider, D. (1963). Electrophysiological investigation of insect olfaction, in *Olfaction and Taste*, ed. Y. Zotterman, Pergamon Press, New York, pp. 85–103

Shepherd, G. M. (1970). The olfactory bulb as a simple cortical system: experimental analysis and functional implications, in *The Neurosciences. Second Study Program*, ed. F. O. Schmitt, Rockefeller University Press, New York, pp. 539–552

Shepherd, G. M. (1972). Synaptic organization of the mammalian olfactory bulb, *Physiol. Rev.*, 52(4), 864–917

Shepherd, G. M., Getchell, T. V. and Kauer, J. S. (1975). Analysis of structure and function in the olfactory pathway, in *The Nervous System*, vol. 1, ed. D. B. Tower, Raven Press, New York, pp. 207–220

Wright, R. H. (1964). *The Science of Smell*, Basic Books, New York

Wright, R. H. and Burgess, R. E. (1970). Specific physicochemical mechanisms of olfactory stimulation, in *Taste and Smell in Vertebrates*, eds G. E. W. Wolstenholme and J. Knight, J. & A. Churchill, London, pp. 325–342

Original Papers

Adrian, E. D. (1942). Olfactory reactions in the brain of the hedgehog, *J. Physiol. (Lond.)*, 100, 459–473

Adrian, E. D. (1950). The electrical activity of the mammalian olfactory bulb, *Electroencephalogr. Clin. Neurophysiol.*, 2, 377–388

Adrian, E. D. and Ludwig, C. (1938). Nervous discharges from the olfactory organs of fish, *J. Physiol.*, 94, 441–460

Amoore, J. E. (1963). Stereochemical theory of olfaction, *Nature*, 198, 271–272

Amoore, J. E. (1970). Computer correlation of molecular shape with odour: A model for structure–activity relationships, in *Taste and Smell in Vertebrates*, eds G. E. W. Wolstenholme and J. Knight, J. & A. Churchill, London, pp. 293–312

Duchamp, A., Revial, M. F., Holley, A. and MacLeod, P. (1974). Odor discrimination by frog olfactory receptors, *Chem. Senses Flavor*, 1, 213–233

Døving, K. B. and Pinching, A. J. (1973). Selective degeneration of neurones in the olfactory bulb following prolonged odour exposure, *Brain Res.*, 52, 115–129

Døving, K. B., Selset, R. and Thommesen, G. (1980). Olfactory sensitivity to bile acids in salmonid fishes, *Acta Physiol. Scand.*, 108, 123–131

Gasser, H. S. (1956). Olfactory nerve fibers, *J. Gen. Physiol.*, 39, 473–496

Gesteland, R. C., Lettvin, J. Y. and Pitts, W. H. (1965). Chemical transmission in the nose of the frog, *J. Physiol. (Lond.)*, 181, 525–559

Gesteland, R. C., Lettvin, J. Y., Pitts, W. H. and Rojas, A. (1963). Odor specificities of the frog's olfactory receptors, in *Olfaction and Taste*, ed. Y. Zotterman, Pergamon Press, New York, pp. 19–34

Getchell, T. V. (1973). Analysis of unitary spikes recorded extracellularly from frog olfactory receptor cells and axons, *J. Physiol. (Lond.)*, 234, 533–551

Getchell, T. V. (1974). Electrogenic sources of slow voltage transients recorded from frog olfactory epithelium, *J. Neurophysiol.*, 37, 1115–1130

Getchell, T. V. (1977). Mechanisms of excitation in vertebrate olfactory receptors and sustentacular cells, in *Food Intake and Chemical Senses*, eds Y. Katsuki, M. Sato, S. F. Takagi and Y. Oomura, Japan Scientific Societies Press, pp. 3–11

Getchell, T. V. and Shepherd, G. M. (1978). Responses of olfactory receptor cells to step pulses of odour at different concentrations in the salamander, *J. Physiol. (Lond.)*, 282, 521–540

Getchell, T. V. and Shepherd, G. M. (1978). Adaptive properties of olfactory receptors analysed with odour pulses of varying durations, *J. Physiol. (Lond.)*, 282, 541–560

Graziadei, P. P. C. and Graziadei, G. A. M. (1979). Neurogenesis and neuron regeneration in the olfactory system of mammals. I. Morphological aspects of differentiation and structural organization of the olfactory sensory neurons, *J. Neurocytol.*, 8, 1–18

Holley, A., Duchamp, A., Rivial, M. F., Juge, A. and MacLeod, P. (1974). Qualitative and quantitative discrimination in the frog olfactory receptors: analysis from electrophysiological data, *Ann. N. Y. Acad. Sci.*, 237, 102–114

Kauer, J. S. (1974). Response patterns of amphibian olfactory bulb neurones to odour stimulation, *J. Physiol. (Lond.)*, **243**, 675–715

Kauer, J. S. (1980). Some spatial characteristics of central information processing in the vertebrate olfactory pathway, in *Olfaction and Taste*, vol. VII, ed. H. Van der Starre, IRL, London, pp. 227–236

Kauer, J. S. and Moulton, D. G. (1974). Responses of olfactory bulb neurones to odour stimulation of small nasal areas in the salamander, *J. Physiol. (Lond.)*, **243**, 717–737

Kauer, J. S. and Shepherd, G. M. (1977). Analysis of the onset phase of olfactory bulb unit responses to odour pulses in the salamander, *J. Physiol. (Lond.)*, **272**, 495–516

Ohloff, G. (1980). Stereochemistry–activity relationships in human odour sensation: 'The triaxial rule', in *Olfaction and Taste*, vol. VII, ed. H. Van der Starre, IRL, London, pp. 3–11

Ottoson, D. (1956). Analysis of the electrical activity of the olfactory epithelium, *Acta Physiol. Scand.*, **35**, *Suppl.* 122, 1–83

Ottoson, D. (1958). Studies on the relationship between olfactory stimulating effectiveness and physico-chemical properties of odorous compounds, *Acta Physiol. Scand.*, **43**, 167–181

Ottoson, D. (1959). Studies on slow potentials in the rabbit's olfactory bulb and nasal mucosa, *Acta Physiol. Scand.*, **47**, 136–148

Ottoson, D. (1970). Electrical signs of olfactory transducer action, in *Taste and Smell in Vertebrates*, eds G. E. W. Wolstenholme and J. Knight, J. & A. Churchill, London, pp. 343–356

Pinching, A. J. and Powell, T. P. S. (1971). The neuropil of the glomeruli of the olfactory bulb, *J. Cell Sci.*, **9**, 347–377

Rall, W., Shepherd, G. M., Reese, T. S. and Brightman, M. W. (1966). Dendrodendritic synaptic pathway for inhibition in the olfactory bulb, *Exp. Neurol.*, **14**, 44–56

Seifert, K. (1970). *Die Ultrastruktur des Riechespithels beim Makrosmatiker, Normale und Pathologische Anatomie*, vol. 21, Georg Thieme Verlag, Stuttgart

Shepherd, G. M. (1963). Responses of mitral cells to olfactory nerve volleys in the rabbit. *J. Physiol. (Lond.)*, **168**, 89–100

Shepherd, G. M. (1963). Neuronal systems controlling mitral cell excitability, *J. Physiol. (Lond.)*, **168**, 101–117

Sicard, G., Duchamp, A., Revial, M. F. and Holley, A. (1980). Odour discrimination by frog olfactory receptor cells: a recapitulative study, in *Olfaction and Taste*, vol. VII, ed. H. Van der Starre, IRL, London, pp. 171–174

Tactile Sensations, etc.

Suggested Reading

Baldessarini, R. J. (1979). The pathophysiological basis of tardive dyskinesia, *Trends in Neurosci.*, **2**(5), 133–135

Blix, M. (1884). Experimentelle Beiträge zur Lösung der Frage über die specifische Energie der Hautnerven, *Z. Biol.*, **10**, 141–156

Burgess, P. R. and Perl, E. R. (1973). Cutaneous mechanoreceptors and nociceptors, in *Somatosensory System, Handbook of Sensory Physiology*, vol. II, ed. A. Iggo, Springer-Verlag, Heidelberg, pp. 29–78

Dodt, E. and Zotterman, Y. (1952). Mode of action of warm receptors, *Acta Physiol. Scand.*, **26**, 345–357

Dodt, E. and Zotterman, Y. (1952). The discharge of specific cold fibres at high temperature (the paradoxical cold), *Acta Physiol. Scand.*, **26**, 358–365

Goodwin, G. M., McCloskey, D. I. and Matthews, P. B. C. (1972). The contribution of muscle afferents to kinaesthesia shown by vibration induced illusions of movement and by the effects of paralysing joint afferents, *Brain*, **95**, 705–748

Hallin, R. G. and Torebjörk, H. E. (1973). Electrically induced A and C fibre responses in intact human skin nerves, *Exp. Brain Res.*, **16**, 309–320

Hensel, H. (1952). Physiologie der Thermorezeption, *Ergebn. Physiol.*, **47**, 166–368

Iggo, A. and Ramsey, R. L. (1976). Thermosensory mechanisms in the spinal cord of monkeys, in *Sensory Functions of the Skin in Primates, with Special Reference to Man*, ed. Y. Zotterman, Pergamon Press, New York, pp. 285–302

Johansson, R. S. (1978). Tactile sensibility in the human hand: Receptive field characteristics of mechanoreceptive units in the glabrous skin area, *J. Physiol. (Lond.)*, **281**, 101–123

Johansson, R. S. (1979). Tactile afferent units with small and well demarcated receptive fields in the glabrous skin area of the human hand, in *Sensory Functions of the Skin of Humans*, ed. D. R. Kenshalo, Plenum, New York, pp. 129–145

Järvilehto, T., Hämäläinen, H. and Kekoni, J. (1976). Mechanoreceptive unit activity in human skin nerves correlated with touch and vibratory sensations, in *Sensory Functions of the Skin in Primates*, ed. Y. Zotterman, Pergamon Press, Oxford, pp. 215–230

Knibestöl, M. (1975). Stimulus response functions of slowly adapting mechanoreceptors in the human glabrous skin area, *J. Physiol. (Lond.)*, **245**, 63–80

Knibestöl, M. and Vallbo, Å. B. (1980). Intensity of sensation related to activity of slowly adapting mechanoreceptive units in the human hand, *J. Physiol. (Lond.)*, **300**, 251–267

Matthews, P. B. C. (1977). Muscle afferents and kinaesthesia, *Br. Med Bull.*, **33**, 137–142

McCloskey, D. I. (1978). Kinesthetic sensibility, *Physiol. Rev.*, **58** (4), 763–820

Mountcastle. V. B. and Powell, T. P. S. (1957). Central nervous mechanisms subserving position sense and kinesthesis, *Bull. Johns Hopkins Hosp.*, **105**, 173–200

Necker, R. (1981). Thermoreception and temperature regulation in homeothermic vertebrates, in *Progress in Sensory Physiology*, vol. 2, ed. D. Ottoson, Springer-Verlag, Heidelberg

Oscarsson, O. and Rosen, I. (1963). Projection to cerebral cortex of large muscle-spindle afferents in forelimb nerves of the cat, *J. Physiol. (Lond.)*, **169**, 924–945

Vallbo, Å. B. and Johansson, R. S. (1976). Skin mechanoreceptors in the human hand: neural and psychophysical thresholds, in *Sensory Functions of the Skin in Primates*, ed. Y. Zotterman, Pergamon Press, Oxford, pp. 185–199

Vallbo, Å. B., and Hagbarth, K. E. (1968). Activity from skin mechanoreceptors recorded percutaneously in awake human subjects, *Exp. Neurol.*, **21**, 270–289

Vallbo, Å. B., Hagbarth, K. E., Torebjörk, H. E. and Wallin, B. G. (1979). Somatosensory, proprioceptive, and sympathetic activity in human peripheral nerves, *Physiol. Rev.*, **59**, 919–957

Werner, G. and Mountcastle, V. B. (1965). Neural activity in mechanoreceptive cutaneous afferents: stimulus–response relations, Weber functions, and information transmission, *J. Neurophysiol.*, **28**, 359–397

Zotterman, Y. (1939). Touch, pain and tickling: an electrophysiological investigation on cutaneous sensory nerves, *J. Physiol. (Lond.)*, **95**, 1–28

Zotterman, Y. (1959). Thermal sensations, in *Handbook of Physiology*, eds Field, Magoun and Hall, American Physiological Society, Washington, pp. 1–43

Zotterman, Y. (ed.) (1976). *Int. Symp. on Sensory Functions of the Skin in Primates*, Pergamon Press, Oxford and New York

Pain

Suggested Reading and Reviews

An Outline of Chinese Acupuncture, Foreign Languages Press, Peking (1975)

Akil, H. and Watson, S. J. (1980). The role of endogenous opiates in pain control, in *Pain and Society, Life Sci. Res. Rep.* 17, eds H. W. Kosterlitz and L. Y. Terenius, Verlag Chemie, Weinheim, pp. 201–222

Andersson, S. A. and Holmgren, E. (1975). On acupuncture analgesia and the mechanism of pain, *Am. J. Clin. Med.*, **3**(4), 311–334

Basbaum, A. I. (1980). The anatomy of pain and pain modulation, in *Pain and Society, Life Sci. Res. Rep.* 17, eds H. W. Kosterlitz and L. Y. Terenius, Verlag Chemie, Weinheim, pp. 93–122

Basbaum, A. I., Clanton, C. H. and Fields, H. L. (1976). Opiate and stimulus-produced analgesia: functional anatomy of a medullospinal pathway, *Proc. Natl Acad. Sci. USA*, **73**, 4685–4688

Basbaum, A. I. and Fields, H. L. (1978). Endogenous pain control mechanisms: review and hypothesis, *Ann. Neurol.*, **4** (5), 451–462

Besson, J. M. (1977). Analgésie et morphine, in *La Recherche en Neurobiologie*, Editions du Seuil, Paris, pp. 316–324

Besson, J. M. R. (1980). Supraspinal modulation of the segmental transmission of pain, in *Pain and Society, Life Sci. Res. Rep.* 17, eds H. W. Kosterlitz and L. Y. Terenius, Verlag Chemie, Weinheim, pp. 161–182

Bonica, J. J. (ed.) (1974). *Pain, Advances in Neurology*, vol. 4, Raven Press, New York

Bonica, J. J. (ed.) (1980). *Pain, Res. Publ.: Assoc. Res. Nerv. Mental Dis.*, vol. 58, Raven Press, New York

Cervero, F. (1980). Deep and visceral pain, in *Pain and Society, Life Sci. Res. Rep.* 17, eds H. W. Kosterlitz and L. Y. Terenius, Verlag Chemie, Weinheim, pp. 263–282

Chang, H.-T. (1978). Neurophysiological basis of acupuncture analgesia, *Scientia Sinica*, **21** (6), 829–846

Chapman, C. R. (1980). The measurement of pain in man, in *Pain and Society, Life Sci. Res. Rep.* 17, eds H. W. Kosterlitz and L. Y. Terenius, Verlag Chemie, Weinheim, pp. 339–354

Costa, E. and Trabucchi, M. (eds) (1978). *The Endorphins*, Raven Press, New York

Dubner, R., Hayes, R. L. and Hoffman, D. S. (1980). Neural and behavioral correlates of pain in the trigeminal system, in *Pain, Assoc. Res. Nerv. Mental Dis.*, vol. 58, ed. J. J. Bonica, Raven Press, New York, pp. 63–76

Fields, H. L. and Basbaum, A. I. (1978). Brainstem control of spinal pain transmission neurons, *Ann. Rev. Physiol.*, **40**, 193–221

Garratt, A. C. (1860). *Electrophysiology and Electrotherapeutics*, Tricknor and Fields, Boston

Han, J. S. (1982). Neurochemical basis of acupuncture analgesia, *Ann. Rev. Pharmacol. Toxicol.*, **22**, 193–220

Handwerker, H. O. (1980). Pain producing substances, in *Pain and Society, Life Sci. Res. Rep.* 17, eds H. W. Kosterlitz and L. Y. Terenius, Verlag Chemie, Weinheim, pp. 325–338

Katz, R. L., Kao, C. Y., Spiegel, H. and Katz, G. J. (1974). Pain, acupuncture, hypnosis, in *Pain, Advances in Neurology*, vol. 4, ed. J. J. Bonica, Raven Press, New York, pp. 819–825

Keele, K. D. (1957). *Anatomies of Pain*, Blackwell, Oxford

Keele, C. A. and Amstrong, D. (1964). *Substances Producing Pain and Itch*, Edward Arnold, London

Keele, C. A. and Smith, R. (1962). *The Assessment of Pain in Man and Animals*, E. S. Livingstone, Edinburgh

Kerr, F. W. L. and Casey, K. L. (eds) (1978). *Pain, Neurosci. Res. Prog.* **16**(1)

Kosterlitz, H. W. and Terenius, L. Y. (eds) (1980). *Pain and Society, Life Sci. Res. Rep.* 17, Verlag Chemie, Weinheim

Liebeskind, J. C. (1976). Pain modulation by central nervous system stimulation, in *Advances in Pain Research and Therapy*, vol. 1, eds J. J. Bonica and D. G. Albe-Fessard, Raven Press, New York, pp. 445–453

Liebeskind, J. C., Mayer, D. J. and Akil, H. (1974). Central mechanisms of pain inhibition: studies of analgesia from focal brain stimulation, in *Pain, Advances in Neurology*, vol. 4, ed. J. J. Bonica, Raven Press, New York, pp. 261–268

Livingston, W. K. (1976). *Pain Mechanisms. A Physiologic Interpretation of Causalgia and its Related States*, Plenum Press, New York

Melzack, R. (1973). *The Puzzle of Pain*, Penguin Books, Harmondsworth

Melzack, R. and Casey K. L. (1968). Sensory, motivational and central control determinants of pain, in *The Skin Senses*, C. C. Thomas, Springfield

Perl, E. R. (1980). Afferent basis of nociception

and pain: Evidence from the characteristic of sensory receptors and their projections to the spinal dorsal horn, in *Pain, Assoc. Res. Nerv. Mental Dis.*, vol. 58, ed. J. J. Bonica, Raven Press, New York, pp. 19–45

Prescott, F. (1965). *The Control of Pain*, T. Y. Crowell, New York

Quarti, C. and Renaud, J. (1972). *Neuropsychologie de la Douleur*, Hermann, Paris

Sjölund, B. H. and Eriksson, M. B. E. (1980). Stimulation techniques in the management of pain, in *Pain and Society, Life Sci. Res. Rep. 17*, eds H. W. Kosterlitz and L. Y. Terenius, Verlag Chemie, Weinheim, pp. 415–430

Snyder, S. H. (1977). Opiate receptors in the brain, *N. Engl. J. Med.*, **296**, 266–271

Snyder, S. H. (1977). Opiate receptors and internal opiates, *Scient. Am.*, **236**, 44–56

Soulairac, A., Cahn, J. and Charpentier, J. (1968). *Pain*, Academic Press, London

Wall, P. D. (1980). The role of substantia gelatinosa as a gate control, in *Pain, Assoc. Res. Nerv. Mental Dis.*, vol. 58, ed. J. J. Bonica, Raven Press, New York, pp. 205–231

Wall, P. D. and Dubner, R. (1972). Somatosensory pathways, *Ann. Rev. Physiol.*, **34**, 315–336

Weisenberg, M. (1975). *Pain, Clinical and Experimental Perspectives*, C. V. Mosby, St Louis

Willis, W. D. (1980). Neurophysiology of nociception and pain in the spinal cord, in *Pain, Assoc. Res. Nerv. Mental Dis.*, vol. 58, ed. J. J. Bonica, Raven Press, New York, pp. 77–92

Wolff, B. B. (1980). Measurement of human pain, in *Pain, Assoc. Res. Nerv. Mental Dis.*, vol. 58, ed. J. J. Bonica, Raven Press, New York, pp. 173–189

Wolff, H. G. and Wolf, S. (1958). *Pain*, Blackwell, Oxford

Zimmermann, M. (1976). Neurophysiology of nociception, *Int. Rev. Physiol. Neurophysiol. II*, **10**, 179–221

Original Papers

Akil, H., Mayer, D. J. and Liebeskind, J. C. (1976). Antagonism of stimulation-produced analgesia by naloxone, a narcotic antagonist, *Science*, **191**, 961–962

Albe-Fessard, D., Levante, A. and Lamour, Y. (1974). Origin of spino-thalamic tract in monkeys, *Brain Res.*, **65**, 503–509

Boivie, J. (1971). The termination of the spino-thalamic tract in the cat. An experimental study with silver impregnation methods, *Exp. Brain Res.*, **12**, 331–353

Capps, J. A. and Coleman, G. H. (1932). *An Experimental and Clinical Study of Pain in the Pleura, Pericardium and Peritoneum*, Macmillan, New York

Elde, R., Hökfelt, T., Johansson, O. and Terenius, L. (1976). Immunohistochemical studies using antibodies to leu-enkephalin: initial observations on the nervous system of the rat, *Neuroscience*, **1**, 349–351

Eriksson, M. B. E., Sjölund, B. H. and Nielzen, S. (1979). Long term results of peripheral conditioning stimulation as an analgesic measure in chronic pain, *Pain*, **6**, 335–347

Fields, H. L., Basbaum, A. I., Clanton, C. H. and Anderson, S. D. (1977). Nucleus raphe magnus inhibition of spinal cord dorsal horn neurons, *Brain Res.*, **126**, 441–454

Grant, G. (1962). Spinal course and somatotopically localized termination of the spinocerebellar tracts. An experimental study in the cat, *Acta Physiol. Scand.*, **56**, *Suppl.* 193, 1–45

Hallin, R. G. and Torebjörk, H. E. (1976). Studies on cutaneous A and C fibre afferents, skin nerve blocks and perception, in *Sensory Functions of the Skin in Primates, with Special Reference to Man*, ed. Y. Zotterman, Pergamon Press, New York, pp. 137–148

Han, J. S., Tang, J., Huang, B., Liang, X. and Zhang, N. (1979). Acupuncture tolerance in rats, *Chin. Med. J.*, **92** (9), 625–627

Handwerker, H. O., Iggo, A. and Zimmermann, M. (1975). Segmental and supraspinal actions on dorsal horn neurons responding to noxious and non-noxious skin stimuli, *Pain*, **1**, 147–165

Hardy, J. D., Goodell, H. and Wolff, H. G. (1951). The influence of skin temperature upon the pain threshold as evoked by thermal radiation, *Science*, **114**, 149–150

Hardy, J. D., Wolff, H. G. and Goodell, H. (1952). *Pain Sensations and Reactions to Pain*, Williams & Wilkins, Baltimore

Heinbecker, P., Bishop, G. H. and O'Leary, J. (1933). Pain and touch fibers in peripheral nerves, *Arch. Neurol. Psychiatr.*, **29**, 771–789

Henderson, G., Hughes, J. and Kosterlitz, H. W. (1978). In vitro release of leu- and met-enkephalin from the corpus striatum, *Nature*, **271**, 677–679

Hilgard, E. R. (1967). A quantitative study of pain and its reduction through hypnotic suggestion, *Proc. Natl Acad. Sci.*, **57**, 1581–1586

Hughes, J., Smith, T. W., Kosterlitz, H. W., Fothergill, L. A., Morgan, B. A. and Morris, H. R. (1975). Identification of two related pentapeptides from the brain with potent opiate agonist activity, *Nature*, **258**, 577–579

Johansson, O., Hökfelt, T., Elde, R. P., Schultzberg, M. and Terenius, L. (1978). Immunohistochemical distributions of enkephalin neurons, in *The Endorphins*, eds E. Costa and M. Trabucchi, Raven Press, New York, pp. 51–70

Kerr, F. W. L. (1975). Neuroanatomical substrates of nociception in the spinal cord, *Pain*, **1**, 325–356

Kerr, F. W. L. (1975). The ventral spinothalamic tract and other ascending systems of the ventral funiculus of the spinal cord, *J. Comp. Neurol.*, **159**, 335–356

Kolmodin, G. M. and Skoglund, C. R. (1960). Analysis of spinal interneurons activated by tactile and nociceptive stimulation, *Acta Physiol. Scand.*, **50**, 337–355

Leeman, S. E. and Mroz, E. A. (1974). Substance P, *Life Sci.*, **15**, 2033–2044

Lembeck, F. (1953). Zur Frage der Zentralen Übertragung afferenter Impulse, III. Das Vorkommen und die Bedeutung der Substanz P in den dorsalen Wurzeln des Ruckenmarks, *Naunyn-Schmiedebergs Arch. Exp. Pathol. Pharmakol.*, **219**, 197–213

Liebeskind, J. C., Guilbaud, G., Besson, J. M. and Oliveras, J. L. (1973). Analgesia from electrical stimulation of the periaqueductal gray matter in the cat: behavioral observations and inhibitory effects on spinal cord interneurons, *Brain Res.*, **50**, 441–446

Light, A. R. and Metz, C. B. (1978). The morphology of the spinal cord efferent and afferent neurons contributing to the ventral roots of the cat, *J. Comp. Neurol.*, **179**, 501–515

Lim, R. K. S., Liu, C. N., Guzman, F. and Braun, C. (1962). Visceral receptors concerned in visceral pain and the pseudoaffective response to intra-arterial injection of bradykinin and other algesic agents, *J. Comp. Neurol.*, **118**, 269–294

Lindblom, U. F. and Ottoson, J. O. (1957). Influence of pyramidal stimulation upon the relay of coarse cutaneous afferents in the dorsal horn, *Acta Physiol. Scand.*, **38**, 309–318

Mayer, D. J. and Price, D. D. (1976). Central nervous system mechanisms of analgesia, *Pain*, **2**, 379–404

Mehler, W. R. (1974). Central pain and the spinothalamic tract, in *Advances in Neurology*, vol. 4, *Int. Symp. on Pain*, ed. J. J. Bonica, Raven Press, New York, pp. 127–146

Melzack, R. and Wall, P. D. (1965). Pain mechanisms: a new theory, *Science*, **150**, 971–979

Nashold, B. S., Jr (1975). Dorsal columns stimulation for control of pain: a three-year follow-up, *Surg. Neurol.*, **4**, 146–147

Nashold, B. S., Jr, Wilson, W. P. and Slaughter, D. G. (1969). Sensations evoked by stimulation in the midbrain of man, *J. Neurosurg.*, **30**, 14–24

Nathan, P. W. (1976). The gate-control theory of pain: a critical review, *Brain*, **99**, 123–158

Oliveras, J. L., Besson, J. M., Guilbaud, G. and Liebeskind, J. C. (1974). Behavioral and electrophysiological evidence of pain inhibition from midbrain stimulation in the cat, *Exp. Brain Res.*, **20**, 32–44

Oliveras, J. L., Hosobuchi, Y., Redjemi, F., Guilbaud, G. and Besson, J. M. (1977). Opiate antagonist, naloxone, strongly reduces analgesia induced by stimulation of a raphe nucleus (centralis inferior), *Brain Res.*, **120**, 221–229

Oliveras, J. L., Redjemi, F., Guilbaud, G. and Besson, J. M. (1975). Analgesia induced by electrical stimulation of the inferior centralis nucleus of the raphe in the cat, *Pain*, **1**, 139–145

Orne, M. T. (1980). Hypnotic control of pain: Toward a clarification of the different psychological processes involved, in *Pain Assoc. Res. Nerv. Mental Dis.*, vol. 58, ed. J. J. Bonica, Raven Press, New York, pp. 155–172

Perl, E. R. (1968). Myelinated afferent fibres innervating the primate skin and their response to noxious stimuli, *J. Physiol. (Lond.)*, **197**, 593–615

Pert, A. and Yaksh, T. (1974). Site of morphine induced analgesia in the primate brain: relation to pain pathways, *Brain Res.*, **80**, 135–140

Pert, C. B., Kuhar, M. J. and Snyder, S. H. (1976). Opiate receptor: autoradiographic localization in rat brain, *Proc. Natl Acad. Sci. USA*, **73**, 3729–3733

Ralston, H. J. (1968). The fine structure of neurons in the dorsal horn of the cat spinal cord, *J. Comp. Neurol.*, **132**, 275–302

Reynolds, D. V. (1969). Surgery in the rat during electrical analgesia induced by focal brain stimulation, *Science*, **164**, 444–445

Sjölund, B., Terenius, L. and Eriksson, M. (1977). Increased cerebrospinal fluid levels of endorphins after electroacupuncture, *Acta Physiol. Scand.*, **100**, 382–384

Terenius, L. and Wahlström, A. (1975). Morphine-like ligand for opiate receptors in human CSF, *Life Sci.*, **16**, 1759–1764

Torebjörk, H. E. (1974). Afferent C units responding to mechanical thermal and chemical stimuli in human non-glabrous skin, *Acta Physiol. Scand.*, **92**, 374–390

Wall, P. D. and Sweet, W. H. (1967). Temporary abolition of pain in man, *Science*, **155**, 108–109

Willis, W. D., Haber, L. H. and Martin, R. F. (1977). Inhibition of spinothalamic tract cells and interneurons by brain stem stimulation in the monkey, *J. Neurophysiol.*, **40**, 968–981

Wolff, H. G. and Goodell, H. (1943). The relation of attitude and suggestion to the perception of and reaction to pain, *Res. Nerv. Ment. Dis. Proc.*, **23**, 434–448

Yaksh, T. L., Yeung, J. C. and Rudy, T. A. (1976). Systematic examination in the rat of brain sites sensitive to the direct application of morphine: observation of differential effects within the periaqueductal gray, *Brain Res.*, **114**, 83–103

Zhang, A., Pan, X., Xu, S., Cheng, J. and Mo, W. (1980). Endorphins and acupuncture analgesia, *Chin. Med. J.*, **93** (10), 673–680

Zotterman, Y. (1933). Studies in the peripheral nervous mechanisms of pain, *Acta Med. Scand.*, **80**, 185–242

Sensory deprivation

Suggested Reading

Riesen, A. H. (1975). *The Developmental Neuropsychology of Sensory Deprivation*, Academic Press, New York

Index

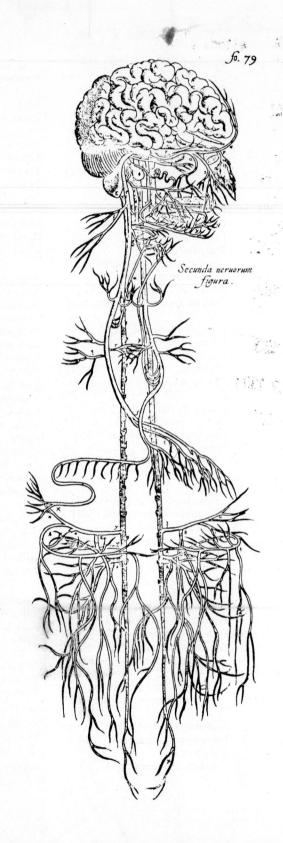

Secunda neruorum figura.